S0-DGK-643

TRANSFORMED *by* GOD'S NATURE

Finding Hope in God's Character *in the* Midst of Suffering

Sisters, Oregon

ISBN: 978-0-578-65533-8

Contents

Preface

How do I know that God is good when my life is not? Can I believe that God is just when injustice surrounds me? I have believed in God all of my life, but what kind of God is He? And does it really even matter to my everyday life? Is faith even relevant when life hurts so much?

These sound like the questions of a skeptic. In reality, these are the questions that I wrestled with in the midst of great trials after decades of following Jesus Christ. People that I had trusted betrayed that trust. Deep pain caused me to question whether faith in God was enough. Whether God Himself was enough.

So I started looking for answers to my tough questions in the Bible. I searched for verses on forgiveness…on goodness…on knowing God. This person who had never had any formal training in theology became a theologian—not to learn lofty ideas or get an advanced degree but because I needed answers. Nothing about the faith that I had lived to that point in my life made sense any more. I had served God, and it seemed that He had failed me. But I knew in the deepest parts of my soul that if I couldn't find answers in the Bible, I wouldn't find them anywhere else. I felt a kinship with Peter, who said to Jesus, "Lord, to whom shall we go? You have the words of eternal life" (Jn. 6:68).

It has now been ten years since I began wrestling with God in His Word. I have learned so much about who He is. He has patiently guided me through one lesson after another. Many people more educated than I am have written about the attributes of God, and I have learned from these resources as well. But I believe that God has called me to write specifically about what His character means to those who are suffering. And since my vocation for the majority of my life has been an illustrator, I believe He has called me to bring the writing to life with art. My goal is to communicate Biblical information regarding God's nature in small daily doses with words, images, and action steps that move us closer to knowing Him day by day.

My understanding of God was limited and incorrect, but God has answered my cry to know Him more. This book is my attempt, by His grace, to answer His call to communicate what I have learned. I have found so much comfort in leaning on the character of God, and it is my hope that others can find this as well. Please keep in mind as you work through this book that it is extremely important for each reader to seek God in the pages of Scripture for themselves. Always check my words against Scripture and seek the truths of God on your own. Pray for His guidance to discover truth about His nature beyond what I have written.

My prayer now is that others can spend time in these studies, pursue more of the Word of God on their own, and find rest in the true God, avoiding the pain and confusion that result when we lean on an incorrect view of Him.

Introduction

Before we jump into daily readings, it is important to explore some general ideas about God's nature as well as define a few terms.

According to the *Merriam-Webster* online dictionary:

Attribute: a quality, character, or characteristic ascribed to someone or something
Character: one of the attributes or features that make up and distinguish an individual
Characteristic: a distinguishing trait, quality, or property
Nature: the inherent character or basic constitution of a person or thing: essence

These words seem to be synonyms that can be easily interchanged with one another. They are all used to define each other! As I have studied and prepared to write this book, one of these terms has emerged to me as a personal favorite. The word *nature* feels best to me to describe God. I have nothing against the other words, and I will most definitely use them repeatedly. But let me explain why I personally believe *nature* works best.

God is infinite. That is one of the attributes that we will study. Everything about Him is infinite. So when we talk about His love, it's infinite. Justice? That's infinite, too. His faithfulness goes on forever as well. His attributes are also connected. Infinity and love cannot be separated when we consider God. *All* of His attributes are interconnected. We cannot break God into parts. He is not love at this moment and justice in the next moment and faithful after that. He is all of His attributes all of the time forever and ever. Everything He wills and everything He speaks is consistent with His very being—which includes *all* of His attributes. When God administers justice, it is perfect in love and grace. When He loves, He does so at the same time that He has infinite knowledge of our sin. In my mind, when we speak of attributes and characteristics, it implies separate parts. When we speak of His nature, it is a singular word. As *Merriam-Webster* defines it, this is His essence. God is unified. He is all of His attributes, all of the time; they are wrapped up into His being, which cannot be contained in the pages of a book or in the human mind.

I have attempted an illustration (at left) to symbolize these concepts. The five sets of circular shapes represent five different attributes of God. For simplicity in the illustration, I am only showing five unnamed attributes, but we will be covering much more than five. Each set of circles extends off of the page because the attribute is infinite. Notice that the attributes overlap each other. In reality, they cannot be separated from one another, and they should be drawn stacked right on top of each other. There is not a good part of God and a holy part of God and a sovereign part of God. All of God is all of His characteristics. A perfect depiction, if I could have thought of a way to draw it, would have been all of the attributes filling all of the page and all of the next page, spilling out of the book, and covering the bookshelf and all of the shelves in the universe.

This is all very difficult for our human minds to get in focus. As a result, we need to discuss one attribute at a time. Our minds can only begin to understand God when we break Him into parts, even though He cannot be separated. In the illustration, the circles are not stacked directly on top of each other because our eyes would not be able to distinguish one set from the other. As the illustrator, I have pulled each series of colored circles away from the center so that we can see them as parts of the whole. Try to imagine a cohesiveness between the circles where, if we could lift them up off the page, they would snap back into alignment with one another to make one unified, infinite whole. This pulling out is what we are doing to the nature of God when we study one attribute by itself. Remember that each attribute is always part of one unified, infinite, incomprehensible God.

The infinite nature of God means that we cannot ever fully explore any one of His attributes. The fact that He is all of His nature all of the time and we can only study Him by breaking His attributes apart means that we cannot ever fully comprehend His nature. But God calls us into relationship with Him to know Him. He reveals Himself to us through His Spirit as we study His Word. If we submit to follow Him into this process of knowing Him, the rewards will be more than we could ever imagine.

God reveals Himself to humanity through both Scripture and creation:

> ***For his invisible attributes, namely, his eternal power and divine nature, have been clearly perceived, ever since the creation of the world, in the things that have been made.***
>
> ***Romans 1:20***

This verse teaches that the spectacular beauty and thoughtful design of creation bear witness to the glory, power, and existence of God. But, as I have studied Scripture intently in the writing of this book, I believe God's self-revelation in creation goes further than just a general statement of His glory. Because He communicates with humans, He uses the language of humans, which consists of both literal words and the images of creation from the world in which we live. All throughout Scripture, God uses images of creation to speak to us about Himself. He compares Himself with human roles (a bridegroom, a shepherd, an architect), He describes His actions as if He had human body parts (a face, hand, eyes), and He likens Himself to nonhuman elements of creation (a rock, a fire, a lion). These are just a few examples of the many, many times that God chooses to use His finite creation to help us understand His infinite nature and ways. Every single piece of God's creation has its origin in Him and in His will. Therefore, every element of His creation has potential for God to reveal something of Himself in it. God declared in Romans 1 His intent to include revelation of Himself in creation. He provided examples throughout Scripture of how to see glimpses of His nature in His creation. It would be wise for His faithful followers to pay close attention to Scripture and to understand the ways that God has revealed Himself in the created world.

Using this Book

The illustrations throughout this book are intended to serve multiple purposes. At first glance, they are images from nature used to picture some truth about God's nature. On another level, the illustrations remind the reader on every page that we are only seeing a brief glimpse of the infinite being of God. Each daily reading is accompanied by a small excerpt of a broader image—for example, a mountain scene. These close-up views of the overall image allow us to see more details in the art, just as we pause daily in the Scriptures to see some of the details of God's nature. The more deeply we study the whole counsel of Scripture, the more we can appreciate the depth of His character. When you combine all of the small pieces of the mountain scene for the week, you get an overall image of most of the mountains in that scene, just as our daily studies combine to give us a bigger picture over the week of one attribute. But there is more of the broad scene flowing off of the page, reminding us that even in the full week's study, we have only considered a part of that attribute. In fact, to fully explore that attribute, we would have to study all of the "mountain ranges" in the world and, even then, assume that we have only seen them in part.

Two things that should come out of studying God's nature are a greater reverence for Him and a greater resemblance in us to Jesus Christ. Theologians sometimes divide God's attributes into two categories: communicable (those He shares with us, such as love) and incommunicable (those that are unique to His nature, such as infiniteness). To me, a more practical division of His attributes is the following:

1. the attributes that should drive us to reverence, which would be all of them because He is infinitely perfect in all of them, and

2. the attributes that He expects to see in us as we are conformed to the image of Jesus Christ.

The theme of this book—the one crucial message that I hope we can all get a clearer picture of—is that we can only effectively reflect God's image to the extent that we are conformed to Christ in *all* of the attributes that He shares with us. Picking a favorite attribute of God and reflecting only that quality in our own lives is analogous to breaking God Himself into parts. We do not bear His image correctly if we do not bring the fullness of Christ-likeness in the strength of the Holy Spirit. For example, a believer seeking justice without bringing love to the situation as well is not reflecting God's justice.

Romans 12:2 teaches that we are transformed by the renewal of our minds. Studying the Bible is crucial to having our minds renewed. Every day's reading begins with Scripture, and it is important to carefully read those verses before considering the rest of the daily reading. Please keep in mind as you work through this book that it is vital for each reader to pursue God in the pages of Scripture for yourself. Always check my words against Scripture and seek the truths of God on your own. Pray for His guidance to discover truth about His nature beyond what I have written.

Each day's reading finishes with an action step. Some of the action steps will include opportunities to fall on our knees before a holy God, who is far more awesome than anything He has created. Other action steps will be designed to renew our minds to be transformed into His image. Participating in these action steps is a huge part of cementing an understanding of God's character into your mind and heart. The action steps that involve prayer are vital because we can only understand God to the extent that He reveals Himself to us—cry out for understanding! The action steps that involve additional Scripture reading are important to round out a larger view of His revelation. The action steps that invite you into some kind of physical activity (walking, writing, etc.) are especially necessary for those whose learning style is more hands-on. Action steps that ask you to interact with other people are important, not only because God calls us to love others and be in relationships with them, but also because the process of looking for opportunities to communicate with others keeps the Scripture being studied at a more conscious level in your mind.

Wherever you see this image on the page, it is a visual reminder that God's attributes are connected. Look for a place in the text on that page where one of His attributes is connected to another. All of His nature is consistent in all of His acts.

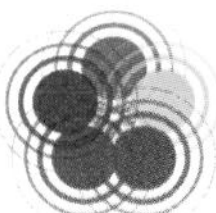

Part I

In Part I of this book, we will consider the attributes of God that are unique to Him. These attributes should drive us to worship and reverence for the glory of who God is. His character and perfections are unlike any other. To study God's nature is to behold His glory as He has revealed it in Scripture. There is no better exercise to bring us to a humble posture before the Almighty God. We will begin our Scripture study with a week of readings that look into reasons for spending our lives increasing our knowledge of God.

WEEK 1

Why Study God's Nature?

The highest science, the loftiest speculation, the mightiest philosophy, which can ever engage the attention of a child of God, is the name, the nature, the person, the work, the doings, and the existence of the great God whom he calls his Father. There is something exceedingly improving to the mind in a contemplation of the Divinity. It is a subject so vast, that all our thoughts are lost in its immensity; so deep, that our pride is drowned in its infinity. Other subjects we can compass and grapple with; in them we feel a kind of self-content, and go our way with the thought, "Behold I am wise." But when we come to this master-science, finding that our plumb-line cannot sound its depth, and that our eagle eye cannot see its height, we turn away with the thought, that vain man would be wise, but he is like a wild ass's colt; and with the solemn exclamation, "I am but of yesterday, and know nothing." No subject of contemplation will tend more to humble the mind, than thoughts of God. We shall be obliged to feel—

"Great God, how infinite art thou,
What worthless worms are we!"

But while the subject humbles *the mind, it also* expands *it. He who often thinks of God, will have a larger mind than the man who simply plods around this narrow globe. He may be a naturalist, boasting of his ability to dissect a beetle, anatomize a fly, or arrange insects and animals in classes with well-nigh unutterable names; he may be a geologist, able to discourse of the megatherium and the plesiosaurus, and all kinds of extinct animals; he may imagine that his science, whatever it is, ennobles and enlarges his mind. I dare say it does, but after all, the most excellent study for expanding the soul, is the science of Christ, and him crucified, and the knowledge of the Godhead in the glorious Trinity. Nothing will so enlarge the intellect, nothing so magnify the whole soul of man, as a devout, earnest, continued investigation of the great subject of the Deity. And, whilst humbling and expanding, this subject is eminently* consolatory. *Oh, there is, in contemplating Christ, a balm for every wound; in musing on the Father, there is a quietus for every grief; and in the influence of the Holy Ghost, there is a balsam for every sore. Would you lose your sorrows? Would you drown your cares? Then go, plunge yourself in the Godhead's deepest sea; be lost in his immensity; and you shall come forth as from a couch of rest, refreshed and invigorated. I know nothing which can so comfort the soul; so calm the swelling billows of grief and sorrow; so speak peace to the winds of trial, as a devout musing upon the subject of the Godhead.*

Charles H. Spurgeon, *The Immutability of God*, 1855

And so, from the day we heard, we have not ceased to pray for you, asking that you may be filled with the knowledge of his will in all spiritual wisdom and understanding, so as to walk in a manner worthy of the Lord, fully pleasing to him, bearing fruit in every good work and increasing in the knowledge of God.

Colossians 1:9-10

Thus says the Lord*: "Let not the wise man boast in his wisdom, let not the mighty man boast in his might, let not the rich man boast in his riches, but let him who boasts boast in this, that he understands and knows me, that I am the* Lord *who practices steadfast love, justice, and righteousness in the earth. For in these things I delight, declares the* Lord*."*

Jeremiah 9:23-24

Why Study God's Nature?

Knowing God 1

In our relationships with other people, we use the word *know* in different ways. For example, I may ask you, "Do you know Emily?" Experience tells me that most others understand me to be asking, "Do you know who Emily is?" But the question could also be interpreted to mean, "Do you know Emily well? Do you know what she likes and doesn't like? Do you know how she might behave in a certain situation? Do you know what's important to her?"

Often in our Christian jargon, we refer to someone as "knowing the Lord," and by that we mean simply that person has trusted Jesus as Savior. That is certainly the first step to knowing God, for anyone who has trusted Jesus has the Holy Spirit residing within (Eph. 1:13-18), as apart from the Holy Spirit we cannot know or understand God (1 Cor. 2:10-13).

Colossians 1:10 makes it quite clear that it is possible to increase in the knowledge of God. If knowing the Lord starts and ends with trusting Jesus as Savior, there would be no way to increase our knowledge of Him.

Jeremiah 9 suggests there is a knowledge of God that involves understanding His nature—that He delights in love, justice, and righteousness. Man's own wisdom, power, and wealth are not of value to God, but man's relationship with Him is. Knowledge and understanding of the Lord can come from observing His works and His revelation of Himself in Scripture. Just as in our example with our friend, Emily, when you spend time learning about another, a relationship is developed that goes beyond knowing who that person is into understanding that person's nature.

So at least two stages of "knowing God" are part of the Christian life:

1. a saving knowledge of the Lord that occurs at the time one places faith in Jesus and
2. knowing God increasingly and understanding His nature through seeing examples of how He interacts with people and reveals Himself in His Word.

It is this deeper knowledge that is the goal of this book. But factual knowledge of God is not sufficient. We will attempt to apply our knowledge to worship Him in our daily walks and conduct our lives in a manner worthy of Him. Knowing God Himself must be the end goal of any growth of knowledge about Him. As we know Him and love Him more, we will be transformed by that knowledge.

Action Step: We cannot know God without the guidance of the Holy Spirit, who comes to minister to us when we acknowledge Jesus as our Savior. Have you trusted Jesus as your Savior and thus taken this important first step toward knowing the Lord?

Paul prayed for the Colossians that they "may be filled with the knowledge of his will in all spiritual wisdom and understanding." Spend some time in prayer asking God to fill you with knowledge and understanding of Him as you discipline yourself to study His Word.

For I desire steadfast love and not sacrifice, the knowledge of God rather than burnt offerings.

Hosea 6:6

"With what shall I come before the LORD, and bow myself before God on high? Shall I come before him with burnt offerings, with calves a year old? Will the LORD be pleased with thousands of rams, with ten thousands of rivers of oil? Shall I give my firstborn for my transgression, the fruit of my body for the sin of my soul?" He has told you, O man, what is good; and what does the LORD require of you but to do justice, and to love kindness, and to walk humbly with your God?

Micah 6:6-8

Why Study God's Nature?

2 Seek Knowledge of God's Ways in Scripture

Hosea teaches that the desire of God is for people to come to Him with love and to seek knowledge of Him, rather than just to bring sacrifices. Outward religious acts are meaningless to Him if we do not come with hearts submitted to Him.

Micah elaborates on this. Notice the progression of value of the sacrifices that are proposed by Micah: a calf, followed by a thousand rams, escalating to ten thousand rivers of oil, and finishing with the abhorrent offering of a firstborn child! None of these is really what God wants! What does He require instead? For us to do justice, love kindness, and walk humbly with our God. We will get into details of what justice and loving kindness look like in God's nature later in this book. For now, what does it look like to "walk humbly with your God"?

I am not an expert outdoorsman, but I live in a region in which many people are. If I was to set out to summit one of our local mountains, I would be wise to travel with someone who had done it before—someone with expertise in climbing the mountain who could guide me on the best trails according to my abilities. My well-being would be dependent on the guide. While on the trail, I would stick close to my guide and submit to his instructions, thus following the ways of an expert mountaineer.

God wants our lives to look something like that mountain adventure. He has a path set out for us. I am not referring here to a calling in life like a vocation or where to live. I am referring to the simple path of walking with Him (Ps. 16:11). On every page of the Bible, He has revealed to us what He is like. This is the path on which He wants us to walk humbly. Walking humbly includes submitting to His ways. And we cannot submit to His ways unless we have a fuller understanding of the ways He wants us to walk in keeping with His character. God desires devotion to Him and faithfulness to walk in His ways. The first step in that adventure is to seek knowledge of His ways in Scripture.

Action Step: Evaluate yourself. Are you willing to submit to God to walk in His ways? Spend some time in prayer asking God to reveal places where you may prefer to walk in your own ways rather than in His.

When Jesus had spoken these words, he lifted up his eyes to heaven, and said, "Father, the hour has come; glorify your Son that the Son may glorify you, since you have given him authority over all flesh, to give eternal life to all whom you have given him. And this is eternal life, that they know you, the only true God, and Jesus Christ whom you have sent."

John 17:1-3

Why Study God's Nature?

Jesus Shows Us the Character of God 3

John 17 records Jesus' beautiful prayer for Himself, His disciples, and later His believers, including us. Part of the prayer is His affirmation that eternal life is defined by knowing God and His Son, Jesus Christ.

Eternal life, throughout Scripture, is used both to refer to life that never ends and to refer to a quality of life that is abundant, based in an ongoing fellowship with God.

The tense of the verb in the phrase "that they know you" is present and ongoing. It is not a past-tense action that happened once and is completed, as would be the case if the wording was "that they came to know you." Eternal life—both never-ending and abundant—is available to us to begin now, and the key to beginning it is an ongoing process of knowing God and Jesus.

We will be entering into a brief study on the Trinity later in this book, but it is important to note here that knowing God and knowing Jesus are one in the same. Jesus is "the radiance of the glory of God and the exact imprint of his nature" (Heb. 1:3). Jesus came, in part, to show us the Father (Jn. 1:18, 14:8-11). Throughout our study of Scripture to understand God's nature, we need to remember that our best concrete example of the character of God is the character of Jesus.

Action Step: Look through the book of John and find a story to read about Jesus. Your Bible may have headlines that explain what is going on in each passage that will help you pick a story. The book of John is really one story about Jesus after another. Read a story and think of one adjective that describes Jesus that is evidenced by that story. This is one step in beginning to understand the character of Jesus.

1 *My son, if you receive my words and treasure up my commandments with you,*
2 *making your ear attentive to wisdom and inclining your heart to understanding;*
3 *yes, if you call out for insight and raise your voice for understanding,*
4 *if you seek it like silver and search for it as for hidden treasures,*
5 *then you will understand the fear of the LORD and find the knowledge of God.*
6 *For the LORD gives wisdom; from his mouth come knowledge and understanding;*
7 *he stores up sound wisdom for the upright; he is a shield to those who walk in integrity,*
8 *guarding the paths of justice and watching over the way of his saints.*
9 *Then you will understand righteousness and justice and equity, every good path;*
10 *for wisdom will come into your heart, and knowledge will be pleasant to your soul;*
11 *discretion will watch over you, understanding will guard you,*
12 *delivering you from the way of evil, from men of perverted speech,*
13 *who forsake the paths of uprightness to walk in the ways of darkness,*
14 *who rejoice in doing evil and delight in the perverseness of evil,*
15 *men whose paths are crooked, and who are devious in their ways.*

Proverbs 2:1-15

The fear of the Lord is the beginning of wisdom, and the knowledge of the Holy One is insight.

Proverbs 9:10

Why Study God's Nature?
All Knowledge Comes from The Lord 4

Receive my words...treasure my commandments...make your ear attentive to wisdom.... Incline your heart to understanding...call out for insight...raise your voice for understanding. God most certainly expects some effort on our parts to know Him. If you undertake all that action and all that effort, "then you will understand the fear of the Lord and find the knowledge of God." Great effort experiences great rewards.

It is interesting to note, though, (Prov. 2:6) that it is the Lord that gives wisdom, knowledge, and understanding. Even with all of our efforts, we are still dependent upon Him. Yet He still wants our efforts, because all of those activities recognize that He is the source for all that we are seeking.

Next, note in verses 9-12 the transformation into godly living that comes from our efforts and God's gifts: understanding righteousness, justice, and equity; every good path; wisdom in the heart; knowledge pleasant to the soul; discretion; understanding; delivery from evil. The more we work toward knowing God, the more we become like Him!

If we back up to verse 5, we note that the other benefit of our efforts is understanding "the fear of the Lord." This fear is not a terror that causes us to run from relationship with Him. It is a reverent awe and respect for the majesty and power of who He is, which causes us to be drawn to Him. The more we study God and understand His nature, the more we will revere Him. Reverent love of God is vital to our faith. It is the source of our praise and worship and our desire to obey Him, and it inspires us to grow in faith and continue our pursuit of knowing Him.

This continuing cycle of the pursuit of wisdom leading to the fear of the Lord, which in turn leads back to wisdom, is supported by Proverbs. Proverbs 2:1-5 shows that the pursuit of wisdom leads to the fear of the Lord. Proverb 9:10 teaches that the fear of the Lord is the beginning of wisdom. The most important thing to keep in mind during this cycle is that, ultimately, all knowledge, understanding, and wisdom come from the Lord.

Action Step: Read Psalm 89:1-18 carefully. Note all the ways the author shows reverence to the Lord. Prayerfully consider whether your own thoughts of God are as high and lofty.

And we know that the Son of God has come, and he has given us understanding so that we can know the true God. And now we live in fellowship with the true God because we live in fellowship with his Son, Jesus Christ. He is the only true God, and he is eternal life. Dear children, keep away from anything that might take God's place in your hearts.

1 John 5:20-21 (NLT)

Put to death therefore what is earthly in you: sexual immorality, impurity, passion, evil desire, and covetousness, which is idolatry.

Colossians 3:5

Why Study God's Nature?
Seek the True God

5

The true God. Three times here John refers to Him as the *true* God. One obvious point he is making is that some people worship other gods who are not true. In Old Testament times, people sometimes worshiped animal images, wooden poles, or various gods of other nations. In New Testament times, the Roman gods were worshiped, including Caesar. We dismiss these easily, knowing that we would never worship such ridiculous "gods."

Many Christian leaders today warn about modern equivalents of false gods. Anything that we value more highly than God is an idol. If we look to find fulfillment and security in anything other than God, we are practicing idolatry. We can give our own physical appearance, our children, our money, our pleasure, or our reputation so much importance that they become more precious to us than God. Paul teaches in Colossians 3:5 that desires of the human heart that displace God are idolatry.

There is another kind of false god that can be even more dangerous because it takes so much more effort to spot. This is the god that we contrive in our own minds when we take pieces of the true God and add to that attributes of our own design. When we struggle over a Scriptural account that is difficult, decide not to include that in our concept of God, and instead add our own accounts of what we would prefer Him to be like—this is idolatry. Even a simple lack of knowledge of the true God as He reveals Himself in Scripture can lead to a false image of God.

Scripture leads us into an understanding of God's nature. It is vital that we study the Bible and seek to understand God to the best of our ability as He has revealed Himself so that we are not inventing a false god that we are more comfortable with than the true God.

Action Step: Ask God to help you identify anything that you may be valuing more than Him. Then prayerfully consider whether you might be creating a false God by refusing to accept Scriptural accounts of God's work in this world. Ask Him to begin revealing His true nature to you in His Word.

So God created man in his own image, in the image of God he created him; male and female he created them.

Genesis 1:27

...you have put off the old self with its practices and have put on the new self, which is being renewed in knowledge after the image of its creator.

Colossians 3:9-10

Why Study God's Nature?
Our Beliefs Determine Our Behavior 6

God created men and women in His image. We are not an exact representation of Him. But in some ways, we bear His likeness. To what degree we show His image is dependent on what we believe about Him.

An atheist believes there is no God, so she is free to bear her own image, determining herself the behavior, actions, and attitudes that she chooses.

A deist believes in God but believes Him to have separated Himself from His creation. This man's ethical conduct depends on natural laws determined not by God's revelation, but by man's moral code. His image will be one of man's righteousness.

The woman who constructs a god of her own design, piecing together attributes that are comfortable and make sense to her, will reflect the image of that false god.

The man who believes in God and His Word but sees God as a collection of attributes or parts is missing that God cannot be divided. This man, in his desire to be an image-bearer, may fall short by applying grace alone to one situation and justice alone to another situation.

The woman who believes in God but struggles to trust in His goodness may spend her life distant from God due to an unhealthy fear of Him. This woman will find it hard to bear the image of God when she has never drawn close to Him.

But the man who understands and believes God as He has revealed Himself in Scripture and trusts in Jesus Christ, resting in the promises of His Word, will spend his life transforming into the image of Jesus.

It is logical that who we believe God to be is the greatest contributor to who we are as individuals and to how we behave.

Paul wrote to the Colossians that the new self (the believing self) "is being renewed in knowledge after the image of its creator." "Is being renewed" indicates an ongoing process. How is it being renewed? In knowledge. A deep, intimate knowledge of God results in growing more and more into the image of God in Christ. This is fulfilling the design that God had in mind when He first created mankind.

Let's take steps toward being renewed after the image of the Creator by seeking knowledge about His nature.

Action Step: Think carefully about what you believe to be true about God. Would you fall somewhere within the descriptions that I have offered? Are you willing to expand your knowledge about God from Scripture and be renewed after the image of your Creator?

Weekly Summary
Key Points

1. At least two stages of "knowing God" are part of the Christian life: 1) a saving knowledge of the Lord that occurs at the time one places faith in Jesus and 2) knowing God increasingly and understanding His nature through seeing examples of how He interacts with people and reveals Himself in His Word.

2. God desires devotion to Him and faithfulness to walk in His ways. The first step in that adventure is to seek knowledge of His ways in Scripture.

3. Our best concrete example of the character of God is the character of Jesus.

4. The more we work toward knowing God, the more we become like Him. Ultimately, all knowledge, understanding, and wisdom come from the Lord.

5. It is vital that we study the Bible and seek to understand God exactly as He has revealed Himself so that we are not inventing a false God that we are more comfortable with than the true God.

6. To what degree we show God's image is dependent on what we believe about Him. A deep, intimate knowledge of God results in growing more and more into the image of God in Christ.

Why Study God's Nature?
Action Steps

7

Go back through the action steps and complete any that you have not yet completed or repeat one that was meaningful:

1. We cannot know God without the guidance of the Holy Spirit, who comes to minister to us when we acknowledge Jesus as our Savior. Have you trusted Jesus as your Savior and thus taken this important first step toward knowing the Lord?

   Paul prayed for the Colossians that they "may be filled with the knowledge of his will in all spiritual wisdom and understanding." Spend some time in prayer asking God to fill you with knowledge and understanding of Him.

2. Evaluate yourself. Are you willing to submit to God to walk in His ways? Spend some time in prayer asking God to reveal places where you may prefer to walk in your own ways rather than in His.

3. Look through the book of John and find a story to read about Jesus. Your Bible may have headlines that explain what is going on in each passage that will help you pick a story. The book of John is really one story about Jesus after another. Read a story and think of one adjective that describes Jesus that is evidenced by that story. This is one step in beginning to understand the character of Jesus.

4. Read Psalm 89:1-18 carefully. Note all the ways the author shows reverence to the Lord. Prayerfully consider whether your own thoughts of God are as high and lofty.

5. Ask God to help you identify anything that you may be valuing more than Him. Then prayerfully consider whether you might be creating a false God by refusing to accept Scriptural accounts of God's work in this world. Ask Him to begin revealing His true nature to you in His Word.

6. Think carefully about what you believe to be true about God. Are you willing to expand your knowledge about God from Scripture and be renewed after the image of your Creator?

WEEK 2
Incomprehensible

When we try to imagine what God is like we must of necessity use that-which-is-not-God as the raw material for our minds to work on; hence whatever we visualize God to be, He is not, for we have constructed our image out of that which He has made and what He has made is not God.

A.W. Tozer, *The Knowledge of the Holy*

"To whom will you compare me?
Who is my equal?" asks the Holy One.
Look up into the heavens.
Who created all the stars?
He brings them out like an army, one after another,
calling each by its name.
Because of his great power and incomparable strength,
not a single one is missing.

Isaiah 40:25-26 (NLT)

Great is the LORD, and greatly to be praised, and his greatness is unsearchable.

Psalms 145:3

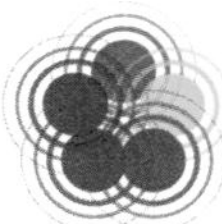

Incomprehensible
God Cannot Be Measured 1

When the Lord wanted to demonstrate to Abram how numerous his offspring would be, He brought Abram outside and challenged him to number the stars. The stars cannot be numbered, and yet God created every one of them. What a fitting illustration of God's great power to keep the promise to Abram (Gen. 15).

Our family lives in an area with relatively easy access to night skies virtually unaffected by light pollution. It is astounding to camp under the night sky and consider the vastness of outer space with thousands of points of light visible, many in reality as big or bigger than our own sun. In fact, some of those points of light represent entire galaxies!

Technology on board the Hubble Space Telescope has led astronomers to estimate the existence of about two trillion galaxies in the universe. Scientists estimate that there may be as many as one hundred billion stars in our galaxy, the Milky Way. Multiply those numbers (two trillion × one hundred billion), and you arrive at man's best efforts at counting the number of stars that God spoke into existence. If that number seems too large to comprehend, then just try to wrap your mind around the fact that God calls each one by name, and He is aware that not a single one is missing.

The concept of "name" in the Bible goes beyond a word label. To know someone by name was to know a person's character and nature. God calling each star "by its name" may mean that He assigned a word label to every star, but it furthermore means that God knows each star's characteristics, location, and movement in the universe. Not only is He familiar with every single star in the universe, but those stars are subject to His sovereignty. The intended audience for Isaiah 40 is thought to be the Israelites in Babylonian captivity. The Babylonians practiced astrology, seeking direction from gods that were visible in the night sky. Isaiah's words assured the Israelites that God rules over the stars and the false gods of Babylon.

The universe is beyond our measurements. Even more so is the God who created it. We are finite creatures, while God is infinite. There is no one equal to God. No one can rival Him. This should lead us to praise and worship of Him.

Action Step: Contemplate the stars tonight. If you live in an area where the skies are dark enough and the sky is clear, go outside, find a place where you have a clear view of the stars, and try to count their number. If the stars are not visible for you, look for Hubble Space Telescope photos to consider instead. Try to count the stars in the photo, or see if you can find out how many stars are in the galaxy pictured. Worship God, who placed those stars along with innumerable others.

6 *"Seek the Lord while he may be found; call upon him while he is near;*
7 *let the wicked forsake his way, and the unrighteous man his thoughts; let him*
return to the Lord, that he may have compassion on him, and to our God, for
he will abundantly pardon.
8 *For my thoughts are not your thoughts, neither are your ways my ways,*
declares the Lord.
9 *For as the heavens are higher than the earth, so are my ways higher than your*
ways and my thoughts than your thoughts.

10 *"For as the rain and the snow come down from heaven and do not return*
there but water the earth, making it bring forth and sprout, giving seed to the
sower and bread to the eater,
11 *so shall my word be that goes out from my mouth; it shall not return to me*
empty, but it shall accomplish that which I purpose, and shall succeed in the
thing for which I sent it."

Isaiah 55:6-11

Incompleteprehensible

God Reveals Himself through His Word

2

This passage starts out with a call to repentance—an invitation to turn from our own ways and thoughts to submit to God's ways. The Christian life is one of continued repentance. Repentance is an act of turning away from our sinful ways and toward His perfect ways where we will find His grace. In the same way that we cannot climb to the heavens from the earth on our own strength, we cannot comprehend God's thoughts or achieve His ways on our own.

Left to our own human nature, we attempt to reduce God to something that we can understand completely or control. Our thoughts of Him are confined to the way we view ourselves. We get angry with Him when life doesn't go our way. Our way is an easy, successful life of minimal hardship. In God's way, He allows us to experience weakness, brokenness, and hardship so we can experience His strength.

How do we begin to forsake our own thinking and seek His ways? Verses 10-11 explain that it is His word that accomplishes His purpose. In the Hebrew language, *word* is *dabar*. It is used in many ways in the Old Testament, but in relation to the word of the Lord, it includes everything that God communicates to man. Everything that God speaks or purposes will come to pass.

Included in His purpose is the redemption of mankind. His way is the way of restoring relationship with His creation. God created us for fellowship with Him, and He reveals both His nature and His plan for redeeming us through His word. Just as rain falls from the heavens with a purpose to water the earth, God's word is sent out to reveal Himself and His redemption plan to us. It will accomplish that purpose.

The disconnect between the infinite God and finite humanity can only be crossed when God speaks comprehension and understanding to us. He uses images from creation and earth throughout Scripture to describe Himself in ways that we can comprehend, yet He exists infinitely beyond creation. It is important to appreciate the distance between man and God to keep us humble before Him. As we listen to His words, we draw near to Him and He will draw near to us (Jms. 4:8).

Action Step: Water something. If it is summer, water your lawn or garden. Water a houseplant. If nothing else, fill a glass with water, find any patch of dirt, and pour the water slowly onto the dirt. Watch what happens to the water. If the soil is porous, the water should slowly seep into the soil, filling the tiny empty spaces and trickling deep into the soil, changing the soil from dry to wet. If the soil is hard and clay-like, the water may run off the surface rather than penetrating. Using a garden tool or something sharp, rough up the hard soil, and create holes in it to allow the water to penetrate.

Consider how the water is like God's Word in the soil of your heart. If your heart is porous and soft, His Word will penetrate deeply and change your character according to His purpose. If your heart is hard, you may be running the risk of God using sharp, challenging circumstances to soften your heart to His Word.

9 *But, as it is written,*
"What no eye has seen, nor ear heard, nor the heart of man imagined,
what God has prepared for those who love him"—
10 *these things God has revealed to us through the Spirit. For the Spirit searches*
everything, even the depths of God.
11 *For who knows a person's thoughts except the spirit of that person, which is in*
him? So also no one comprehends the thoughts of God except the Spirit of God.
12 *Now we have received not the spirit of the world, but the Spirit who is from*
God, that we might understand the things freely given us by God.
13 *And we impart this in words not taught by human wisdom but taught by the*
Spirit, interpreting spiritual truths to those who are spiritual.
14 *The natural person does not accept the things of the Spirit of God, for they*
are folly to him, and he is not able to understand them because they are
spiritually discerned.
15 *The spiritual person judges all things, but is himself to be judged by no one.*
16 *"For who has understood the mind of the Lord so as to instruct him?" But we*
have the mind of Christ.

1 Corinthians 2:9-16

Incomprehensible
God Reveals Himself through the Holy Spirit

3

We have seen that God is beyond human comprehension. We can only understand Him to the extent that He reveals Himself by sending forth His Word. Yet we still need more help in receiving His Word. These verses from 1 Corinthians teach that help comes from the Holy Spirit.

Verse 9 of this passage is often taken out of context and interpreted as referring to heaven. Certainly, other Biblical teaching about heaven confirms that it is beyond what we can imagine, and Paul could have had eternity in his thoughts here. But that cannot be *all* that Paul was teaching about here. The next verse goes on to explain that the things beyond our imagination that God has prepared He "*has* revealed" through the Spirit. The broader context of this passage is a discussion of the wisdom of God, especially as revealed in the gospel.

I can spend my entire life in a relationship with another person, but they will only know me as much as I choose to reveal. No one can read my mind or know my thoughts or plans unless I tell them. Even then, I may only tell part of the truth. Can they really trust what I am sharing of myself? We are only known by other people to the extent that we reveal ourselves to them.

The Spirit of God can reveal to us the depths of God because He is of one mind with God. At the same time, we who have trusted Christ have received "the Spirit who is from God, that we might understand the things freely given us by God." The things freely given us by God include a knowledge of His nature and His plan for redemption. And what God discloses of Himself can absolutely be trusted as true. The Spirit helps us to understand the truths in Scripture and to have the mind of Christ. To have the mind of Christ is to have our minds in understanding and submission to God's ways, just as Christ submitted to the Father (Phil. 2:5-8). Scripture also describes the Holy Spirit as "the Spirit of wisdom and of revelation," giving us knowledge of Jesus Christ and enlightening "the eyes of our hearts" (Eph. 1:17-18). It is the Holy Spirit that enables us to see what the Father is doing in the gospel of Jesus Christ and to know God more deeply.

The fact that God is so far beyond our understanding and still chooses to make Himself known so we can enjoy a relationship with Him should lead us to humility and reverence before Him.

Action Step: Set aside some time today to spend with a friend or loved one. Share something of yourself that the other person doesn't know. It could be a silly childhood memory or a hidden fear or something that you have always dreamed of doing. Ask the other person if they would be willing to share likewise. As you share, think of how revealing something that has been hidden about you helps that other person know more of your character. This is a small representation of how your time reading the Bible under the guidance of the Holy Spirit helps you to learn about God's character.

"All things have been handed over to me by my Father, and no one knows the Son except the Father, and no one knows the Father except the Son and anyone to whom the Son chooses to reveal him."

Matthew 11:27

For the law was given through Moses; grace and truth came through Jesus Christ. No one has ever seen God; the only God, who is at the Father's side, he has made him known.

John 1:17-18

He is the image of the invisible God, the firstborn of all creation.

Colossians 1:15

Incomprehensible

God Reveals Himself in Jesus Christ

4

God reveals Himself to us through His Word, as interpreted to us by His Spirit. In addition, God has revealed Himself by coming from heaven to earth in the person of Jesus Christ, the Word made flesh (Jn. 1:14). Everything that Jesus is and does and says shows us the Father (Jn. 14:8-11).

In the book of Exodus, God led the nation of Israel out of slavery in Egypt and into a land that He had promised to Abraham's descendants hundreds of years earlier. God called Moses to lead the nation of Israel in a special agreement with God called a covenant. A covenant is a binding agreement between parties that is based in promises made to one another. God promised to lead Israel and to give them a land, and the people promised to obey God and worship Him alone. The people of Israel broke the covenant almost immediately when they fashioned a golden calf to worship. In Exodus 33-34, Moses came before the Lord again to renew the covenant after the Israelites sinned. Moses asked the Lord to show him His glory. The Lord told Moses, "You cannot see my face, for man shall not see me and live." Still, to honor Moses' request, the Lord passed by Moses, placing Moses in a cleft of the rock and covering him with His hand as He passed by, allowing Moses to see His back. Moses then spent forty days with the Lord, and he returned to camp with his face shining because he had been talking with God. After his personal encounter with God, Moses was able to share with Israel the words the Lord had revealed to him even though the people of Israel were afraid to come near him because his face shone.

In contrast, John 1:18 says that Jesus came from the Father's side. Jesus, being God Himself, for all eternity existed with the Father. The Father did not hide His face from the Son. The Father, Son, and Holy Spirit share the same nature. Jesus is in the Father, and the Father is in Jesus (Jn. 14:10). No man has ever seen the fullness of God, but Jesus has. If Moses—a mere man unable to look on God's face—was able to share with the Israelites something of God's heart for His people, how much more qualified is Jesus to show us the Father?

As I have read the book of Exodus over the years, I have often imagined how amazing it must have been for the Israelites to follow God Himself in the "pillar of cloud by day and the pillar of fire by night" (Ex. 13:22). How spectacular to see a visible manifestation of the Lord! In those moments of imagination, I am losing sight of the tremendous advantage we have in the age of the church. God has stepped into humanity in the person of Jesus Christ, not only as a visible manifestation but as the only begotten Son. His words and actions are recorded for us in Scripture. And after His ascension to the Father, He has given those who trust Him the Holy Spirit to guide us into all truth. We ourselves are the temple that God dwells in (1 Cor. 3:16). What a privilege to be in this intimate relationship with an incomprehensible God!

Action Step: Read John 1:1-18 carefully. Keep in mind that "the Word" refers to Jesus Christ. Note places throughout the passage that speak of the connection and intimacy between God (the Father) and the Word (the Son).

Oh, the depth of the riches and wisdom and knowledge of God! How unsearchable are his judgments and how inscrutable his ways!
"For who has known the mind of the Lord, or who has been his counselor?"

Romans 11:33-34

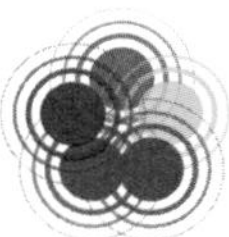

Incomprehensible
God's Ways Lead Us to Praise

5

The book of Romans is the Apostle Paul's most comprehensive presentation of the gospel of Jesus Christ. And the good news of the gospel is that the life, death, and resurrection of Jesus Christ gives us the ability, through faith, to have the right relationship with God. Paul spends most of the letter to the Romans explaining the following:

1. our need to repair our relationship with God,
2. faith as a means to repair our relationship with God, and
3. the abundant blessings of a right relationship with God.

In Romans 11:33-34, after laying out his arguments, Paul breaks out in praise of the One who conceived and carried out this gospel plan. The wisdom and knowledge of God are beyond our abilities to fully comprehend.

The immediate context of Romans 11 discusses how the failure of the nation of Israel to recognize Jesus as the Messiah has led to the inclusion of the Gentiles in God's reconciliation plan, which in turn will lead to the salvation of Israel. What human mind would possibly turn the nation of Israel's failures into a plan of salvation for all the world? Who could possibly counsel the Lord to come up with such a magnificent plan? The answer, of course, is that no one could. The wisdom, knowledge, judgment, and ways of the Lord are perfect and infinite.

We can never completely understand all of His ways, but what He has revealed should lead us to passionate worship. It should also lead us to evaluate ourselves as to whether we are ready to trust His ways even when they are beyond our understanding.

Action Step: Evaluate yourself. Do you trust God completely, even in the areas that you do not understand? For example, do you trust His plan of salvation by faith alone, or do you often feel that you are not good enough to be "worthy" of His redemption? (Hint: none of us are.) Do you find it difficult to trust God when you are in the midst of suffering that just doesn't seem to make sense? Spend some time in prayer asking God to show you places where you only trust Him to the point that you understand Him. Praise Him for His unsearchable wisdom and knowledge.

1 *O Lord, you have searched me and known me!*
2 *You know when I sit down and when I rise up; you discern my thoughts from*
afar.
3 *You search out my path and my lying down and are acquainted with all my*
ways.
4 *Even before a word is on my tongue, behold, O Lord, you know it altogether.*
5 *You hem me in, behind and before, and lay your hand upon me.*
6 *Such knowledge is too wonderful for me; it is high; I cannot attain it.*

7 *Where shall I go from your Spirit? Or where shall I flee from your presence?*
8 *If I ascend to heaven, you are there! If I make my bed in Sheol, you are there!*
9 *If I take the wings of the morning and dwell in the uttermost parts of the sea,*
10 *even there your hand shall lead me, and your right hand shall hold me.*
11 *If I say, "Surely the darkness shall cover me, and the light about me be night,"*
12 *even the darkness is not dark to you; the night is bright as the day, for darkness*
is as light with you.

13 *For you formed my inward parts; you knitted me together in my mother's*
womb.
14 *I praise you, for I am fearfully and wonderfully made. Wonderful are your*
works; my soul knows it very well.
15 *My frame was not hidden from you, when I was being made in secret,*
intricately woven in the depths of the earth.
16 *Your eyes saw my unformed substance; in your book were written, every one*
of them, the days that were formed for me, when as yet there was none of
them.
17 *How precious to me are your thoughts, O God! How vast is the sum of them!*
18 *If I would count them, they are more than the sand. I awake, and I am still*
with you.

Psalms 139:1-18

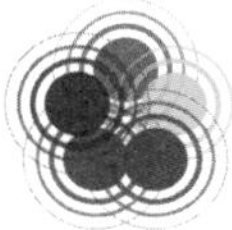

Incomprehensible

We Will Never Learn All about God 6

Psalm 139 is an exploration by David of how intimately God knows him. God's intimate knowledge is not unique to David. The Lord knows everyone's heart to this extent.

The first section (v. 1-6) affirms God's personal knowledge of our actions, thoughts, and words. Then David stated, "Such knowledge is too wonderful for me; it is high; I cannot attain it." God's knowledge of us goes deeper than our knowledge of ourselves.

The next section (v. 7-12) proclaims God's presence to be everywhere. If we did not have a full picture of God's nature, verse 7 could potentially give us reason for terror—we cannot flee from His presence! But this incomprehensible God, whose knowledge knows no bounds, is also limitless in love. God's loving care is described in verse 10, "even there your hand shall lead me, and your right hand shall hold me."

God's power and creativity in His creation is praised in verses 13-18. God intricately wove us together for His purposes before we were even born.

This passage then turns to praise God for the vastness of His thoughts (v. 17-18). His thoughts are so limitless that we will continue to grow in knowledge of Him throughout all eternity because we will never learn all that there is to know about Him. Our God has knowledge so great that He fully knows the extent of our sin and yet He loves us still. This is too wonderful to comprehend and a source of tremendous comfort.

Action Step: Spend some time in prayer praising God for His limitless knowledge and thoughts. Praise Him for His omnipresence–that wherever we go, He is there. Praise Him that, even when you are in the darkest times, He still sees you. Ask Him to help you comprehend Him and His ways.

Weekly Summary

Key Points

1. The universe is beyond our measurements. Even more so is the God who created it. We are finite creatures, while God is infinite. There is no one equal to God. No one can rival Him.

2. The disconnect between the infinite God and finite humanity can only be crossed when God speaks comprehension and understanding to us.

3. The Spirit helps us to understand the truths in Scripture and to have the mind of Christ.

4. In addition, God has revealed Himself by coming from heaven to earth in the person of Jesus Christ, the Word made flesh. Everything that Jesus is and does and says shows us the Father.

5. The wisdom and knowledge of God are beyond our abilities to fully comprehend, but they should lead us to praise.

6. His thoughts are so limitless that we will continue to grow in knowledge of Him throughout all eternity because we will never learn all that there is to know about Him.

Incomprehensible
Action Steps

7

Go back through the action steps and complete any that you have not yet completed or repeat one that was meaningful:

1. Contemplate the stars tonight. If you live in an area where the skies are dark enough and the sky is clear, go outside, find a place where you have a clear view of the stars, and try to count their number. If the stars are not visible for you, look for Hubble Space Telescope photos to consider instead. Try to count the stars in the photo, or see if you can find out how many stars are in the galaxy pictured. Worship God, who placed those stars along with innumerable others.

2. Water something. If it is summer, water your lawn or garden. Water a houseplant. If nothing else, fill a glass with water, find any patch of dirt, and pour the water slowly onto the dirt. Watch what happens to the water. If the soil is porous, the water should slowly seep into the soil, filling the tiny empty spaces and trickling deep into the soil, changing the soil from dry to wet. If the soil is hard and clay-like, the water may run off the surface rather than penetrating. Using a garden tool or something sharp, rough up the hard soil, and create holes in it to allow the water to penetrate. Consider how the water is like God's Word in the soil of your heart. If your heart is porous and soft, His Word will penetrate deeply and change your character according to His purpose. If your heart is hard, you may be running the risk of God using sharp, challenging circumstances to soften your heart to His Word.

3. Set aside some time today to spend with a friend or loved one. Share something of yourself that the other person doesn't know. It could be a silly childhood memory or a hidden fear or something that you have always dreamed of doing. Ask the other person if they would be willing to share likewise. As you share, think of how revealing something that has been hidden about you helps that other person know more of your character. This is a small representation of how your time reading the Bible under the guidance of the Holy Spirit helps you to learn about God's character.

4. Read John 1:1-18 carefully. Keep in mind that "the Word" refers to Jesus Christ. Note places throughout the passage that speak of the connection and intimacy between God (the Father) and the Word (the Son).

5. Evaluate yourself. Do you trust God completely, even in the areas that you do not understand? For example, do you trust His plan of salvation by faith alone, or do you often feel that you are not good enough to be "worthy" of His redemption? (Hint: none of us are.) Do you find it difficult to trust God when you are in the midst of suffering that just doesn't seem to make sense? Spend some time in prayer asking God to show you places where you only trust Him to the point that you understand Him. Praise Him for His unsearchable wisdom and knowledge.

6. Spend some time in prayer praising God for His limitless knowledge and thoughts. Praise Him for His omnipresence—that wherever we go, He is there. Praise Him that, even when you are in the darkest times, He still sees you. Ask Him to help you comprehend Him and His ways.

WEEK 3
Triune

We worship one God in trinity and the Trinity in unity, neither confusing the persons nor dividing the divine being.

For the Father is one person, the Son is another, and the Spirit is still another.

But the deity of the Father, Son, and Holy Spirit is one, equal in glory, coeternal in majesty.

What the Father is, the Son is, and so is the Holy Spirit.

Uncreated is the Father; uncreated is the Son; uncreated is the Spirit. The Father is infinite; the Son is infinite; the Holy Spirit is infinite.

Eternal is the Father; eternal is the Son; eternal is the Spirit: And yet there are not three eternal beings, but one who is eternal; as there are not three uncreated and unlimited beings, but one who is uncreated and unlimited.

Almighty is the Father; almighty is the Son; almighty is the Spirit: And yet there are not three almighty beings, but one who is almighty.

Thus the Father is God; the Son is God; the Holy Spirit is God: And yet there are not three gods, but one God.

Thus the Father is Lord; the Son is Lord; the Holy Spirit is Lord: And yet there are not three lords, but one Lord.

As Christian truth compels us to acknowledge each distinct person as God and Lord, so catholic religion forbids us to say that there are three gods or lords.

The Father was neither made nor created nor begotten; the Son was neither made nor created, but was alone begotten of the Father; the Spirit was neither made nor created, but is proceeding from the Father and the Son.

Thus there is one Father, not three fathers; one Son, not three sons; one Holy Spirit, not three spirits.

And in this Trinity, no one is before or after, greater or less than the other; but all three persons are in themselves, coeternal and coequal; and so we must worship the Trinity in unity and the one God in three persons.

excerpt from ***The Athanasian Creed***

"Hear, O Israel: The LORD *our God, the* LORD *is one. You shall love the* LORD *your God with all your heart and with all your soul and with all your might."*

Deuteronomy 6:4-5

You believe that God is one; you do well. Even the demons believe—and shudder!

James 2:19

Triune
God Is One

1

Triune describes something that is three in one. It is an adjective referring to the Trinity. The Trinity is a description of God as He has revealed Himself—one God in three persons. The word *Trinity* comes from the root *tri*, meaning three, and *unity*, which means the state of being joined as a whole. Though the word *Trinity* never occurs in the Bible, the concept of one God in three persons runs throughout the Bible.

Scripture makes it very clear that God is one. The book of Deuteronomy is a review of the law by Moses. Moses took this opportunity, before his death, to remind the Israelites what God had done for them and what the Israelites had agreed to under the covenant with God initiated at Mount Sinai. Moses had just reviewed the Ten Commandments and reminded the people to keep His commandments "that it may go well with you." It was at this moment that Moses declared, "Hear, O Israel: The LORD our God, the LORD is one. You shall love the LORD your God with all your heart and with all your soul and with all your might."

To the Jews, both past and present, this declaration is a basic confession of their monotheistic faith. As they entered the Promised Land, they were surrounded by cultures that worshiped many gods, but this confession reminded God's people that there is only one true God, and He alone is to be worshiped. To Jesus, this statement was the first and greatest commandment (Mk. 12:29). Jesus Himself affirmed that there is one true God.

There is some difference of opinion among scholars as to the translation of the word for *one*, which is *echad* in Hebrew. It can mean *one*, translating to the "...LORD is one." *Echad* may also translate to *alone*, yielding a translation "...the LORD alone." *Echad* does not conflict with the doctrine of the Trinity, however, because the word carries a meaning of unity as well. In any case, the Deuteronomy verses make it clear that God is unlike any other—there are not multiple gods.

The verse from James restates in brief the faith confession of the Deuteronomy verses and commends the Jewish audience for believing that God is one: "You believe that God is one; you do well." James goes on to say that the demons believe as well, but the belief of the demons is an empty intellectual knowledge of the oneness of God. The demons do not trust God, they simply acknowledge something about His nature. In other words, James is confirming as correct doctrine the idea that God is one, but correct doctrine, by itself, is not enough.

A vibrant, active faith will take this first step of recognizing the oneness of God, then push further into understanding more of the Trinity and more of His nature, allowing it to change our hearts and our lives.

Action Step: Spend some time in prayer today asking God to help you understand more about the Trinity. Remember that we can only understand Him to the extent that He reveals Himself to us in Scripture and through insight given by the Holy Spirit. Call out to Him for opportunities to learn about this very difficult-to-grasp doctrine. As you pray, keep in mind that our times of prayer can also be seen as joining into a conversation that is already initiated between the Father, the Son, and the Holy Spirit.

In the beginning was the Word, and the Word was with God, and the Word was God. He was in the beginning with God. All things were made through him, and without him was not any thing made that was made.

John 1:1-3

Philip said to him, "Lord, show us the Father, and it is enough for us." Jesus said to him, "Have I been with you so long, and you still do not know me, Philip? Whoever has seen me has seen the Father. How can you say, 'Show us the Father'? Do you not believe that I am in the Father and the Father is in me? The words that I say to you I do not speak on my own authority, but the Father who dwells in me does his works."

John 14:8-10

For in him the whole fullness of deity dwells bodily.

Colossians 2:9

Do you not know that you are God's temple and that God's Spirit dwells in you?

1 Corinthians 3:16

Triune
Jesus Christ Is God, the Holy Spirit Is God 2

The deity of Jesus Christ is essential to the gospel and is clearly taught in the New Testament. John opens his gospel with a discussion of "the Word," revealed as Jesus in verse 14. John begins with, "In the beginning was the Word." This phrase parallels the opening of the book of Genesis: "In the beginning, God…" Immediately, John makes clear that Jesus was there alongside the Father at creation and before time began, even in eternity past. He continues with, "the Word was with God," suggesting that there is some distinction between God and the Word for them to be with one another. He finishes that first sentence with "the Word was God." In one sentence, John has pointed to Jesus' deity, while also distinguishing Him from God the Father. In verse 3, John leaves no room for doubt that Jesus Christ was present in the Creation and that nothing was made apart from Jesus Christ.

Later, in John 14, the exchange between Philip and Jesus reaffirms His unity with the Father. The Father is in Jesus, and Jesus is in the Father. Whoever has seen Jesus has seen the Father. This deepens the mystery: Jesus and the Father are *with* one another, and yet they are one. Colossians 2:9 makes clear the deity of Christ. The whole fullness of deity dwells in Him.

And what does Scripture say about the deity of the Holy Spirit? The book of 1 Kings includes an account of the construction of the temple of the Lord by King Solomon. God had ordained that Solomon would be the one to build His dwelling place among His people. When the temple was completed and furnished, the leaders of Israel assembled, and the priests brought the ark of the covenant to the Most Holy Place in the temple. "And when the priests came out of the Holy Place, a cloud filled the house of the Lord, so that the priests could not stand to minister because of the cloud, for the glory of the Lord filled the house of the Lord" (1 Ki. 8:10-11). God, who had led the Israelites out of Egypt as a pillar of cloud by day and a pillar of fire by night, appeared before His people once again in the form of a cloud to occupy the temple.

1 Corinthians 3:16 states that we are God's temple and His Spirit dwells in us. Paul pointed the Corinthians to an illustration of the Holy Spirit dwelling in the New Testament church as likened to God occupying His temple. In doing so, he makes clear that the Holy Spirit is God.

Jesus Christ is God. The Holy Spirit is God. All of the attributes that we are studying about God are completely true of each person of the Trinity, and each person of the Trinity is fully God. Father, Son, and Holy Spirit are one in nature or essence.

Action Step: Read through the Athanasian Creed excerpt on page 39. This creed is named for Athanasius, an early church leader who fought hard against heresies regarding the Trinity. Athanasius died in 373 AD, and modern scholars are in agreement that this creed was written well after his death, probably during the sixth century (c. 500 AD) at the earliest, so Athanasius was not likely the author. Do the statements in the Athanasian Creed line up with Scriptural teaching on the Trinity? As we study the Bible this week on the subject of the Trinity, watch for verses that affirm the Athanasian Creed.

Then God said, "Let us make man in our image, after our likeness. And let them have dominion over the fish of the sea and over the birds of the heavens and over the livestock and over all the earth and over every creeping thing that creeps on the earth."

Genesis 1:26

Then the LORD God said, "Behold, the man has become like one of us in knowing good and evil. Now, lest he reach out his hand and take also of the tree of life and eat, and live forever—"
Genesis 3:22

And Jacob was left alone. And a man wrestled with him until the breaking of the day. When the man saw that he did not prevail against Jacob, he touched his hip socket, and Jacob's hip was put out of joint as he wrestled with him. Then he said, "Let me go, for the day has broken." But Jacob said, "I will not let you go unless you bless me." And he said to him, "What is your name?" And he said, "Jacob." Then he said, "Your name shall no longer be called Jacob, but Israel, for you have striven with God and with men, and have prevailed." Then Jacob asked him, "Please tell me your name." But he said, "Why is it that you ask my name?" And there he blessed him. So Jacob called the name of the place Peniel, saying, "For I have seen God face to face, and yet my life has been delivered."
Genesis 32:24-30

So the LORD said to Moses, "Take Joshua the son of Nun, a man in whom is the Spirit, and lay your hand on him."
Numbers 27:18

Triune

The Trinity in the Old Testament 3

There are many hints in the Old Testament that God exists as one and yet is diverse. In just the opening few chapters of Genesis, there are several times when God is referred to as plural. "Then God said, 'Let *us* make man in *our* image, after *our* likeness.'" Even the Hebrew used here for *God* is *Elohim*, which is a plural form of God.

There are several suggestions as to why a plural form is used. Some have said that the use is similar to historic kings speaking of themselves in plural form, ascribing majesty to the position. Others suggest that God is having a conversation with angels, yet nowhere in Scripture is it taught that mankind is created in the likeness of angels. But, when viewed with the teaching on the Trinity in the New Testament, it seems most likely that God is hinting at a mysterious plurality of persons within Himself, more fully revealed in the New Testament.

This pattern of use is repeated in Genesis 3:22, when "the LORD God (*Elohim*) said, 'Behold, the man has become like one of *us* in knowing good and evil.'" Both passages in Genesis imply that God speaks to Himself as a plural being.

In Genesis 32, Jacob returned to Canaan, the land of his birth, with his wives, children, and herds. Jacob was fearful of his brother Esau, whom he deceived. Jacob humbly asked God for deliverance from the hand of his brother and stayed by himself that night in camp. This is when "a man wrestled with him until the breaking of the day." After they wrestled, the man said, "you have striven with God and with men, and have prevailed." In saying this, the "man" identified Himself as God. This and other appearances of God as a man in the Old Testament (see Genesis 18) foreshadow the incarnation of Jesus Christ.

The Spirit of God is mentioned many times in the Old Testament. But the passage from Numbers is interesting in that there is some distinction made between the Lord, who is speaking to Moses, and the Spirit, who is in Joshua. The Lord seems to speak of the Spirit as a separate person from Himself.

These glimpses of the Trinity in the Old Testament do not, in themselves, give us much understanding of the Trinity. Yet, they do affirm that God did not change at the incarnation. He simply revealed more of Himself to all believers in the person of Jesus Christ and the sending of the Holy Spirit.

Action Step: One popular illustration given to describe the Trinity is an apple. The apple has skin, a core, and the fruit itself, which taken together make an apple. The illustration compares this to the Father, Son, and Holy Spirit together being God. Is this a good representation of the Trinity? The parts of the apple can be separated from one another, and a core, by itself, is definitely not an apple. If you are in doubt, try offering a child an apple core as a snack. In contrast, God is not made up of parts. All persons in the Godhead are fully God, but they cannot be separated into sections. There is no illustration from nature that can represent the Trinity. The Trinity is not revealed in nature, but only in Scripture. Anything from the created world used as a tool to imagine the Trinity will fail to do so accurately. Illustrations of the Trinity are therefore best used to show what the triune Godhead is *not* like. Think of any other illustrations of the Trinity that you have heard and evaluate how they may introduce a false concept of God.

"Go therefore and make disciples of all nations, baptizing them in the name of the Father and of the Son and of the Holy Spirit,"

Matthew 28:19

Now there are varieties of gifts, but the same Spirit; and there are varieties of service, but the same Lord; and there are varieties of activities, but it is the same God who empowers them all in everyone.

1 Corinthians 12:4-6

The grace of the Lord Jesus Christ and the love of God and the fellowship of the Holy Spirit be with you all.

2 Corinthians 13:14

There is one body and one Spirit—just as you were called to the one hope that belongs to your call—one Lord, one faith, one baptism, one God and Father of all, who is over all and through all and in all.

Ephesians 4:4-6

So then you are no longer strangers and aliens, but you are fellow citizens with the saints and members of the household of God, built on the foundation of the apostles and prophets, Christ Jesus himself being the cornerstone, in whom the whole structure, being joined together, grows into a holy temple in the Lord. In him you also are being built together into a dwelling place for God by the Spirit.

Ephesians 2:19-22

Triune

The Trinity in the New Testament 4

I love listening to music. The gifts of voice, music composition, and ability to play instruments are not something that I possess, but I appreciate them in others. There is something otherworldly about the rhythm, flow, and creativity of music. It is mathematical. It is poetic. It is artistic. God Himself is the creator of music—just listen to the rhythm of any songbird.

Rhythm is the best word that I can come up with to describe the repeated pattern of the New Testament speaking of the Father, the Son, and the Holy Spirit. Time and again the New Testament writers mention them in unison. They are there together in baptism (Matt. 3 and 28). They are all a part of the spiritual gifting of believers (1 Cor. 12). Paul closes his second letter to the Corinthians with wishes for a relationship between the believers and all three persons of the Trinity (2 Cor. 13). The unity of believers relies on all three (Eph. 4). The household of God is built by their partnership (Eph. 2). The Father, the Son, and the Holy Spirit are joined in one stanza after another in the song of the New Testament.

C. S. Lewis, in *Mere Christianity*, has described their relationship as a dance:

> *...in Christianity God is not a static thing—not even a person—but a dynamic, pulsating activity, a life, almost a kind of drama. Almost, if you will not think me irreverent, a kind of dance. The union between the Father and the Son is such a live concrete thing that this union itself is also a Person.... What grows out of the joint life of the Father and Son is a real Person, is in fact the Third of the three Persons who are God.*
>
> *This third Person is called, in technical language, the Holy Ghost, or the "spirit" of God. Do not be worried or surprised if you find it (or Him) rather vaguer or more shadowy in your mind than the other two. I think there is a reason why that must be so. In the Christian life you are not usually looking* at *Him. He is always acting through you. If you think of the Father as something "out there," in front of you, and of the Son as someone standing at your side, helping you to pray, trying to turn you into another son, then you have to think of the third Person as something inside you, or behind you.**

The three Persons of the Trinity have been participating in this dance for all eternity. And now God invites us into this relationship with Him. The life of a believer in Jesus Christ is a life of fellowship with the Trinity. What a privilege to be invited into the dance!

Action Step: Galatians 5:25 says, "If we live by the Spirit, let us also keep in step with the Spirit." Keeping in step with the Spirit brings to mind following along with a leader in the same way that one partner will follow the lead of the other partner in a dance. The Father, Son, and Holy Spirit established the dance of life. The Holy Spirit walks with us to lead us in the dance. We must follow His lead to best participate in a life that honors God. What can you do today to follow His lead? Is there someone with whom He would direct you to share God's loving kindness today?

** Mere Christianity by CS Lewis © copyright CS Lewis Pte Ltd 1042, 1943, 1944, 1952.*

Jesus answered him, "If anyone loves me, he will keep my word, and my Father will love him, and we will come to him and make our home with him."

John 14:23

"But the Helper, the Holy Spirit, whom the Father will send in my name, he will teach you all things and bring to your remembrance all that I have said to you."

John 14:26

"But when the Helper comes, whom I will send to you from the Father, the Spirit of truth, who proceeds from the Father, he will bear witness about me."

John 15:26

"Nevertheless, I tell you the truth: it is to your advantage that I go away, for if I do not go away, the Helper will not come to you. But if I go, I will send him to you."

John 16:7

"I still have many things to say to you, but you cannot bear them now. When the Spirit of truth comes, he will guide you into all the truth, for he will not speak on his own authority, but whatever he hears he will speak, and he will declare to you the things that are to come. He will glorify me, for he will take what is mine and declare it to you. All that the Father has is mine; therefore I said that he will take what is mine and declare it to you."

John 16:12-15

"Father, I desire that they also, whom you have given me, may be with me where I am, to see my glory that you have given me because you loved me before the foundation of the world."

John 17:24

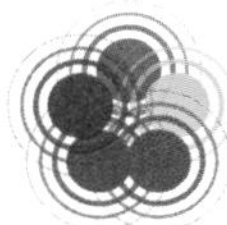

Triune

The Trinity Is Relational

5

John 14-17 gives an account of Jesus and His disciples gathered for some of their last moments together before His arrest. We are given the blessed opportunity to listen to what Jesus said to His disciples and what He prayed to the Father. We are learning about the Trinity by listening to conversations within the Trinity! I am struck in studying these chapters at the incredible focus in His teaching on relationships. Jesus tells His disciples that He is leaving and that where He is going they cannot follow. They are understandably confused and troubled. Jesus sets out to encourage them with teaching on their continuing relationship through the Holy Spirit. There does not seem to be any other section in the Bible that gives us so much insight into the intimate relationship between the Father, the Son, and the Holy Spirit.

Here are some highlights of what we can learn in John 14-17 about the personal relationship that exists within the Godhead:

Jesus is in the Father, and the Father is in Him. (14:9)
Jesus sends the Spirit of truth from the Father to bear witness about Jesus. (15:26)
The Spirit will glorify Jesus by declaring truths about Jesus to His disciples. (16:14)
Everything that the Father has also belongs to Jesus. (16:15)
Jesus was not alone—the Father was with Him. (16:32)
Jesus and the Father shared glory and love before the world existed. (17:5, 24)

These truths suggest that for all eternity, the Trinity has been in loving relationship within their unity. Jesus and the Spirit submit to the will of the Father, suggesting that they are in complete agreement with one another. They are always pleased with each other (Jn. 8:29), and they glorify each other. Even without the presence of mankind, God is triune and relational.

In the beauty of studying the connections within the Trinity revealed in this passage, we must not miss the place that we have been granted in the relationship as well:

Jesus Christ is in us, and we are in Jesus Christ. (14:20)
Jesus asks the Father to give the Spirit to dwell in the disciples and in us. (14:16-17)
The Holy Spirit will teach us truth and bring it to our remembrance. (14:26)
Jesus prayed that we may be one just as Jesus is in the Father and the Father is in Jesus, and that we may be in them. (17:20-21)

This brief study of the perfect loving relationship within the Godhead leaves me in awe not only of my limits in understanding One who is so much higher than I, but also of the ways that we are invited into that relationship and have our own lives forever changed.

Action Step: Print out a copy of the gospel of John, chapters 14-17. Use one color of highlighting pen to mark all of the phrases in these four chapters having to do with the relationship among the persons of the Trinity. Some examples might be "the Father is in me" or "the Holy Spirit, whom the Father will send in my name"–anything that mentions connections or communication between the Father, the Son, and the Holy Spirit. Use a second color to highlight phrases that have to do with the relationship or connections between any member of the Trinity and believers. For example, "Abide in me" or "he will guide you into all the truth." You may be surprised to find that these relational highlights cover a large percentage of this text. Save your highlighted copy, as we will come back to it later in this book.

Peter, an apostle of Jesus Christ, To those who are elect exiles of the Dispersion in Pontus, Galatia, Cappadocia, Asia, and Bithynia, according to the foreknowledge of God the Father, in the sanctification of the Spirit, for obedience to Jesus Christ and for sprinkling with his blood: May grace and peace be multiplied to you.

1 Peter 1:1-2

But when the fullness of time had come, God sent forth his Son, born of woman, born under the law, to redeem those who were under the law, so that we might receive adoption as sons. And because you are sons, God has sent the Spirit of his Son into our hearts, crying, "Abba! Father!"

Galatians 4:4-6

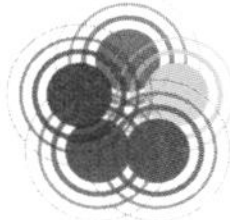

Triune
Trinity Roles in Salvation 6

The triune nature of God is not spelled out in Scripture in clear wording like many other teachings. The uniqueness of this doctrine is that it is revealed by the Father sending the Son and the Holy Spirit to *show* us His triune nature. This sending and revelation is paired with God's revelation of the plan for mankind's salvation. The Bible then testifies to the appearance of the Son and the Spirit and further explains God's acts of redemption.

In Peter's first epistle, there is a tremendous amount of teaching packed into his opening greeting. The recipients of his letter are "elect exiles." This refers to believers who are exiles in the sense that the world is no longer their home. They are citizens of the kingdom of heaven. Peter's opening teaches that God has chosen and foreknown them. The Father initiates a relationship with His people. Jesus fulfills the mission required for a holy God to have a relationship with sinful people through the sacrificial shedding of His blood—His death on the cross. The Spirit applies redemption to the believer by convicting us of sin, giving us faith, and continuing to make us more like Jesus (sanctification). Obedience is the result of sanctification, as seen in the phrase "sanctification of the Spirit, *for* obedience to Jesus Christ." Obedience is not the entry ticket into covenant or relationship with God. Peter shows here that obedience is the objective or the end result of sanctification by the Spirit.

The sprinkling of Jesus' blood accomplishes the forgiveness of sins when we fail to obey. Under the Old Covenant, God set up a sacrificial system in which the blood of animal sacrifices made atonement for their sins (Lev. 17:11). Under the New Covenant, the truth remains that "without the shedding of blood there is no forgiveness of sins" (Heb. 9:22), but it is the once-for-all sacrifice of Jesus that accomplishes the atonement (Heb. 10:10-12).

In his epistle to the Galatians, Paul also gives a short summary of how the Trinity works together to accomplish salvation. God is the sender. Jesus was born under the law, the Old Covenant, to live a life that perfectly obeyed the law and die to redeem those who are unable to fulfill the law. His shed blood purchased our pardon, allowing us to be adopted as sons. One of the privileges of being sons is receiving the righteous record of Jesus Christ, which grants us access to a perfectly holy God. Also, with adoption comes the Spirit of His Son, the Holy Spirit, giving us the ability to recognize ourselves that we are sons of God.

The Father initiated the plan of salvation by sending the Son and the Spirit, the Son fulfilled it in history, and the Spirit fulfills it in the individual human heart. The Son speaks and acts based on what He hears from the Father, and the Spirit enables us to understand what the Son has spoken and accomplished.

As in any study of the nature of God, we are forced to accept that we cannot fully understand the Trinity. Though our understanding of the Trinity is limited, we do not want the understanding that we do have to be in error.

Action Step: The doctrine of the Trinity is one of the most difficult for the human mind to grasp because it is so unlike anything that we experience. God's nature is completely unique! Spend some time today in praise and worship for the God who is three-in-one. Praise Him for who He is and the fact that He has chosen to reveal His triune nature to us and to invite us to participate in that fellowship.

Weekly Summary
Key Points

1. God is one, and He is unlike any other.
2. God the Father is God. Jesus Christ is God. The Holy Spirit is God.
3. The Old Testament contains hints and glimpses of the Trinity.
4. The Trinity is further revealed in the New Testament.
5. For all eternity, the Trinity has been in loving relationship within their unity.
6. Every member of the Trinity is involved in and takes a unique role in the salvation of believers.

Triune

Action Steps

7

Go back through the action steps and complete any that you have not yet completed or repeat one that was meaningful:

1. Spend some time in prayer today asking God to help you understand more about the Trinity. Remember that we can only understand Him to the extent that He reveals Himself to us in Scripture and through insight given by the Holy Spirit. Call out to Him for opportunities to learn about this very difficult-to-grasp doctrine.

2. Read through the Athanasian Creed excerpt on page 39. This creed is named for Athanasius, an early church leader who fought hard against heresies regarding the Trinity. Athanasius died in 373 AD, and modern scholars are in agreement that this creed was written well after his death, probably during the sixth century (c. 500 AD) at the earliest, so Athanasius was not likely the author. Do the statements in the Athanasian Creed line up with Scriptural teaching on the Trinity? As we study the Bible this week on the subject of the Trinity, watch for verses that affirm the Athanasian Creed.

3. There is no illustration from nature that can represent the Trinity. The Trinity is not revealed in nature, but only in Scripture. Anything from the created world used as a tool to imagine the Trinity will fail to do so accurately. Illustrations of the Trinity are therefore best used to show what the triune Godhead is not like. Think of any illustrations of the Trinity that you have heard and evaluate how they may introduce a false concept of God.

4. Galatians 5:25 says, "If we live by the Spirit, let us also keep in step with the Spirit." Keeping in step with the Spirit brings to mind following along with a leader in the same way that one partner will follow the lead of the other partner in a dance. The Father, Son, and Holy Spirit established the dance of life. The Holy Spirit walks with us to lead us in the dance. We must follow His lead to best participate in a life that honors God. What can you do today to follow His lead? Is there someone He would direct you with whom to share God's loving kindness today?

5. Print out a copy of the gospel of John, chapters 14-17. Use one color of highlighting pen to mark all of the phrases in these four chapters having to do with the relationship among the persons of the Trinity. Some examples might be "the Father is in me" or "the Holy Spirit, whom the Father will send in my name"—anything that mentions connections or communication between the Father, the Son, and the Holy Spirit. Use a second color to highlight phrases that have to do with the relationship or connections between any member of the Trinity and believers. For example, "Abide in me" or "he will guide you into all the truth." You may be surprised to find that these relational highlights cover a large percentage of this text. Save your highlighted copy, as we will come back to it later in this book.

6. The doctrine of the Trinity is one of the most difficult for the human mind to grasp because it is so unlike anything that we experience. God's nature is completely unique! So, how can we respond to something that we cannot thoroughly understand? Worship the Father and the Son and the Holy Spirit! Spend some time today in praise and worship for the God who is three-in-one.

WEEK 4

Eternal

God that hath neither beginning nor end, that is our God; who hath not only immortality in himself, but immortality to give out to others. As he hath "abundance of spirit" to quicken them… so he hath abundance of immortality to continue them.

Stephen Charnock, *The Existence and Attributes of God*

Lord, you have been our dwelling place in all generations. Before the mountains were brought forth, or ever you had formed the earth and the world, from everlasting to everlasting you are God.

Psalms 90:1-2

In the beginning, God created the heavens and the earth.

Genesis 1:1

The Lord will reign forever, your God, O Zion, to all generations. Praise the Lord!

Psalms 146:10

How great are his signs, how mighty his wonders! His kingdom is an everlasting kingdom, and his dominion endures from generation to generation.

Daniel 4:3

And the four living creatures, each of them with six wings, are full of eyes all around and within, and day and night they never cease to say, "Holy, holy, holy, is the Lord God Almighty, who was and is and is to come!"

Revelation 4:8

Eternal
God's Duration Is Perpetual 1

To begin to consider the eternal nature of God, let's first consider His existence as endless days. Psalm 90 is believed to be the only psalm that was written by Moses, though Scripture gives more than one account of Moses leading the nation of Israel in worship through song (Exodus 15:1; Deuteronomy 31:30). In Psalm 90, the limited and passing days of men and women are contrasted with the endless days of God. He is our dwelling place and refuge in all generations. From everlasting to everlasting, He is God. The Hebrew word here translated as *everlasting* can mean a vanishing point or time out of mind, or it can be a reference to eternity. Everlasting, then, is that time and place that we cannot see no matter how much we strain our eyes or imaginations. Therefore, the meaning of this phrase is that from before a time that the human mind can conceive until a time beyond what we can see, He is God.

"In the beginning, God created the heavens and the earth." The beginning of Creation is the beginning of time that we can conceive. Before that time, He was God. The creator must have existed before the creation. The concept of someone existing before us is not hard to grasp. It is a fact that we are aware of from childhood. Our parents existed before us. Our children will likely live past us. If we think of time as a number line that proceeds from this moment in both directions—before us and after us—we can think of God existing throughout the line of time. But Genesis 1:1 teaches that time began with the creation of the world—that the Creation is the beginning of time. This is affirmed in verse 5: "And there was evening and there was morning, the first day." The first day implies the beginning of time. So our number line of time has a defined beginning, and God existed before that. God existed before time began.

In Daniel 3, King Nebuchadnezzar of Babylon cast Shadrach, Meshach, and Abednego into the fiery furnace for refusing to worship his golden image. The king himself saw the three men in the fire along with a mysterious fourth man, who appeared "like a son of the gods." The king had the three men retrieved from the fire unharmed, and Nebuchadnezzar was led to praise God: "How great are his signs, how mighty his wonders! His kingdom is an everlasting kingdom, and his dominion endures from generation to generation." How amazing for the most powerful king in the known world—a Gentile king—to point out that God's kingdom is unique in its duration for ever and ever. Not only did God exist before Creation, His reign will last forever.

The number line of time has a defined beginning, but God's years endure infinitely beyond time. Pick any point on the timeline, even if it does extend infinitely in both directions, and the proclamation from Revelation 4:8 remains true: God was before that point, and He is at that point, and He is to come after that point.

Action Step: Psalm 146 parallels the praise of Nebuchadnezzar. Read Psalm 146 and note the advice to place your trust in the God who will reign forever rather than kings of this earth who endure only for one generation. As the Psalm ends in praise, allow it to lead you into praise to God for His eternal nature.

For thus says the One who is high and lifted up, who inhabits eternity, whose name is Holy: "I dwell in the high and holy place, and also with him who is of a contrite and lowly spirit, to revive the spirit of the lowly, and to revive the heart of the contrite."

Isaiah 57:15

For a thousand years in your sight are but as yesterday when it is past, or as a watch in the night.

Psalms 90:4

But do not overlook this one fact, beloved, that with the Lord one day is as a thousand years, and a thousand years as one day.

2 Peter 3:8

Eternal
God Inhabits Eternity

2

We are very familiar with time. We are aware that a moment passes, and it cannot be retrieved. Just as that moment has passed, we continue into another moment. We can anticipate the coming moments as well. And so it goes with years, as well as moments. This is the nature of time and its passing.

God inhabits eternity. Eternity is unaffected by the notion of time. His whole essence or nature is in one permanent state where there is no passing of time. He is aware of time, for He has created time, but He is not constrained by it. The Creator cannot be contained or held captive by His creation. All at once He knows what is, what has been, and what will be. He is always what He was, and He is always what He will be.

There are times in Scripture when the language of time is used to describe the eternity of God. But these words are always for our benefit, so that we are able to use the experience of Creation to gain a limited understanding of the infinite nature of God. Psalm 90:4 is one such example. Assuming we have healthy minds, you and I can remember most of what occurred yesterday. We remember the work that was accomplished, the people we saw, and topics of the conversations that we had. But pick an average day from ten years ago and try to do the same. It is very difficult to remember anything with clarity from ten years ago, unless it was a very significant event. In contrast, any day a thousand years ago to God is just as yesterday is to you and me.

Peter adapts the Psalm and adds the inverse: "with the Lord one day is as a thousand years." God experiences one day as if it goes on for a thousand years without end. Our eternal God is so unaffected by the passage of time that the passage of that one day is the same as the passage of a thousand years. Yet we need to remind ourselves that a thousand years is still a time period that is described for our benefit. In reality, the thousand-year time period is representative of all of eternity.

Let's assume it was possible to empty the oceans (though it's not possible—where would we put all that water?). Then assume that emptying the oceans would not affect the rest of the earth's water cycle (though it would, since ninety percent of evaporating water that supplies the water cycle comes from the ocean). Picture the biggest river that you have ever seen flowing at its normal rate. Now imagine all of earth's mighty rivers and the immensity of their collective flow. All of those rivers and streams flowing at their normal rate would take over thirty-six thousand years to refill that empty ocean. Imagining the vastness of the volume of water in the ocean is another imperfect exercise in getting our limited minds to understand the vastness of God's eternal nature. The length of each of our lives is a tiny mountain brook relative to the volume of God's eternal existence.

Action Step: Have some fun pondering numbers today. The National Oceanic and Atmospheric Administration website says that there is enough water in the ocean to fill about 352,670,000,000,000,000,000 gallon-sized milk containers. If you had the pleasure of a beachfront home and you walked to the water's edge to fill a gallon-sized milk jug with ocean water every day for 352,670,000,000,000,000,000 days to drain the ocean dry, God would still be on the throne after your task was finished. How do you even pronounce a number with 16 zeros in it?

Then Moses said to God, "If I come to the people of Israel and say to them, 'The God of your fathers has sent me to you,' and they ask me, 'What is his name?' what shall I say to them?" God said to Moses, "I AM WHO I AM." And he said, "Say this to the people of Israel, 'I AM has sent me to you.'" God also said to Moses, "Say this to the people of Israel, 'The LORD, the God of your fathers, the God of Abraham, the God of Isaac, and the God of Jacob, has sent me to you.' This is my name forever, and thus I am to be remembered throughout all generations."

Exodus 3:13-15

"Your father Abraham rejoiced that he would see my day. He saw it and was glad." So the Jews said to him, "You are not yet fifty years old, and have you seen Abraham?" Jesus said to them, "Truly, truly, I say to you, before Abraham was, I am." So they picked up stones to throw at him, but Jesus hid himself and went out of the temple.

John 8:56-59

"Remember the former things of old; for I am God, and there is no other; I am God, and there is none like me, declaring the end from the beginning and from ancient times things not yet done, saying, 'My counsel shall stand, and I will accomplish all my purpose,'"

Isaiah 46:9-10

Eternal
God Experiences All of Time as Present 3

Exodus 3 recounts God's appearance to Moses in the burning bush to call Moses to lead His people out of Egypt. Moses, feeling vastly underqualified for such a task, asked God for a bit of backing, possibly a name to "drop." God answered, "'I AM WHO I AM.' And he said, 'Say this to the people of Israel, I AM has sent me to you.'" Three times in one verse the Lord described Himself with a form of the Hebrew word meaning "to be" or "to exist." Wrapped up in this name that God has revealed of Himself is His self-existence and His unchanging and eternal nature. God's description of Himself in the present tense is meant to be understood that He is always in the present. He is the same God that He was to Abraham, Isaac, and Jacob.

This eternal implication of His name is confirmed by the fact that, one thousand five hundred years after Moses, Jesus used the same name in the same present tense to describe Himself. In John 8, Jesus was not merely claiming to be over two thousand years old and alive at the time of Abraham, which would be a miraculous claim in itself. Jesus used the same name that God used with Moses at the burning bush. He used present tense—existing always—language to clearly claim not only to be eternal but to be the very God who appeared to Moses. Listeners very clearly understood His claim, as they immediately picked up stones to execute Jesus for what they saw as blasphemy.

In this name, God conveyed that "I AM" is in the past, "I AM" is in the present, and "I AM" is in the future. "I AM" is what He will be in all moments of time and in all eternity. God exists in eternal duration. He experiences all things as present, seeing from the beginning to the end in one view. God's foreknowledge is not merely an ability to look ahead and know the future. God is just as present in the future as He is in this moment in addition to the past. It is as if our timeline that we discussed two days ago is completely contained within God. God's eternal existence is a perfect whole that encompasses all of time and all of eternity.

Action Step: Meditate on who God is and His record of faithfulness and continuous presence, both in the past, in Scripture, and in your own life, in the present. Consider His presence with His people suffering as slaves in Egypt and His call to Moses to lead them out of slavery. Compare this with any trials that you may be enduring in the present. The same eternal God who was aware of the cry of His people in Egypt is present with you and aware of your cries. Pray for understanding of His eternal nature as we continue to study Scripture that reveals this characteristic of God.

Behold my servant, whom I uphold, my chosen, in whom my soul delights; I have put my Spirit upon him; he will bring forth justice to the nations. He will not cry aloud or lift up his voice, or make it heard in the street; a bruised reed he will not break, and a faintly burning wick he will not quench; he will faithfully bring forth justice. He will not grow faint or be discouraged till he has established justice in the earth; and the coastlands wait for his law… "Behold, the former things have come to pass, and new things I now declare; before they spring forth I tell you of them."

Isaiah 42:1-4, 9

But when the fullness of time had come, God sent forth his Son, born of woman, born under the law, to redeem those who were under the law, so that we might receive adoption as sons.

Galatians 4:4-5

"Behold, the days are coming, declares the Lord, when I will establish a new covenant with the house of Israel and with the house of Judah, not like the covenant that I made with their fathers on the day when I took them by the hand to bring them out of the land of Egypt. For they did not continue in my covenant, and so I showed no concern for them, declares the Lord. For this is the covenant that I will make with the house of Israel after those days, declares the Lord: I will put my laws into their minds, and write them on their hearts, and I will be their God, and they shall be my people."

Hebrews 8:8-10

Eternal

God Takes Action in Time 4

Although God is eternal and is not constrained by time, He does act in specific moments in the human timeline. He even tells of His intended actions through Old Testament prophecy at a point in time long before the human timeline experiences His acts. God uses the progression of time and history to accomplish His purposes and reveal His glory.

Isaiah 42:1-9 is referred to as a "Servant Song," one of several in Isaiah that point toward the Messiah. (In fact, the first four verses of this Servant Song are quoted in Matthew 12:18-21 as being fulfilled in Jesus.) The people of Isaiah's time were living under the Old Covenant given to Moses on the mountain, but Israel had failed to keep their covenant responsibilities. The Northern Kingdom of Israel was exiled for their covenant failures during Isaiah's ministry. The Southern Kingdom of Judah was exiled for their disobedience about one hundred years after Isaiah's life and ministry. Isaiah's prophetic book includes warning and judgment for all the people of Israel. But it is also filled with promises of new things that will come. God will put His Spirit upon the Messiah, and He will ultimately bring justice to the whole earth, including the nation of Israel.

Now let's move forward in time and God's use of it to the New Testament. The book of Galatians is an explanation of the gospel of Jesus Christ and a description of the New Covenant, in which believers in Jesus Christ do not have to fulfill the ceremonial requirements of the Mosaic covenant. In Galatians 4:4, Paul describes the timing of God sending the Son as "the fullness of time." God had directed all of world history for this perfect moment in time for all nations to be prepared for the life and ministry of Jesus Christ and the subsequent spread of the gospel throughout the world. God did not have to wait for the right cultural and political events to occur to accomplish His purposes, He orchestrated them. The promises of God's redemption of His people—promises made as far back as Genesis 3:15—are fulfilled in Jesus Christ.

A clear contrast between the Old Covenant, broken through unbelief, and the new and better covenant, is discussed in Hebrews 8. Included in this discussion is God's promise to put His law into our minds and write His commands on our hearts. These verses in Hebrews are quoted from Jeremiah 31:31-34, making it clear that Jesus is the fulfillment of this prophecy. God had revealed to Jeremiah a redemptive new covenant to come for His people.

God's intent for a living relationship between Him and people of faith is part of His eternal plan. These verses are just a sample of the moments in time when God spoke prophetically or acted intentionally to accomplish the plan that is eternally in His nature.

Action Step: Draw a timeline and label all of these dates, events, and prophecies: 1) Creation, the fall, and the Genesis 3:15 promise of redemption by Eve's offspring (assume 4000 BC for this exercise, though not all Christians are in agreement on this); 2) Isaiah's Servant Song prophecy and the exile of Israel (c. 700 BC); 3) Jeremiah's prophecy of a new covenant and Judah's exile (c. 600 BC); 4) The life, death, and resurrection of Jesus, fulfilling the promise of the new covenant (c. 0 AD); 5) The writing of the books of Galatians and Hebrews (c. 50-70 AD); 6) Today's date and the status of your personal participation in God's redemptive plan. After completing the timeline, consider that God is eternally present in all of those events.

"I am the Alpha and the Omega," says the Lord God, "who is and who was and who is to come, the Almighty."

Revelation 1:8

"You, Lord, laid the foundation of the earth in the beginning, and the heavens are the work of your hands; they will perish, but you remain; they will all wear out like a garment, like a robe you will roll them up, like a garment they will be changed. But you are the same, and your years will have no end."

Hebrews 1:10-12

Of old you laid the foundation of the earth, and the heavens are the work of your hands. They will perish, but you will remain; they will all wear out like a garment. You will change them like a robe, and they will pass away, but you are the same, and your years have no end.

Psalms 102:25-27

Eternal, All-Powerful, and Unchanging 5

God's eternal nature is so closely tied to His other attributes that it is nearly impossible to discuss eternity without taking notice of some of His other attributes. As stated in this book's introduction, we have to emphasize that He cannot be divided into parts. Yet our minds are so limited that we find it difficult to comprehend any of Him without narrowing our vision to just one or two attributes at a time. Still, there are times when we cannot successfully separate the attributes of God!

If God is all-powerful (omnipotent), then He must be eternal. If He is powerful over everything else that exists, then there is nothing that could have brought Him into existence, because that thing would be more powerful than God. Likewise, if He is all-powerful, nothing can prevent Him from continuing to exist.

Alpha and Omega are the first and last letters of the Greek alphabet. God calls Himself the Alpha and Omega because He was the Creator at the beginning, and He will be the Ruler forever. It is worth noting that in the same statement, He refers to Himself as "the Almighty." He is the first and the last—everything from A to Z—and coupled with that His power is absolute. God's almighty nature will accomplish His eternal plan for re-creating the earth when His kingdom is established as set forth in the book of Revelation.

Similarly, God's unchanging character and eternal nature are inseparable and interdependent. If He were not eternal, then that would mean He would change. Ceasing to exist or beginning to exist is certainly a change. Jesus Christ is the same yesterday and today and forever (Heb. 13:8). He never has changed, and He never will change; therefore, He is eternal.

Psalm 102 is given a title: "A prayer of one afflicted, when he is faint and pours out his complaint before the LORD." It is a cry of distress that ends with a proclamation that the eternal God is where we find our hope. The psalmist links God's unchanging character—"you are the same"—with His eternal nature—"your years have no end." The author of Hebrews cites this Psalm as referring to the Son (Heb. 1:8-12), as he opens his book with evidence for the deity and supremacy of Christ.

We think of the earth as "solid as a rock," or lasting forever. Yet these verses from Psalm 102 point out that the earth will be rolled up like worn-out clothes. The earth will be replaced, but God will never change. God is an everlasting rock (Is. 26:4). Comfort for the afflicted and security for the faithful are found throughout all generations in the unchanging and everlasting nature of all three Persons of the Trinity.

Action Step: Jude closes his short epistle with the following:

"Now to him who is able to keep you from stumbling and to present you blameless before the presence of his glory with great joy, to the only God, our Savior, through Jesus Christ our Lord, be glory, majesty, dominion, and authority, before all time and now and forever. Amen." Jude 1:24-25

How are God's glory, majesty, dominion, and authority enriched by His eternal nature? For example, would His authority be as significant if He was not eternal?

He has put eternity into man's heart, yet so that he cannot find out what God has done from the beginning to the end.

Ecclesiastes 3:11

"Truly, truly, I say to you, whoever hears my word and believes him who sent me has eternal life. He does not come into judgment, but has passed from death to life."
John 5:24

Then the angel showed me the river of the water of life, bright as crystal, flowing from the throne of God and of the Lamb through the middle of the street of the city; also, on either side of the river, the tree of life with its twelve kinds of fruit, yielding its fruit each month.

Revelation 22:1-2

Eternal

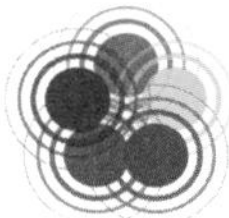

We Will Not Experience Eternity in the Infinite Way that God Does

6

Men and women are created in the image of God. As part of making us His image-bearers, He has placed eternity into our hearts. We have a sense that this world is not all there is and that our lives were made for something more. Our souls are indeed created for eternal life, but we will likely never experience all time as present the way that God does. God is infinite, and we will always be finite creatures.

God's source of life is in Himself (Jn. 5:26). He is self-existent. Because He does not have need of anything outside of Himself to continue to exist, He is eternal. God exists eternally because that is His nature. Our source of life is in God (Acts 17:28). We live forever and ever only because God has granted us life that never ends through faith in Jesus Christ. We will be forever reliant on God as a fountain of life (Ps. 36:9).

The Bible does not give much clear, concrete description of what eternal life will look like in the new heaven and new earth, our forever home. "The dwelling place of God is with man.... He will wipe away every tear from their eyes, and death shall be no more...the former things have passed away.... No longer will there be anything accursed, but the throne of God and of the Lamb will be in it, and his servants will worship him. They will see his face, and his name will be on their foreheads. And night will be no more. They will need no light of lamp or sun, for the Lord God will be their light, and they will reign forever and ever" (excerpts from Rev. 21 and 22). Just a few details are added in other New Testament passages, such as a mention of the wedding feast for the Bride of Christ and Christ's statement that there will be no marriage or giving in marriage.

These are not all the words used to describe our eternal existence in the entire Bible, but there isn't much detail beyond this. There are actually more vivid words and descriptions for the appearance of the holy city of New Jerusalem in the last two chapters of the Bible than there are for what our lives will be like. Will we experience the passing of time? It would seem so, based on the description of the tree of life yielding its fruit each month. That yield seems to be a successive event. As resurrected human beings, we may still experience the passage of time, but time, like all things in heaven, will be perfected. Time will never be confining or limiting or negative in any way. The most important aspect of heaven is the presence of God. We will dwell with Him for endless days. God has designed mankind with just enough of His eternal nature to give us the opportunity, through faith, to spend eternity with Him.

Action Step: A Pharisee once asked Jesus, "Which is the great commandment in the law?" Jesus answered, "You shall love the Lord your God with all your heart and with all your soul and with all your mind. This is the great and first commandment. And a second is like it: You shall love your neighbor as yourself. On these two commandments depend all the Law and the Prophets" (Matt. 22:37-40). If these commandments carry that much importance, it seems that this will be what we will be spending most of eternity doing–loving God and loving people. Who can you actively show love to today to begin enjoying eternal life?

Weekly Summary
Key Points

1. God's duration is perpetual—from before time began and forever and ever.
2. God does not experience the passing of time within Himself.
3. God experiences all of time as the present.
4. God enters into creation and takes action at specific moments in time.
5. God's all-powerful, unchanging, and eternal essence are interwoven.
6. God has granted eternal life to men and women, but we will not experience eternity in the infinite way that God does.

Eternal
Action Steps

7

Go back through the action steps and complete any that you have not yet completed or repeat one that was meaningful:

1. Read Psalm 146 and note the advice to place your trust in the God who will reign forever rather than kings of this earth who endure only for one generation. As the Psalm ends in praise, allow it to lead you into praise to God for His eternal nature.

2. Have some fun pondering numbers today. The National Oceanic and Atmospheric Administration website says that there is enough water to fill about 352,670,000,000,000,000,000 gallon-sized milk containers in the ocean. If you had the pleasure of a beachfront home and you walked to the water's edge to fill a gallon-sized milk jug with ocean water every day for 352,670,000,000,000,000,000 days to drain the ocean dry, God would still be on the throne after your task was finished. How do you even pronounce a number with 16 zeros in it?

3. Meditate on who God is and His record of faithfulness and continuous presence, both in the past, in Scripture, and in your own life, in the present. Pray for understanding of His eternal nature as we continue to study Scripture that reveals this characteristic of God.

4. Draw a timeline and label all of these dates, events, and prophecies: 1) Creation, the fall, and the Genesis 3:15 promise of redemption by Eve's offspring (assume 4000 BC for this exercise, though not all Christians are in agreement on this); 2) Isaiah's Servant Song prophecy and the exile of Israel (c. 700 BC); 3) Jeremiah's prophecy of a new covenant and Judah's exile (c. 600 BC); 4) The life, death, and resurrection of Jesus, fulfilling the promise of the new covenant (c. 0 AD); 5) The writing of the books of Galatians and Hebrews (c. 50-70 AD); 6) Today's date and the status of your personal participation in God's redemptive plan. After completing the timeline, consider that God is currently present in all of those events.

5. Jude closes his short epistle with the following: "Now to him who is able to keep you from stumbling and to present you blameless before the presence of his glory with great joy, to the only God, our Savior, through Jesus Christ our Lord, be glory, majesty, dominion, and authority, before all time and now and forever. Amen" (Jude 1:24-25). How are God's glory, majesty, dominion, and authority enriched by His eternal nature? For example, would His authority be as significant if He was not eternal?

6. A Pharisee once asked Jesus, "Which is the great commandment in the law?" Jesus answered, "You shall love the Lord your God with all your heart and with all your soul and with all your mind. This is the great and first commandment. And a second is like it: You shall love your neighbor as yourself. On these two commandments depend all the Law and the Prophets" (Matt. 22:37-40). If these commandments carry that much importance, it seems that this will be what we will be spending most of eternity doing—loving God and loving people. Who can you actively show love to today to begin enjoying eternal life?

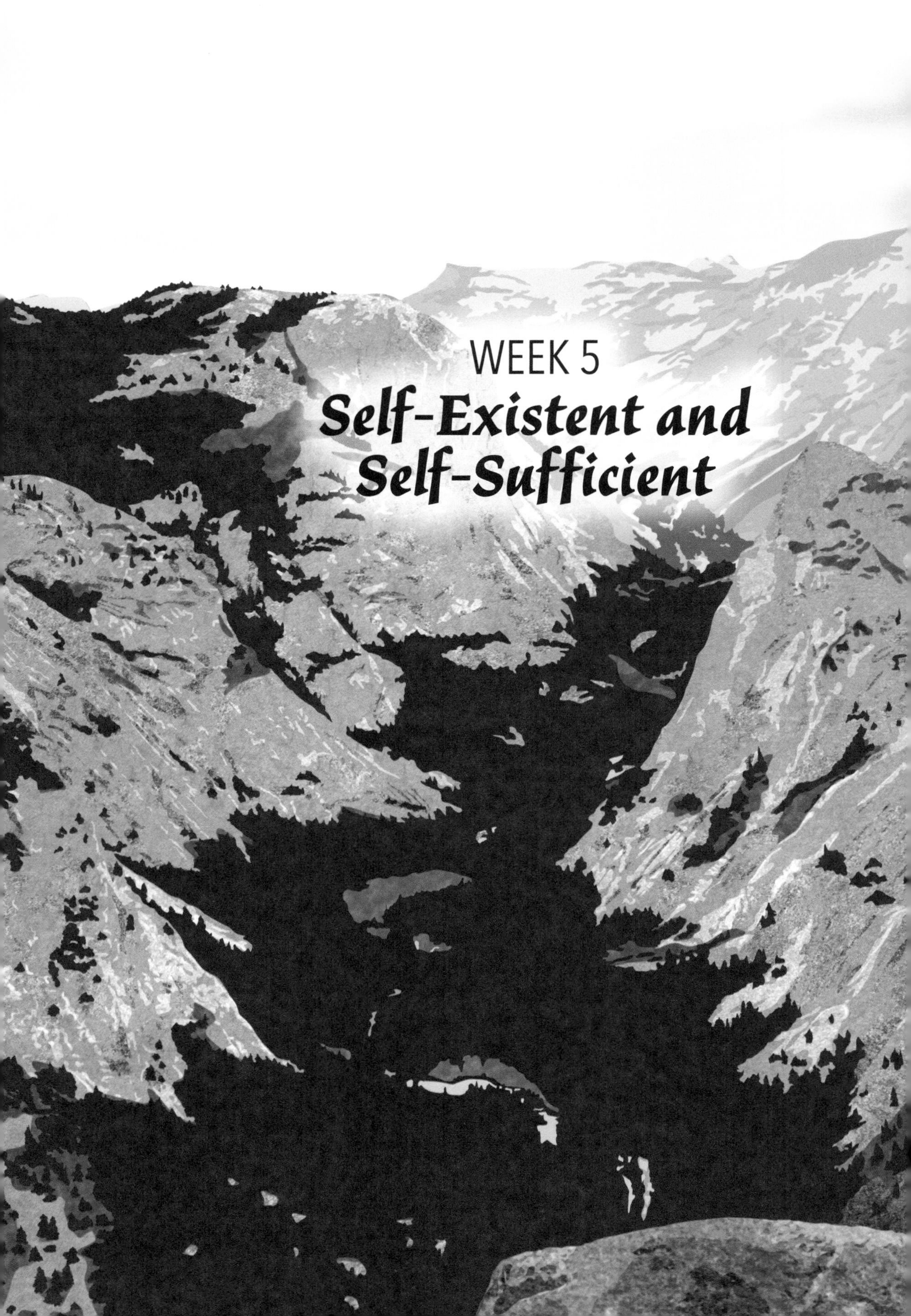

WEEK 5

Self-Existent and Self-Sufficient

The life of God…is not a gift from another. Were there another from whom God could receive the gift of life, or indeed any gift whatever, that other would be God in fact. An elementary but correct way to think of God is as the One who contains all, who gives all that is given, but who Himself can receive nothing that He has not first given.

A.W. Tozer, *The Knowledge of the Holy*

"For as the Father has life in himself, so he has granted the Son also to have life in himself."

John 5:26

Then Moses said to God, "If I come to the people of Israel and say to them, 'The God of your fathers has sent me to you,' and they ask me, 'What is his name?' what shall I say to them?" God said to Moses, "I AM WHO I AM." And he said, "Say this to the people of Israel, 'I AM has sent me to you.'" God also said to Moses, "Say this to the people of Israel, 'The LORD, the God of your fathers, the God of Abraham, the God of Isaac, and the God of Jacob, has sent me to you.' This is my name forever, and thus I am to be remembered throughout all generations."

Exodus 3:13-15

Thus says the LORD, the King of Israel and his Redeemer, the LORD of hosts: "I am the first and I am the last; besides me there is no god. Who is like me? Let him proclaim it. Let him declare and set it before me, since I appointed an ancient people. Let them declare what is to come, and what will happen. Fear not, nor be afraid; have I not told you from of old and declared it? And you are my witnesses! Is there a God besides me? There is no Rock; I know not any."

Isaiah 44:6-8

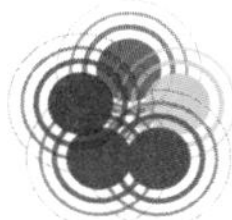

Self-Existent and Self-Sufficient

God Has No Origin

1

The giant rock that is Half Dome in Yosemite National Park is a breathtaking sight. If you visit this natural wonder, you might ask how it came to be. You might believe that it was thrust up from deep within the earth in a prehistoric shifting of tectonic plates. You might believe that glaciers and erosion carved away the softer soils, leaving the hardened granite shape that we see today. You might believe that God spoke it into existence in its present form on the third day of Creation, when He let the dry land appear on the earth. Regardless of where Half Dome came from, it had an origin. Everything that we see, touch, and are familiar with in this world had its origin from something outside of itself.

God has no such origin. God is self-existent—His source of life is in Himself. He had no beginning, and His existence cannot be credited to anything or anyone else. As we studied God's eternal nature, we looked at Exodus 3:13-15, when God stated to Moses, "I AM WHO I AM." As we saw then, the Hebrew word used for "I AM" means "to be" or "to exist." Another possible translation of this Hebrew phrase into English could be, "I exist that I exist." To come back to our Half Dome comparison, we could say, "Half Dome exists because ________." (Fill in the blank with the answer that matches your understanding.) God has proclaimed that He exists because He exists. This statement is difficult for us to make sense of. That is because there is nothing else in existence like God. There is nothing else that simply exists without origin.

In Isaiah 44, the prophet spoke for God, explaining the absurdity of idol-worship. God declared, "besides me there is no god." The people of Israel were witnesses of the promises that He made and fulfilled. He is the only one who is sufficient in Himself to keep His promises. No one else can proclaim the future—certainly not idols. God is unique, and there is no other that exists without origin.

Action Step: There are several correct responses to the question, "Why did Jesus come to earth?" He came to redeem mankind. He came to show us the Father. He came that we might have life. A different question would be, "Why does Jesus exist?" None of the previous answers are true for this question because Jesus Christ is the eternal Son, part of the triune Godhead from everlasting. Jesus Christ exists because He exists. Spend some time in prayer meditating on the self-existence of the Trinity. Again and again, as we study God's nature, we should be moved to humble worship of the God who is so unique and worthy of praise.

The earth is the LORD's and the fullness thereof, the world and those who dwell therein,

Psalms 24:1

"Who has first given to me, that I should repay him? Whatever is under the whole heaven is mine."

Job 41:11

"For every beast of the forest is mine, the cattle on a thousand hills. I know all the birds of the hills, and all that moves in the field is mine. If I were hungry, I would not tell you, for the world and its fullness are mine. Do I eat the flesh of bulls or drink the blood of goats? Offer to God a sacrifice of thanksgiving, and perform your vows to the Most High, and call upon me in the day of trouble; I will deliver you, and you shall glorify me."

Psalms 50:10-15

He is the image of the invisible God, the firstborn of all creation. For by him all things were created, in heaven and on earth, visible and invisible, whether thrones or dominions or rulers or authorities—all things were created through him and for him. And he is before all things, and in him all things hold together.

Colossians 1:15-17

The king's heart is a stream of water in the hand of the LORD; he turns it wherever he will.

Proverbs 21:1

He is the radiance of the glory of God and the exact imprint of his nature, and he upholds the universe by the word of his power.

Hebrews 1:3

"The God who made the world and everything in it, being Lord of heaven and earth, does not live in temples made by man, nor is he served by human hands, as though he needed anything, since he himself gives to all mankind life and breath and everything."

Acts 17:24-25

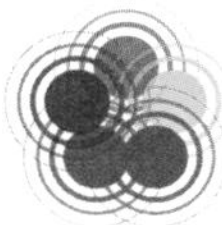

Self-Existent and Self-Sufficient
God Has No Need

2

Verse after verse in both the Old and New Testament declare that God is the Creator, Sustainer, and Owner of the heavens and the earth and everything in them. Every cow, bird, and beast of the forest or field is His. Everything visible and invisible was created and is held together by Him. Even a world ruler's heart "is a stream of water in the hand of the LORD; he turns it wherever he will." The entire universe is dependent on His power for its continued existence. It is clear that God has no need of anything from any man or anything else in creation. God has within Himself all attributes, all power, all resources, and all abilities to be complete. This is God's self-sufficiency.

In Psalm 50 the worshipers sing of what it means to be God's people. One of the main subjects is that God is not in need of their empty sacrifices. If God owns all of the beasts, including cattle and birds, why would He need to be provided with such things through the offerings of His people? In verses 14-15, God makes clear that His desire is thanksgiving and dependence on Him. God does not need to be provided for by His people. There is nothing we can give to God that is not already His.

Acts 17 includes a description of Paul's visit to Athens, Greece. The Athenians of the time loved hearing and discussing philosophy, and Paul had some new ideas to share. He was invited by some Athenians to teach them what he had been presenting to others in the city. Paul started by pointing out an Athenian altar that he had seen, inscribed with "To the unknown god." He then proceeded to tell them about the one true God, who can be known. The first thoughts that Paul shared about God is that He made everything, and He does not need to be served by humans in a temple. The God who gives life and breath and everything to mankind certainly does not need anything from man. If everything in the world originated in God and He freely shares that with us, why would He need anything from us? God is the source of all and has no need outside of Himself.

Action Step: In the United States, nearly everyone is familiar with the iconic Uncle Sam poster first created as the US entered World War I. The character of Uncle Sam was first conceived of in the previous century, but he became a cultural icon when he was painted with white hair and a stern expression and a finger pointed directly at the viewer as a recruiting poster for the Army. "I WANT YOU FOR U.S. ARMY," Uncle Sam demands. Adaptations and spoofs of this poster are too numerous to count, and the image is imprinted on every American's mind from an early age. If you aren't as familiar with it, just search for the image online, and it will not be difficult to find.

How many of us have allowed this image to taint our view of God? Have you ever perceived of God as a white-haired, stern-faced man pointing His finger at you and demanding your service? The Army needed recruits for war. God is not in need of our service. Neither does He force it. God will accomplish His plan whether we cooperate with Him or not.

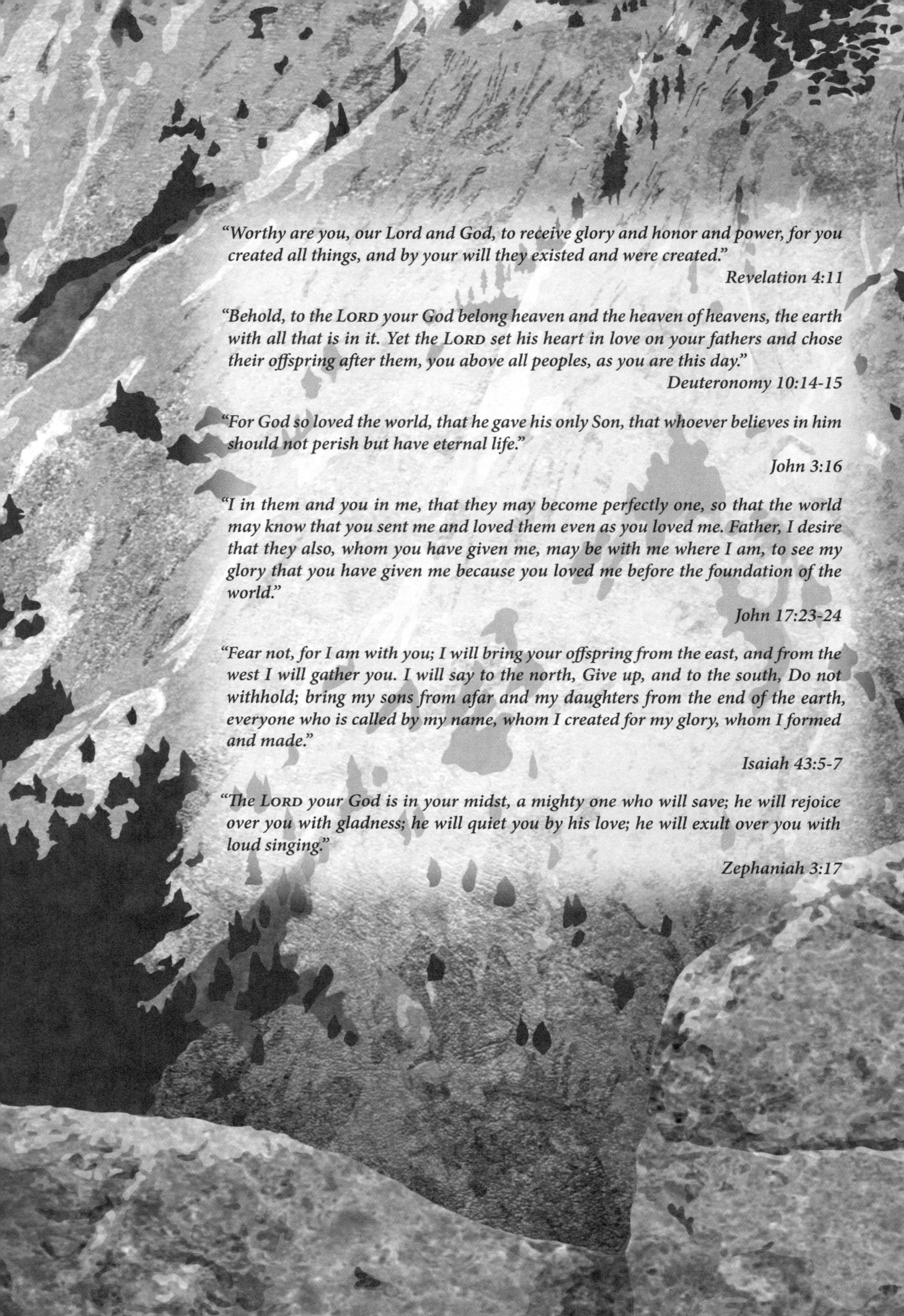

"Worthy are you, our Lord and God, to receive glory and honor and power, for you created all things, and by your will they existed and were created."

Revelation 4:11

"Behold, to the Lord *your God belong heaven and the heaven of heavens, the earth with all that is in it. Yet the* Lord *set his heart in love on your fathers and chose their offspring after them, you above all peoples, as you are this day."*

Deuteronomy 10:14-15

"For God so loved the world, that he gave his only Son, that whoever believes in him should not perish but have eternal life."

John 3:16

"I in them and you in me, that they may become perfectly one, so that the world may know that you sent me and loved them even as you loved me. Father, I desire that they also, whom you have given me, may be with me where I am, to see my glory that you have given me because you loved me before the foundation of the world."

John 17:23-24

"Fear not, for I am with you; I will bring your offspring from the east, and from the west I will gather you. I will say to the north, Give up, and to the south, Do not withhold; bring my sons from afar and my daughters from the end of the earth, everyone who is called by my name, whom I created for my glory, whom I formed and made."

Isaiah 43:5-7

"The Lord *your God is in your midst, a mighty one who will save; he will rejoice over you with gladness; he will quiet you by his love; he will exult over you with loud singing."*

Zephaniah 3:17

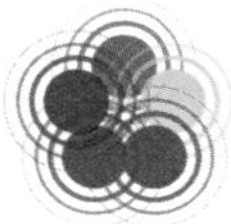

Self-Existent and Self-Sufficient

God Created Mankind out of Love 3

If God has no need and already had relationships within the Persons of the Trinity before time began, why did He create man? He certainly didn't *need* to create us, and yet He *chose* to. As Revelation 4:11 says, *by His will* all things were created—some versions say for His pleasure. Why did He will to have a relationship with mankind? Why would He find pleasure in this? To the extent that we can find an answer, it has to be found in God's revelation of His nature.

In Deuteronomy 10, Moses was speaking to the people of Israel, encouraging them to love and serve the Lord. Moses reminded them that though everything in heaven and on the earth belongs to God—in other words, though He has everything He needs at His disposal—He has chosen to set His heart in love on the people of Israel above all. And in the gospel of Jesus Christ, He has extended that covenant love to all nations. God is love (1 Jn. 4:8), and God's love gives to the point of giving His only Son (Jn. 3:16). As the source of never-ending life and love, God chose to create men and women to give His life and love to. Jesus affirmed in His prayer in John 17 that God loves us, even as He has loved Jesus. The perfect love shared within the Trinity before the foundation of the world is offered to us.

Isaiah 43 gives another reason for God's creation of man—for His glory. Though He has glory in Himself, we can also bring Him glory. Again, He has no need for this, for all glory originates in God. He receives glory from us, not in a way that adds to His glory, but in a way that we proclaim the honor and majesty that He already possesses.

Not only can we bring God glory, He also delights in us. The prophet Zephaniah spoke of God's judgment and blessing to come, both in the near-term for the nation of Israel and the final judgment of the world. In chapter 3, he wrote of the coming conversion of people from all nations to the Lord and the return of some from the nation of Israel to the Lord. Zephaniah described those who "call upon the name of the Lord" (v. 9), those who "serve Him" (v. 9), those who "seek refuge in the name of the Lord" (v. 12), and those who "rejoice and exult with all your heart" (v. 14). These are the people of faith whom God will rejoice over with gladness and exult over with loud singing. God created us to experience life, joy, and love in Him. In turn, the amazing result is that the Creator of all that there is then delights in us!

Action Step: Zephaniah 3:9 looks ahead to a time when all nations "may call upon the name of the Lord and serve him with one accord." Ask God for an opportunity to serve Him today by serving someone in need. Buy someone who is short on cash a bag of groceries. If it's a hot day, deliver a case of cold drinks to a crew working outside. If you have a friend that missed school or work due to illness, stop by or call to check on them. Such acts of service, performed in love and to the glory of God, cause God to "rejoice over you with gladness."

"For my name's sake I defer my anger, for the sake of my praise I restrain it for you, that I may not cut you off. Behold, I have refined you, but not as silver; I have tried you in the furnace of affliction. For my own sake, for my own sake, I do it, for how should my name be profaned? My glory I will not give to another."

Isaiah 48:9-11

Every good gift and every perfect gift is from above, coming down from the Father of lights, with whom there is no variation or shadow due to change.

James 1:17

Beloved, let us love one another, for love is from God, and whoever loves has been born of God and knows God.

1 John 4:7

But we ought always to give thanks to God for you, brothers beloved by the Lord, because God chose you as the firstfruits to be saved, through sanctification by the Spirit and belief in the truth.

2 Thessalonians 2:13

"When the Spirit of truth comes, he will guide you into all the truth, for he will not speak on his own authority, but whatever he hears he will speak, and he will declare to you the things that are to come."

John 16:13

Jesus said to him, "I am the way, and the truth, and the life. No one comes to the Father except through me."

John 14:6

In him was life, and the life was the light of men.

John 1:4

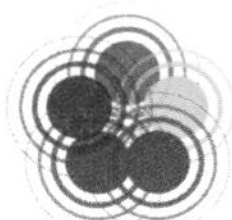

Self-Existent and Self-Sufficient

His Self-Sufficiency Is Not Self-Centered

4

From an early age, we are taught that seeking praise for ourselves is not a desirable behavior. If you watch an interview with a professional athlete and that athlete explains how their own performance that day was superior to anyone else on the team and key to the team's victory, neither you nor the athlete's teammates would think highly of that athlete's attitude. Even if that athlete is the team's star, the comments would be considered egotistical and self-centered. Often, self-centered attitudes like that, possessed by people seeking their own glory, can be rooted in a person's insecurities. They require the praise of others to feel good about themselves.

God reveals in Scripture that He will not share His glory. Throughout the book of Isaiah, God reprimanded the nation of Israel for their disobedience and lack of faith, then came back to proclaim His own faithfulness and hints of His plan for redemption. Why did He persist in rescuing the nation of Israel? Isaiah 48:9-11 explains that it is for His own sake and His glory. God's glory is the end goal of His actions. Does this mean that God is self-centered or insecure? As we have already studied, God does not lack anything or have any need. He cannot be insecure because He does not need the praise of others. Why does He demand all glory?

God is the Creator and source of all life. As we continue to study His nature, we will see that He is also the source of all that is good (Jms. 1:17). All love originates in God (1 Jn. 4:7). Sanctification and holiness come from the Spirit (2 Thess. 2:13). The Spirit guides us into truth (Jn. 16:13), and Jesus is the truth and the life (Jn. 1:4, 14:6). The Trinity is the source of all that we need.

God's goal of receiving glory arises out of His love for us. His love desires what is best for us, and what is best for us is God Himself. God desires glory for Himself to focus our attention on Him, the source of all goodness, love, holiness, truth, and life. He is the only One who can satisfy our needs. If the professional athlete could satisfy all of the needs of his team in every area of life, then he might be right to seek glory. Obviously, no man can provide such satisfaction. God's self-sufficiency and desire for glory is not rooted in self-centeredness or insecurity, but in His love for us.

Action Step: Read all of Isaiah 48. The whole chapter declares God's glory in His faithfulness, His power to act, His patience, and His righteousness. Even in the midst of Israel's discipline for disobedience, He is faithful to His covenant for His own sake. Not all of our suffering in this world is due to our own disobedience. But the faithfulness and glory of God will accompany His children to bring refinement regardless of the source of our afflictions. Look to God today to supply all of your needs, especially in your trials. "And my God will supply every need of yours according to his riches in glory in Christ Jesus." (Philippians 4:19)

For by grace you have been saved through faith. And this is not your own doing; it is the gift of God, not a result of works, so that no one may boast. For we are his workmanship, created in Christ Jesus for good works, which God prepared beforehand, that we should walk in them.

Ephesians 2:8-10

But he said to me, "My grace is sufficient for you, for my power is made perfect in weakness." Therefore I will boast all the more gladly of my weaknesses, so that the power of Christ may rest upon me. For the sake of Christ, then, I am content with weaknesses, insults, hardships, persecutions, and calamities. For when I am weak, then I am strong.

2 Corinthians 12:9-10

What then is Apollos? What is Paul? Servants through whom you believed, as the Lord assigned to each. I planted, Apollos watered, but God gave the growth. So neither he who plants nor he who waters is anything, but only God who gives the growth. He who plants and he who waters are one, and each will receive his wages according to his labor. For we are God's fellow workers. You are God's field, God's building. According to the grace of God given to me, like a skilled master builder I laid a foundation, and someone else is building upon it. Let each one take care how he builds upon it. For no one can lay a foundation other than that which is laid, which is Jesus Christ.

1 Corinthians 3:5-11

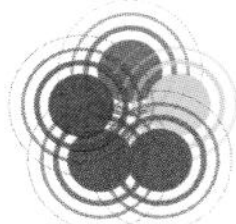

Self-Existent and Self-Sufficient

God Invites Us to Join in His Work 5

What if your favorite music artist invited you to help write a song? Imagine the scenario. Pick your favorite artist of all time in any music genre. What if that artist invited you personally to meet them in the studio and help to write the next big hit? It is doubtful the artist actually needs your help. He or she has already written enough music to become a star—why would they need the help of someone with less training and fame? Could you really add anything that the artist doesn't already bring? Yet imagine the privilege and joy of being invited into the process!

God doesn't *need* us to accomplish His plan, but He invites us to be part of it. Human efforts or works are not the things that save us (Eph. 2:8), but God has prepared in advance for us to do good works as participants in His kingdom (Eph. 2:10). Through faith we are new creations—"his workmanship"—and in faith and the Spirit we are able to do good works.

In 2 Corinthians 12, Paul explains the power of Christ working in his weakness and enabling Paul to serve. Paul's weakness was precisely the thing that demonstrated the power of Christ. God accomplishes His purposes right through our human weakness, including suffering. In fact, the weaker the human, the more clearly we can see God's power. My insufficiencies are not a reason to avoid serving God. He wants us to come from a place of weakness and rely on His power.

1 Corinthians 3 describes a real-life example of workers partnering with God to accomplish a task—the growth of the Corinthian church. Paul explains that he and Apollos were just like workers in a field, with Paul planting and Apollos watering. But behind all of their labor, God is the one who gives growth. Neither worker is anything in himself. Paul and Apollos are expected to labor together as "God's fellow workers"—partners under His authority. Then Paul moves on to a building analogy to remind his readers that underneath all the work of building the church is the secure foundation of Jesus Christ.

God alone is credited for the success of our works and service. He is the one who can transform human hearts, and He is not in need of our assistance to do that. Yet we are fulfilling the life God designed for us when we work in cooperation with Him in Christ's strength. What a privilege and joy to be invited into God's work!

Action Step: 1 Corinthians 10:31 says, "So, whether you eat or drink, or whatever you do, do all to the glory of God." Whatever your tasks are today, focus on doing them for God's glory. If someone praises you for a job well done, don't be ashamed to say that you were working today for God's glory. As we have opportunities to bring glory to Him, we are pointing others to the source of life and love and holiness.

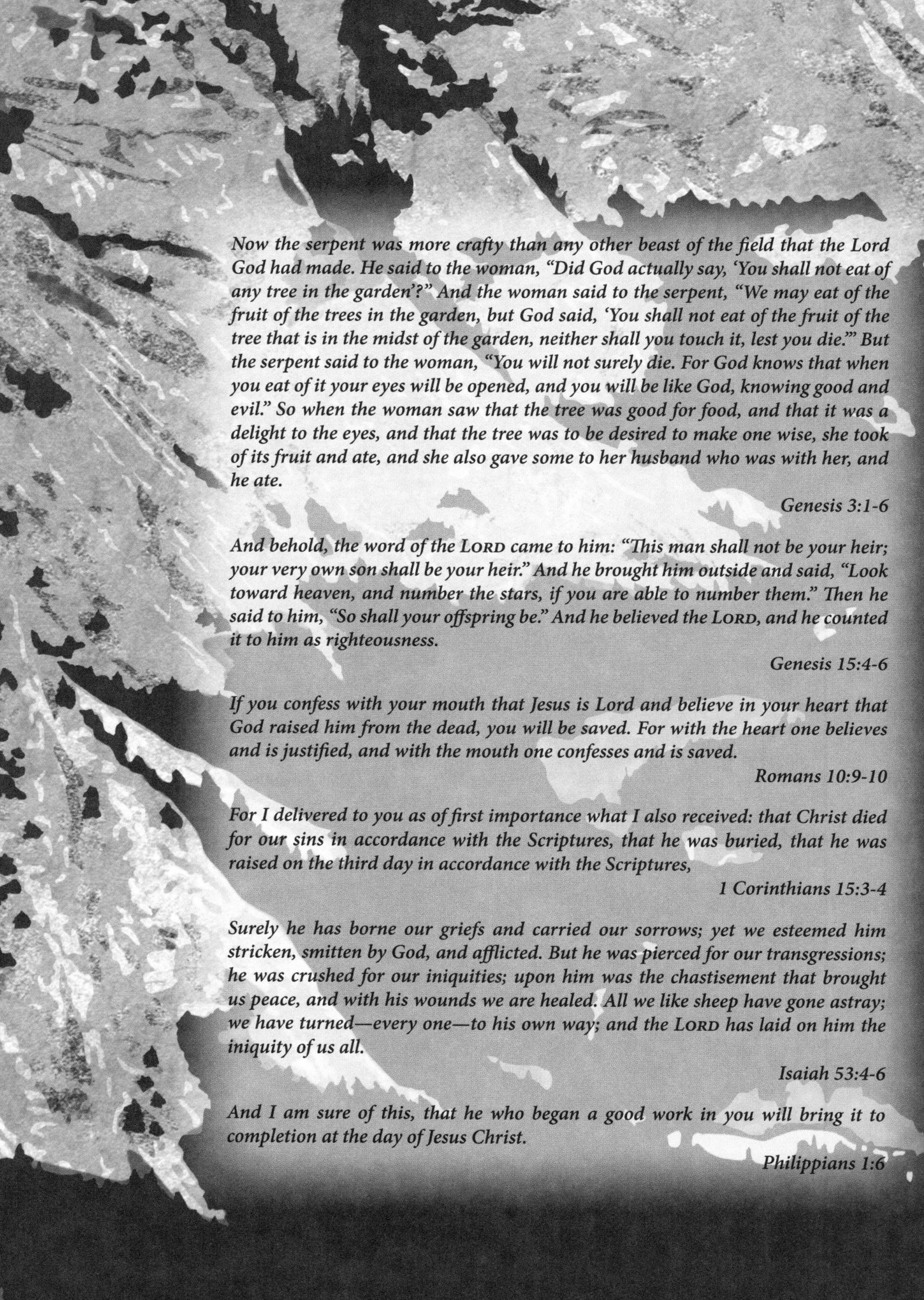

Now the serpent was more crafty than any other beast of the field that the Lord God had made. He said to the woman, "Did God actually say, 'You shall not eat of any tree in the garden'?" And the woman said to the serpent, "We may eat of the fruit of the trees in the garden, but God said, 'You shall not eat of the fruit of the tree that is in the midst of the garden, neither shall you touch it, lest you die.'" But the serpent said to the woman, "You will not surely die. For God knows that when you eat of it your eyes will be opened, and you will be like God, knowing good and evil." So when the woman saw that the tree was good for food, and that it was a delight to the eyes, and that the tree was to be desired to make one wise, she took of its fruit and ate, and she also gave some to her husband who was with her, and he ate.

Genesis 3:1-6

And behold, the word of the LORD came to him: "This man shall not be your heir; your very own son shall be your heir." And he brought him outside and said, "Look toward heaven, and number the stars, if you are able to number them." Then he said to him, "So shall your offspring be." And he believed the LORD, and he counted it to him as righteousness.

Genesis 15:4-6

If you confess with your mouth that Jesus is Lord and believe in your heart that God raised him from the dead, you will be saved. For with the heart one believes and is justified, and with the mouth one confesses and is saved.

Romans 10:9-10

For I delivered to you as of first importance what I also received: that Christ died for our sins in accordance with the Scriptures, that he was buried, that he was raised on the third day in accordance with the Scriptures,

1 Corinthians 15:3-4

Surely he has borne our griefs and carried our sorrows; yet we esteemed him stricken, smitten by God, and afflicted. But he was pierced for our transgressions; he was crushed for our iniquities; upon him was the chastisement that brought us peace, and with his wounds we are healed. All we like sheep have gone astray; we have turned—every one—to his own way; and the LORD has laid on him the iniquity of us all.

Isaiah 53:4-6

And I am sure of this, that he who began a good work in you will bring it to completion at the day of Jesus Christ.

Philippians 1:6

Self-Existent and Self-Sufficient

Faith Is Believing in the Sufficiency of God for Us

6

God is sufficient in Himself and has no need outside of Himself. If we believe that, are we willing to take the step into believing that God is sufficient for *us*? The essence of faith is believing that God is sufficient to meet our greatest needs.

The story of the fall of man in Genesis 3 is a story of the serpent convincing Eve that God and His instructions were not enough. The serpent persuaded Eve that there was something better for her outside of what God had supplied. At its most basic level, Adam and Eve's action of taking the fruit and eating it was an act of trusting in human sufficiency to do what is best for oneself. It was a failure to trust in God's sufficient provision for their needs. All sin has at its root the belief in sufficiency of the human self and a lack of trust in God.

A contrasting Old Testament example is Abram's belief in Genesis 15. God promised Abram (soon to be Abraham) that he would have a son to be his heir and that his offspring would be as numerous as the stars. In that moment, Abram believed that God was sufficient to fulfill this promise. And Abram's faith was counted as righteousness. Abram had a trusting response to God's revelation about Himself and His plans. Unfortunately, as the continuing story in Genesis shows, Abram's trust did waver at times, and he had moments of trusting in his own human efforts to make God's promises come true. We all have those moments, but we must be willing to call those lapses in trust in God's abilities what they are—sin.

The New Testament reveals that the subject of our faith, God, should also include His Son, Jesus Christ. Saving faith is trusting in this revelation of Jesus and in His work to make us right with God (Rom. 10:9). His work included His death on the cross and His resurrection from the dead (1 Cor. 15:3-4). His death was a substitutionary payment for our sins (Is. 53:4-6). When we trust in the sufficiency of Jesus' work, we are saved. Like Abram, when we have a trusting response to Jesus' revelation about Himself and His plans, we are declared righteous. Like Adam and Eve, when we question God's plan and attempt to add something in our own strength to what He has provided for us, we are in sin. Whether it is in first coming to faith or in the process of being made holy by faith, we should trust that God is sufficient to complete the work that He started in us (Phil. 1:6).

Action Step: In Paul's letter to the Philippians, he points out how we are to cooperate with God in our continued faith: "Therefore, my beloved, as you have always obeyed, so now, not only as in my presence but much more in my absence, work out your own salvation with fear and trembling, for it is God who works in you, both to will and to work for his good pleasure" (Phil. 2:12-13). We are to take action in the process of being made new, but everything worthy that is accomplished is God working in us. Is your faith strong enough to trust that God will transform you? Is your faith strong enough to trust that God will transform those around you? Pray that God will give you the faith that trusts that God is sufficient.

Weekly Summary
Key Points

1. God has no origin.
2. God has no need.
3. God created mankind out of love.
4. His self-sufficiency is not self-centered.
5. God invites us to join in His work.
6. Faith is believing in the sufficiency of God for us.

Self-Existent and Self-Sufficient

Action Steps 7

Go back through the action steps and complete any that you have not yet completed or repeat one that was meaningful:

1. There are several correct responses to the question, "Why did Jesus come to earth?" He came to redeem mankind. He came to show us the Father. He came that we might have life. A different question would be, "Why does Jesus exist?" None of the previous answers are true for this question because Jesus Christ is the eternal Son, part of the triune Godhead from everlasting. Jesus Christ exists because He exists. Spend some time in prayer meditating on the self-existence of the Trinity. Again and again, as we study God's nature, we should be moved to humble worship of the God who is so unique and worthy of praise.

2. How many of us have allowed a character like Uncle Sam to taint our view of God? Have you ever perceived of God as a white-haired, stern-faced man pointing His finger at you and demanding your service? The Army needed recruits for war. God is not in need of our service. Neither does He demand it. God will accomplish His plan whether we cooperate with Him or not.

3. Zephaniah 3:9 looks ahead to a time when all nations "may call upon the name of the Lord and serve him with one accord." Ask God for an opportunity to serve Him today by serving someone in need. Buy someone who is short on cash a bag of groceries. If it's a hot day, deliver a case of cold drinks to a crew working outside. If you have a friend that missed school or work due to illness, stop by or call to check on them. Such acts of service, performed in love and to the glory of God, cause God to "rejoice over you with gladness."

4. Read all of Isaiah 48. The whole chapter declares God's glory in His faithfulness, His power to act, His patience, and His righteousness. Look to God today to supply all of your needs. "And my God will supply every need of yours according to his riches in glory in Christ Jesus." (Philippians 4:19)

5. 1 Corinthians 10:31 says, "So, whether you eat or drink, or whatever you do, do all to the glory of God." Whatever your tasks are today, focus on doing them for God's glory. If someone praises you for a job well done, don't be ashamed to say that you were working today for God's glory. As we have opportunities to bring glory to Him, we are pointing others to the source of life and love and holiness.

6. In Paul's letter to the Philippians, he points out how we are to cooperate with God in our continued faith: "Therefore, my beloved, as you have always obeyed, so now, not only as in my presence but much more in my absence, work out your own salvation with fear and trembling, for it is God who works in you, both to will and to work for his good pleasure" (Phil. 2:12-13). We are to take action in the process of being made new, but everything worthy that is accomplished is God working in us. Is your faith strong enough to trust that God will transform you? Is your faith strong enough to trust that God will transform those around you? Pray that God will give you the faith that trusts that God is sufficient.

WEEK 6
Spirit and Infinite

God is a Spirit, in and of himself infinite in being, glory, blessedness, and perfection; all-sufficient, eternal, unchangeable, incomprehensible, every where present, almighty, knowing all things, most wise, most holy, most just, most merciful and gracious, long-suffering, and abundant in goodness and truth.

Westminster Larger Catechism

God is a Spirit, infinite, eternal, and unchangeable, in his being, wisdom, power, holiness, justice, goodness, and truth.

Westminster Shorter Catechism

The woman said to him, "Sir, I perceive that you are a prophet. Our fathers worshiped on this mountain, but you say that in Jerusalem is the place where people ought to worship." Jesus said to her, "Woman, believe me, the hour is coming when neither on this mountain nor in Jerusalem will you worship the Father. You worship what you do not know; we worship what we know, for salvation is from the Jews. But the hour is coming, and is now here, when the true worshipers will worship the Father in spirit and truth, for the Father is seeking such people to worship him. God is spirit, and those who worship him must worship in spirit and truth."

John 4:19-24

Spirit and Infinite
God Is Spirit

1

John 4 contains the account of Jesus meeting the Samaritan woman at the well. In the encounter, Jesus ignored some social norms by speaking to a Samaritan woman and asking for a drink of water from a well used by Samaritans. In doing so, He showed that reaching the lost with His message was more important to Him than following divisive social practices. Jesus began a discussion with the woman about "living water," and, though she didn't quite understand what He was offering to her, she was intrigued. Jesus lovingly confronted her about her broken lifestyle, knowing in His divine nature of her past and present relationships with men. It was at this point that she redirected the conversation to a religious debate about proper places of worship.

Jesus continued to surprise the woman when He did not take sides in an argument about where to worship, but He instead introduced a completely new pattern for worship. Because God is spirit, He must be worshiped in spirit and in truth. God is not confined to any physical location, such as a mountain in Samaria or a temple in Jerusalem. As Spirit, He is not a material being. Spirit, in fact, is the opposite of material. God, as Spirit, is present in any location where we seek to worship Him.

How can man, a material being with physical senses, even relate to God, who is Spirit and has no material form? One answer is that God has created men and women with a spirit, allowing us to worship a spiritual being. But also significant in this passage is Jesus' statement that "the hour is coming, and is now here." The ministry of Jesus Christ, including His death, resurrection, and ascension to the Father, followed by the sending of the Holy Spirit, gives believers the ability to worship God in spirit and in truth. We have access to God the Father through His Son and in the Holy Spirit (Eph. 2:18).

In their conversation, the woman refers to their fathers—the Samaritan fathers. The New Testament Greek here uses the work *pater*, the common word used in the language for a parent. This is also the Greek word that is used to record Jesus' many personal references to His Father in heaven—the first Person of the Trinity—both in this passage and throughout the New Testament. It is interesting to note that when He states that "God is spirit," Scripture uses the Greek word *theos*, which refers to the essence of God, the divine nature that Jesus shares with the Father. "God is spirit" is a description of all Persons of the Trinity, including Jesus Himself. Jesus took on flesh in the incarnation, but in His divine nature He is Spirit.

Action Step: The Bible teaches that God created man with a spirit, which connects us to God and helps us to understand (Job 32:8). Our spirits then return to God when we die (Ecc. 12:7). Medical science generally makes a practice of only addressing the physical part of men and women. In recent years, however, some research has been done looking into quantum processes occurring in tiny structures within the brain cells. A theory proposes that these quantum vibrations may be related to human consciousness. The researchers are attempting to define consciousness and whether it can exist outside of the body. Those who believe the Bible to be true do not need the support of research to trust that the human spirit exists. Neither do we need to feel threatened by the possibility that scientists may eventually identify human consciousness. Do you believe that your spirit originated from God and finds its home at some point in returning to Him?

"Can you find out the deep things of God? Can you find out the limit of the Almighty? It is higher than heaven—what can you do? Deeper than Sheol—what can you know? Its measure is longer than the earth and broader than the sea."

Job 11:7-9

"But will God indeed dwell on the earth? Behold, heaven and the highest heaven cannot contain you; how much less this house that I have built!"

1 Kings 8:27

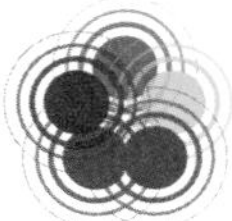

Spirit and Infinite

God Is Without Limits or Bounds 2

A ponderosa pine tree stands about fifty feet tall outside our home. That tree drops pine cones onto the lawn daily. Our family can't effectively run the lawn mower with dozens of pine cones scattered across the grass. Every time we cut the lawn, we have to toss all of the pine cones off the lawn. This is an ongoing project. We have lived in our home for ten years, and for ten years the supply of pine cones dropping on our lawn looks to be without limits. It would seem that I could spend the rest of my life picking up pine cones and never see the end of it. Is there really no limit to the pine cones? In reality, the tree has a defined size. It is no easy task to measure the height of a tree, but it can be done. Also, the tree's age is finite. Eventually, the tree will either die of disease, get knocked down in a windstorm, or possibly be cut down by homeowners that have grown weary of the pine cones. Even as long as the tree lives, there are still limits to the number of pine cones that it can produce.

God's height cannot be measured as if He were a tree or any other physical object. It may help to understand God's existence as Spirit by understanding what He is *not*. In this case, He is *not finite*. Finite is defined as "having limits or bounds." He is *in*finite. We cannot "find out the limit of the Almighty" because He has no limit. The endless supply of the outflow of His attributes cannot be counted like so many pine cones. The fact that God is Spirit means that He has no spatial limitations and His presence encompasses the entire universe. The fullness of all that He is exists in every place. God's infinity does not just define Him as infinitely higher than mankind. We are finite, and He is infinite; therefore, He is of a different essence than us.

1 Kings 8 records Solomon's prayer of dedication for the newly completed temple. Solomon recognized that God is not contained by the new temple or limited to it because God existed before the temple. God cannot be confined in a certain place. Even when His presence is manifested in the temple, He exists infinitely beyond the temple. If the highest heaven cannot contain Him, how much less can a building do so on earth? God's choice to dwell in the temple alongside His people is an act of His love and grace, an evidence of the infinite God desiring a relationship with His finite creation.

Action Step: God's infinite nature, being so foreign to us, is another quality that is so difficult to grasp. Pray for understanding and that the Spirit will help you gain a glimpse of understanding of His existence without limits.

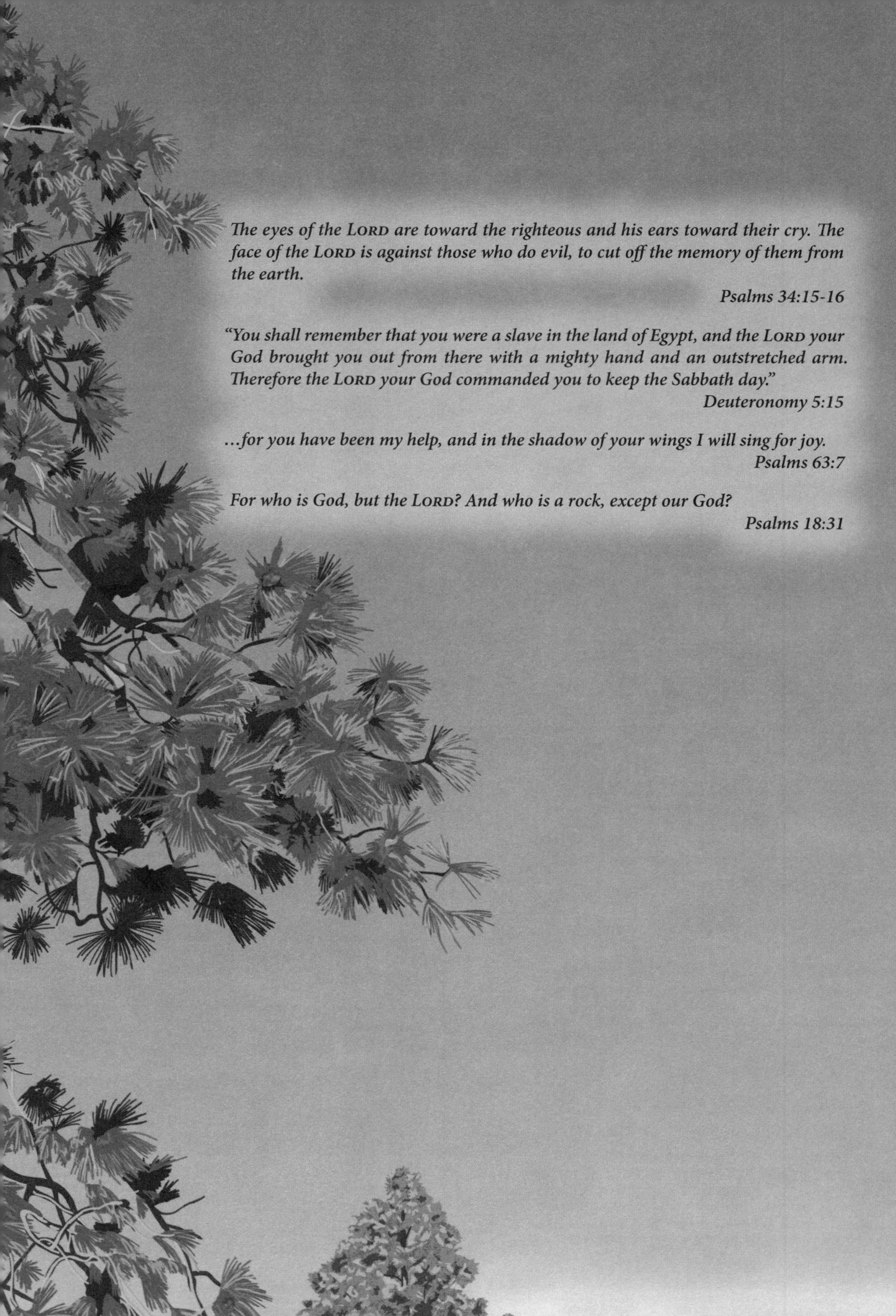

The eyes of the LORD are toward the righteous and his ears toward their cry. The face of the LORD is against those who do evil, to cut off the memory of them from the earth.

Psalms 34:15-16

"You shall remember that you were a slave in the land of Egypt, and the LORD your God brought you out from there with a mighty hand and an outstretched arm. Therefore the LORD your God commanded you to keep the Sabbath day."

Deuteronomy 5:15

...for you have been my help, and in the shadow of your wings I will sing for joy.

Psalms 63:7

For who is God, but the LORD? And who is a rock, except our God?

Psalms 18:31

Spirit and Infinite

God Has No Body

3

The nature of God is without physical composition or body parts. Just as God is *not finite*, He is *not flesh*. Yet there are many occasions in Scripture referring to the hand, arm, or eye of the Lord. Those descriptions might lead one to imagine that God looks like us. These verses are examples of God communicating to us on our own terms. The references to body parts describe God's actions as being similar to actions we would make with those body parts.

For example, in Psalm 34, "The eyes of the LORD are toward the righteous and his ears toward their cry" suggests that God's attention is directed to those who trust Him. In contrast, "The face of the LORD is against those who do evil" refers to how when we turn our faces away from a task, we are no longer giving attention to it and allowing it to continue its natural course on its own. When God turns His face against those who do evil, He is leaving them to continue on their own path. The reader is left to decide whether he or she wants God's attention and guidance or whether they would like to be left alone by God to their own consequences. The verses are not intended to teach about a physical appearance of God.

Likewise, in Deuteronomy 5, the "mighty hand" and "outstretched arm" of the Lord represent His abundant power and far-extending reach in the miraculous rescue of the people of Israel from the land of Egypt. If we assumed that these descriptions indicated actual body parts of God, then we would have to logically conclude that God has wings as well, since "in the shadow of your wings I will sing for joy." The term "shadow of your wings" is used in Scripture to point to a safe shelter. Finally, this pattern of thinking would suggest that, based on Psalm 18, God looks like a rock, when the verse is actually conveying that He is the only solid and unchanging one.

We should always be aware as we read Scripture and find places where God describes Himself with terms from creation that He exists outside of creation. The fact that He is not limited by a physical body, but He exists as Spirit, is consistent with His repeated promises that He will "not leave you or forsake you." We can take comfort in the knowledge that His "outstretched arm" reaches wherever we are.

Action Step: One of the ways God reaches us is through the community of believers. God has no physical body, but the sum of all believers for all time is the body of Christ (1 Cor. 12:12-31). As the body of Christ, we are called to care for one another, suffer together, and rejoice together. Is there someone in your life today who needs care for whom you can be God's outstretched arm?

No one has ever seen God; the only God, who is at the Father's side, he has made him known.

John 1:18

"Everyone who has heard and learned from the Father comes to me—not that anyone has seen the Father except he who is from God; he has seen the Father."

John 6:45-46

To the King of the ages, immortal, invisible, the only God, be honor and glory forever and ever. Amen.

1 Timothy 1:17

I charge you in the presence of God, who gives life to all things, and of Christ Jesus, who in his testimony before Pontius Pilate made the good confession, to keep the commandment unstained and free from reproach until the appearing of our Lord Jesus Christ, which he will display at the proper time—he who is the blessed and only Sovereign, the King of kings and Lord of lords, who alone has immortality, who dwells in unapproachable light, whom no one has ever seen or can see. To him be honor and eternal dominion. Amen.

1 Timothy 6:13-16

"But," he said, "you cannot see my face, for man shall not see me and live."

Exodus 33:20

"Blessed are the pure in heart, for they shall see God."

Matthew 5:8

No longer will there be anything accursed, but the throne of God and of the Lamb will be in it, and his servants will worship him. They will see his face, and his name will be on their foreheads.

Revelation 22:3-4

See what kind of love the Father has given to us, that we should be called children of God; and so we are. The reason why the world does not know us is that it did not know him. Beloved, we are God's children now, and what we will be has not yet appeared; but we know that when he appears we shall be like him, because we shall see him as he is.

1 John 3:1-2

Spirit and Infinite

God Is Invisible

4

God is Spirit. We have seen that He is *not finite* and *not flesh*. Today's verses teach that God is *not visible*. We cannot experience God with our physical senses. John says in his gospel that "no one has ever seen God," but that Jesus has made Him known. Jesus also said that no one has seen the Father other than Jesus Himself. Paul, in his letter to Timothy, calls God "invisible" and describes Him as the One "whom no one has ever seen or can see." Even logic tells us that, if God is present everywhere and we were able to see Him with our physical eyes, all we would see would be God everywhere we look!

It is actually a good thing that we cannot see God everywhere we look because God told Moses, "man shall not see me and live." His divine glory would overpower and destroy our sinful flesh (Is. 6:5). God has made Himself visible to people in different forms throughout the Old Testament, such as wrestling with Jacob as a man, appearing as a pillar of cloud or fire in the Exodus, and emerging as a burning bush to Moses. These, and other appearances of God in the Old Testament, may be forecasts of the incarnation of Christ, but they are not occasions where people looked on the spiritual nature and full essence of God's divine being. It is this full essence of God, in all His glory, that sinful man cannot look on and survive the experience.

In the New Testament are promises that some will see God. Jesus said that the pure in heart will see God. Revelation gives a description of the servants of God worshiping at the throne of God and of the Lamb and promises that they will see His face. The Apostle John wrote that "when he appears we shall be like him, because we shall see him as he is." Is this consistent with the teaching that God is not visible and we cannot look at Him and live? One clear explanation is that we will see Jesus. 1 John 3 refers to "when he appears," pointing to the return of Jesus Christ. When Jesus appears, we will be like Jesus, and we will see Jesus as He is in His resurrected state. The verse in Revelation describes a future scene in the new heaven and the new earth in which God's servants will see His face. This could be another reference to the face of Jesus, since the setting is "the throne of God and of the Lamb." Jesus is "the Lamb of God, who takes away the sin of the world" (Jn. 1:29). It is also possible that in our sinless, glorified state we have the capacity to see all persons of the Trinity. Since we will be without sin, the incompatibility of unholy sinners before a holy God will be removed.

Action Step: What does it look like to "see" God now, as we walk through our lives on earth? God is invisible, and Jesus Christ has ascended and is no longer visible on earth. In Ephesians 1:18, Paul describes "having the eyes of your hearts enlightened" to see the gospel and the hope, riches, and power that come with it. Read Ephesians 1:15-23 and reflect on the things Paul prayed for when he asked the Spirit to help the Ephesians to see with their hearts. Faith and the work of the Holy Spirit allow us to see the powerful results of God's work on our behalf, even when we can't see Him with physical eyes.

"See my hands and my feet, that it is I myself. Touch me, and see. For a spirit does not have flesh and bones as you see that I have."

Luke 24:39

"And behold, I am with you always, to the end of the age."

Matthew 28:20

And we know that the Son of God has come and has given us understanding, so that we may know him who is true; and we are in him who is true, in his Son Jesus Christ. He is the true God and eternal life.

1 John 5:20

Spirit and Infinite
Our Own View of God Is Too Small 5

Consider a power screwdriver. In fact, think of the most high-end power screwdriver that money can buy. It has more power and more features than any other on the market. When you drive a screw into the hardest surface, this tool turns the screw in as if the surface was butter. It is a finely crafted tool and a tribute to the creativity and innovation of its maker. Now take this tool to a job site and attempt to use it to dig a hole for the foundation of a new home. That would be ridiculous! The manufacturer did not design it for that job. In the same way, God did not create our finite minds with the intention of comprehending His infinite nature. Our thoughts are too small for the job.

Studying His infinite nature is an impossible exercise without the assistance that God has provided by revealing Himself in the Scriptures and in the Word made flesh, Jesus Christ. We have considered that God is *not finite*, *not flesh*, and *not visible*. Yet the human body that Jesus put on *is* finite *and* flesh *and* visible. In order to properly appreciate the miracle of the incarnation of Jesus Christ, it can be helpful to understand some of the truths behind the mystery of the Son of God made flesh. A doctrine finalized at a church council in 451 AD, which is accepted by the vast majority of Catholic, Protestant, and Orthodox churches, states that Jesus Christ is one Person with two natures—divine and human. The divine nature is spirit and infinite and of one essence within the Trinity. The human nature is fully man and finite—exactly like the nature of you and I, but without sin. In Jesus, one Person of the infinite Godhead has condescended to take on finite, human form. Wayne Grudem, in *Systematic Theology*, summarizes this doctrine:

> *It is by far the most amazing miracle of the entire Bible—far more amazing than the resurrection and more amazing even than the creation of the universe. The fact that the infinite, omnipotent, eternal Son of God could become man and join himself to a human nature forever, so that infinite God became one person with finite man, will remain for eternity the most profound miracle and the most profound mystery in all the universe.**

This is a doctrine that is not declared in a straightforward way in one place in Scripture but is supported by the whole of Scripture. A very basic Biblical defense can be presented by combining Luke 24:39 and Matthew 28:20. Both are appearances by Jesus to His disciples after His resurrection. In Luke 24, Jesus appeared to His disciples, who were afraid, thinking He was a spirit. Jesus invited them to touch His body, "For a spirit does not have flesh and bones as you see that I have." Even after His resurrection, Jesus had human form and flesh. In the verse from Matthew, Jesus promised to be with His followers "always, to the end of the age." This must be referring to His divine nature, which is infinite. His finite human form can't be with all of His followers all of the time as they go to separate nations. This one Person with two natures is Jesus Christ, who has "come and has given us understanding." It is through looking at Jesus Christ that we can begin to see the Father.

Action Step: Spend some time in prayer and meditation on the Son of God. Praise God that the eternal Son, who has always existed in perfect, loving relationship within the Trinity, humbled Himself to take on human form in order to redeem mankind.

But you, O Lord, are enthroned forever; you are remembered throughout all generations.

Psalms 102:12

Jesus Christ is the same yesterday and today and forever.

Hebrews 13:8

O Lord, how manifold are your works! In wisdom have you made them all; the earth is full of your creatures.

Psalms 104:24

"Ah, Lord God! It is you who have made the heavens and the earth by your great power and by your outstretched arm! Nothing is too hard for you."

Jeremiah 32:17

"The Rock, his work is perfect, for all his ways are justice. A God of faithfulness and without iniquity, just and upright is he."

Deuteronomy 32:4

The Lord passed before him and proclaimed, "The Lord, the Lord, a God merciful and gracious, slow to anger, and abounding in steadfast love and faithfulness,"

Exodus 34:6

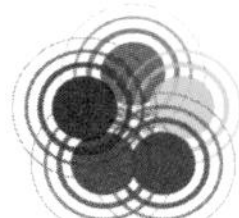

Spirit and Infinite

The Infinity of God Is in All of His Attributes

6

Because God's spirit is infinite and has no limits, it is impossible for us to fully grasp His nature. However, with the example of the perfect Son of God before us in Scripture and the illumination of the Holy Spirit giving us understanding, we can at least begin to see the nature of the Father. Perhaps the best way to appreciate the infinite aspect of His nature is to see examples in Scripture of the way that all of His attributes are without limits. Infinite can be seen as one of God's attributes, but infinite can also be used as a description for each and every one of His other attributes.

The verses at left are just a small sample of the everlastingness of God's characteristics. His majesty is *forever*. He is *forever* unchanging. *Nothing* is too hard for His power. *All* His ways are justice. He is *abounding* in steadfast love and faithfulness. It is easy to see that every aspect of God's nature is infinite.

The Westminster Assembly was a gathering of theologians and other students of Scripture in England and Scotland in the 1640s. They published the *Westminster Confession* in 1647 as a reformation movement in the Church of England. This was followed by the writing of more concise catechisms—the *Westminster Larger* and *Shorter Catechisms*. These were statements of faith in the form of questions, followed by Biblically supported answers. The Confession and Catechisms are still widely used in Christian churches today, though they are always subordinate to the Bible.

I have included on page 87 the answers from both the *Larger* and *Shorter Catechisms* to the question: "What is God?" It is worth noting that in both versions, following the statement that God is a Spirit, the next word used to describe Him is "infinite." I am unaware of anything recorded as to the reasoning behind the order of the attributes listed in the response. It is almost certainly not intended to be a list in order of importance. Yet in both the *Larger* and *Shorter* responses, there does seem to be a sense in the wording affirming that the infinity of God's essence runs through all of the other descriptive words. His infinite nature is integral to all of who God is.

Action Step: Read the *Catechism* responses to the question "What is God?" on page 87. Note especially the references to what God is infinite *in*. God is infinite in "being, glory, blessedness, and perfection" and "wisdom, power, holiness, justice, goodness, and truth." Read each of them individually. For example, "God is infinite in being. God is infinite in glory. God is infinite in blessedness." Continue through all of the listed characteristics, and consider how this impacts your view of Him.

Weekly Summary

Key Points

1. God is Spirit.
2. God is without limits or bounds.
3. God has no body.
4. God is invisible.
5. Our own view of God is too small.
6. The infinity of God is in all of His attributes.

Spirit and Infinite
Action Steps

7

Go back through the action steps and complete any that you have not yet completed or repeat one that was meaningful:

1. The Bible teaches that God created man with a spirit, which connects us to God and helps us to understand (Job 32:8). Our spirits then return to God when we die (Ecc. 12:7). Medical science generally makes a practice of only addressing the physical part of men and women. In recent years, however, some research has been done looking into quantum processes occurring in tiny structures within the brain cells. A theory proposes that these quantum vibrations may be related to human consciousness. The researchers are attempting to define consciousness and whether it can exist outside of the body. Those who believe the Bible to be true do not need the support of research to trust that the human spirit exists and can exist outside of the physical body. Neither do we need to feel threatened by the fact that scientists may eventually quantify the human spirit. Do you believe that your spirit originated from God and finds its home at some point in returning to Him?

2. God's infinite nature, being so foreign to us, is another quality that is so difficult to grasp. Pray for understanding and that the Spirit will help you gain a glimpse of understanding of His existence without limits.

3. One of the ways God reaches us is through the community of believers. God has no physical body, but the sum of all believers for all time is the body of Christ (1 Cor. 12:12-31). As the body of Christ, we are called to care for one another, suffer together, and rejoice together. Is there someone in your life today who needs care for whom you can be God's outstretched arm?

4. What does it look like to "see" God now, as we walk through our lives on earth? God is invisible, and Jesus Christ has ascended and is no longer visible on earth. In Ephesians 1:18, Paul describes "having the eyes of your hearts enlightened" to see the gospel and the hope, riches, and power that come with it. Read Ephesians 1:15-23 and reflect on the things Paul prayed for when he asked the Spirit to help the Ephesians to see with their hearts. Faith and the work of the Holy Spirit allow us to see the powerful results of God's work in our lives, even when we can't see Him with physical eyes.

5. Spend some time in prayer and meditation on the Son of God. Praise God that the eternal Son, who has always existed in perfect, loving relationship within the Trinity, humbled Himself to take on human form in order to redeem mankind.

6. Read the *Catechism* responses to the question "What is God?" on page 87. Note especially the references to what God is infinite *in*. God is infinite in "being, glory, blessedness, and perfection" and "wisdom, power, holiness, justice, goodness, and truth." Read each of them individually. For example, "God is infinite in being. God is infinite in glory. God is infinite in blessedness." Continue through all of the listed characteristics, and consider how this impacts your view of Him.

WEEK 7

Sovereign

God is sovereign. His will is supreme. So far from God being under law of "right," He is a law unto Himself, so that whatsoever He *does is right.*

Arthur W. Pink, *The Attributes of God*, 42-43.

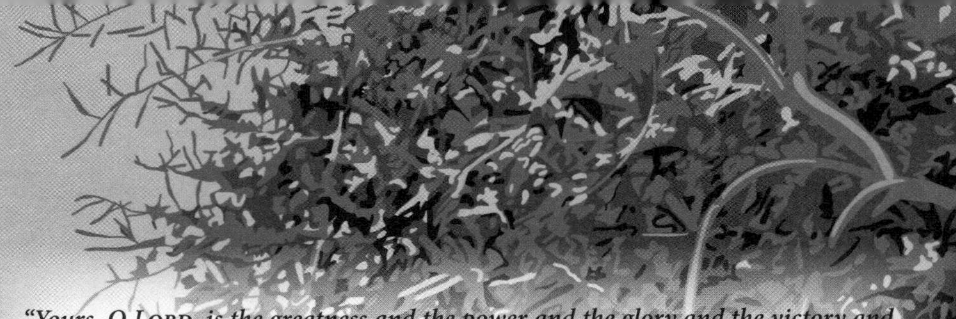

"Yours, O Lord, is the greatness and the power and the glory and the victory and the majesty, for all that is in the heavens and in the earth is yours. Yours is the kingdom, O Lord, and you are exalted as head above all. Both riches and honor come from you, and you rule over all. In your hand are power and might, and in your hand it is to make great and to give strength to all. And now we thank you, our God, and praise your glorious name."

1 Chronicles 29:11-13

"You are the Lord, you alone. You have made heaven, the heaven of heavens, with all their host, the earth and all that is on it, the seas and all that is in them; and you preserve all of them; and the host of heaven worships you."

Nehemiah 9:6

"For the Lord your God is God of gods and Lord of lords, the great, the mighty, and the awesome God, who is not partial and takes no bribe."

Deuteronomy 10:17

Our God is in the heavens; he does all that he pleases.

Psalms 115:3

The Lord has established his throne in the heavens, and his kingdom rules over all.

Psalms 103:19

I charge you in the presence of God, who gives life to all things, and of Christ Jesus, who in his testimony before Pontius Pilate made the good confession, to keep the commandment unstained and free from reproach until the appearing of our Lord Jesus Christ, which he will display at the proper time—he who is the blessed and only Sovereign, the King of kings and Lord of lords, who alone has immortality, who dwells in unapproachable light, whom no one has ever seen or can see. To him be honor and eternal dominion. Amen.

1 Timothy 6:13-16

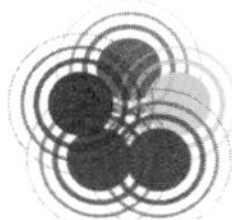

Sovereign
Definition 1

The word *sovereign* may appear many times in the version of the Bible that you use, or it may only appear a few times. Some Bible translations use *master* or *Lord* to describe God in the same place where others translate the Greek or Hebrew language into *sovereign*. Regardless of whether a given version of the Bible uses the word, the concept of God's sovereignty runs through all of Scripture.

Dictionary definitions of *sovereign* usually include a description such as "having supreme rank or authority." A political definition of a sovereign state is one that is not dependent on or under the power of any other state. So a basic English definition of the word sovereign might be "having complete control."

The best way to build a Biblical definition of God's sovereignty is to look at Scripture that considers His rank, authority, or control. Based only on the verses on the left page, here are some descriptions of God's sovereignty:

Greatness, power, glory, victory, majesty
All that is in the heavens and earth is His
Exalted as head above all
Ruler over all
In His hand are power and might
Maker of heaven and earth
God of gods, Lord of lords
Awesome
He does all that He pleases
His kingdom rules over all
Eternal dominion

God is free to do all that He chooses to do. Of course, He will only choose to do the things that are consistent with His nature. The idea of a human being with absolute control and authority can be terrifying. God does possess absolute dominion over the earth, the heavens, and everything contained within, but His rule is one that is consistent with love, wisdom, righteousness, justice, and the rest of His perfections. It would be both logical and Biblical to say that God deserves sovereignty as the Creator of all things. It would also be reasonable to say that the complete excellency of His nature justifies His authority.

Action Step: From the list of descriptive phrases above, write out your own full definition of God's sovereignty. You might even look for additional verses to add depth to your definition.

"I know that you can do all things, and that no purpose of yours can be thwarted."
Job 42:2

For I know that the LORD is great, and that our Lord is above all gods. Whatever the LORD pleases, he does, in heaven and on earth, in the seas and all deeps.
Psalms 135:5-6

The LORD of hosts has sworn: "As I have planned, so shall it be, and as I have purposed, so shall it stand,"
Isaiah 14:24

Consider the work of God: who can make straight what he has made crooked? In the day of prosperity be joyful, and in the day of adversity consider: God has made the one as well as the other, so that man may not find out anything that will be after him.
Ecclesiastes 7:13-14

Then Moses stretched out his hand over the sea, and the LORD drove the sea back by a strong east wind all night and made the sea dry land, and the waters were divided. And the people of Israel went into the midst of the sea on dry ground, the waters being a wall to them on their right hand and on their left.
Exodus 14:21-22

So to keep me from becoming conceited because of the surpassing greatness of the revelations, a thorn was given me in the flesh, a messenger of Satan to harass me, to keep me from becoming conceited. Three times I pleaded with the Lord about this, that it should leave me. But he said to me, "My grace is sufficient for you, for my power is made perfect in weakness." Therefore I will boast all the more gladly of my weaknesses, so that the power of Christ may rest upon me.
2 Corinthians 12:7-9

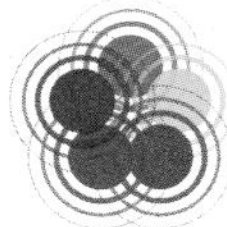

Sovereign

Sovereignty and Power

2

The sovereignty or authority of God is closely tied to His power, though we should understand the differences. If I were to invite a friend to stay at my home with me for a weekend, that does not mean she has been given ownership of my home. Suppose I woke after the first night of my friend's stay to discover that my living room furniture had been moved out and replaced with something different. That would be quite a surprise and outside of normal social expectations. I am the owner of the home and the furniture. Therefore, the final word of authority as to placement of furniture in the home really should be mine. You might say that I possess a tiny amount of sovereignty over my home.

Let's look at the same scene with respect to power. I am advancing in years, and I don't have the strength that I used to. Suppose my house guest is in the prime of her life, trains for triathlons, and competes professionally. If I want to move my living room furniture out of the house, I don't have the power to do so. After the first night of her stay, my friend has proven that she definitely has the strength to do the job. I have the authority but lack the power. My friend has the strength but lacks the authority.

God possesses all authority and all strength. He has the right of ownership to do as He pleases and complete power to bring about His will. No one can prevent Him from completing His sovereign plan. God reigns over the earth and all that is in it to accomplish His purposes, whether His plan is prosperity or adversity for His people.

One of the most well-known stories of the Old Testament is the account of God parting the Red Sea for the nation of Israel to safely escape from the pursuing Egyptians. Our familiarity with this story may cause us to minimize how incredible this was. God created the earth with certain physical laws, including gravity. He completely overrode laws of His own physical creation on a large scale in this event. The waters of the Red Sea had been settled within its shores since the Genesis flood had receded. God's powerful wind divided the waters, creating a wall of water on each side and dry ground at the bottom of the sea despite every natural force on earth acting in opposition to the wind. According to Exodus 14:21, these walls of water stood *all night long*. God's sovereign plan to rescue His people from slavery and His power over all of creation met in a spectacular victory for Israel at the Red Sea.

We also know that God's sovereign plan for His people may include adversity. Even the Apostle Paul, in the midst of his great calling to preach the gospel, was faced with "a thorn in the flesh, a messenger of Satan." He pleaded with the Lord to remove it from him, but God made it clear to Paul that this adversity had a purpose—to keep him from becoming conceited. In this case, God's sovereign plan to bring the gospel to the nations met with His power over Paul's body to bring adversity to Paul's life. Whether the path through the Red Sea is smooth or the path through Paul's life is rocky, God has established His sovereign will, and His ultimate purposes are realized.

Action Step: Pray that God will give you understanding of the extent of His sovereignty. Worship and praise Him for His reign over the earth and all that is in it.

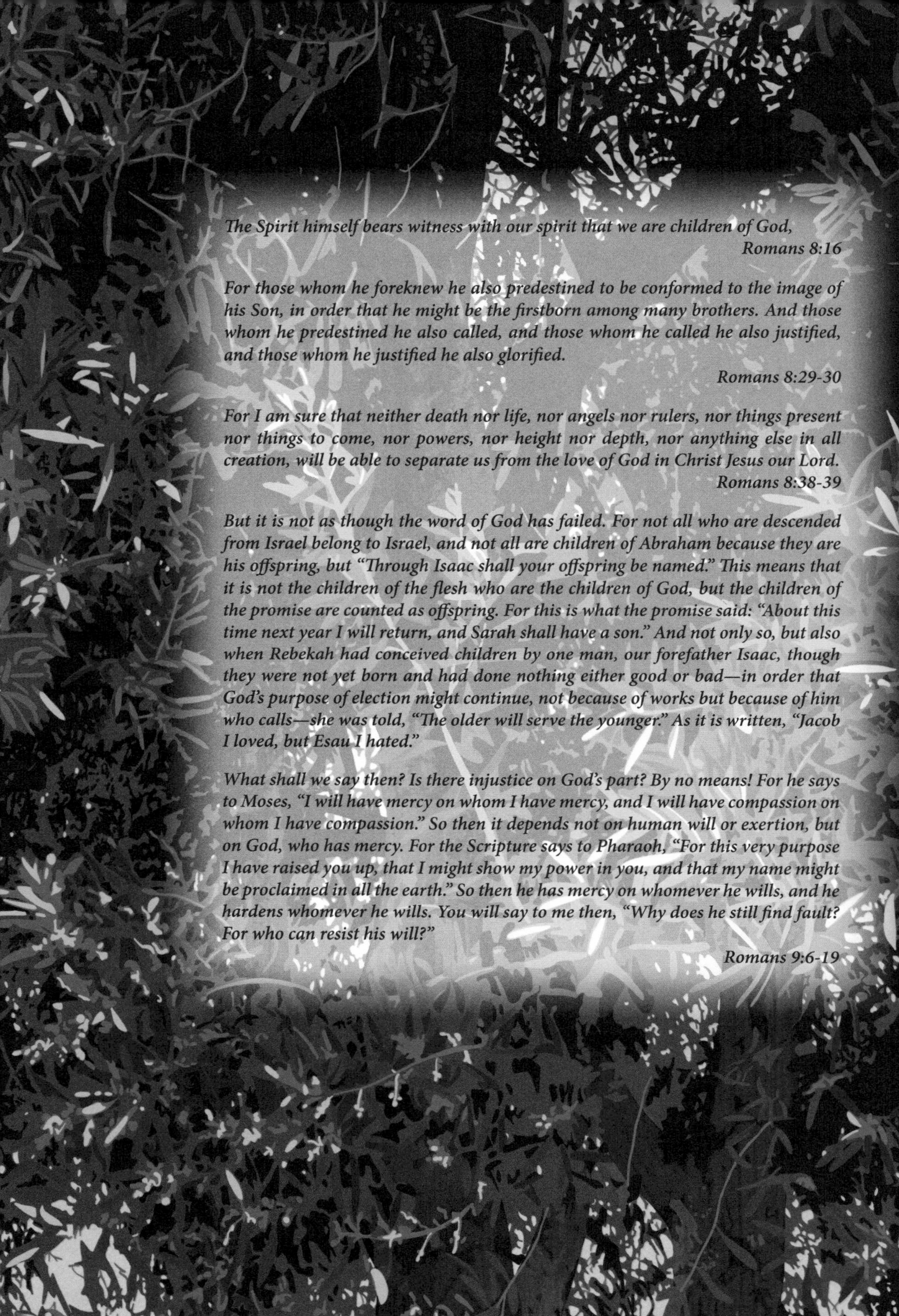

The Spirit himself bears witness with our spirit that we are children of God,

Romans 8:16

For those whom he foreknew he also predestined to be conformed to the image of his Son, in order that he might be the firstborn among many brothers. And those whom he predestined he also called, and those whom he called he also justified, and those whom he justified he also glorified.

Romans 8:29-30

For I am sure that neither death nor life, nor angels nor rulers, nor things present nor things to come, nor powers, nor height nor depth, nor anything else in all creation, will be able to separate us from the love of God in Christ Jesus our Lord.

Romans 8:38-39

But it is not as though the word of God has failed. For not all who are descended from Israel belong to Israel, and not all are children of Abraham because they are his offspring, but "Through Isaac shall your offspring be named." This means that it is not the children of the flesh who are the children of God, but the children of the promise are counted as offspring. For this is what the promise said: "About this time next year I will return, and Sarah shall have a son." And not only so, but also when Rebekah had conceived children by one man, our forefather Isaac, though they were not yet born and had done nothing either good or bad—in order that God's purpose of election might continue, not because of works but because of him who calls—she was told, "The older will serve the younger." As it is written, "Jacob I loved, but Esau I hated."

What shall we say then? Is there injustice on God's part? By no means! For he says to Moses, "I will have mercy on whom I have mercy, and I will have compassion on whom I have compassion." So then it depends not on human will or exertion, but on God, who has mercy. For the Scripture says to Pharaoh, "For this very purpose I have raised you up, that I might show my power in you, and that my name might be proclaimed in all the earth." So then he has mercy on whomever he wills, and he hardens whomever he wills. You will say to me then, "Why does he still find fault? For who can resist his will?"

Romans 9:6-19

Sovereign
God's Sovereignty in Choosing a People 3

The Apostle Paul spends much of the first half of the book of Romans outlining the tremendous hope that believers have in the gospel of Jesus Christ. This culminates in Romans 8, a celebration of the assurance that those who are in Christ Jesus are led by God's Spirit and are adopted as God's children. They are foreknown, predestined, called, and justified by God, and absolutely nothing in all creation can separate them from God's love. Immediately following this celebration, at the beginning of Romans 9, Paul changes to lament for his fellow Jews who have not received Jesus as Messiah.

The reality in the church at the time Paul wrote this letter was that many Gentiles had received and believed the gospel, but most of the nation of Israel had not. The promised Messiah had come, and God's people had missed it! This absence of many Jewish believers was an agonizing situation for Paul since the nation of Israel—Paul's kinsmen—were God's chosen people who had been given the promise of adoption into God's family, the glory of God in the temple, the covenants, the law, and more. Even the physical descent of Jesus Christ came through the nation of Israel. Now the Gentiles were receiving these promises of God. What then of God's promises to Abraham and his descendants? Had God's promises failed? Worse yet, was God unjust? If God was not keeping promises to the nation of Israel, how could Gentiles be assured that He would be faithful to His promises to them?

Romans chapters 9-11 are Paul's carefully worded response to these questions in which he outlines the justice behind God's sovereign actions. The short answer is, "God is just, and His promises never fail." Paul begins his argument in chapter 9 with a quick tour through the Old Testament looking at the process of God sovereignly choosing people to receive His promises. God's original covenant was with Abraham. Abraham had two sons, Ishmael and Isaac. Isaac was chosen for the promises. Isaac and Rebekah had twin sons, Esau and Jacob. Before either of these twins were born, before either of them had done anything good or bad, God chose Jacob to receive the promises. Paul explains to his readers that God will show mercy to those whom He chooses. God's election of those who will receive His promises is based entirely in God's mercy and has nothing to do with earning His favor. No man or woman deserves God's mercy, no matter how hard we try to work for it. Yet His sovereign will remains to choose a people for Himself. Throughout the Old Testament, God has never chosen all of Abraham's descendants to receive His promises. God has always selected a people from within the larger nation of Israel to be faithful to Him. God calling a small group of Jews to believe that Jesus is their Messiah is consistent with the way God has always called people to faith.

Romans 9:19 asks another crucial question: "You will say to me then, 'Why does he still find fault? For who can resist his will?'" Paul anticipates the reader's question—the same question that people ask God today. If God predestines and calls specific people to faith, how can God hold people responsible who don't believe? Paul has set himself up perfectly in this letter to outline the full theological explanation for how to balance God's sovereign election of people with man's freedom to choose whether to believe. As we will see in tomorrow's reading, Paul's explanation takes an unexpected turn.

Action Step: Carefully read all of Romans chapters 9-11 to get an overall view of the Scripture for today and the next two days.

You will say to me then, "Why does he still find fault? For who can resist his will?" But who are you, O man, to answer back to God? Will what is molded say to its molder, "Why have you made me like this?" Has the potter no right over the clay, to make out of the same lump one vessel for honorable use and another for dishonorable use? What if God, desiring to show his wrath and to make known his power, has endured with much patience vessels of wrath prepared for destruction, in order to make known the riches of his glory for vessels of mercy, which he has prepared beforehand for glory—even us whom he has called, not from the Jews only but also from the Gentiles?

Romans 9:19-24

The word that came to Jeremiah from the LORD: "Arise, and go down to the potter's house, and there I will let you hear my words." So I went down to the potter's house, and there he was working at his wheel. And the vessel he was making of clay was spoiled in the potter's hand, and he reworked it into another vessel, as it seemed good to the potter to do.

Then the word of the LORD came to me: "O house of Israel, can I not do with you as this potter has done? declares the Lord. Behold, like the clay in the potter's hand, so are you in my hand, O house of Israel. If at any time I declare concerning a nation or a kingdom, that I will pluck up and break down and destroy it, and if that nation, concerning which I have spoken, turns from its evil, I will relent of the disaster that I intended to do to it. And if at any time I declare concerning a nation or a kingdom that I will build and plant it, and if it does evil in my sight, not listening to my voice, then I will relent of the good that I had intended to do to it."

Jeremiah 18:1-10

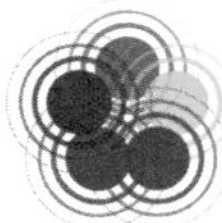

Sovereign
The Potter and His Clay

4

Here in Romans 9, God's justice and righteousness are being questioned. Not by Paul himself, but Paul has presented the questions that, in his experience, are on his readers' minds. Is God being fair to hold Israel, and others, responsible for not believing in Jesus as Messiah when God is the one who chooses who He will call? We might think this would be the perfect place for Paul to share with his readers that in-depth explanation of how God's sovereignty meets human freedom. But Paul doesn't attempt to explain the mystery. Instead, he essentially asks, "Can finite people explain what an infinite God is doing?" God is sovereign, and we are not.

Jeremiah was a prophet to Judah, the southern kingdom within the nation of Israel. His prophetic ministry began while the people of Judah were still in their homeland and extended until the exile of Judah to Babylon. During his ministry, God called him to observe a potter working with clay as an illustration of God's work with His people. As Jeremiah watched the potter, the vessel was spoiled—the clay had apparently been resistant to the work of the potter. The potter started over with the clay. He had an image in mind of what he wanted the clay to shape into, and he continued to work it until the shape had been achieved. Just as the potter reworked the clay, God was continuing to reshape Israel and the other nations. The people of Judah would be sent into exile in Babylon, but it would be to bring a rebellious people to repentance so that God could remake them.

Paul picked up this illustration to underscore God's sovereignty over His creation. God has both the power and authority to shape a people to follow Him. On top of this, He has the wisdom to do this perfectly. Doesn't the potter have the right to design different pots for different purposes? Instead of explaining God to justify Him, Paul focuses on what God had planned for the clay—shaping a chosen people into vessels that will make known the riches of His glory. He is molding clay pots—people of faith—into the shape of Jesus for God's glory. The process of God reshaping clay pots is not an unfaithful act to His promises but part of the fulfillment of His promises.

In His wisdom and sovereignty, God has chosen vessels of mercy—the people that He has called to faith. Though there are none that deserve His mercy and all deserve His wrath (Rom. 3:23), in His love He has chosen to show mercy to some. Paul is content to answer readers' questions about God's sovereignty and human freedom with a call to submit to God's sovereignty. God's will is always consistent with all of His nature, and our response should be one of surrender and trust.

Action Step: Proverbs 3 includes the following commands: "Trust in the LORD with all your heart, and do not lean on your own understanding... Be not wise in your own eyes; fear the LORD, and turn away from evil." Seeking knowledge of God's ways from Scripture is to honor God. Refusing to trust God because you don't completely understand His ways is rebellious. Examine your own heart to see if there are areas where your trust in God falls short because you don't fully understand Him.

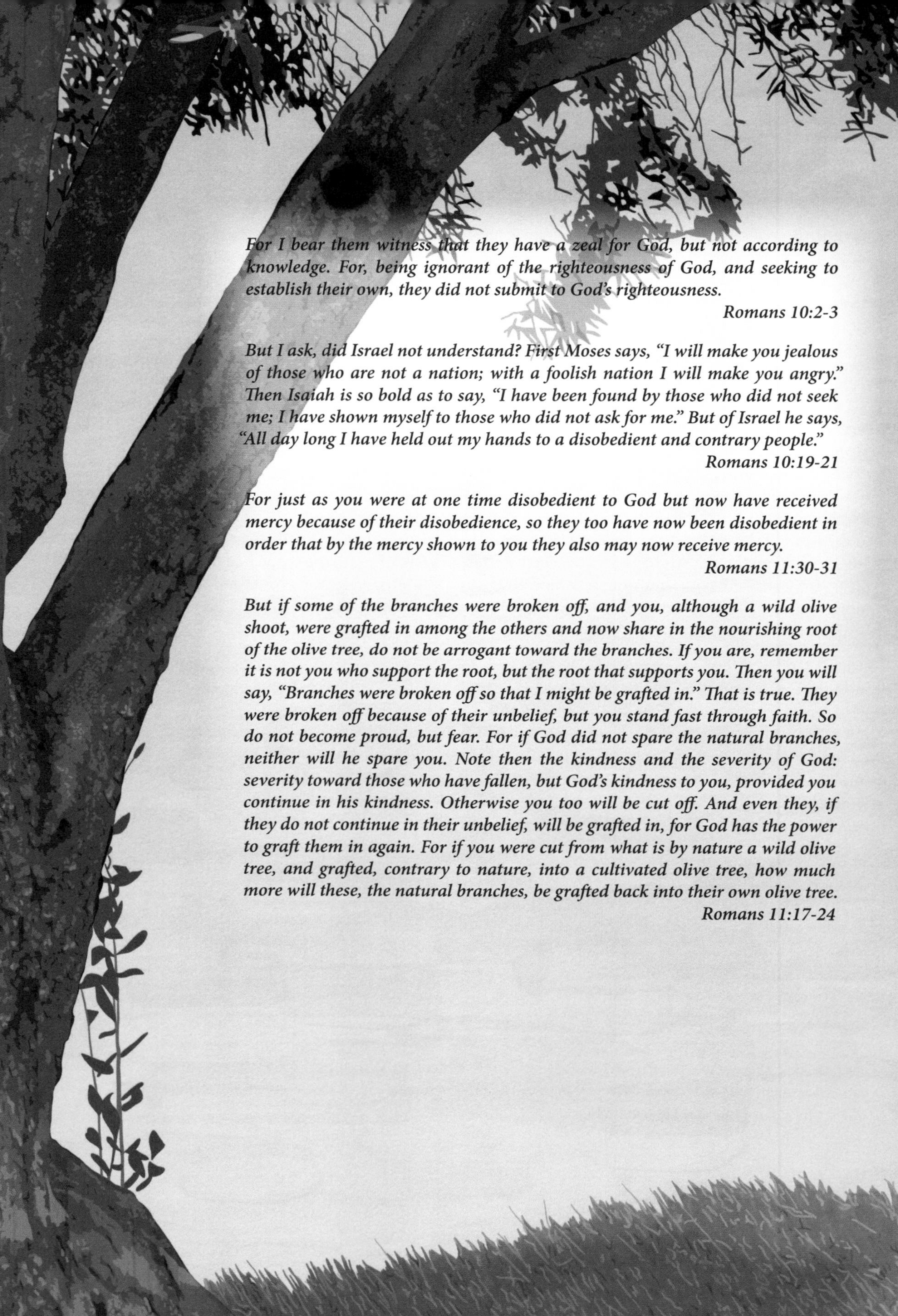

For I bear them witness that they have a zeal for God, but not according to knowledge. For, being ignorant of the righteousness of God, and seeking to establish their own, they did not submit to God's righteousness.

Romans 10:2-3

But I ask, did Israel not understand? First Moses says, "I will make you jealous of those who are not a nation; with a foolish nation I will make you angry." Then Isaiah is so bold as to say, "I have been found by those who did not seek me; I have shown myself to those who did not ask for me." But of Israel he says, "All day long I have held out my hands to a disobedient and contrary people."

Romans 10:19-21

For just as you were at one time disobedient to God but now have received mercy because of their disobedience, so they too have now been disobedient in order that by the mercy shown to you they also may now receive mercy.

Romans 11:30-31

But if some of the branches were broken off, and you, although a wild olive shoot, were grafted in among the others and now share in the nourishing root of the olive tree, do not be arrogant toward the branches. If you are, remember it is not you who support the root, but the root that supports you. Then you will say, "Branches were broken off so that I might be grafted in." That is true. They were broken off because of their unbelief, but you stand fast through faith. So do not become proud, but fear. For if God did not spare the natural branches, neither will he spare you. Note then the kindness and the severity of God: severity toward those who have fallen, but God's kindness to you, provided you continue in his kindness. Otherwise you too will be cut off. And even they, if they do not continue in their unbelief, will be grafted in, for God has the power to graft them in again. For if you were cut from what is by nature a wild olive tree, and grafted, contrary to nature, into a cultivated olive tree, how much more will these, the natural branches, be grafted back into their own olive tree.

Romans 11:17-24

Sovereign
God's Sovereignty Gives Us Free Choice 5

Following the description of the potter and the clay, Paul begins to point out Israel's unbelief. While the Gentiles were pursuing righteousness by faith, Israel pursued righteousness by the law. Israel failed to believe in God's righteousness, which comes through confessing and believing in Jesus Christ. Had Israel not heard or understood God's message? Yes, they had! Both Moses and Isaiah prophesied that Israel would be jealous of other nations and that those who did not previously seek God would find Him. Israel had been disobedient. They were responsible for their own unbelief.

In God's sovereign plan for creation, He has willed that mankind should have a certain amount of free choice. By giving the freedom to choose, the possibility exists to choose disobedience and unbelief. This disobedience has brought evil into God's good creation. It is also part of God's sovereign plan for creation to execute justice by holding people responsible for the choices made. Israel heard, but they did not obey. As Paul wrote his letter to the Romans, there was a believing remnant of Jews. However, the rest of the nation of Israel was being held responsible for their unbelief through a partial hardening. But Paul assures his readers in Romans 11 that this hardening will not last for all time. Because of Israel's failure, salvation came to other nations. Paul was confident that Israel would be jealous of the Gentiles' blessings and they would then believe, receive mercy, and be included in the promises.

Paul illustrates this plan of God with an olive tree with roots in God's promises to Abraham, Isaac, and Jacob. Originally, only Israel had branches in the tree. Some of Israel's branches were broken off so that wild shoots—the Gentiles—could be grafted in. But Paul reminds his readers that the root of the tree is still from Israel. Continuing life for the entire tree is drawn from God's faithfulness to His promises to the patriarchs. Those from Israel who believe will be grafted back in again, and the tree will be complete—a full, thriving tree with both Jews and Gentiles receiving God's promises. This is God's sovereign plan for choosing a people for Himself who also choose to love and trust Him.

Romans 9 focuses on God's sovereignty in calling people to faith. Romans 10 and 11 focus on Israel's responsibility for their failure to believe. Yes, God is sovereign, and He chooses for Himself a people. Yes, people have been given a range of choices to make in life, and God will hold them accountable for their choices. Paul lets both of these realities exist right next to each other in his letter to the Romans, and he never offers a tidy explanation about where the two meet. This would indicate that we also need to accept both realities in faith. Yet again, we see that our finite minds cannot fully grasp any one of God's attributes.

Action Step: In Romans 10:14-15, Paul is in the midst of his argument that Israel had indeed heard the message of Christ and the inclusion of the Gentiles in God's chosen people. In this context, he issues a great call for the gospel to be preached: "How then will they call on him in whom they have not believed? And how are they to believe in him of whom they have never heard? And how are they to hear without someone preaching? And how are they to preach unless they are sent? As it is written, 'How beautiful are the feet of those who preach the good news!'" Look for an opportunity today to preach the good news to someone who may not have heard it. Just a simple statement that your hope is found in the gospel of Jesus Christ can open up an opportunity to be a part of God's calling in someone's life.

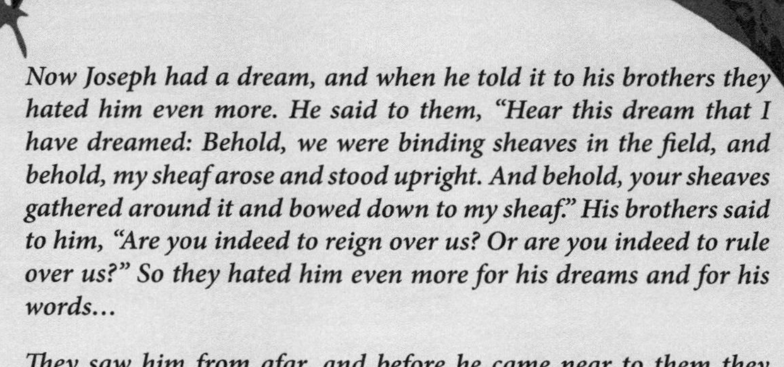

Now Joseph had a dream, and when he told it to his brothers they hated him even more. He said to them, "Hear this dream that I have dreamed: Behold, we were binding sheaves in the field, and behold, my sheaf arose and stood upright. And behold, your sheaves gathered around it and bowed down to my sheaf." His brothers said to him, "Are you indeed to reign over us? Or are you indeed to rule over us?" So they hated him even more for his dreams and for his words…

They saw him from afar, and before he came near to them they conspired against him to kill him. They said to one another, "Here comes this dreamer. Come now, let us kill him and throw him into one of the pits. Then we will say that a fierce animal has devoured him, and we will see what will become of his dreams…"
So when Joseph came to his brothers, they stripped him of his robe, the robe of many colors that he wore. And they took him and threw him into a pit…

Then Judah said to his brothers, "What profit is it if we kill our brother and conceal his blood? Come, let us sell him to the Ishmaelites, and let not our hand be upon him, for he is our brother, our own flesh." And his brothers listened to him. Then Midianite traders passed by. And they drew Joseph up and lifted him out of the pit, and sold him to the Ishmaelites for twenty shekels of silver. They took Joseph to Egypt.

Genesis 37:5-8, 18-20, 23-24, 26-28

Many are the plans in the mind of a man, but it is the purpose of the LORD *that will stand.*

Proverbs 19:21

Sovereign

God Is Sovereign over Evil

6

The entire life of Joseph recorded in Genesis 37-50 demonstrates God's sovereignty. From the beginning, Joseph's brothers hated him for the favoritism that their father, Jacob, showed toward him. Then he had two dreams that suggested that he might one day rule over his brothers. Since Joseph was the second youngest of twelve sons, this possibility seemed ridiculous, and the brothers hated him even more for telling them of his dreams.

When the brothers were tending flocks, Jacob sent Joseph to check on them, and the brothers devised a plan to do away with Joseph. Notice that their motivation was to destroy his dream. These sons of Jacob must have had some idea that God can use dreams to reveal His plans to His people. Their father had at least two such dreams (Gen. 28:12, 31:10). It seems that they were uncomfortable with the possibility of being ruled by their little brother, and they decided to put a stop to the plan even if it might have been from God. Initially, they wanted to kill Joseph, but they changed their minds when they saw an opportunity to make a profit from selling him into slavery. Midianite traders came by at just the right time—one hint that God was in control of this situation. But the most startling example of God's sovereignty in this story is that the brothers were trying to get rid of Joseph to kill his dreams, and they unknowingly contributed to fulfilling them. By selling Joseph into slavery in Egypt, the brothers put him right where God wanted him to be. Joseph ascended to power in Egypt, famine came to the land, and Jacob sent his sons to Egypt to buy food from none other than their little brother. God had a sovereign plan for the nation of Israel, and He saw to it that even those who worked in opposition to His plan were actually contributing to it. By the end of the story, Joseph told his brothers, "As for you, you meant evil against me, but God meant it for good, to bring it about that many people should be kept alive, as they are today" (Gen. 50:20). God's sovereignty uses even those who intend evil to bring about His good purposes.

The most significant New Testament example of this principle is at the cross of Jesus Christ. Satan attempted to orchestrate the death and defeat of the Son of God. He did not realize that He was actually playing a part in God's plan. Satan may have even temporarily felt victory when Jesus died on the cross. He probably did not realize at that point that Jesus' death actually sealed Satan's destruction (Heb. 2:14). But when Jesus rose from the grave, it had to have become clear that God had used Satan's evil schemes to accomplish His sovereign will. Joseph's words are surprisingly relevant again—what Satan meant for evil, God meant for good, to bring it about that many people should have eternal life. God did not create evil. God has permitted evil to exist in this world, but it exists always under His authority to be used as He sees fit to fulfill His plan.

Action Step: When Joseph was being carted off to Egypt by Midianites, he had absolutely no way of seeing how God could use this horrible injustice for anything good. He was being taken away from everything he knew and the family that he loved. All of his brothers had betrayed and disowned him. He was seemingly being taken away from the promise of being part of the chosen people of God. He was a slave who lost complete control of his own life. Is there a circumstance right now in your life that you see as an unjust evil? Pray that God will sovereignly use that circumstance as part of His good plan. Keep in mind that about twenty years passed from the time Joseph's brothers threw him into the well until his brothers came to Egypt and Joseph saw the good purposes of God's plan.

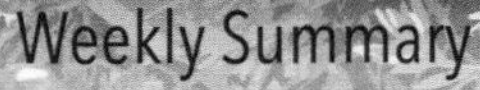

Weekly Summary

Key Points

1. The definition of God's sovereignty includes His rank, authority, and control.
2. The sovereignty or authority of God is closely tied to His power.
3. God is sovereign in choosing a people for Himself.
4. God has both the power and authority to shape a people to follow Him, just as a potter shapes clay vessels according to his design.
5. God's sovereignty gives humanity free choices.
6. God is sovereign over evil.

Sovereign

Action Steps

7

Go back through the action steps and complete any that you have not yet completed or repeat one that was meaningful:

1. From the list of descriptive phrases on page 105, write out your own full definition of God's sovereignty. You might even look for additional verses to add depth to your definition.

2. Pray that God will give you understanding of the extent of His sovereignty. Worship and praise Him for His reign over the earth and all that is in it.

3. Carefully read all of Romans chapters 9-11 to get an overall view of this key Scripture for this week.

4. Proverbs 3 includes the following commands: "Trust in the Lord with all your heart, and do not lean on your own understanding… Be not wise in your own eyes; fear the Lord, and turn away from evil." Seeking knowledge of God's ways from Scripture is to honor God. Refusing to trust God because you don't completely understand His ways is rebellious. Examine your own heart to see if there are areas where your trust in God falls short because you don't fully understand Him.

5. In Romans 10:14-15, Paul is in the midst of his argument that Israel had indeed heard the message of Christ and the inclusion of the Gentiles in God's chosen people. In this context, he issues a great call for the gospel to be preached: "How then will they call on him in whom they have not believed? And how are they to believe in him of whom they have never heard? And how are they to hear without someone preaching? And how are they to preach unless they are sent? As it is written, 'How beautiful are the feet of those who preach the good news!'" Look for an opportunity today to preach the good news to someone who may not have heard it. Just a simple statement that your hope is found in the gospel of Jesus Christ can open up an opportunity to be a part of God's calling in someone's life.

6. When Joseph was being carted off to Egypt by Midianites, he had absolutely no way of seeing how God could use this horrible injustice for anything good. He was being taken away from everything he knew and the family that he loved. All of his brothers had betrayed and disowned him. He was seemingly being taken away from the promise of being part of the chosen people of God. He was a slave who lost complete control of his own life. Is there a circumstance right now in your life that you see as an unjust evil? Pray that God will sovereignly use that circumstance as part of His good plan. Keep in mind that about twenty years passed from the time Joseph's brothers threw him into the well until his brothers came to Egypt and Joseph saw the good purposes of God's plan.

WEEK 8
Unchanging

The doctrine of God's immutability is highly significant for religion. The difference between the Creator and the creature hinges on the contrast between being and becoming. All that is creaturely is in process of becoming. It is changeable, constantly striving, in search of rest and satisfaction, and finds this rest only in him who is pure being without becoming. This is why, in Scripture, God is so often called the Rock.

Herman Bavinck, *Reformed Dogmatics, Vol. 2,* 156.

God said to Moses, "I AM WHO I AM." And he said, "Say this to the people of Israel, 'I AM has sent me to you.'"

Exodus 3:14

"For I the LORD do not change; therefore you, O children of Jacob, are not consumed."

Malachi 3:6

Every good gift and every perfect gift is from above, coming down from the Father of lights with whom there is no variation or shadow due to change.

James 1:17

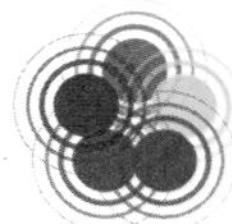

Unchanging

God's Nature Is Unchanging

1

Change makes me uncomfortable. Take technology, for example. When I was in high school, I purchased music on vinyl records. In college, cassette tapes were the norm—they worked great for listening in the car. At about the time that I graduated from college, the music standard turned to compact discs—CDs. This remained the standard technology for a satisfying twenty years until a certain computer company released a handheld device that stored music you could purchase online one song at a time. I resisted for nearly ten years, content with my growing CD library, until I discovered that I could download my CDs onto my computer and transfer all of that music onto this one device that could fit in my pocket—and now the device could make phone calls, too! I was satisfied with my leap into the twenty-first century. It has only been in the last few years that this same computer company has turned from their download format as the standard and now promotes a music subscription service. Now I have to figure out how to get the subscription playlist to find all of my preferred music. And what in the world am I supposed to do with the vinyls and cassettes I still have in a closet?

At times it feels as though this world is spinning by, and my life, including the people in it, are changing faster than I can keep up with. Fashions, language, and even moral standards are pushed aside in favor of the next new thing. In the midst of this pace, there is a God who never changes. We have touched earlier on God's self-described name that He announced to Moses in Exodus: "I AM WHO I AM." The repetition of "I AM" suggests that He is exactly the same at that moment as He was before time began and as He is today. The fact that God proclaimed this as His name states that this is inherent in His nature. God never changes.

When the Father of lights created the heavens and the earth, He set it all in motion in a rhythmic pattern of change. The earth repeats its cycles of interaction with the sun and the moon to give us days and seasons. As the seasons change, we see a succession of loss of life and new growth. As the years pass, so do generations, which are replaced by new generations. This stands in stark contrast to God's unchanging nature. Theologians refer to this attribute as God's *immutability*. Mutations are changes. So immutability describes the fact that every single one of God's attributes is the same forever and ever. Change implies adding something or taking something away—a modification of some sort. This is incompatible with God's perfect and infinite nature. If something is added to God, then He was not infinite or perfect to begin with. If something is taken away from God, then He is not infinite or perfect after the subtraction. Scripture directly teaches that God does not change, and change is inconsistent with everything that the Bible teaches about His nature.

As we helplessly watch the world race by us and move on to the next new thing, we can take comfort in the fact that God is always the same. The same God who fashioned Adam from the dust of the earth and made a covenant with Abraham and sent His Son to earth to reconcile sinful humanity with Himself remains the God—in every aspect of His character—who seeks a relationship with you and me.

Action Step: Try to conceive of an existence in which God changed. For example, what if His goodness was modified? If God, who defines good for all creation, changed His standard for goodness, how would we know what is good? Worship God for His unchanging nature.

Blessed be the God and Father of our Lord Jesus Christ, who has blessed us in Christ with every spiritual blessing in the heavenly places, even as he chose us in him before the foundation of the world, that we should be holy and blameless before him.

Ephesians 1:3-4

To me, though I am the very least of all the saints, this grace was given, to preach to the Gentiles the unsearchable riches of Christ, and to bring to light for everyone what is the plan of the mystery hidden for ages in God who created all things, so that through the church the manifold wisdom of God might now be made known to the rulers and authorities in the heavenly places. This was according to the eternal purpose that he has realized in Christ Jesus our Lord,

Ephesians 3:8-11

Many are the plans in the mind of a man, but it is the purpose of the LORD that will stand.

Proverbs 19:21

"God is not man, that he should lie, or a son of man, that he should change his mind. Has he said, and will he not do it? Or has he spoken, and will he not fulfill it?"

Numbers 23:19

"But he is unchangeable, and who can turn him back? What he desires, that he does. For he will complete what he appoints for me, and many such things are in his mind."

Job 23:13-14

This is the purpose that is purposed concerning the whole earth, and this is the hand that is stretched out over all the nations. For the LORD of hosts has purposed, and who will annul it? His hand is stretched out, and who will turn it back?

Isaiah 14:26-27

The counsel of the LORD stands forever, the plans of his heart to all generations.

Psalms 33:11

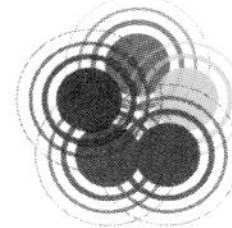

Unchanging
God's Plan is Unchanging 2

In the beginning, God had a plan. Much of His plan is revealed to us in Scripture. Some of it is not. His revealed plan includes the creation of the world and the creation of man and woman in His image. It includes giving humanity freedom to choose to obey Him or not. And His plan has always, from before Creation, included the perfect path for a chosen people to find redemption from our sinful choices and to live in holiness before Him. According to Ephesians 1, God "chose us in him before the foundation of the world." Paul states in Ephesians 3 that God graced him to preach to the Gentiles "the plan of the mystery hidden for ages in God who created all things...according to the eternal purpose that he has realized in Jesus Christ our Lord." God's plan, like His nature, has never changed.

Many imagine the God of the Old Testament and the God of the New Testament to be different in character. But His nature has not changed across time—He exists outside of time. "Well," we may think, "He is the same, but His plan has certainly changed." But that is not correct either. God has unfolded His plan to us in stages through different covenants and through hints from the mouths of His prophets. But there has always, from eternity past, only been one plan for His relationship with mankind—salvation through Jesus Christ our Lord.

We humans are accustomed to making plans. We purpose to do something, but there is no guarantee that we will accomplish the thing. Unforeseen circumstances get in the way. We don't live up to our potential, or our potential is not what we thought it was. Any number of things can interfere, and we have to reevaluate and change course. Because God is infinite in power and wisdom and knowledge, there is never any need for Him to change plans to adapt to an unforeseen circumstance. He knows all that will come to pass, and He possesses all power to bring His plans to completion.

One of the most humorous accounts in all of Scripture has to be the story of Balaam in Numbers 22-24. The Israelites were moving into the Promised Land, defeating nations along the way as God went before them. They ended up camping in the plains of Moab, which left Balak, the king of Moab, very afraid. So Balak sent for Balaam, a pagan prophet who apparently had a reputation for being able to curse and bless people. Getting Balaam to come was quite a story in itself, including payments for divination services, conversations between God and Balaam, wrong motives on Balaam's part, a talking donkey, and an appearance by the angel of the Lord! Eventually, Balaam arrived at the plains of Moab, where Balak the King showed him the people of Israel camped out. Three times the king asked Balaam to speak a curse over the nation of Israel. Three times Balaam spoke a *blessing* over the Israelites. It was during one of these blessings that Balaam spoke the words recorded in Numbers 23:19. As you can imagine, Balak was pretty furious. It didn't get any better when Balaam's next speech turned out to include a curse against Moab. God had purposed to deliver His people to the Promised Land, and His power accomplished it. A pagan prophet was unable to even speak against God's people. A donkey was given sight and words of wisdom beyond the man who rode him. And no earthly king could possibly hope to change God's mind or prevent Him from fulfilling His promise.

Action Step: Read Numbers 22-24 in one sitting, if possible. Enjoy the humor of the story but appreciate also the serious lesson: God's plans will be accomplished, and no human power will prevail against them.

All flesh is grass, and all its beauty is like the flower of the field. The grass withers, the flower fades when the breath of the Lord *blows on it; surely the people are grass. The grass withers, the flower fades, but the word of our God will stand forever.*

Isaiah 40:6-8

Forever, O Lord*, your word is firmly fixed in the heavens.*

Psalms 119:89

But you are near, O Lord*, and all your commandments are true. Long have I known from your testimonies that you have founded them forever.*

Psalms 119:151-152

The sum of your word is truth, and every one of your righteous rules endures forever.

Psalms 119:160

"Do not think that I have come to abolish the Law or the Prophets; I have not come to abolish them but to fulfill them. For truly, I say to you, until heaven and earth pass away, not an iota, not a dot, will pass from the Law until all is accomplished."

Matthew 5:17-18

"But it is easier for heaven and earth to pass away than for one dot of the Law to become void."

Luke 16:17

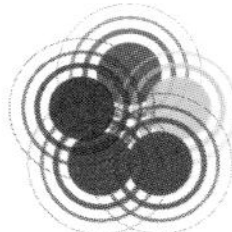

Unchanging

God's Word Is Unchanging

3

In Isaiah 40, God spoke comfort to His people through the mouth of the prophet Isaiah. The people faced exile because of their rebellious disobedience. But God assured His people that He would still be faithful to His promises. He compared people in their flesh to grass and flowers in the field. Human flesh is weak, and life will pass, but in contrast, the Lord's promised blessings do not change or fail. God had promised Abraham that He would bless all of the nations through him (Gen. 22:18). God had promised David that his heir would reign forever (2 Sam. 7:16). God had promised Israel that He would write His law on their hearts (Jer. 31:33). These promises would certainly be fulfilled. God will not change His mind about His promises. A temporary discipline would not deter Him from His plan to redeem mankind. His character never changes, and His infinite power guarantees the fulfillment of His promises. The Word of our God will stand forever, even in the midst of our unfaithfulness and frailty.

Psalm 119 is the longest chapter in the Bible. The author is clearly captivated by the beauty of God's Word, and the entire psalm is a poetic tribute to the gift of Scripture. A long list of synonyms is used for the Word, including law, testimonies, ways, precepts, statutes, commandments, rules, promise, and word of truth. A careful search of the psalm shows that, of the 176 verses, only 8 do not directly refer to the Word with one of these synonyms. One goal of this psalm is to build a deep appreciation for the Word that will result in a life shaped by its teaching. Among the themes of love for the Word, the truth of the Word, and blessings that come from obedience to the Word, the permanence of God's Word is also emphasized.

A beautiful word picture is painted in verse 89: "Forever, O Lord, your word is firmly fixed in the heavens." The image that comes to my mind is of a night sky with immovable stars that spell out the total of God's Word. In my mind, those stars will hold their places forever proclaiming the truth of God's ways. But this picture is imperfect. Jesus taught in the gospels that it is easier for heaven and earth to pass away than for the tiniest speck of God's Word to become void. The stars will not even last long enough to forever proclaim the unchanging message of God's Word. The Law and the prophets have always pointed to Jesus as their complete fulfillment, and none of these words could possibly pass away until all of God's plan is accomplished in Christ's ultimate reign over heaven and earth.

Action Step: Because the Word of God is unchanging, it is always relevant to our lives. Do you fully accept God's Word as always trustworthy in your life? For example, multiple times in Scripture, God promised His people, "I will never leave you nor forsake you." Are there moments when you feel that verse does not apply to you because you believe God has abandoned you? Pray and ask God to help you trust the relevance of His promises to your daily life.

For when God made a promise to Abraham, since he had no one greater by whom to swear, he swore by himself, saying, "Surely I will bless you and multiply you." And thus Abraham, having patiently waited, obtained the promise. For people swear by something greater than themselves, and in all their disputes an oath is final for confirmation. So when God desired to show more convincingly to the heirs of the promise the unchangeable character of his purpose, he guaranteed it with an oath, so that by two unchangeable things, in which it is impossible for God to lie, we who have fled for refuge might have strong encouragement to hold fast to the hope set before us. We have this as a sure and steadfast anchor of the soul, a hope that enters into the inner place behind the curtain, where Jesus has gone as a forerunner on our behalf, having become a high priest forever after the order of Melchizedek.

Hebrews 6:13-20

Jesus Christ is the same yesterday and today and forever.

Hebrews 13:8

Unchanging

Jesus Christ is Unchanging 4

The book of Hebrews was written to an audience of believers as a means to encourage them to persevere in their faith in Jesus Christ. The author spends most of the book building arguments as to how Jesus is superior to the Old Covenant and how, in fact, He is the fulfillment of the promises of the Old Covenant. From the opening verses of the book, the author makes clear that Jesus Christ is the Son of God, the heir of all things, Creator of the world, the exact imprint of God's nature, and the upholder of the universe. Despite any persecution they may be enduring, the author presents Christ as the One who is worthy of their faith.

Jesus Christ is described in Hebrews as superior to angels (1:4), worthy of more glory than Moses (3:3), a greater high priest than those who had to sacrifice for their own sins (4:14-15), and a guarantor of a better covenant that is enacted on better promises (7:22, 8:6). Christ entered into holy places in heaven itself by means of His own blood, not into a man-made copy in an earthly tabernacle (9:11, 24). Christ offered a better sacrifice—the once-for-all sacrifice of Himself, which perfects for all time those who are being sanctified (9:26, 10:14).

Jesus Christ is superior to every aspect of the Old Covenant because the Old Covenant was always designed to point to Jesus as its fulfillment. Jesus fulfilled the Law of Moses by never sinning. He fulfilled every Old Testament prophecy about His birth, life, death, and resurrection. Hebrews points out that Jesus does away with the first covenant in order to establish the second (10:9). The law was just a "shadow of the good things to come instead of the true form of these realities" (10:1). But through the Holy Spirit, God has fulfilled His promise: "I will put my laws on their hearts, and write them on their minds" (10:16).

In Hebrews 6, the author explains how the fulfillment of God's promises demonstrates to us the "unchangeable character of his purpose." Just as Abraham could rely on God's promises because of God's unchanging purpose and oath, we can trust Jesus as our high priest forever. In Jesus Christ, we are placing our hope in the originator of the same unchanging purpose and oath that Abraham relied on. This is summarized by the writer of Hebrews near the end of the book: "Jesus Christ is the same yesterday and today and forever." Some may question whether the Son of God changed with the incarnation. In the incarnation, the divine nature of the Son of God that existed eternally was joined to His human nature. However, the divine nature remained unchanged and will remain that way for eternity.

Action Step: The rapid change of this world and the people in it has contributed to a reality that has been referred to as "the generation gap." This term was first used in the 1960s to describe the vastly different cultures and views between parents and their children's generations. This gap can make it difficult for individuals from different generations to relate to one another and even sometimes to worship God together. Yet God does not change; therefore, He does not have different standards for how we should approach Him across different generations. How can we use this idea to connect with individuals from a separate generation than our own? Schedule a coffee or meal with someone from a different generation and explore how you can connect, in spite of your differences, over a God who does not change.

"For I the Lord do not change; therefore you, O children of Jacob, are not consumed. From the days of your fathers you have turned aside from my statutes and have not kept them. Return to me, and I will return to you, says the Lord of hosts."

Malachi 3:6-7

Then the word of the Lord came to Jonah the second time, saying, "Arise, go to Nineveh, that great city, and call out against it the message that I tell you." Jonah began to go into the city, going a day's journey. And he called out, "Yet forty days, and Nineveh shall be overthrown!" And the people of Nineveh believed God. They called for a fast and put on sackcloth, from the greatest of them to the least of them…

When God saw what they did, how they turned from their evil way, God relented of the disaster that he had said he would do to them, and he did not do it.

Jonah 3:1-2, 4-5, 10

"If you are not careful to do all the words of this law that are written in this book, that you may fear this glorious and awesome name, the Lord your God…

"the Lord will scatter you among all peoples, from one end of the earth to the other, and there you shall serve other gods of wood and stone, which neither you nor your fathers have known."

Deuteronomy 28:58, 64

"And when all these things come upon you, the blessing and the curse, which I have set before you, and you call them to mind among all the nations where the Lord your God has driven you, and return to the Lord your God, you and your children, and obey his voice in all that I command you today, with all your heart and with all your soul, then the Lord your God will restore your fortunes and have mercy on you, and he will gather you again from all the peoples where the Lord your God has scattered you."

Deuteronomy 30:1-3

"If at any time I declare concerning a nation or a kingdom, that I will pluck up and break down and destroy it, and if that nation, concerning which I have spoken, turns from its evil, I will relent of the disaster that I intended to do to it. And if at any time I declare concerning a nation or a kingdom that I will build and plant it, and if it does evil in my sight, not listening to my voice, then I will relent of the good that I had intended to do to it."

Jeremiah 18:7-10

Unchanging

In Different Situations, God Responds Differently to People

5

There are several occasions in Scripture where it would seem that God had changed His mind. This may leave us wondering whether He is indeed unchanging. Malachi 3:6-7 is a good place to start to answer our questions. In verse 6, God proclaimed that He does not change. In fact, that is why the children of Jacob were not consumed. God has chosen the nation of Israel, and He will not change His plan. If He destroyed them for their disobedience, He would not be fulfilling His promises to Abraham, Isaac, and Jacob. But in verse 7, He showed that He will change His behavior when they change their hearts. "Return to me, and I will return to you." God's essence does not change. His plan and His Word do not change. But His actions toward us do change, according to our behavior and attitude toward Him.

This principle is also demonstrated in the story of Jonah. God called Jonah to go to the city of Nineveh to warn the people of His coming judgment for their evil ways. Jonah resisted but reconsidered after having a few days inside the belly of a giant fish to think over his choices. So Jonah did go to Nineveh, and he did warn that it would be overthrown in forty days. These are the very words that God gave Jonah to speak. But the people of Nineveh repented. From the greatest to the least they repented. The king of Nineveh even called for repentance throughout the city. The people believed God and "God relented of the disaster that he had said he would do to them." Some versions of the Bible use the words "repented" or "changed His mind" instead of "relented." But God has no need for repentance, and He does not truly "change His mind." Instead, He changes His behavior toward people who believe in Him.

The changing of God's actions according to people's behavior is part of God's character. God has always hated sin. God has always extended mercy toward repentant sinners. His concerns are for righteous behavior on the part of His people and a people who submit to Him. He has directly revealed this to be true in Scripture. In the book of Deuteronomy, before Israel had even entered into the Promised Land, Moses reviewed the Law with them. Included in this review was the promise that a disobedient Israel would be taken from their land and scattered among other nations. But if Israel returned to the Lord, He would return them to their land. In the book of Jeremiah, eight hundred years after the promises of Deuteronomy, God extended this to other nations as well. If a nation does evil, God will withdraw the good that He had intended for it. If a nation turns from its evil, God will relent. The fact that God relents when people turn to Him is not contrary to His unchanging nature but actually confirms it because He has revealed this to be part of who He is.

Action Step: Sometimes it is so very easy to see when another person needs to repent. Even in the pages of the Old Testament it is obvious to any observant reader that the Israelites failed in their covenant with God again and again. Yet it can sometimes be so difficult to recognize our own patterns of sin. Spend some time in prayer today asking God to reveal where you need repentance. If you are a believer in Jesus, you have likely repented of general sin with the result of salvation, but the Christian life is one of ongoing repentance in order to maintain fellowship with God (1 Jn. 1:5-10).

Since we have such a hope, we are very bold, not like Moses, who would put a veil over his face so that the Israelites might not gaze at the outcome of what was being brought to an end. But their minds were hardened. For to this day, when they read the old covenant, that same veil remains unlifted, because only through Christ is it taken away. Yes, to this day whenever Moses is read a veil lies over their hearts. But when one turns to the Lord, the veil is removed. Now the Lord is the Spirit, and where the Spirit of the Lord is, there is freedom. And we all, with unveiled face, beholding the glory of the Lord, are being transformed into the same image from one degree of glory to another. For this comes from the Lord who is the Spirit.

2 Corinthians 3:12-18

I appeal to you therefore, brothers, by the mercies of God, to present your bodies as a living sacrifice, holy and acceptable to God, which is your spiritual worship. Do not be conformed to this world, but be transformed by the renewal of your mind, that by testing you may discern what is the will of God, what is good and acceptable and perfect.

Romans 12:1-2

Unchanging
The Blessing of Change in Our Lives 6

God's unchanging nature is a blessing that we can take comfort in. The changing nature of this world and the people in it can be frustrating. But the fact that we humans can change is also a tremendous blessing that we should be thankful for. From the first disobedience of Adam and Eve, mankind has existed in a broken state, separated from God. But, because God has placed in us the capacity for change, we have the potential to be transformed into holy creatures with the ability to come before a holy God.

In 2 Corinthians 3, Paul contrasts the Old Covenant given through Moses against the New Covenant given through the Spirit. When the Lord gave the Ten Commandments tablets to Moses on Mt. Sinai (Ex. 34), Moses returned to the Israelites with his face shining from the encounter with God's glory. Moses put a veil on to cover his face because the Israelites were afraid to come near him. The veil over Moses' face was representative of a veil over their hearts that prevented them from seeing God's glory and truth. The Law never had the power to transform the Israelites, and its work was brought to an end. But through the work of Jesus Christ and the ministry of the Holy Spirit, the veil over our hearts can be removed so that we can behold the glory of the Lord and the truth of the gospel. Not only can we behold it, we can be transformed into His image "from one degree of glory to another." The blessing of change in our lives is that when one turns to the Lord in faith, the Holy Spirit slowly remakes in us the image of God that was lost when Adam and Eve sinned in the garden.

Paul addresses this transformation again in his letter to the Romans. The word "therefore" in verse 1 of chapter 12 indicates that he is referring back to what he had previously written. Likely, he is referring to *all* that he wrote in chapters 1-11, which is a great exposition on the gospel of Jesus Christ. So Paul asks his readers to present their bodies—physically, emotionally, and spiritually—as sacrifices to God and acts of worship *because of the truths of the gospel*. Because of the love that God has demonstrated to us in the good news of Jesus Christ, we should have no hesitation to present ourselves as sacrifices to Him. Along with this sacrifice comes a process of transformation. Our minds are renewed by the work of the Spirit as we follow with some conscious effort on our own part to pursue the truth and to not be conformed to the world. The result is that our lives are transformed to come into alignment with God's standards—what is good, acceptable, and perfect. The change initiated in our lives through the work of the Trinity in the gospel is essential to our salvation and is the only way that we can be transformed into the image of Christ.

Action Step: A caterpillar is an immature stage of a butterfly. The caterpillar hatches from its egg with its body parts optimized for its main purpose–eating. The caterpillar has short stubby legs that are perfect for crawling across the surface of the leaf it is consuming and mouth parts that are perfect for chewing. At just the right time, the caterpillar encloses itself in a pupa, where it undergoes a metamorphosis into a butterfly. When the butterfly emerges, it is equipped with just the right body parts for its new main purpose–reproduction. The butterfly has longer legs, more complex eyes, and wings, all of which it needs to move to a new area, mate, and lay eggs. The change to a new appearance accomplishes its new mission. Consider how our new birth in Christ is like the butterfly's metamorphosis. Before our new life in Christ, our purpose is self-oriented. Once we are transformed, our purpose is to bear God's image and glorify Him. Does your life have a completely different appearance as you are living out this new mission?

Weekly Summary

Key Points

1. God's nature is unchanging.
2. God's plan is unchanging.
3. God's word is unchanging.
4. Jesus Christ is unchanging.
5. In different situations, God responds differently to people.
6. Change is a blessing in our lives.

Unchanging
Action Steps

7

Go back through the action steps and complete any that you have not yet completed or repeat one that was meaningful:

1. Try to conceive of an existence in which God changed. For example, what if His goodness was modified? If God, who defines good for all creation, changed His standard for goodness, how would we know what is good? Worship God for His unchanging nature.

2. Read Numbers 22-24 in one sitting, if possible. Enjoy the humor of the story but appreciate also the serious lesson: God's plans will be accomplished, and no human power will prevail against them.

3. Because the Word of God is unchanging, it is always relevant to our lives. Do you fully accept God's Word as always trustworthy in your life? For example, multiple times in Scripture, God promised His people, "I will never leave you nor forsake you." Are there moments when you feel that verse does not apply to you? Pray and ask God to help you trust the relevance of His promises to your daily life.

4. The rapid change of this world and the people in it has contributed to a reality that has been referred to as "the generation gap." This term was first used in the 1960s to describe the vastly different cultures and views between parents and their children's generations. This gap can make it difficult for individuals from different generations to relate to one another and even sometimes to worship God together. Yet God does not change; therefore, He does not have different standards for how we should approach Him across different generations. How can we use this idea to connect with individuals from a separate generation than our own? Schedule a coffee or meal with someone from a different generation and explore how you can connect, in spite of your differences, over a God who does not change.

5. Sometimes it is so very easy to see when another person needs to repent. Even in the pages of the Old Testament it is obvious to any observant reader that the Israelites failed in their covenant with God again and again. Yet it can sometimes be so difficult to recognize our own patterns of sin. Spend some time in prayer today asking God to reveal where you need repentance. If you are a believer in Jesus, you have likely repented of general sin with the result of salvation, but the Christian life is one of ongoing repentance in order to maintain fellowship with God (1 Jn. 1:5-10).

6. Consider how our new birth in Christ is like the butterfly's metamorphosis. Before our new life in Christ, our purpose is self-oriented. Once we are transformed, our purpose is to bear God's image and glorify Him. Does your life have a completely different appearance as you are living out this new mission?

WEEK 9

Far Above Creation and Intimately Involved in Creation

God is not trifling with us in the gospel but opening up in the most intimate way his very heart. Of course, God remains incomprehensible, mysterious, and far above all created things in a way that is not at all diminished by the way he makes himself lavishly available to fallen humanity in the economy of salvation. But his infinite transcendence over all created things cannot be construed as any kind of reserve or standoffishness. The Father's giving of the Son renders that interpretation impossible.
Fred Sanders, *The Deep Things of God*
© 2010 Fred Sanders, Reprinted and used by permission

"Yours, O Lord, is the greatness and the power and the glory and the victory and the majesty, for all that is in the heavens and in the earth is yours. Yours is the kingdom, O Lord, and you are exalted as head above all."
1 Chronicles 29:11
Great is the Lord, and greatly to be praised, and his greatness is unsearchable.
Psalms 145:3
The Lord is high above all nations, and his glory above the heavens!
Who is like the Lord our God, who is seated on high,
who looks far down on the heavens and the earth?
Psalms 113:4-6

Far Above, Intimately Involved

God Is Completely Other Than Creation 1

As men and women who are part of God's creation, when we study and contemplate the Creator, we become aware of a canyon that cannot be crossed between His nature and our own. His being is completely other than that of any human. His ways are completely other than our ways. God's existence is independent from creation. He is not just simply above creation, He is altogether of another essence than His creation.

This attribute of God is referred to as His *transcendence.* One dictionary definition of transcendence, given by *Merriam-Webster,* is "being beyond the limits of all possible experience and knowledge." This definition is a great place to start with a human-language attempt to describe God, who is beyond the limits of our comprehension.

King David had a deep respect for God's transcendence. 1 Chronicles 29 records David's call to the people of Israel for offerings to build the temple. God revealed to David that his son, Solomon, would be the one to oversee the building of a temple for the Lord. But David provided a generous offering of materials for the construction, and he asked for others to follow his lead. David then prayed over the offering with praise to God for providing to them the very gifts that they were offering back to Him. It was in this context that he spoke the words of praise in verse 11, including "you are exalted as head above all." David expressed his understanding that God is not part of creation, but head over all creation. Because God is transcendent over all, He is ruler over all. Thus, His transcendence is closely tied to His sovereignty.

Many psalms, some of which were also written by David, touch on the transcendence of God. Psalm 145 is credited to David; here he describes God's greatness as "unsearchable." Throughout this psalm, David seems to use every word at his disposal to attempt to express his praise to God—extol, bless, praise, greatness, commend, declare, splendor, wondrous, awesome, abundant—yet still David is left with a description of God's greatness as "unsearchable." Psalm 113 proclaims that God is "high above all nations" and "his glory is above the heavens." It goes on to suggest that there is no one like God "who looks far down on the heavens and the earth." Throughout Scripture there are many attempts to describe with human words the vast distance between God's nature and our own.

Action Step: Read the verses on the left page carefully and slowly, possibly even out loud. Meditate on the message that David is communicating about God. Write your own definition of God's transcendence, and appreciate that you are attempting to define One who is beyond our limits of expression.

In the year that King Uzziah died I saw the Lord sitting upon a throne, high and lifted up; and the train of his robe filled the temple. Above him stood the seraphim. Each had six wings: with two he covered his face, and with two he covered his feet, and with two he flew. And one called to another and said:

"Holy, holy, holy is the Lord of hosts; the whole earth is full of his glory!"

And the foundations of the thresholds shook at the voice of him who called, and the house was filled with smoke. And I said: "Woe is me! For I am lost; for I am a man of unclean lips, and I dwell in the midst of a people of unclean lips; for my eyes have seen the King, the Lord of hosts!"

Then one of the seraphim flew to me, having in his hand a burning coal that he had taken with tongs from the altar. And he touched my mouth and said: "Behold, this has touched your lips; your guilt is taken away, and your sin atoned for."

And I heard the voice of the Lord saying, "Whom shall I send, and who will go for us?" Then I said, "Here I am! Send me." And he said, "Go, and say to this people..."

Isaiah 6:1-9

Getting into one of the boats, which was Simon's, he asked him to put out a little from the land. And he sat down and taught the people from the boat. And when he had finished speaking, he said to Simon, "Put out into the deep and let down your nets for a catch." And Simon answered, "Master, we toiled all night and took nothing! But at your word I will let down the nets." And when they had done this, they enclosed a large number of fish, and their nets were breaking. They signaled to their partners in the other boat to come and help them. And they came and filled both the boats, so that they began to sink. But when Simon Peter saw it, he fell down at Jesus' knees, saying, "Depart from me, for I am a sinful man, O Lord." For he and all who were with him were astonished at the catch of fish that they had taken, and so also were James and John, sons of Zebedee, who were partners with Simon. And Jesus said to Simon, "Do not be afraid; from now on you will be catching men." And when they had brought their boats to land, they left everything and followed him.

Luke 5:3-11

Far Above, Intimately Involved

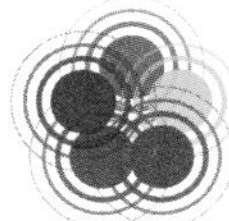

A Holy God Cannot Be Approached by Unholy Mankind

2

God's transcendence becomes even more clear when His holiness is considered. Holiness is a complete separation from all that is evil, corrupt, and sinful. A holy God is unapproachable by fallen and sinful mankind. In Isaiah 6, the prophet described his calling by God. Isaiah had a vision in which he saw God enthroned in the temple.

Heavenly beings, seraphim, were present, and even the seraphim covered their faces with their wings because of their insufficiency to look on the glory of God. The seraphim proclaimed Him to be "holy, holy, holy," affirming and praising the absolute holiness of God. Isaiah's reaction to this experience was one of fear and awe. He immediately recognized that his uncleanness rendered him unfit to live in the face of God's holiness. He was overwhelmed with a recognition of his sin and the sins of his people. Isaiah confessed his sin, and one of the seraphim purified his lips with a burning coal from the altar while assuring Isaiah that his guilt was removed through the process. Once this purification was complete, Isaiah was able to answer the Lord's call. God provided a way for Isaiah's cleansing so the prophet could speak with God and volunteer for the mission God had for him.

The impurity of our sin is humbling in the presence of God's perfect holiness. Simon Peter experienced this as well when Jesus called him to be His disciple. He told Peter and the other fishermen to let down their nets during a time of day when they knew they would not catch any fish. The astonishing number of fish in the nets demonstrated Jesus' authority over creation. Peter recognized this miraculous catch of fish as a sign of the presence of God. Like Isaiah, Peter was convicted of his sin in the presence of holiness. Jesus assured Simon Peter that he did not need to be afraid and then charged him with a new calling to become a fisher of men. Again, the Lord provided what His servant needed to fulfill the calling.

Action Step: Note in Isaiah's story that he confessed his own sin and the sin of his people: "Woe is me! For I am lost; for I am a man of unclean lips, and I dwell in the midst of a people of unclean lips." There is no attempt to minimize his sin just because everyone else around him is guilty of the same sin. Have you ever minimized sin in your own life because it is a "common" sin, like dishonesty or gossiping? When it comes to relationship with the perfectly holy God, all sin—even the sins that we perceive as minor—hinder our fellowship with Him. Pray and ask God to reveal all sin in your life, including those that you may be dismissing as irrelevant.

"In his hand is the life of every living thing and the breath of all mankind."
Job 12:10
You make springs gush forth in the valleys; they flow between the hills;
they give drink to every beast of the field; the wild donkeys quench their thirst.
Beside them the birds of the heavens dwell; they sing among the branches.
From your lofty abode you water the mountains; the earth is satisfied with the fruit of your work.
Psalms 104:10-13
…one God and Father of all, who is over all and through all and in all.
Ephesians 4:6
And he is before all things, and in him all things hold together.
Colossians 1:17
He is the radiance of the glory of God and the exact imprint of his nature, and he upholds the universe by the word of his power.
Hebrews 1:3

Far Above, Intimately Involved

God Is Intimately Involved in All Creation 3

God's transcendence over all of creation is an incomplete picture without addressing God's presence throughout creation. Job declared the life of every living thing to be in God's hand. This is not a universe that God spoke into existence only to distance Himself after setting it into motion. God's hand *continues* to hold the life of every creature. Psalm 104 gives images to God's provision. He provides springs for animals to quench their thirst, skies and trees for birds to make their homes, and rain to water the mountains. Waters that continue to gush forth and supply the water cycle across the planet are continuously refreshed by the hand of God. His ongoing tender care is visible throughout the world as animals find shelter and food and drink.

Ephesians 4 begins with a beautiful description of the unity shared within the body of Christ. Paul's list of things that unite us concludes with the statement that the Father is "over all and through all and in all." God is everywhere present and engaged at the same time; He is transcendent over all. Scripture makes clear that Jesus Christ is actively involved and holding all things in the world together and upholding the universe by the word of His power.

On January 28, 1986, Space Shuttle Challenger lifted off from its launchpad at NASA's Kennedy Space Center in Cape Canaveral, Florida. Seven astronauts were on board. Just over one minute after liftoff, as the vehicle climbed into the clear blue Florida skies, there was an explosion. All seven astronauts tragically lost their lives that day. The investigation that followed determined that an O-ring seal failed between segments of the solid rocket boosters. The rubber O-ring lost its flexibility in the unusually cold temperatures. The resulting gaps where the seal failed to hold the segments together allowed heated exhaust and flames to escape from the rocket booster, which damaged adjacent fuel tanks and caused the explosion. One of the most complex machines ever built by mankind was destroyed by a human failure to respect the limits of rubber—a substance that people have been working with for centuries.

As complex a machine as a space shuttle is, the universe is unimaginably more complex, with an infinite number of moving pieces. From the largest ball of potentially explosive gases that we see as a star in our night sky to the tiniest indivisible part of a carbon atom in a human cell, Jesus Christ holds all of it together. There is no risk of Jesus failing under any extreme conditions. He is aware of the physical limits of every particle in the universe, and He upholds it all by His command. If it were not for God's continued involvement in creation, the universe as we know it could not continue to exist.

Action Step: Spend some time in prayer praising God for His continuous involvement in and care for our world and all that is in it.

"The God who made the world and everything in it, being Lord of heaven and earth, does not live in temples made by man, nor is he served by human hands, as though he needed anything, since he himself gives to all mankind life and breath and everything. And he made from one man every nation of mankind to live on all the face of the earth, having determined allotted periods and the boundaries of their dwelling place, that they should seek God, and perhaps feel their way toward him and find him. Yet he is actually not far from each one of us, for "'In him we live and move and have our being'; as even some of your own poets have said, "'For we are indeed his offspring.'"

Acts 17:24-28

Who is like the LORD our God, who is seated on high, who looks far down on the heavens and the earth?
He raises the poor from the dust and lifts the needy from the ash heap, to make them sit with princes, with the princes of his people.
He gives the barren woman a home, making her the joyous mother of children. Praise the LORD!

Psalms 113:5-9

He will tend his flock like a shepherd; he will gather the lambs in his arms; he will carry them in his bosom, and gently lead those that are with young.

Isaiah 40:11

"Be strong, all you people of the land, declares the LORD. Work, for I am with you, declares the LORD of hosts, according to the covenant that I made with you when you came out of Egypt. My Spirit remains in your midst. Fear not."

Haggai 2:4-5

The LORD is near to all who call on him, to all who call on him in truth.

Psalms 145:18

"It is the LORD who goes before you. He will be with you; he will not leave you or forsake you. Do not fear or be dismayed."

Deuteronomy 31:8

Far Above, Intimately Involved

God Is Intimately Involved in Individual Lives

4

In our study of God's self-existence and self-sufficiency, we looked at the Acts 17 account of Paul's visit to Athens. Paul addressed the Athenians by first contrasting their "unknown" god with God who can be known. He points out that God does not need anything from man, but in fact, God "gives to all mankind life and breath and everything." Paul then goes on to describe how God "determined allotted periods and the boundaries of their dwelling place." Every breath that we take, the life that we live, and the time and place where we dwell is given by God. He is very much involved in people's lives. Paul even gives the reason why God remains involved: "that they should seek God, and perhaps feel their way toward him and find him." God is not far from each one of us because His desire is for us to seek Him and find Him.

The reading on Day 1 of this week looked at God's transcendence in Psalm 113, where the Lord is described as "high above all nations." But a transition is seen in the next few verses (v. 5-9) in which God is very involved with His people by raising the poor, lifting the needy, and blessing the barren woman with children. In Isaiah 40, we see the tender image of God caring for His flock like a shepherd, gathering them in His arms, and gently leading those with young. Keep in mind that the flock that He is tending is His people. We are the sheep of His pasture (Ps. 95:7). As you read these verses in Isaiah, don't miss the picture that God will gather *you* in His arms and carry *you* in His bosom. And if you have children that you care for in your family, hold onto the truth that He is gently leading you with an extra measure of attention. These descriptions are of a God who has a deep loving care for every person in His flock.

Throughout Scripture, the Lord promises that He is with those who are in covenant with Him and near to those who call on Him, and He will not leave or forsake His people. God chooses to have a personal fellowship with those who live by faith. He is always aware of the weak, and He is "near to the brokenhearted and saves the crushed in spirit" (Ps. 34:18).

Action Step: God inspired the writers of Scripture to consistently compare people with sheep, and much commentary has been written about the similarities. The flock mentality and fearfulness of sheep are often seen as similar to human nature. There is some recent evidence that sheep can be rather intelligent and scheming as well. In the United Kingdom, a flock of sheep perfected a means of crossing a cattle guard to find greener pastures. When the sheep discovered that they could not walk across the cattle guard, they discovered a new way to move—they rolled! One observer was quoted, "They lie down on their side, or sometimes their back, and just roll over and over the grids until they are clear. I've seen them doing it. It is quite clever." The thought of this comical scene might lead you to consider ways in which you circumvent the boundaries that the Good Shepherd has established for His people. Are there ways that you are intentionally bypassing the guidelines that God has lovingly set up to care for His flock?

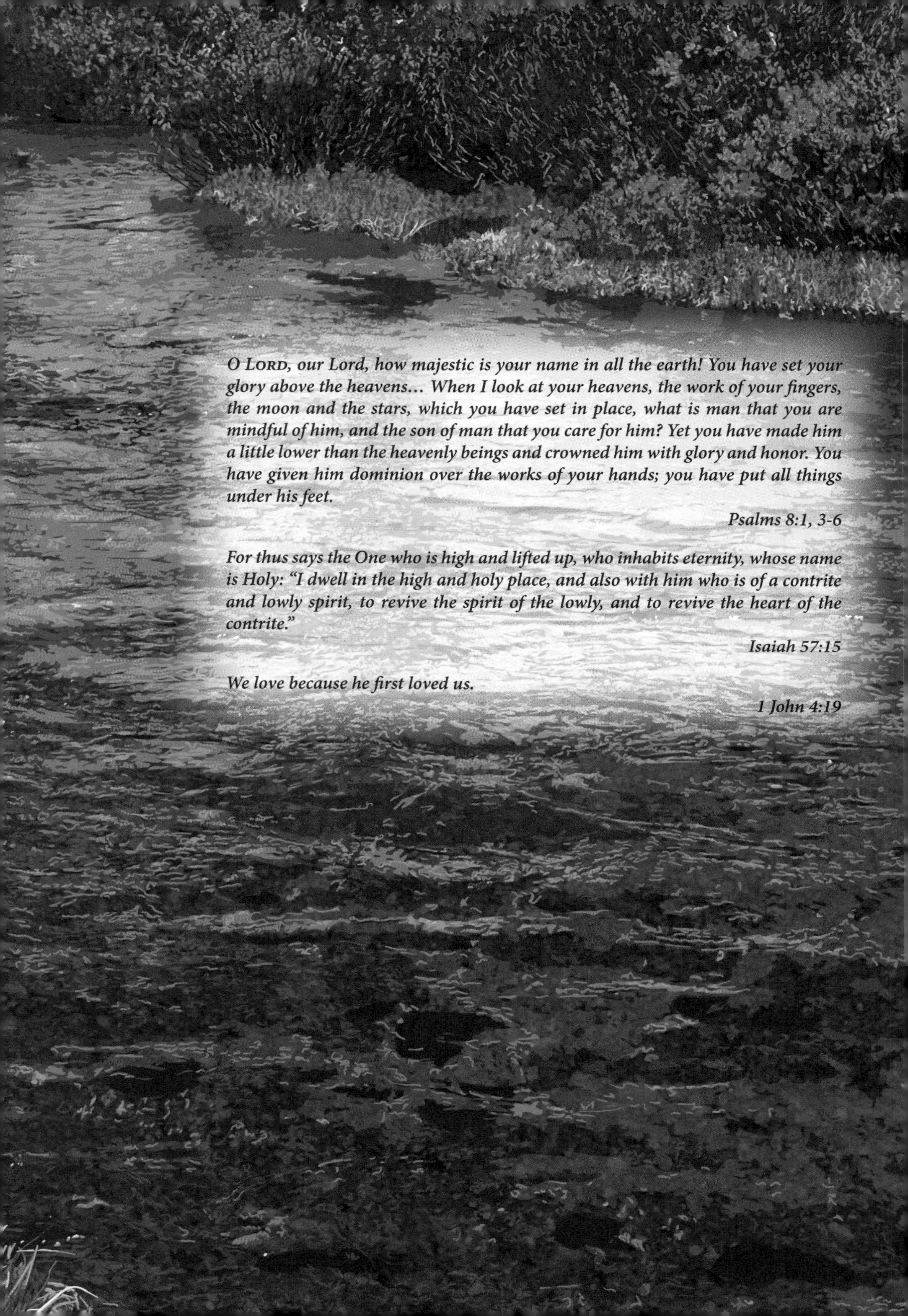

O LORD, *our Lord, how majestic is your name in all the earth! You have set your glory above the heavens… When I look at your heavens, the work of your fingers, the moon and the stars, which you have set in place, what is man that you are mindful of him, and the son of man that you care for him? Yet you have made him a little lower than the heavenly beings and crowned him with glory and honor. You have given him dominion over the works of your hands; you have put all things under his feet.*

Psalms 8:1, 3-6

For thus says the One who is high and lifted up, who inhabits eternity, whose name is Holy: "I dwell in the high and holy place, and also with him who is of a contrite and lowly spirit, to revive the spirit of the lowly, and to revive the heart of the contrite."

Isaiah 57:15

We love because he first loved us.

1 John 4:19

Far Above, Intimately Involved

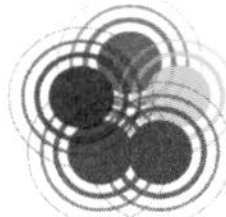

We Can Approach God Only Because He First Approached Us

God is transcendent. He exists completely apart from creation, and we cannot search Him out with our own resources and senses. We have also seen that God is *immanent*—the term used for the reality that God is intimately involved within His creation. *Merriam-Webster* gives one definition of immanent as "being within the limits of possible experience or knowledge." This definition is exactly the opposite of the definition given for transcendent: "being beyond the limits of all possible experience and knowledge." How can He be both?

The answer starts with God's regard for mankind. It pleased God to make mankind in His image, after His likeness—both males and females (Gen. 1:26-27). According to Psalm 8, the Lord made humanity "a little lower than the heavenly beings and crowned him with glory and honor." He gave mankind dominion and put all things in our care. This was God's choice, and it had nothing to do with what men and women have earned or deserved. It is His good pleasure. The Lord, whose name is majestic in all the earth, chose to have fellowship with man. However, when Adam and Eve disobeyed in the Garden of Eden, the sinful nature that they took on and passed to all the human race has made us incompatible with the holy God. The New Testament cites Psalm 8 on several occasions, pointing to Jesus as the ideal human fulfilling the role that God intended for all of mankind. Despite human sin and failure, God still takes the initiative to reveal Himself to us so that we can have fellowship with Him.

Isaiah 57:15 is just one Old Testament verse that addresses how God deals with the human dilemma of incompatibility with the holy God. He dwells in the high and holy place and also with him who is of a contrite and lowly spirit. Although God is altogether of another essence than His creation, He chooses to restore a relationship with mankind. He has provided a way for sinful creatures who cannot approach Him to be remade into His image so that we can have fellowship with Him. The word translated as *contrite* in this verse is a word that means crushed, as in broken into dust or powder. God chooses to come near to people who are so broken and humbled by their sin that they recognize that they are as dust before the holiness of God. When we repent of our sin and turn toward Him, He restores His image in us to the extent that a relationship is possible. The unholy creature puts on God's holiness to fellowship with Him. When God calls us to draw near to Him (Jms. 4:8), He is not calling us to a new physical location, but a new spiritual location. Rather than consulting a map on our phones for which route to take to reduce the miles between us and our Creator, He calls us to consult His Word and our hearts to reduce the spiritual distance between His image and our own.

Action Step: On several occasions in the Old Testament, people are said to "repent in dust and ashes." That the Hebrew word for *contrite* communicates a picture of being crushed into dust is reminiscent of the humble posture of actually covering oneself in dust and ashes. The application of ashes to the forehead on Ash Wednesday that is practiced in Catholic and several Protestant denominations is rooted in this picture of repentance. Whether you physically participate in applying ashes to your body or not, this could be a valuable image to have in mind when you catch yourself in sin. Are you so broken and devastated by your sin that in your heart you are repenting in dust and ashes?

But as he considered these things, behold, an angel of the Lord appeared to him in a dream, saying, "Joseph, son of David, do not fear to take Mary as your wife, for that which is conceived in her is from the Holy Spirit. She will bear a son, and you shall call his name Jesus, for he will save his people from their sins." All this took place to fulfill what the Lord had spoken by the prophet:

"Behold, the virgin shall conceive and bear a son, and they shall call his name Immanuel" (which means, God with us).

Matthew 1:20-23

Because of Christ and our faith in him, we can now come boldly and confidently into God's presence.

Ephesians 3:12 (NLT)

We implore you on behalf of Christ, be reconciled to God. For our sake he made him to be sin who knew no sin, so that in him we might become the righteousness of God.

2 Corinthians 5:20-21

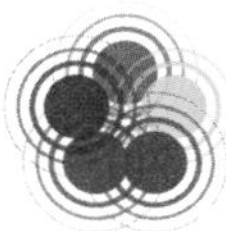

Far Above, Intimately Involved

Immanuel, God with Us

6

In the Old Testament, God spoke through the prophet Isaiah to King Ahaz of Judah. The Lord wanted to give a sign to Ahaz to strengthen his faith. Ahaz refused to ask for a sign, but God spoke anyway through Isaiah with a sign—the promise of Immanuel. When Matthew opened his gospel, he made clear that the birth of Jesus was the ultimate and final fulfillment of Isaiah's Immanuel prophecy.

The English word *immanent* has its roots in Latin. The prefix *im-* is sometimes interchangeable with *in-* and can be used to mean *in*. The Latin word *manere* means *remain*. So, the literal meaning of immanent is *remain in*. The English translation of the Hebrew word *Immanuel* is very similar in spelling to the word *immanent*, but the roots for the words are in two different languages. The Hebrew word *Immanuel* comes from the following roots: *Im-* (with, among, in), *-anu-* (we or us), and *-el* (God). Immanuel translates to *with us God*. Despite the difference in word origins, the ultimate, tangible delivery of God's immanence is Immanuel—Jesus Christ.

Jesus' life, teaching, death, and resurrection make up the climax of God's plan to restore fellowship with mankind. As Ephesians 3 states, because of Christ and our faith in Him, we have access to God. Jesus' atonement for our sins is the link that connects our repentance to God's restoration of our fellowship with Him. God is just, and there must be consequences for our sin. Our faith in Christ is faith in Him bearing the penalty for our sins on the cross so that we can be restored to a relationship with our holy God. Paul describes in 2 Corinthians 5 the interchange that is accomplished at the cross—Jesus taking on our sin so that we can take on His righteousness. Jesus became like us so that we would be able to be like Him. We approach God with confidence and boldness only because we are wearing the righteousness of Jesus Christ.

God's transcendence and His immanence meet in His loving, eternal plan for our redemption. God has already announced in Revelation 21 that, at the end of time, His dwelling place will be with man. The majestic, holy, transcendent God will be eternally and intimately in relationship with His people.

Action Step: Read Revelation 21:1-4. Focus on the passages that describe the relationship between God and man. This is the fellowship that believers will enjoy for everlasting days.

Weekly Summary

Key Points

1. God is completely other than creation.
2. A holy God cannot be approached by unholy mankind.
3. God is intimately involved in all creation.
4. God is intimately involved in individual lives.
5. We can approach God only because He first approached us.
6. Jesus Christ is Immanuel, God with us.

Far Above, Intimately Involved

Action Steps

7

Go back through the action steps and complete any that you have not yet completed or repeat one that was meaningful:

1. Read the verses on page 136 carefully and slowly, possibly even out loud. Meditate on the message that David is communicating about God. Write your own definition of God's transcendence, and appreciate that you are attempting to define One who is beyond our limits of expression.

2. Note in Isaiah's story that he confessed his own sin and the sin of his people: "Woe is me! For I am lost; for I am a man of unclean lips, and I dwell in the midst of a people of unclean lips." There is no attempt to minimize his sin just because everyone else around him is guilty of the same sin. Have you ever minimized sin in your own life because it is a "common" sin, like dishonesty or gossiping? When it comes to relationship with the perfectly holy God, all sin—even the sins that we perceive as minor—hinder our fellowship with Him. Pray and ask God to reveal all sin in your life, including those that you may be dismissing as irrelevant.

3. Spend some time in prayer praising God for His continuous involvement in and care for our world and all that is in it.

4. God inspired the writers of Scripture to consistently compare people with sheep, and much commentary has been written about the similarities. The flock mentality and fearfulness of sheep are often seen as similar to human nature. There is some recent evidence that sheep can be rather intelligent and scheming as well. In the United Kingdom, a flock of sheep perfected a means of crossing a cattle guard to find greener pastures. When the sheep discovered that they could not walk across the cattle guard, they discovered a new way to move—they rolled! One observer was quoted, "They lie down on their side, or sometimes their back, and just roll over and over the grids until they are clear. I've seen them doing it. It is quite clever." The thought of this comical scene might lead you to consider ways in which you circumvent the boundaries that the Good Shepherd has established for His people. Are there ways that you are intentionally bypassing the guidelines that God has lovingly set up to care for His flock?

5. On several occasions in the Old Testament, people are said to "repent in dust and ashes." That the Hebrew word for *contrite* communicates a picture of being crushed into dust is reminiscent of the humble posture of actually covering oneself in dust and ashes. The application of ashes to the forehead on Ash Wednesday that is practiced in Catholic and several Protestant denominations is rooted in this picture of repentance. Whether you physically participate in applying ashes to your body or not, this could be a valuable image to have in mind when you catch yourself in sin. Are you so broken and devastated by your sin that in your heart you are repenting in dust and ashes?

6. Read Revelation 21:1-4. Focus on the passages that describe the relationship between God and man. This is the fellowship that believers will enjoy for everlasting days.

WEEK 10
Father

You sum up the whole of New Testament teaching in a single phrase, if you speak of it as a revelation of the Fatherhood of the holy Creator. In the same way, you sum up the whole of New Testament religion if you describe it as the knowledge of God as one's holy Father. If you want to judge how well a person understands Christianity, find out how much he makes of the thought of being God's child, and having God as his Father. If this is not the thought that prompts and controls his worship and prayers and his whole outlook on life, it means that he does not understand Christianity very well at all. For everything that Christ taught, everything that makes the New Testament new, and better than the Old, everything that is distinctively Christian as opposed to merely Jewish, is summed up in the knowledge of the Fatherhood of God. "Father" is the Christian name for God.

J. I. Packer, *Knowing God*

"Then you shall say to Pharaoh, 'Thus says the LORD, Israel is my firstborn son, and I say to you, "Let my son go that he may serve me." If you refuse to let him go, behold, I will kill your firstborn son."'

Exodus 4:22-23

"Is this the way you repay the LORD, you foolish and senseless people? Isn't he your Father who created you? Has he not made you and established you?

For the people of Israel belong to the LORD; Jacob is his special possession….

Like an eagle that rouses her chicks and hovers over her young, so he spread his wings to take them up and carried them safely on his pinions,"

Deuteronomy 32:6, 9, 11 (NLT)

"With weeping they shall come, and with pleas for mercy I will lead them back, I will make them walk by brooks of water, in a straight path in which they shall not stumble, for I am a father to Israel, and Ephraim is my firstborn."

Jeremiah 31:9

Yet the number of the children of Israel shall be like the sand of the sea, which cannot be measured or numbered. And in the place where it was said to them, "You are not my people," it shall be said to them, "Children of the living God."

Hosea 1:10

And when his parents saw him, they were astonished. And his mother said to him, "Son, why have you treated us so? Behold, your father and I have been searching for you in great distress." And he said to them, "Why were you looking for me? Did you not know that I must be in my Father's house?" And they did not understand the saying that he spoke to them. And he went down with them and came to Nazareth and was submissive to them. And his mother treasured up all these things in her heart.

Luke 2:48-51

Father

God Has Revealed Himself as Father

1

Thus far in our study of God's nature, we have kept most of our focus on His character as revealed in specific attributes—adjectives that attempt to describe His being. But we have also touched on the significance of names in the Bible. To know someone by name often included knowing a person's character and nature. God uses many names for Himself throughout Scripture, each of which reveal something of who He is. Yet there is a strong argument that the most significant name for God in Scripture is the name that Jesus Christ, the Son of God, used for Him—Father. A study of the ways that God has revealed Himself to be Father in Scripture will yield rich results in a search to know Him more deeply.

Even in the Old Testament, God is occasionally referred to as Father, both by prophets and by His own words. These Old Testament references usually portray Him as a Father to the nation of Israel collectively. In Exodus 4, as the Lord gave instructions to Moses on what he was to say to Pharaoh, He referred to Israel as His "firstborn son." God remembered His covenant with Abraham and heard the cries of His people, who had been enslaved in Egypt for four hundred years. And the Lord intended to set His son free. By referring to Israel as His firstborn son, the Lord demonstrated His commitment to the nation that He had called out as first priority to reveal His faithfulness to the whole world. Near the end of his life, Moses reminded the people that God is their Father, even comparing God's care of Israel to that of a mother eagle hovering over her young. The psalms provide guidance to sing of the God who is a Father to the fatherless (Ps. 68:5) and the God who shows compassion to His children like a father (Ps. 103:13). The prophet Jeremiah spoke on behalf of the Lord to remind Israel that God would lead the nation back from exile because He is their Father and they are His firstborn. And the book of Hosea, which teaches of Israel's continuing unfaithfulness and God's persistent redeeming love, shows that even Israel's failure to obey the covenant, though it brought discipline from the Lord, would not remove their status as children of the living God.

The New Testament revelation of God as Father greatly expands on the Old Testament revelation and also adds an unexpected turn. Jesus Christ referred to the God and Father of the nation of Israel as *His* Father. In Luke 2, Scripture gives us one brief glimpse into Jesus' early adolescent years. Jesus' parents had traveled with Him to Jerusalem to celebrate the Passover. When they left Jerusalem, they discovered that Jesus was no longer with them. It took them three days of searching to find Jesus in the temple conversing with the teachers. As He addressed His parents, He referred to the temple as "my Father's house." Even though He was only twelve years old, Jesus was already revealing His unique relationship with His Father in heaven. His parents did not understand Him, but Jesus expanded on the truth throughout His life that He was the Son of God, continuing to address God as His Father and then teaching His followers to do the same.

Action Step: Deuteronomy 32:11 was part of a song composed by Moses at the end of his life to prepare Israel to enter the Promised Land. These verses are not a scientific commentary on the way that an eagle cares for its young, but a reminder to the people of Israel that they are God's special possession, and He will provide and care for them as He faithfully fulfills His promises to His children. If a powerful bird with predatory instincts can stoop gently to care for its young, how much more will our loving Father care for His children? Pray and praise the Father for His care for you.

This was why the Jews were seeking all the more to kill him, because not only was he breaking the Sabbath, but he was even calling God his own Father, making himself equal with God.

John 5:18

"Father, I desire that they also, whom you have given me, may be with me where I am, to see my glory that you have given me because you loved me before the foundation of the world."

John 17:24

"For God so loved the world, that he gave his only Son, that whoever believes in him should not perish but have eternal life."

John 3:16

And we have seen and testify that the Father has sent his Son to be the Savior of the world.

1 John 4:14

Long ago, at many times and in many ways, God spoke to our fathers by the prophets, but in these last days he has spoken to us by his Son, whom he appointed the heir of all things, through whom also he created the world.

Hebrews 1:1-2

Jesus said to them, "My food is to do the will of him who sent me and to accomplish his work."

John 4:34

"For I have come down from heaven, not to do my own will but the will of him who sent me."

John 6:38

"And he who sent me is with me. He has not left me alone, for I always do the things that are pleasing to him."

John 8:29

"I and the Father are one."

John 10:30

When Jesus had spoken these words, he lifted up his eyes to heaven, and said, "Father, the hour has come; glorify your Son that the Son may glorify you,"

John 17:1

"For the Father loves the Son and shows him all that he himself is doing. And greater works than these will he show him, so that you may marvel."

John 5:20

"but I do as the Father has commanded me, so that the world may know that I love the Father. Rise, let us go from here."

John 14:31

Father

God Is Father Eternally to His Son

2

When speaking *of* the Father throughout the gospels, Jesus referred to Him as both "God" and "Father." However, when directly speaking *to* Him, Jesus almost always addressed Him as "Father." The intimate relationship that Jesus demonstrated with the Father stood out as very different and even had the Jews seeking to kill Him.

In the New Testament, God does not primarily reveal His Fatherhood as a comparison to human fathers or even as the Father of creation. The basis of His revelation of Fatherhood is in His relationship to the Son of God, Jesus Christ. One significant aspect of this Father-Son relationship is that it is eternal. God did not become the Father nor Jesus the Son when Jesus was born as a human. They have always eternally co-existed as Father and Son. John 17:24 speaks of the Father loving the Son before the foundation of the world. And there are many verses that describe the Father sending His Son—His own Son (Rom. 8:32), His only Son (Jn. 1:14, 3:16), and His beloved Son (Mt. 3:17)—into the world to redeem mankind. This implies that He was already the Son when He was sent. The second Person of the Trinity was the Son before He was sent, before creation, and from eternity.

When we studied the Trinity earlier in this book, we saw that each Person—Father, Son, and Holy Spirit—takes a different role in human salvation. We have also seen that each Person of the Trinity is fully God and shares the same attributes. Yet there are distinctions between the Persons, and this is revealed in Scripture both in the ways that the Persons function in the world and in the ways that the Persons relate to one another. Therefore, a search in Scripture for the character of God that is revealed in His Fatherhood should start with His relationship to His Son.

Scripture indicates that the Father gives the Son (Jn. 3:16; Rom. 8:32), sends the Son (1 Jn. 4:14), and speaks through the Son (Heb. 1:1-2). Jesus describes Himself as obedient to the Father's will (Jn. 4:34, 6:38). This would imply that, within the relationships of the Trinity, the Father is the initiator, and the Son exhibits obedience that is in perfect agreement with the Father's will. There is uninterrupted fellowship between the Father and Son, and they are one (Jn. 8:29, 10:30). The Father and Son glorify one another (Jn. 17:1). Their relationship includes perfect love—the Father loves the Son (Jn. 5:20, 17:24), and the Son loves the Father (Jn. 14:31). So an examination of the Father-Son relationship reveals that the Father initiates actions, seeks fellowship, gives and receives glory, and loves perfectly. It is in God's eternal nature as Father to exhibit these characteristics.

Action Step: On Day 5 in our study of the Trinity (page 49), the Action Step involved printing out John 14-17 and highlighting the relational phrases in those chapters. Review the phrases that you highlighted in one color having to do with the relationship among the Persons of the Trinity. As you read through those, focus on statements about the Father. Mark any phrases that confirm the Father as initiating, having fellowship, giving and receiving glory, and loving and receiving love. You should find examples of all of these actions of the Father in just these four chapters. You may even find that nearly everything you had highlighted about the Father represents one of these four actions.

Blessed be the God and Father of our Lord Jesus Christ, who has blessed us in Christ with every spiritual blessing in the heavenly places, even as he chose us in him before the foundation of the world, that we should be holy and blameless before him. In love he predestined us for adoption as sons through Jesus Christ, according to the purpose of his will, to the praise of his glorious grace, with which he has blessed us in the Beloved.

Ephesians 1:3-6

But now that faith has come, we are no longer under a guardian, for in Christ Jesus you are all sons of God, through faith.

Galatians 3:25-26

For all who are led by the Spirit of God are sons of God. For you did not receive the spirit of slavery to fall back into fear, but you have received the Spirit of adoption as sons, by whom we cry, "Abba! Father!" The Spirit himself bears witness with our spirit that we are children of God,

Romans 8:14-16

But to all who did receive him, who believed in his name, he gave the right to become children of God, who were born, not of blood nor of the will of the flesh nor of the will of man, but of God.

John 1:12-13

"That which is born of the flesh is flesh, and that which is born of the Spirit is spirit."
John 3:6

Father

All Who Believe Are Children of God 3

The Fatherhood of God exists eternally in His relationship with the Son. But when the Father sent the Son to accomplish His plan for salvation, He took the amazing step of enabling people to become children of God. While the Son of God has eternally been in a relationship with the Father, through the redemptive work of Christ, believers are now privileged to be adopted into His family. The radical message to the people of God is that He is not simply Father to a nation, as portrayed in the Old Testament, but He is the adoptive Father of every individual who trusts in Jesus Christ for salvation.

When a person places faith in Jesus Christ, several things happen. The believer is *justified.* Jesus Christ's death on the cross is applied to their own personal sin, erasing the penalty owed by that sinner, and Jesus Christ's perfect righteousness is applied to them so that God declares the sinner to be righteous (Rom. 5:1; 2 Cor. 5:21). Justification is a legal term referring to our status before God. The believer is also *adopted.* Adoption is another legal term referring to our status before God. Galatians 3:26 says that "in Christ Jesus you are all sons of God, through faith." In Galatians 4, a few sentences later, Paul refers to the same process as "adoption as sons." Further, the believer is *gifted with the Holy Spirit.* Romans 8:9 teaches that if the Spirit is not dwelling in us, we do not belong to Christ. Therefore, at the moment we place our faith in Jesus Christ, the Holy Spirit comes to dwell in us. These three together—justification, adoption, and the indwelling of the Holy Spirit—are wrapped up together as immediate gifts when a person believes in Jesus Christ.

Although justification and adoption are transactions that refer to our status before God, the gift of the indwelling Holy Spirit is much more. The Holy Spirit is referred to as the "Spirit of adoption" in Romans 8:15. He "bears witness with our spirit that we are children of God." The gifts that God gives to people of faith bring a desperately needed change in status before God, but included in the gift is God Himself dwelling in us. Thus, justification and adoption into God's family become much more than legal transactions. God gives His Spirit to assure us of our status as children and to remake us into His image. The power of the Holy Spirit in our lives goes beyond giving us status in God's family, to mature us into bearing a resemblance to our Father and His Son.

This is what it looks like to be "born of God," as described in John 1:12-13. Being born of blood or born of the will of the flesh or of man all describe a human birth—a child coming into a family by being physically born or adopted into it. Being born of God comes from faith, and it is a transfer of spiritual life that can only come from our Father in heaven. God is interested in adopting us so that we bear the family image—so much so that He sends His Spirit to seal the adoption and equip every believer for their new life.

Action Step: For most couples today, the choice to have children is a decision of their own will. Whether they have their own biological children or adopt children or both, becoming a parent is within reach for almost every adult. In contrast, it is not within the reach of the will of the parent that their children are born of God, as described in John 1. Parents can certainly raise a child to understand Scripture and the Christian faith, but adoption into God's family comes from God. What we *can* do is pray for our children and the children of those around us. Choose a child that you know–your own or someone else's–and pray for that child to believe in the name of Jesus and become a child of God.

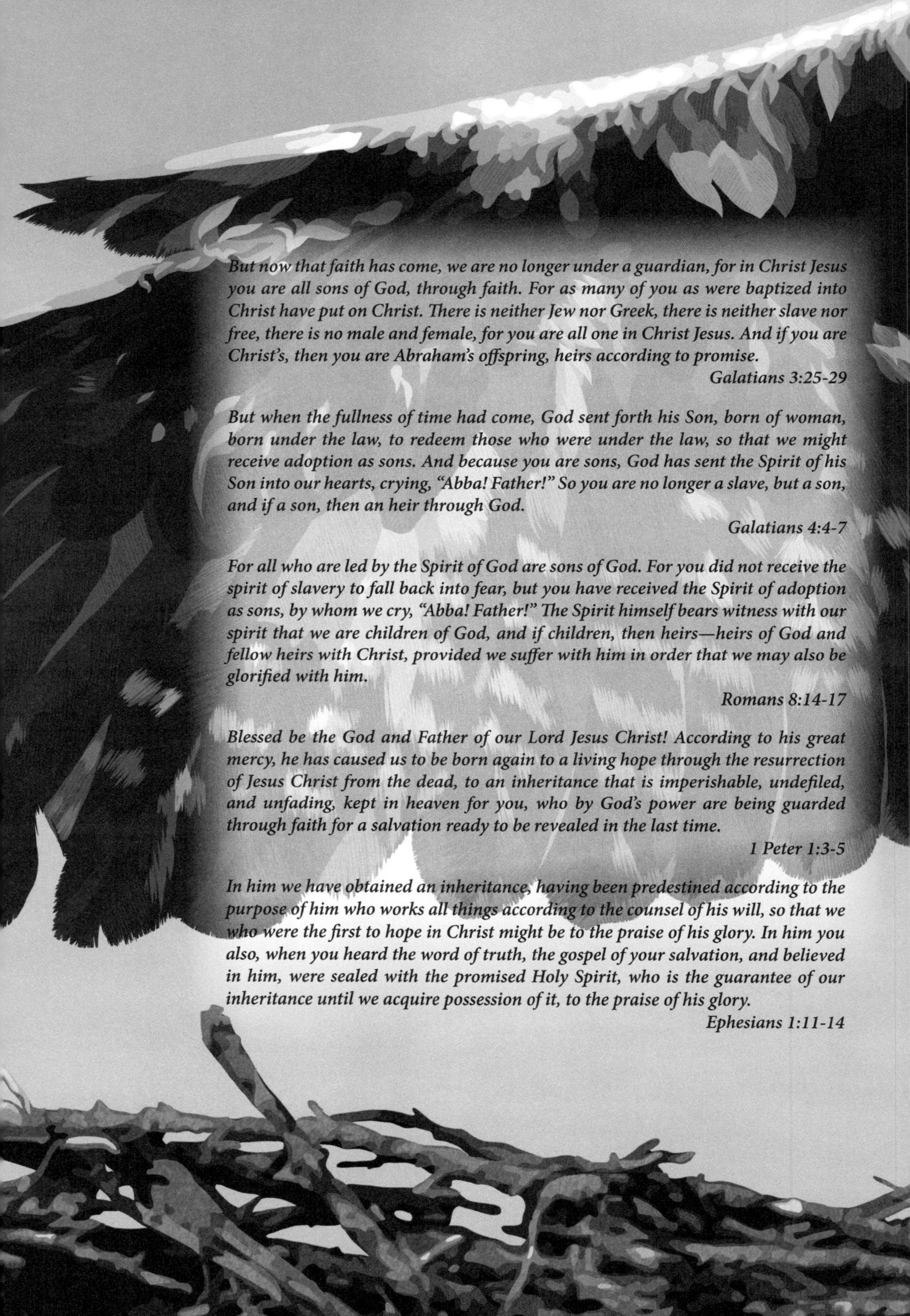

But now that faith has come, we are no longer under a guardian, for in Christ Jesus you are all sons of God, through faith. For as many of you as were baptized into Christ have put on Christ. There is neither Jew nor Greek, there is neither slave nor free, there is no male and female, for you are all one in Christ Jesus. And if you are Christ's, then you are Abraham's offspring, heirs according to promise.

Galatians 3:25-29

But when the fullness of time had come, God sent forth his Son, born of woman, born under the law, to redeem those who were under the law, so that we might receive adoption as sons. And because you are sons, God has sent the Spirit of his Son into our hearts, crying, "Abba! Father!" So you are no longer a slave, but a son, and if a son, then an heir through God.

Galatians 4:4-7

For all who are led by the Spirit of God are sons of God. For you did not receive the spirit of slavery to fall back into fear, but you have received the Spirit of adoption as sons, by whom we cry, "Abba! Father!" The Spirit himself bears witness with our spirit that we are children of God, and if children, then heirs—heirs of God and fellow heirs with Christ, provided we suffer with him in order that we may also be glorified with him.

Romans 8:14-17

Blessed be the God and Father of our Lord Jesus Christ! According to his great mercy, he has caused us to be born again to a living hope through the resurrection of Jesus Christ from the dead, to an inheritance that is imperishable, undefiled, and unfading, kept in heaven for you, who by God's power are being guarded through faith for a salvation ready to be revealed in the last time.

1 Peter 1:3-5

In him we have obtained an inheritance, having been predestined according to the purpose of him who works all things according to the counsel of his will, so that we who were the first to hope in Christ might be to the praise of his glory. In him you also, when you heard the word of truth, the gospel of your salvation, and believed in him, were sealed with the promised Holy Spirit, who is the guarantee of our inheritance until we acquire possession of it, to the praise of his glory.

Ephesians 1:11-14

Father

If We Are Children of God, Then We Are Heirs

4

An inheritance was a hard thing to come by for a woman in the ancient world. Possessions and land passed from fathers to sons with very few exceptions. When Israel entered the Promised Land, the land was portioned according to a census of male descendants of the twelve tribes of Israel. But an exception was made for the five daughters of Zelophehad because there were no sons in the family. The Lord said to Moses, "If a man dies and has no son, then you shall transfer his inheritance to his daughter" (Num. 27:8). Roman women in the first century were also limited in rights to own and inherit property.

This was the law and cultural context when Paul wrote the book of Galatians. Notice that when he uses the imagery of inheritance, he is careful to explain how human laws of inheritance do not apply to spiritual inheritance. All are sons of God through faith—whether they are Jews or Greeks, slave or free, male or female—and all have the same status as Abraham's offspring and heirs. This must have been astonishing for the Gentiles, slaves, and women in Paul's audience! If they belonged to Christ, they were equal heirs of God's promise! So whenever Paul wrote in any of his letters references to believers as *sons* and heirs, he is not leaving out women, but smashing any notion that cultural norms apply to God's inheritance. Both men and women are equal heirs of God, just as sons were of property in their culture.

The slave analogy in Galatians 4 and Romans 8 refers to the freedom gained from slavery to sin when a person puts faith in Jesus. Before Christ, God's people were unable to obey the Old Testament law because they were trapped in sin and fear for the consequences of their sin. Old Covenant life under the law was like slavery, but New Covenant life brings freedom because we are no longer slaves to a master, but sons of God who are led by the Spirit of God, possessing all the rights as heirs and able to approach the Father with joy and intimacy. Not only are we heirs, but we are *fellow* heirs with Christ! All that belongs to the Son as the natural heir of the Father also belongs to us as adopted heirs by grace! But let's not rush past the last part of Romans 8:17. Being an heir with Christ includes suffering as well as glory. This is confirmed in many places in Scripture—our lives on this earth will include suffering, trials, and persecution. But the result of our suffering is endurance, character, hope, and steadfast faith (Rom. 5:3-4; Jms. 1:2-3).

1 Peter 1 describes our inheritance as "imperishable, undefiled, and unfading, kept in heaven for you." Our inheritance is not fully realized on this earth or in this life, but it is guaranteed by the Holy Spirit until we acquire possession of it (Eph. 1:14). Yet in Ephesians 1:11, Paul wrote in the past tense: "we have obtained an inheritance." The same present/ future conflict exists in Romans 8, where we "are children of God" (v. 17) and "we wait eagerly for adoption as sons" (v. 23). There is some sense that we have already received our inheritance but that it is also waiting for us in heaven. Those who have faith in Jesus Christ already have their names written in the Father's list of heirs. Positionally, we are adult sons. But here on earth, we remain children, still maturing into the image of the Son.

Action Step: To get an overall view of Paul's teaching on connections between faith, justification, adoption, and the Holy Spirit in the book of Galatians, read Galatians 2:15-4:7, 5:16-25 in one sitting.

His divine power has granted to us all things that pertain to life and godliness, through the knowledge of him who called us to his own glory and excellence, by which he has granted to us his precious and very great promises, so that through them you may become partakers of the divine nature, having escaped from the corruption that is in the world because of sinful desire.

2 Peter 1:3-4

that which we have seen and heard we proclaim also to you, so that you too may have fellowship with us; and indeed our fellowship is with the Father and with his Son Jesus Christ.

1 John 1:3

And I heard a loud voice from the throne saying, "Behold, the dwelling place of God is with man. He will dwell with them, and they will be his people, and God himself will be with them as their God."

Revelation 21:3

Father

What Is Our Inheritance?

5

All who have faith in Christ are children of God and heirs. Scripture promises that we have obtained an inheritance and it is being kept for us in heaven. But what is the inheritance? A big clue to the answer is in Romans 8:17, where Scripture tells us we are "fellow heirs with Christ." Our inheritance is Christ's inheritance! God's plan for people of faith is to share an inheritance with the Son of God!

Do we dare to claim anything that belongs to Jesus Christ? Revelation 11:15 tells us that "The kingdom of the world has become the kingdom of our Lord and of his Christ, and he shall reign forever and ever." It would be pretty presumptuous of us to just assume that we could reign over the world. But Scripture tells us we will! 2 Timothy 2:12 says that we will "reign with him," and Revelation 5:10 promises that the people Jesus ransomed for God "shall reign on the earth."

Another element of Jesus' inheritance is the glorified body with which He was resurrected. Our resurrection at the time of Jesus' return will include a transformation of our bodies to be like Jesus' glorified body (Phil. 3:20-21). Our broken, aging bodies will be redeemed and glorified and also share in His inheritance.

But even more immediate than these future promises is the spiritual change included in our inheritance. Peter wrote that through our knowledge of Christ, God's divine power has granted us everything we need, including the Holy Spirit, to partake in the divine nature. This is not that we will be divine, but that we will share aspects of His nature. He will instill in us the characteristics that He expects to see in His family. In addition, we are promised fellowship with the Father and His Son Jesus Christ along with other believers (1 Jn. 1:3). Being a child of God includes sharing in the deep, intimate relationship that the Trinity has enjoyed eternally. This is the greatest privilege of our inheritance. And this is the portion of our inheritance that we can begin to take hold of even now. The fellowship that we enjoy with the Father and His Son Jesus Christ in the power of the Holy Spirit empowers us to escape "from the corruption that is in the world because of sinful desire." In Jesus' prayer recorded in John 17, He asked, "that they may all be one, just as you, Father, are in me, and I in you, that they also may be in us, so that the world may believe that you have sent me." Our fellowship with God and the godly character that flows from that relationship leads to other people believing in Jesus. Ultimately, there will be a more direct and eternal fellowship at the end of time when "the dwelling place of God is with man" (Rev. 21:3), and our inheritance will be complete. But right now, as people of faith, we are already part of the family of God. And we should look like it!

Action Step: John wrote in his first epistle that he was sharing what he had seen and heard so that others may join in fellowship with the believers as they fellowship with the Father and His Son Jesus Christ. The fellowship that we share with other believers is also part of our inheritance. We will be enjoying eternity with this family! Consider whether you are consistently connected with a local representation of the family of God. Do you need to find a group of believers with whom you can pray, worship, or study the Bible?

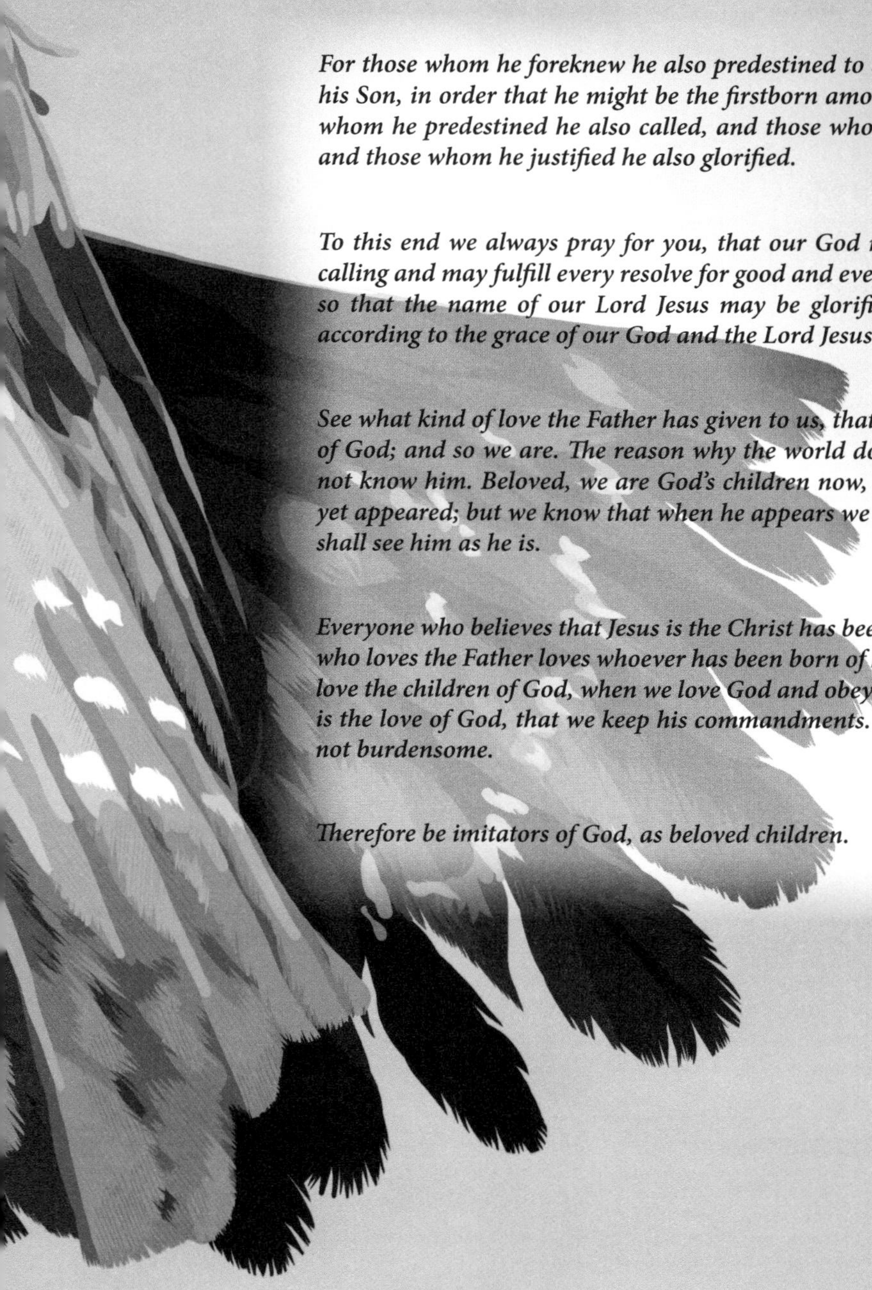

For those whom he foreknew he also predestined to be conformed to the image of his Son, in order that he might be the firstborn among many brothers. And those whom he predestined he also called, and those whom he called he also justified, and those whom he justified he also glorified.

Romans 8:29-30

To this end we always pray for you, that our God may make you worthy of his calling and may fulfill every resolve for good and every work of faith by his power, so that the name of our Lord Jesus may be glorified in you, and you in him, according to the grace of our God and the Lord Jesus Christ.

2 Thessalonians 1:11-12

See what kind of love the Father has given to us, that we should be called children of God; and so we are. The reason why the world does not know us is that it did not know him. Beloved, we are God's children now, and what we will be has not yet appeared; but we know that when he appears we shall be like him, because we shall see him as he is.

1 John 3:1-2

Everyone who believes that Jesus is the Christ has been born of God, and everyone who loves the Father loves whoever has been born of him. By this we know that we love the children of God, when we love God and obey his commandments. For this is the love of God, that we keep his commandments. And his commandments are not burdensome.

1 John 5:1-3

Therefore be imitators of God, as beloved children.

Ephesians 5:1

Father

What Does Our Adoption and Inheritance Teach Us about the Father? 6

As we grow in understanding of what it means to be children of God and heirs, we should reflect back on what this teaches us about the Father. If we are co-heirs with Christ and adopted sons alongside the divine Son, do we dare claim a relationship like the Father has with the Son? The conclusion of Day 2 of this week was that "an examination of the Father-Son relationship reveals that the Father initiates actions, seeks fellowship, gives and receives glory, and loves perfectly." Because we are adopted sons and co-heirs with Christ, this *is* the relationship that we have with the Father.

The Father initiated our lives by creating us individually (Ps. 139:13). He initiated our salvation by sending the Son, and He predestined, called, and justified those who would be conformed to the image of His Son (Rom. 8:29-30). Not only did He initiate our relationship, but He continues to lead by keeping and guiding us (Jd. 24; Prov. 16:9). Therefore, as children of God, we should follow the example of the Son and be obedient to the Father's will. In the Day 5 reading this week, we covered the fellowship that believers share with the Father and the Son. Most Christians are aware of verses teaching that our lives should bring God glory (1 Cor. 10:31; Ps. 115:1). But does God glorify us as His children? He does! In Romans 8:29, the end goal of people being predestined, called, and justified is to be glorified! Isn't God supposed to get all the glory though? He does! Because the glory we as people of faith have comes from God and not from ourselves, our glory points back to God. Our glory is simply being remade into the image of Christ. According to 2 Thessalonians 1, God makes us worthy of His calling and gives us power to do good "so that the name of our Lord Jesus may be glorified in you, and you in him." In John 17, Jesus prays to the Father, "glorify your Son that the Son may glorify you." This is essentially what Paul prayed for the Thessalonians—that they would be made worthy so they could glorify Jesus and He could glorify them.

The last characteristic of the relationship between the Father and the Son is love. This is where we can cry out with the Apostle John, "See what kind of love the Father has given to us, that we should be called children of God"! The very fact that the triune God has initiated our redemption and this relationship with us—in which we can fellowship with Him and give and receive glory—is all the evidence that we need of His love for us! And so our response to Him should be overflowing love—the kind of love that keeps His commandments and loves others. The love the Father has for His children is our motivation to be imitators of God. This love the Father has shown to us by sending the Son and the Holy Spirit gives us both the motive and the ability to share His nature and imitate Him.

Action Step: How can the loving relationship that you share with the Father give you personally the motive and the ability to be obedient to His call to be an imitator of Him? If you haven't already done so, write some thoughts down in this book or in a notebook about the greatness and love of this God who adopts believers into His family. As we complete Part 1 and proceed into Part 2 of this book, we are crossing into the attributes of God that He expects to see in His children as they are conformed to the image of Jesus Christ. If we live our lives out of deep appreciation of who He is and what He has done for us, love and obedience are not burdensome.

Weekly Summary

Key Points

1. God has revealed Himself as Father.
2. God is Father eternally to His Son.
3. All who believe are children of God.
4. If we are children of God, then we are heirs.
5. Our inheritance is Christ's inheritance.
6. Adoption and inheritance teach us about the Father.

Father
Action Steps

7

Go back through the action steps and complete any that you have not yet completed or repeat one that was meaningful:

1. Deuteronomy 32:11 was part of a song composed by Moses at the end of his life to prepare Israel to enter the Promised Land. These verses are a reminder to the people of Israel that they are God's special possession and He will provide and care for them as He faithfully fulfills His promises to His children. If a powerful bird with predatory instincts can stoop gently to care for its young, how much more will our loving Father care for His children? Pray and praise the Father for His care for you.

2. On Day 5 in our study of the Trinity (page 49), the Action Step involved printing out John 14-17 and highlighting the relational phrases in those chapters. Review the phrases that you highlighted having to do with the relationship among the Persons of the Trinity. Focus on statements about the Father. Mark any phrases that confirm the Father as initiating, having fellowship, giving and receiving glory, and loving and receiving love. You should find examples of all of these actions of the Father in just these four chapters. In fact, as I did this exercise, I found that nearly everything I had highlighted about the Father represented one of these four actions.

3. For most couples today, the choice to have children is a decision of their own will. Whether they have their own biological children or adopt children or both, becoming a parent is within reach for almost every adult. In contrast, it is not within the reach of the will of the parent that their children are born of God, as described in John 1. Parents can certainly raise a child to understand Scripture and the Christian faith, but adoption into God's family comes from God. What we *can* do is pray for our children and the children of those around us. Choose a child that you know and pray for that child to believe in the name of Jesus and become a child of God.

4. To get an overall view of Paul's teaching on connections between faith, justification, adoption, and the Holy Spirit, read Galatians 2:15-4:7, 5:16-25 in one sitting.

5. John wrote in his first epistle that he wanted others to join in fellowship with the believers as they fellowship with the Father and His Son Jesus Christ. The fellowship that we share with other believers is also part of our inheritance. We will be enjoying eternity with this family! Consider whether you are consistently connected with a local representation of the family of God. Do you need to find a group of believers with whom you can pray, worship, or study the Bible?

6. How can the loving relationship that you share with the Father give you personally the motive and the ability to be obedient to His call to be an imitator of Him? If you haven't already done so, write some thoughts down in this book or in a notebook about the greatness and love of this God who adopts believers into His family. As we complete Part 1 and proceed into Part 2 of this book, we are crossing into the attributes of God that He expects to see in His children as they are conformed to the image of Jesus Christ. If we live our lives out of deep appreciation of who He is and what He has done for us, love and obedience are not burdensome.

Part II

In Part II of this book, the primary goal is still to bring us to a position of humility and reverence before God in His glory. All of God's attributes—both those explained in Part I and Part II—disclose His perfection and beauty. As we enter into Part II, however, we have the added opportunity (and responsibility) to reflect His glory to a watching world. These are the attributes that God expects to see in us as we are conformed to the image of Jesus Christ. But He does not expect us to imitate Him in our own strength. He has gifted us with the Holy Spirit to bring us power and strength to reflect His nature and His glory.

> ***And we all, with unveiled face, beholding the glory of the Lord, are being transformed into the same image from one degree of glory to another. For this comes from the Lord who is the Spirit.***
>
> *2 Corinthians 3:18*

We will begin this part of the book with a case study of several men who thought that they knew God, but they failed miserably at reflecting His glory.

WEEK 11

When God's Nature Meets Human Brokenness

What Satan could not do by taking away Job's wealth, destroying his family, and assaulting his health, he would accomplish through these so-called 'counselors.' While Job withstood the collapse of his business, the death of his children, and the infliction of disease, what came closest to defeating him was the adverse influence of his friends. These three associates—Eliphaz, Bildad, Zophar—were the devil's deadly instruments. They beat Job down and wore him out.

Steven Lawson, *Job: Holman Old Testament Commentary,* 43.

There was a man in the land of Uz whose name was Job, and that man was blameless and upright, one who feared God and turned away from evil. There were born to him seven sons and three daughters. He possessed 7,000 sheep, 3,000 camels, 500 yoke of oxen, and 500 female donkeys, and very many servants, so that this man was the greatest of all the people of the east. His sons used to go and hold a feast in the house of each one on his day, and they would send and invite their three sisters to eat and drink with them. And when the days of the feast had run their course, Job would send and consecrate them, and he would rise early in the morning and offer burnt offerings according to the number of them all. For Job said, "It may be that my children have sinned, and cursed God in their hearts." Thus Job did continually.

Now there was a day when the sons of God came to present themselves before the LORD, and Satan also came among them. The LORD said to Satan, "From where have you come?" Satan answered the LORD and said, "From going to and fro on the earth, and from walking up and down on it." And the LORD said to Satan, "Have you considered my servant Job, that there is none like him on the earth, a blameless and upright man, who fears God and turns away from evil?" Then Satan answered the LORD and said, "Does Job fear God for no reason? Have you not put a hedge around him and his house and all that he has, on every side? You have blessed the work of his hands, and his possessions have increased in the land. But stretch out your hand and touch all that he has, and he will curse you to your face." And the LORD said to Satan, "Behold, all that he has is in your hand. Only against him do not stretch out your hand." So Satan went out from the presence of the LORD.

Now there was a day when his sons and daughters were eating and drinking wine in their oldest brother's house, and there came a messenger to Job and said, "The oxen were plowing and the donkeys feeding beside them, and the Sabeans fell upon them and took them and struck down the servants with the edge of the sword, and I alone have escaped to tell you." While he was yet speaking, there came another and said, "The fire of God fell from heaven and burned up the sheep and the servants and consumed them, and I alone have escaped to tell you." While he was yet speaking, there came another and said, "The Chaldeans formed three groups and made a raid on the camels and took them and struck down the servants with the edge of the sword, and I alone have escaped to tell you." While he was yet speaking, there came another and said, "Your sons and daughters were eating and drinking wine in their oldest brother's house, and behold, a great wind came across the wilderness and struck the four corners of the house, and it fell upon the young people, and they are dead, and I alone have escaped to tell you."

Then Job arose and tore his robe and shaved his head and fell on the ground and worshiped. And he said, "Naked I came from my mother's womb, and naked shall I return. The LORD gave, and the LORD has taken away; blessed be the name of the LORD."

In all this Job did not sin or charge God with wrong.

Job 1

When God's Nature Meets Human Brokenness

Behind the Scenes

1

The book of Job tackles the problem of human suffering head-on. But if you study the book carefully, there are also lessons in it regarding God's nature and our responsibility to accurately reflect His image. To understand these lessons, we need to start with the setting of Job's suffering.

Many Bible scholars believe that this book may be the oldest book of the Bible. Cultural references in the book date Job's life as likely around the time of Abraham. Job is introduced first as a man who was "blameless and upright, one who feared God and turned away from evil." He was blessed with ten children, and he was very wealthy—"the greatest of all the people of the east." Job cared deeply about his children, taking the initiative to offer sacrifices on their behalf, covering their sins against God.

The first two chapters of the book of Job include a rare glimpse into heaven. We readers have the benefit of being witnesses to conversations between God and Satan. It is important to remember that none of the characters in Job's story were aware of this information that the Spirit-led author has given to readers. Job lived his life as we do, without the benefit of a clear explanation of the spiritual battles around us or the purpose (and sometimes the cause) behind the challenges in our lives.

God pointed to Job as an example of a blameless and upright man and also added the description: "there is none like him on the earth." Satan, always the accuser, claimed that Job was only upright because God had given him so much. In other words, Satan implied that a man will only worship and serve God if there is an earthly reward for it. Satan charged that if everything Job had was taken from him, then he would curse God to His face. The Lord gave Satan permission to touch all that Job had, but not to harm Job himself.

In one day, everything that Job had was taken from him. The oxen, donkeys, and camels were stolen, and the servants tending them were murdered. Fire from heaven burned up the sheep and the servants tending them. The last and most devastating news was that a great wind struck the house that his ten children were in, killing them all. Job's immediate reaction was one of faith, accepting that everything that he had was from the Lord. Job blessed the name of God and did not sin.

On another day, presumably not much later, God presented His servant Job to Satan again, pointing out that Job "still holds fast his integrity, although you incited me against him to destroy him without reason." This time the Lord permitted Satan to give Job sores all over his body. Still, Job's reaction was one of faith: "Shall we receive good from God, and shall we not receive evil?" Job still remained without sin in his response. Satan's claim that Job only served God to gain earthly blessings was immediately shot down.

Action Step: Read all of Job chapters 1-2 to get the full description of the setting and an introduction to the characters in this book. Consider Satan's challenge. Is there evidence in your life that you serve God simply out of love, or is it possible that you may be expecting blessings on earth in return for your worship? Pray and ask for the Holy Spirit to reveal the motives of your heart.

Now when Job's three friends heard of all this evil that had come upon him, they came each from his own place, Eliphaz the Temanite, Bildad the Shuhite, and Zophar the Naamathite. They made an appointment together to come to show him sympathy and comfort him. And when they saw him from a distance, they did not recognize him. And they raised their voices and wept, and they tore their robes and sprinkled dust on their heads toward heaven. And they sat with him on the ground seven days and seven nights, and no one spoke a word to him, for they saw that his suffering was very great.

Job 2:11-13

"Does God pervert justice? Or does the Almighty pervert the right? If your children have sinned against him, he has delivered them into the hand of their transgression. If you will seek God and plead with the Almighty for mercy, if you are pure and upright, surely then he will rouse himself for you and restore your rightful habitation."

Job 8:3-6

"For you have exacted pledges of your brothers for nothing and stripped the naked of their clothing. You have given no water to the weary to drink, and you have withheld bread from the hungry."

Job 22:6-7

"But oh, that God would speak and open his lips to you, and that he would tell you the secrets of wisdom! For he is manifold in understanding. Know then that God exacts of you less than your guilt deserves."

Job 11:5-6

"Agree with God, and be at peace; thereby good will come to you."

Job 22:21

"Is it for your fear of him that he reproves you and enters into judgment with you? Is not your evil abundant? There is no end to your iniquities."

Job 22:4-5

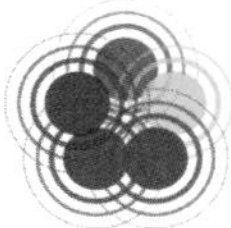

When God's Nature Meets Human Brokenness

When Friends Condemn

2

At the end of Job 2, three of Job's friends gathered together to come visit Job in his grief. This is exactly what we would hope for in the midst of grief—friends who would come alongside of us and weep with us. These men were outwardly examples of godly friends...for seven days. At the end of the week, the spiritual, emotional, and physical exhaustion of grief began to overtake Job. He cursed the day of his birth and expressed a desire to find rest in death. This launched a conversation, covered in Job 4-31, alternating between the advice of the three friends to Job and Job's responses.

Eliphaz was the first friend to speak, introducing the position that all three of Job's friends maintained throughout the conversation—that God punishes the wicked and rewards the righteous. God's justice does demand punishment for sin. God's goodness does reward the upright. However, this is not the sum total of all that God is. For example, God is also patient towards the sinner, wanting them to come to repentance (2 Pet. 3:9).

The three advisers created a narrow theology that insisted that all hardship is the result of sin. Their belief was that God punishes sinners, and Job was greatly suffering; therefore, the only possible conclusion was that Job was a great sinner. Job's three friends turned into condemners. Every time Job responded to defend himself as not being guilty of great sin, their accusations escalated in intensity, and they even accused Job's children of deserving death (8:4) and invented specific sins of which to accuse Job (22:6-7). Zophar spoke truth about God's wisdom, but then claimed that God's wisdom would dictate that Job should have even more punishment (11:5-6)!

Throughout the book of Job, much of what these men said about God's character is true, but it was only *part* of the truth. The friends only reflected a few of God's attributes—mainly His justice and wisdom. They had no concept of God's love or grace. And the truth that they did speak was misplaced in that Job was not wicked, and he was not being punished for sin. Their insistence that Job repent so that God could reward him actually supported Satan's argument that people only serve God to be rewarded. In another ironic twist, in Job 22:4, Eliphaz sarcastically asked Job whether it was because of Job's fear of God that he was being punished. In fact, we know from Job 1:8 that it *was* Job's fear of the Lord that caused God to point Job out as an example to Satan, which *did* lead to his tragic circumstances.

We should recognize that these men did not have access to any written revelation of God as we have today in the Bible. Still, God created men and women in His image, and, as image-bearers, we are called to know Him to the extent that He has revealed Himself and to reflect His nature. Job's friends did a very poor job of image-bearing. These men are examples of people who *abuse* truths about God's attributes because they are only presenting part of God's nature and not the full revealed extent of His nature.

Action Step: Look at the attributes in the Table of Contents of this book. Which are the ones that you find most attractive? Underline several that you are passionate about. These are likely the attributes that you are at risk of overemphasizing as you follow Jesus. Consider a time recently when you may have reflected one of those attributes of God at the expense of His other attributes.

"Shall we receive good from God, and shall we not receive evil?"

Job 2:10

"Oh that my vexation were weighed, and all my calamity laid in the balances! For then it would be heavier than the sand of the sea; therefore my words have been rash."

Job 6:2-3

"I am blameless; I regard not myself; I loathe my life. It is all one; therefore I say, 'He destroys both the blameless and the wicked.'"

Job 9:21-22

"There is no arbiter between us, who might lay his hand on us both."

Job 9:33

"O earth, cover not my blood, and let my cry find no resting place. Even now, behold, my witness is in heaven, and he who testifies for me is on high. My friends scorn me; my eye pours out tears to God, that he would argue the case of a man with God, as a son of man does with his neighbor."

Job 16:18-21

"If indeed you magnify yourselves against me and make my disgrace an argument against me, know then that God has put me in the wrong and closed his net about me. Behold, I cry out, 'Violence!' but I am not answered; I call for help, but there is no justice."

Job 19:5-7

"Today also my complaint is bitter; my hand is heavy on account of my groaning. Oh, that I knew where I might find him, that I might come even to his seat! I would lay my case before him and fill my mouth with arguments. I would know what he would answer me and understand what he would say to me. Would he contend with me in the greatness of his power? No; he would pay attention to me. There an upright man could argue with him, and I would be acquitted forever by my judge."

Job 23:2-7

"Therefore I am terrified at his presence; when I consider, I am in dread of him. God has made my heart faint; the Almighty has terrified me;"

Job 23:15-16

"One should be kind to a fainting friend, but you accuse me without any fear of the Almighty. My brothers, you have proved as unreliable as a seasonal brook that overflows its banks in the spring when it is swollen with ice and melting snow. But when the hot weather arrives, the water disappears. The brook vanishes in the heat."

Job 6:14-17 (NLT)

When God's Nature Meets Human Brokenness

Job in Faith and in Lament 3

Job's immediate reaction to his tragedy was one of faith, accepting that everything that he had was from the Lord. He was prepared to receive both good and difficult circumstances from the Lord. His reaction changed to lament after seven days of grief. He was so deeply grieved that he longed for death. In order to better understand Job, it may help to exercise compassion and figuratively join him in his ash heap of grief.

Tremendous financial pressure fell on Job when he lost all of his livestock to thieves and disaster. He lost essentially all of his worldly possessions. However, Job had hardly found an opportunity to consider his financial loss when it was announced to him that every single one of his ten children had died. Try to imagine the weight of that news. Job loved his children as much as any parent today. He was not detached from them—he offered sacrifices on their behalf. My oldest son died one month after his twenty-first birthday. The grief of that loss was almost more than I could bear. Yet I still had three children left beside me. I cannot imagine the pain of losing all of my children at once. I don't think we can fully understand Job's words until we try to appreciate his pain. He said himself that his rash words were because of the heavy weight of grief (6:3). Adding to his problems, his wife unknowingly encouraged him to take the route that Satan predicted—curse God and die. On top of all of this was the physical pain of his skin sores (30:17, 30).

Job was in agreement with his friends that God's justice punishes the wicked. The problem from Job's view was that he knew that he was not wicked! He did not claim to be sinless, but he knew that he was a man of integrity, no more deserving of this tragedy than the men who counseled him. As his friends escalated their anger and cruelty in their arguments against Job, Job grew in anger in response, both toward his friends and what he saw as injustice from God. He longed for a mediator between himself and God, and he called out for a court proceeding to argue his case. At one point, Job cried out against God for justice and presumed to know how God would answer him, pridefully assuming that he could win an argument with God (23:2-7). In the next moment, Job was terrified to be in God's presence (23:15-16).

Having experienced the grief of losing a child myself, I am left wondering how Job's story might have been different had his friends been content to just weep with him and not counsel him. If his friends had been generous with the kindness, mercy, and love of God, Job might not have raged in confusion the way that he did. What Job most desperately needed was a correct view of God, but his friends led him away from that. Job described the unreliability of his friends as similar to a seasonal brook, where travelers might hope to find refreshment only to be disappointed by it drying up when the need is greatest.

Though Job's immediate reaction to his tragic loss was without sin, he was definitely guilty of sin by the end of his speeches. Job was responsible for his own sin of pride, but his three friends were at least partially responsible for Job's escalating emotion and discouragement.

Action Step: Do you know someone who is grieving? This does not have to be a recent loss. If you know someone who has lost a loved one, even if it was several months or years ago, contact them with a note, phone call, or text message to let them know that you are thinking of them. If you knew the person that they lost, share a favorite memory of them. This is one way to weep with those who weep (Rom. 12:15).

"Or God disciplines people with pain on their sickbeds, with ceaseless aching in their bones. They lose their appetite for even the most delicious food. Their flesh wastes away, and their bones stick out. They are at death's door; the angels of death wait for them.

"But if an angel from heaven appears—a special messenger to intercede for a person and declare that he is upright—he will be gracious and say, 'Rescue him from the grave, for I have found a ransom for his life.' Then his body will become as healthy as a child's, firm and youthful again. When he prays to God, he will be accepted. And God will receive him with joy and restore him to good standing. He will declare to his friends, 'I sinned and twisted the truth, but it was not worth it. God rescued me from the grave, and now my life is filled with light.'"

Job 33:19-28 (NLT)

There were some present at that very time who told him about the Galileans whose blood Pilate had mingled with their sacrifices. And he answered them, "Do you think that these Galileans were worse sinners than all the other Galileans, because they suffered in this way? No, I tell you; but unless you repent, you will all likewise perish. Or those eighteen on whom the tower in Siloam fell and killed them: do you think that they were worse offenders than all the others who lived in Jerusalem? No, I tell you; but unless you repent, you will all likewise perish."

Luke 13:1-5

As he passed by, he saw a man blind from birth. And his disciples asked him, "Rabbi, who sinned, this man or his parents, that he was born blind?" Jesus answered, "It was not that this man sinned, or his parents, but that the works of God might be displayed in him."

John 9:1-3

Servants, be subject to your masters with all respect, not only to the good and gentle but also to the unjust. For this is a gracious thing, when, mindful of God, one endures sorrows while suffering unjustly. For what credit is it if, when you sin and are beaten for it, you endure? But if when you do good and suffer for it you endure, this is a gracious thing in the sight of God.

1 Peter 2:18-20

"My son, do not regard lightly the discipline of the Lord, nor be weary when reproved by him. For the Lord disciplines the one he loves, and chastises every son whom he receives."

It is for discipline that you have to endure. God is treating you as sons. For what son is there whom his father does not discipline? If you are left without discipline, in which all have participated, then you are illegitimate children and not sons. Besides this, we have had earthly fathers who disciplined us and we respected them. Shall we not much more be subject to the Father of spirits and live? For they disciplined us for a short time as it seemed best to them, but he disciplines us for our good, that we may share his holiness. For the moment all discipline seems painful rather than pleasant, but later it yields the peaceful fruit of righteousness to those who have been trained by it.

Hebrews 12:5-11

When God's Nature Meets Human Brokenness

Elihu: Spiritual Insight on Suffering 4

The final player in Job's story was a man named Elihu. Because he was the youngest man on the scene, Elihu withheld his view until all of the others had spoken. Elihu introduced the fresh perspective that God sometimes uses suffering as a form of discipline to bring spiritual growth. Elihu reasoned that sickness and pain could bring a sufferer to humility before God.

Elihu introduced a concept that is developed more fully in New Testament teachings about suffering. God uses life's difficult circumstances for spiritual benefit in the lives of people of faith. In Luke 13, the Jews questioned Jesus about a current event in which Pilate apparently killed some Jews in the midst of their sacrifices. Jesus referred to that incident and another recent event in which a tower fell and killed eighteen people. Jesus clearly stated that the victims of these tragedies did not suffer this fate because of their sin. He did use these tragedies as a reminder that we will all one day face judgment, and we should be prepared by being in a place of repentance. Tragedy can remind us of the brevity of life and direct us to a right relationship with God.

In John 9, the disciples also assumed that sin was involved in causing a man to be born blind. Again, Jesus pointed out that suffering is not always directly because of sin, but "that the works of God might be displayed in him." Jesus' healing of the blind man brought glory to God and was one of many miracles that testified to Jesus being the Son of God (Mk. 2:10).

In Peter's first epistle, he directs servants to submit with respect to their masters, even when the master is unjust. He points out that suffering unjustly is gracious in the sight of God. Patiently enduring unjust suffering of any kind can be evidence of God's grace at work in a believer's life. God will eventually "restore, confirm, strengthen, and establish" the sufferer (1 Pet. 5:10).

The author of Hebrews explains the discipline of the Lord in light of a believer's adoption as a son of God. Just as an earthly father disciplines his children out of love, our Father in heaven much more perfectly disciplines us for our good. God can use difficult, painful circumstances to correct us and bring us to repentance in areas where our lives are lacking in holiness. In Job's case, the suffering had its origin in God's conversation with Satan, but by the end of the book, Job had repented of pride and grown in humility and reverence for God.

There are definitely times in our lives when we experience suffering due to our own poor decisions or the choices of those around us. But there are many examples in Scripture of other reasons for human suffering and ways that God can use it for our benefit. Questioning God about our suffering is not wrong. We may actually see the benefit of suffering in the form of spiritual growth as Job did. However, Job also demonstrated that challenging God and accusing Him of injustice shows pride and is sinful.

Action Step: Read Colossians 2:13-15. The gospel of Jesus Christ shames Satan and other demonic powers. The cross is Christ's final triumph over sin and death. Job's continued faith through his suffering proved Satan wrong and put him to shame. Consider the trials that you are facing today. Is it possible that by placing your faith in Jesus and His finished work on the cross, your perseverance through trials puts spiritual rulers and authorities to shame?

"Then the Lord answered Job out of the whirlwind and said: "Who is this that darkens counsel by words without knowledge? Dress for action like a man; I will question you, and you make it known to me.

"Where were you when I laid the foundation of the earth? Tell me, if you have understanding. Who determined its measurements—surely you know! Or who stretched the line upon it? On what were its bases sunk, or who laid its cornerstone, when the morning stars sang together and all the sons of God shouted for joy?"

Job 38:1-7

"Shall a faultfinder contend with the Almighty? He who argues with God, let him answer it."

Job 40:2

Then Job answered the Lord and said: "Behold, I am of small account; what shall I answer you? I lay my hand on my mouth. I have spoken once, and I will not answer; twice, but I will proceed no further."

Job 40:3-5

"Will you even put me in the wrong? Will you condemn me that you may be in the right?"

Job 40:8

"Can you draw out Leviathan with a fishhook or press down his tongue with a cord? Can you put a rope in his nose or pierce his jaw with a hook? Will he make many pleas to you? Will he speak to you soft words? Will he make a covenant with you to take him for your servant forever? Will you play with him as with a bird, or will you put him on a leash for your girls? Will traders bargain over him? Will they divide him up among the merchants? Can you fill his skin with harpoons or his head with fishing spears? Lay your hands on him; remember the battle—you will not do it again! Behold, the hope of a man is false; he is laid low even at the sight of him. No one is so fierce that he dares to stir him up. Who then is he who can stand before me?"

Job 41:1-10

Then Job answered the Lord and said: "I know that you can do all things, and that no purpose of yours can be thwarted. 'Who is this that hides counsel without knowledge?' Therefore I have uttered what I did not understand, things too wonderful for me, which I did not know. 'Hear, and I will speak; I will question you, and you make it known to me.' I had heard of you by the hearing of the ear, but now my eye sees you; therefore I despise myself, and repent in dust and ashes."

Job 42:1-6

After the Lord had spoken these words to Job, the Lord said to Eliphaz the Temanite: "My anger burns against you and against your two friends, for you have not spoken of me what is right, as my servant Job has. Now therefore take seven bulls and seven rams and go to my servant Job and offer up a burnt offering for yourselves. And my servant Job shall pray for you, for I will accept his prayer not to deal with you according to your folly. For you have not spoken of me what is right, as my servant Job has."

Job 42:7-8

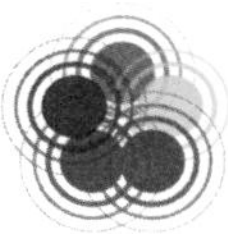

When God's Nature Meets Human Brokenness

God's Response

5

In Job 38, Job's desire to speak before God was fulfilled. But Job discovered that he actually had very little to say. God's voice emerged from a whirling storm, and He began a long series of questions that would help Job realize he was in no way adequate to argue with God.

The Lord reprimanded Job for challenging His ways. The questions pointed out the depth of God's wisdom and knowledge concerning everything that He had created. If Job could not understand the ways that the Almighty God created and continues to manage the earth, how could he find fault with God's management of his life? If Job could not care for the wild animals that God provides for, how could he argue his case that God had not properly provided for him? The same wisdom and sovereignty that God exercises over all of His creation is the wisdom and sovereignty reigning over Job's life.

After God's first series of questions, Job reached a place of humility and promised to speak no longer. Still, the Lord continued in His rebuke of Job, pointing out that he was attempting to place himself in the right and God in the wrong (40:8). God then asked Job to consider carefully two of His most magnificent creatures, which no man could control. By the time God finished His speech, Job finally repented of his pride. Job had an encounter with the true God and found right perspective on his suffering simply in placing his trust in the God who was in control of his circumstances.

It is likely that Job's friends also listened to God's words. If so, it is also possible that they were thinking, "Job, we told you so!" What a surprise it must have been to them when God turned to speak to them, addressing Eliphaz: "My anger burns against you and against your two friends, for you have not spoken of me what is right, as my servant Job has." Job had to listen to a series of corrective questions from God to reach a point of repentance, but these guys were required to have Job offer sacrifices for them and pray to restore them!

What did God mean when He pointed out that the friends did not speak of Him what is right? And what did Job speak that was right? God never corrected Job regarding his integrity before his trials. God only corrected Job's lack of humility in his suffering. Job was right that he was not suffering because of sin. He was right to grieve over his tragic loss. Job was also right to not curse God, as Satan charged that he would, and to repent when confronted with his pride. The friends accused Job of wickedness incorrectly. Their insistence that Job's suffering proved his sin misrepresented the character of God. These men invented their own concept of God, correctly representing some of His attributes and leaving out many others. In doing so, they made God's anger burn against them, and they deeply hurt their friend.

In the end, God never explained His reasons for Job's suffering. But He did reveal Himself and His sovereignty, which was enough for Job. God also restored Job's fortune to twice as much as he had before. Job and his wife also had ten more children. This certainly did not take away the pain of the children they had lost, however. That grief would have stayed with Job for the remaining one hundred forty years he lived on the earth, reminding Job of his lesson about pride.

Action Step: Read Job 38 and 39 (or pick one if you are short on time). As you read it, imagine that God is speaking to you rather than Job. These are valuable chapters to turn to whenever we are tempted to question God. Spend some time in prayer praising God for His wisdom and sovereignty over the earth.

Even though I walk through the valley of the shadow of death, I will fear no evil, for you are with me; your rod and your staff, they comfort me.

Psalms 23:4

"Why is light given to a man whose way is hidden, whom God has hedged in?"

Job 3:23

"He has walled up my way, so that I cannot pass, and he has set darkness upon my paths."

Job 19:8

"The Spirit of the Lord is upon me,
because he has anointed me
to proclaim good news to the poor.
He has sent me to proclaim liberty to the captives
and recovering of sight to the blind,
to set at liberty those who are oppressed,
to proclaim the year of the Lord's favor."

Luke 4:18-19

There is therefore now no condemnation for those who are in Christ Jesus. For the law of the Spirit of life has set you free in Christ Jesus from the law of sin and death.

Romans 8:1-2

When God's Nature Meets Human Brokenness

Job, Meet the Gospel

6

The pain of grief can make the sufferer feel trapped. David describes this experience as "the valley of the shadow of death." Job relates the feeling of being hedged in during his lament in Job 3, and he later portrays it as feeling walled up. It is as though one is imprisoned alone in a canyon with steep sides and no visible way of climbing out. There is comfort in knowing that God is by your side in the canyon. Believers are called to be God's representatives, willing to sit and weep in the canyon and help the grieving person eventually find a way out. The best and most lasting way out of the canyon of suffering is to lean on who God is.

The gospel can provide the tools to comfort the grieving because the gospel is a picture of God's attributes. God, who is **transcendent** over all of creation, has chosen by His **sovereign** will to be ***present*** and **immanent** within creation (Jn. 1:14). The gospel is the ***good*** news of the kingdom of God (Lk. 4:43). The gospel plan reveals God's **infinite *wisdom*** and ***knowledge*** (Rom. 11:33) and has its origin in God's great ***mercy*** and ***love*** (Eph. 2:4). The **Father** sent the Son to reconcile sinful humanity with a ***holy*** God (2 Cor. 5:18-19; Rev. 4:8). Jesus Christ lived a perfectly ***righteous*** life, never committing any sin (1 Pet. 2:22). He died on the cross, taking on the punishment for our sin (1 Cor. 15:1-3). In this way, God's wrath against sin is satisfied and His ***justice*** fulfilled for all who believe in Jesus as Lord (Rom. 3:21-26). When Jesus took on our sin on the cross, He gave us in exchange His ***righteous*** record (2 Cor. 5:21). On the third day, Jesus rose bodily from the grave, completing His victory over sin and death (1 Cor. 15:4, 55-57). We have been saved by God's ***grace*** through faith (Eph. 2:8), and the gospel is referred to as "the gospel of the grace of God" (Acts 20:24). The gospel is the ***power*** of God for salvation for everyone who believes (Rom. 1:16). For people of faith, God is ***faithful*** and ***just*** to forgive our sins when we confess them (1 Jn. 1:9). After Jesus ascended into heaven to sit at the right hand of the Father, the Holy Spirit was poured out on believers, giving us His ***power*** to live ***holy*** lives (Acts 1:8; Rom. 15:16). The Holy Spirit is God ***present*** with us (Rom. 8:11). When the Father sent the Son and the Spirit in His plan for salvation, God revealed His **triune** nature. God, who has existed **eternally** in relationship among the Father, Son, and Spirit and is completely **self-sufficient**, has chosen to grant us eternal life and relationship with Him. This gospel plan has been **eternally** promised by our **unchanging** God (Tit. 1:2). Yet the gospel is **incomprehensible** foolishness to those who are perishing (1 Cor. 1:18).

The gospel includes all of who God has revealed Himself to be in the Son. We should seek to reflect all of the attributes that He shares with us in the power of the Holy Spirit wherever we are. The gospel, given time, brings freedom to captives of grief. Even the more routine trials of life can make us feel trapped, but the gospel and the nature of God that conceived the gospel will set free those who are in Christ Jesus. Jesus is the mediator that Job longed for. Looking to God's nature leads us to the gospel, and the gospel leads us back to who God is because the gospel is the gift of God Himself in the person of Jesus Christ. This is where our strength can be found in the midst of trials and suffering.

Action Step: The words in bold above are attributes of God that we have studied in this book. The words in bold and italic are attributes of God that He also expects to see in our lives as we are conformed to the image of Christ. It is a challenging list that we can never emulate on our own strength. It is only through Christ in the power of the Holy Spirit that we can flourish as image-bearers of God. Pray that God will continue to perfect His image in you as we study these attributes in coming weeks.

Weekly Summary
Key Points

1. There can be spiritual battles and godly purposes behind the trials in our lives that we have no knowledge of.
2. Job's friends created their own concept of God that incorporated only some of His attributes.
3. Job reacted to his tragic circumstances in faith, but the poor counsel of his friends escalated his pain and anger, not only toward his friends, but also toward God.
4. Elihu introduced the principle that God can use suffering for spiritual benefit and not just to punish the wicked.
5. God did respond to Job, but not with explanations. God responded with a revelation of Himself, which was enough for Job. Job had an encounter with the true God and found right perspective on his suffering simply in placing his trust in the God who was in control of his circumstances.
6. The gospel includes all of who God has revealed Himself to be in the Son. The gospel—and the nature of God that conceived it—provides the tools to comfort the grieving.

When God's Nature Meets Human Brokenness 7

Action Steps

Go back through the action steps and complete any that you have not yet completed or repeat one that was meaningful:

1. Read all of Job chapters 1-2 to get the full description of the setting and an introduction to the characters in this book. Consider Satan's challenge. Is there evidence in your life that you serve God simply out of love, or is it possible that you may be expecting blessings on earth in return for your worship? Pray and ask for the Holy Spirit to reveal the motives of your heart.

2. Look at the attributes in the Table of Contents of this book. Which are the ones that you find most attractive? Underline several that you are passionate about. These are likely the attributes that you are at risk of overemphasizing as you follow Jesus. Consider a time recently when you may have reflected one of those attributes of God at the expense of His other attributes.

3. Do you know someone who is grieving? This does not have to be a recent loss. If you know someone who has lost a loved one, even if it was several months or years ago, contact them with a note, phone call, or text message to let them know that you are thinking of them. If you knew the person that they lost, share a favorite memory of them. This is one way to weep with those who weep (Rom. 12:15).

4. Read Colossians 2:13-15. The gospel of Jesus Christ shames Satan and other demonic powers. The cross is Christ's final triumph over sin and death. Job's continued faith through his suffering proved Satan wrong and put him to shame. Consider the trials that you are facing today. Is it possible that by placing your faith in Jesus and His finished work on the cross, your perseverance through trials puts spiritual rulers and authorities to shame?

5. Read Job 38 and 39 (or pick one if you are short on time). As you read it, imagine that God is speaking to you rather than Job. These are valuable chapters to turn to whenever we are tempted to question God. Spend some time in prayer praising God for His wisdom and sovereignty over the earth.

6. The words in bold on page 181 are attributes of God that we have studied in this book. The words in bold and italic are attributes of God that He also expects to see in our lives as we are conformed to the image of Christ. It is a challenging list that we can never emulate on our own strength. It is only through Christ in the power of the Holy Spirit that we can flourish as image-bearers of God. Pray that God will continue to perfect His image in you.

WEEK 12
Love

True love cannot long be dormant. It is like fire, of an active nature; it must be at work. Love longs for expression; it cannot be mute. Command it to be without expression, and you command it not to live. And true love is not satisfied with expressing itself in words. It does use words, but it is painfully conscious of their feebleness, for the full meaning of love is not to be conveyed in any human language. It breaks the backs of words, and crushes them to atoms when it lays upon them all that it means. Love must express itself in deeds, as our old proverb says, "Actions speak more loudly than words." Love delights, too, in sacrifices; she rejoices in self-denials; and the more costly the sacrifice, the better is love pleased to make it. She will not offer that which costs her nothing; she loves to endure pain, and losses, and crosses, and thus she expresses herself best.

Charles H. Spurgeon, 1875

6 *"For you are a people holy to the LORD your God. The LORD your God has*
chosen you to be a people for his treasured possession, out of all the peoples
who are on the face of the earth.
7 *It was not because you were more in number than any other people that the*
LORD set his love on you and chose you, for you were the fewest of all peoples,
8 *but it is because the LORD loves you and is keeping the oath that he swore*
to your fathers, that the LORD has brought you out with a mighty hand and
redeemed you from the house of slavery, from the hand of Pharaoh king of
Egypt.
9 *Know therefore that the LORD your God is God, the faithful God who*
keeps covenant and steadfast love with those who love him and keep his
commandments, to a thousand generations,"

Deuteronomy 7:6-9

The LORD passed before him and proclaimed, "The LORD, the LORD, a God merciful and gracious, slow to anger, and abounding in steadfast love and faithfulness, keeping steadfast love for thousands, forgiving iniquity and transgression and sin, but who will by no means clear the guilty, visiting the iniquity of the fathers on the children and the children's children, to the third and the fourth generation."

Exodus 34:6-7

"In overflowing anger for a moment I hid my face from you, but with everlasting love I will have compassion on you," says the LORD, your Redeemer.

Isaiah 54:8

As for you, O LORD, you will not restrain your mercy from me; your steadfast love and your faithfulness will ever preserve me!

Psalms 40:11

"And I will betroth you to me forever. I will betroth you to me in righteousness and in justice, in steadfast love and in mercy. I will betroth you to me in faithfulness. And you shall know the LORD."

Hosea 2:19-20

"Please pardon the iniquity of this people, according to the greatness of your steadfast love, just as you have forgiven this people, from Egypt until now."

Numbers 14:19

Rise up; come to our help! Redeem us for the sake of your steadfast love!

Psalms 44:26

Let your steadfast love come to me, O LORD, your salvation according to your promise;

Psalms 119:41

He has told you, O man, what is good; and what does the Lord require of you but to do justice, and to love kindness, and to walk humbly with your God?

Micah 6:8

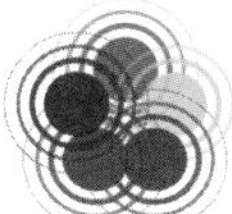

Love
Hesed

1

Since the first pages of this book, the subject of God's love has come up again and again. We have discussed the divine love within the Trinity, the love that God has for mankind that stirs love in our hearts for our God, and the idea that we are called to love one another. But the subject of God's love runs so deep throughout Scripture that we could fill all the pages of this book with nothing but this topic, and we would not run out of verses to study. And so, as we consider the ways that God calls us to reflect His nature, we will turn to love first.

In the Hebrew language of the Old Testament, there are several words used to describe God's love. Deuteronomy 7 alone uses three different words for God's love. Verse 7, "the Lord set his love on you" uses the Hebrew word *chashaq*, which translates to a desire or the idea of being attached to something or someone. In verse 8, "the Lord loves you," the word *ahabah* is used, which is the feminine form of *ahab*. This word, which appears frequently in the Old Testament, is simply translated as love or like or friend. The Hebrew word that we will really fix our attention on here appears in verse 9—*hesed*, translates to steadfast love in the ESV Bible.

Definitions of *hesed* can stretch to multiple pages in Bible dictionaries. Vine's Dictionary describes the term *hesed* as "one of the most important in the vocabulary of Old Testament theology and ethics." The ESV Bible most often translates the word in English as steadfast love, kindness, loyalty, goodness, favor, mercy, or devotion. The best way to grasp the meaning of this word may be to examine the context of its use throughout Scripture. First to note is the occurrence of the words covenant, faithfulness, and compassion alongside steadfast love (*hesed*). The character of *hesed* includes all of these qualities. The covenant aspect of *hesed* is emphasized in the book of Hosea, where God describes Himself as betrothed to His people; this is one of the many times Scripture paints an image of God's relationship with His chosen people as analogous to a marriage covenant. Repeatedly, God's *hesed* is described as everlasting—in fact, every one of the twenty-six verses in Psalm 136 proclaims, "His steadfast love endures forever." There are many times in Scripture where God's people appeal to His *hesed* as a promise, underscoring its reliability and strength. And God's own description of His steadfast love is that He is abounding in *hesed*. God's essence overflows with *hesed*. To summarize all of this in a definition, God's *hesed* is His faithfulness to an everlasting covenant of overflowing steadfast love, in which He loyally devotes Himself to kindness, mercy, and compassion for the good of His people.

But we cannot miss that God is not the only one who can show *hesed*. According to Micah, the Lord requires *hesed* of His people as well. *Hesed* is translated as kindness, or in some versions, mercy, in Micah 6:8. God has shown us His loving kindness, and He expects His people to show it to others as well.

Action Step: Psalm 119:64 proclaims that the earth is full of God's *hesed*. His first act of love directed toward humanity was to create the world and all that is in it. He chose to reveal His nature by creating a place for us to live that cries out of His love. And He chose to create us to image His nature. Pray and praise God for including you in both the revelation and reflection of His abounding love.

"For God so loved the world, that he gave his only Son, that whoever believes in him should not perish but have eternal life."

John 3:16

In this is love, not that we have loved God but that he loved us and sent his Son to be the propitiation for our sins.

1 John 4:10

But God, being rich in mercy, because of the great love with which he loved us, even when we were dead in our trespasses, made us alive together with Christ—by grace you have been saved—and raised us up with him and seated us with him in the heavenly places in Christ Jesus, so that in the coming ages he might show the immeasurable riches of his grace in kindness toward us in Christ Jesus.

Ephesians 2:4-7

Through him we have also obtained access by faith into this grace in which we stand, and we rejoice in hope of the glory of God. Not only that, but we rejoice in our sufferings, knowing that suffering produces endurance, and endurance produces character, and character produces hope, and hope does not put us to shame, because God's love has been poured into our hearts through the Holy Spirit who has been given to us.

For while we were still weak, at the right time Christ died for the ungodly. For one will scarcely die for a righteous person—though perhaps for a good person one would dare even to die—but God shows his love for us in that while we were still sinners, Christ died for us.

Romans 5:2-8

For I am sure that neither death nor life, nor angels nor rulers, nor things present nor things to come, nor powers, nor height nor depth, nor anything else in all creation, will be able to separate us from the love of God in Christ Jesus our Lord.

Romans 8:38-39

Love is patient and kind; love does not envy or boast; it is not arrogant or rude. It does not insist on its own way; it is not irritable or resentful; it does not rejoice at wrongdoing, but rejoices with the truth. Love bears all things, believes all things, hopes all things, endures all things.

Love never ends.

1 Corinthians 13:4-8

Let all that you do be done in love.

1 Corinthians 16:14

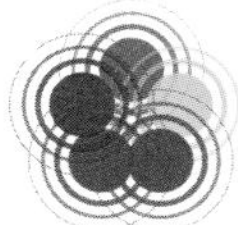

Love

Agape Love

2

If the key word for God's love in the Old Testament Hebrew is *hesed*, then the key word in the New Testament Greek is *agape*. Just as in our study of *hesed*, we can learn much about the meaning of *agape* by the context of its use in Scripture. From John 3:16, we can see that *agape* results in giving to the point of great sacrifice—because of His love (*agape*), God gave His only Son. 1 John 4:10 teaches us that *agape* originates in God, not in us. Both Ephesians 2 and Romans 5 demonstrate that *agape* is not based in merit or worth. We were spiritually dead when God set His love on us. We were ungodly sinners when Christ died for us. God's great love for us is based in His own character, not ours. Ephesians 2 also tells us some benefits of His love for us—He made us alive together with Christ, raised us up with Him, and seated us with Him in the heavenly places. Our citizenship is in heaven, and we are spiritually alive and raised up with Christ. At Christ's return, believers will be physically raised up and seated with Christ. This is how far God's *agape* love goes for us. In summary, a definition of *agape* is God's love that gives sacrificially, not because the loved one deserves it, but simply because He chooses to love for the good of the beloved.

This *agape* love has existed eternally within the Trinity, but it has now been poured into believers' hearts through the Holy Spirit. The end goal of this outpouring of God's love is to show the riches of His grace and kindness toward us in Christ Jesus. A beautiful truth from Romans 8 is that there is absolutely nothing in all of creation that can separate us from this love of God given to us in Christ Jesus.

1 Corinthians 13 gives a detailed description of *agape* love in practice. This chapter is one alongside Paul's teaching on spiritual gifts to the Corinthians. Paul's diversion into a description of *agape* love is to make it preeminent over any of the other gifts. All of our gifts, talents, and actions should be characterized by love. Without love, our actions are fruitless.

It might help us to get a grasp of *agape* if we read the 1 Corinthians passage first as a description of the love that Christ has for us. The list of characteristics of love is divided evenly between things that love does and things that love does not do. The positive characteristics of love are oriented toward others—patience, kindness, rejoicing with the truth, bearing all things, believing all things, hoping all things, and enduring all things. This is the way Jesus Christ loves us. A self-oriented person would envy others, boast of themselves, behave arrogantly or rudely, insist on their own way, act irritably or resentfully, and rejoice at wrongdoing or injustice. The love of Christ is the opposite of all of these self-centered behaviors. The overall message of these statements about *agape* is that it takes action. *Agape* is not confined to feelings, but overflows into visible activity for the sake of the other, even when one has been wronged by the other. Jesus Christ's love for us is not only present when we behave well. He loves unconditionally. Our love should look very much like Christ's model of unconditional *agape* love—considering others before self and putting that thought into action.

Action Step: Luke 15:11-32 tells the story of the Prodigal Son. There are many lessons in this parable, but read it with a particular focus on the father in the story and his love for both of his sons. Note that the father in this story is intended to represent God and His *agape* love for His children.

"Teacher, which is the great commandment in the Law?" And he said to him, "You shall love the Lord your God with all your heart and with all your soul and with all your mind. This is the great and first commandment."

Matthew 22:36-38

For this reason I bow my knees before the Father, from whom every family in heaven and on earth is named, that according to the riches of his glory he may grant you to be strengthened with power through his Spirit in your inner being, so that Christ may dwell in your hearts through faith—that you, being rooted and grounded in love, may have strength to comprehend with all the saints what is the breadth and length and height and depth, and to know the love of Christ that surpasses knowledge, that you may be filled with all the fullness of God.

Ephesians 3:14-19

By this we know that we abide in him and he in us, because he has given us of his Spirit. And we have seen and testify that the Father has sent his Son to be the Savior of the world. Whoever confesses that Jesus is the Son of God, God abides in him, and he in God. So we have come to know and to believe the love that God has for us. God is love, and whoever abides in love abides in God, and God abides in him. By this is love perfected with us, so that we may have confidence for the day of judgment, because as he is so also are we in this world. There is no fear in love, but perfect love casts out fear. For fear has to do with punishment, and whoever fears has not been perfected in love. We love because he first loved us.

1 John 4:13-19

"As the Father has loved me, so have I loved you. Abide in my love. If you keep my commandments, you will abide in my love, just as I have kept my Father's commandments and abide in his love. These things I have spoken to you, that my joy may be in you, and that your joy may be full."

John 15:9-11

"Whoever has my commandments and keeps them, he it is who loves me. And he who loves me will be loved by my Father, and I will love him and manifest myself to him." Judas (not Iscariot) said to him, "Lord, how is it that you will manifest yourself to us, and not to the world?" Jesus answered him, "If anyone loves me, he will keep my word, and my Father will love him, and we will come to him and make our home with him. Whoever does not love me does not keep my words. And the word that you hear is not mine but the Father's who sent me."

John 14:21-24

Love

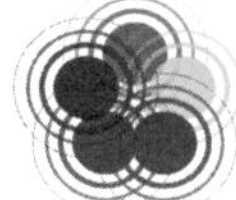

God's Love for Us Leads to Our Love for God

3

Hesed and *agape* love reveal God's devotion to and affection for His children. In Matthew 22, Jesus quoted the Deuteronomy 6:5 command to love God with all your heart, soul, and mind as the first and greatest commandment. This describes a complete devotion of our entire being to God. But where does obedience to this command come from? Does Jesus expect us to just muster from our own selves the will to love God? Not at all.

In the book of Ephesians, Paul expounded on the gospel to the point in chapter 3 where he bowed before the Father in prayer, asking that the Ephesian believers be given strength in the Spirit leading to Christ living in their hearts through faith so that they could be so grounded in love that they might know the love of Christ in a way that surpasses human understanding. The breadth, length, height, and depth give dimension to the vastness of God's love. The end goal of the prayer is that the believers would be filled with all the fullness of God. In other words, experiencing the abounding flood of God's love fills a believer's heart to the point of overflowing love, which is directed first and foremost back to the Lord. The deeper our knowledge of God's love for us, the more we are compelled to love Him. As 1 John 4 says, "We love because he first loved us."

John teaches in both his gospel and epistles that the Father and Son make their home in the believer through the presence of the Holy Spirit. Because God abides in believers, we know and believe the love that He has for us. "God is love." Based on a high school math education, we might be tempted to rewrite that verse as God = love. Based on the entire teaching of Scripture, that would be an error. God is not equal to love, and love is not equal to God. If we allow that thinking to take hold, we elevate His love above His other characteristics, making Him out to be love alone. In fact, "God is love" means that He is the source of all love and everything that He does includes love. In the same way, "God is good" means that He is the source of all good and everything that He does is good (Ps. 119:68).

Jesus taught His disciples in John 15 to abide in His love. To abide is to stay, endure, dwell, or remain in Him. He also taught how to do that—by keeping His commandments. Jesus presented Himself as their model by keeping the Father's commandments and abiding in the Father's love. In John 14, Jesus explained that anyone who loves Him will keep His word, and then the Father and Son will make their home with him. So we abide in Him by keeping His commandments, and when we keep His commandments, He will dwell with us. This is how love is perfected—a mutual abiding. A measuring stick of our love for Christ is obedience to Him because our obedience flows out of our love for Him. There is no point in trying to muster love within our own hearts when we are abiding in the source of perfect love. The result of this enduring relationship is joy that is full!

Action Step: John 15 opens with a beautiful analogy described by Jesus with an image of Him as the vine, the Father as the gardener, and believers as the branches. The vine is the source of life for the branches. The branch can produce absolutely nothing in the way of godly love unless it is attached to–abiding in–the vine. Read John 15:1-11. Pray that God will help you learn to abide in the vine and draw love from its only true source.

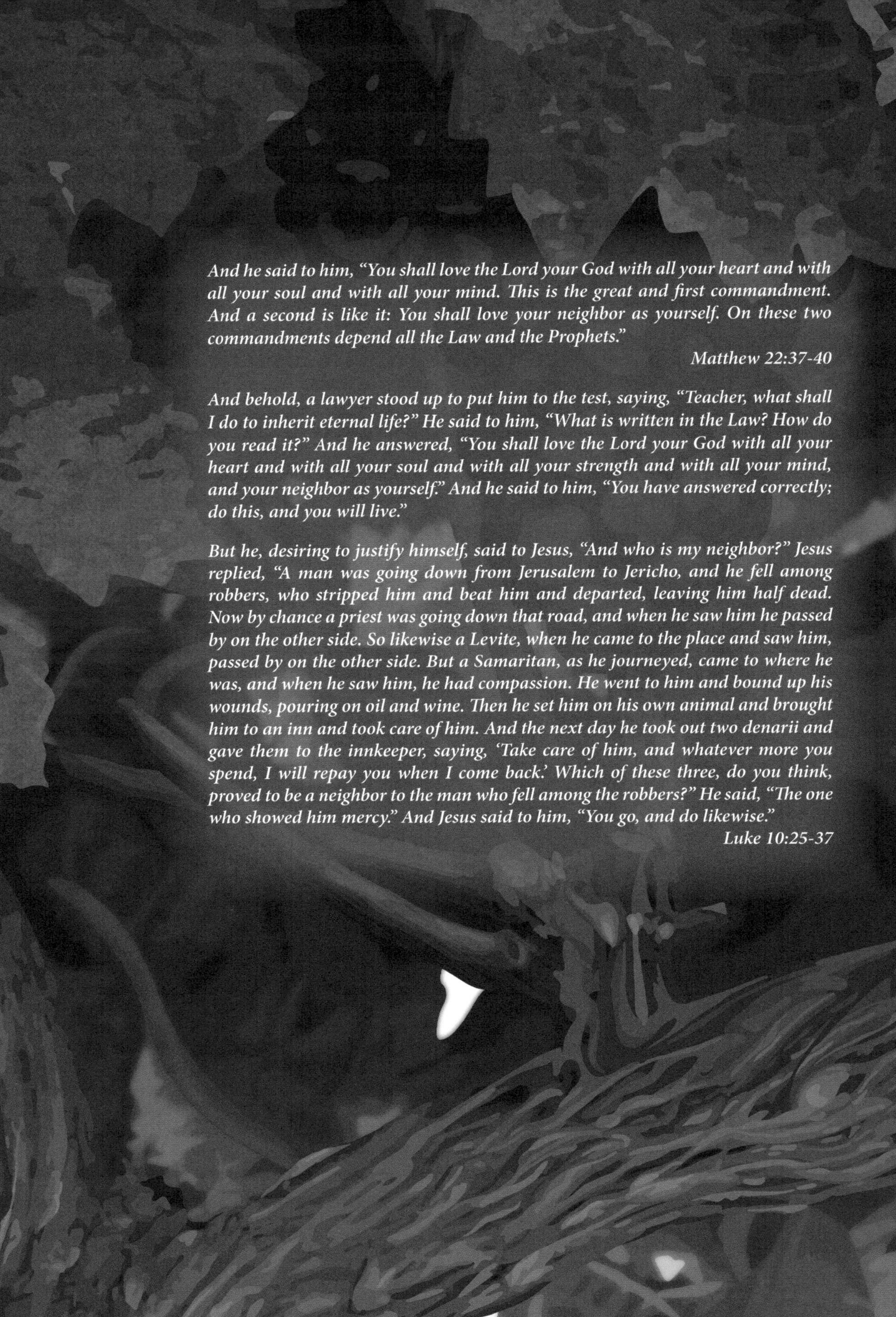

And he said to him, "You shall love the Lord your God with all your heart and with all your soul and with all your mind. This is the great and first commandment. And a second is like it: You shall love your neighbor as yourself. On these two commandments depend all the Law and the Prophets."

Matthew 22:37-40

And behold, a lawyer stood up to put him to the test, saying, "Teacher, what shall I do to inherit eternal life?" He said to him, "What is written in the Law? How do you read it?" And he answered, "You shall love the Lord your God with all your heart and with all your soul and with all your strength and with all your mind, and your neighbor as yourself." And he said to him, "You have answered correctly; do this, and you will live."

But he, desiring to justify himself, said to Jesus, "And who is my neighbor?" Jesus replied, "A man was going down from Jerusalem to Jericho, and he fell among robbers, who stripped him and beat him and departed, leaving him half dead. Now by chance a priest was going down that road, and when he saw him he passed by on the other side. So likewise a Levite, when he came to the place and saw him, passed by on the other side. But a Samaritan, as he journeyed, came to where he was, and when he saw him, he had compassion. He went to him and bound up his wounds, pouring on oil and wine. Then he set him on his own animal and brought him to an inn and took care of him. And the next day he took out two denarii and gave them to the innkeeper, saying, 'Take care of him, and whatever more you spend, I will repay you when I come back.' Which of these three, do you think, proved to be a neighbor to the man who fell among the robbers?" He said, "The one who showed him mercy." And Jesus said to him, "You go, and do likewise."

Luke 10:25-37

Love

God's Love for Us Leads to Our Love for Neighbors

4

When Jesus gave the first and greatest commandment to love God with all your heart, soul, and mind, He went on to give a second command like it: "You shall love your neighbor as yourself." These commandments had been part of the Jewish law for centuries. Jesus combined a commandment from Deuteronomy with one from Leviticus 19:18 to sum up all the Law and the prophets. Love is a summary of God's commandments because if we are actively loving others with *agape* love, we wouldn't consider dishonoring, physically harming, stealing from, or lying to them. A full focus on a love that gives sacrificially for the good of the other is incompatible with offending or acting against them. Again, the source of this kind of love is not in ourselves. It is fully available to believers who are connected to the source of love by abiding in Christ. The love that He has poured into our hearts is the motivation and the equipping that we need to love others. As we abide in Him, we love with *His* love.

In Luke's gospel, just before the parable of the Good Samaritan, these two commandments are revisited. In fact, they were quoted by a lawyer who was trying to test Jesus. The lawyer started with a good and appropriate question about how to inherit eternal life. Jesus turned the question back to him, essentially saying, "Based on what you read in Scripture, what do you think?" The lawyer answered well by quoting the first and second commandments that Jesus had given. But then Jesus challenged him by telling him to now go do this. Loving God with all of your being and loving your neighbor with the same kind of natural instinct that we have to care for our own needs is a nice short summary of the law, but it is really hard to consistently practice. So, in an effort to quantify his accountability, the lawyer asked Jesus, "And who is my neighbor?" This might not look like a misguided question initially. But the lawyer was, consciously or not, looking to create classifications to limit whom he needed to love. "Who is my neighbor?" implies that there is a "not-neighbor" category.

It was here that Jesus stepped in with the story of the Good Samaritan. Any self-respecting priest or Levite would be well aware of the Leviticus command to love your neighbor as yourself. But these two players in Jesus' parable put the injured man into the "not-neighbor" category. The surprising hero in Jesus' story is the Samaritan. Jews did not like or respect Samaritans. Jesus' character casting would have definitely raised some eyebrows among His audience. But it was the Samaritan who displayed self-sacrificing love to the injured man. The Samaritan's love wasn't qualified by who was worthy of his compassion. His compassion took action at a cost to himself. *Agape* love does not spend time categorizing "who is my neighbor" because it is busy being a neighbor to everyone. Abiding in Jesus produces overflowing love for God and for anyone we come into contact with. So Jesus' request to "go, and do likewise" could probably be paraphrased to, "stop considering who is worthy of your love—instead, sacrificially and actively love whoever you encounter."

Action Step: Think of someone you encounter regularly in your life who may have a need for a little help. This might be as small as words of encouragement or as large as help with a home repair or a bag of groceries to feed their family. Make an arrangement today to sacrifice a bit of your time or finances, and take action to be a neighbor to someone in need.

"A new commandment I give to you, that you love one another: just as I have loved you, you also are to love one another. By this all people will know that you are my disciples, if you have love for one another."

John 13:34-35

By this we know love, that he laid down his life for us, and we ought to lay down our lives for the brothers. But if anyone has the world's goods and sees his brother in need, yet closes his heart against him, how does God's love abide in him? Little children, let us not love in word or talk but in deed and in truth.

1 John 3:16-18

In this is love, not that we have loved God but that he loved us and sent his Son to be the propitiation for our sins. Beloved, if God so loved us, we also ought to love one another. No one has ever seen God; if we love one another, God abides in us and his love is perfected in us.

1 John 4:10-12

Love

Our Love for Believers Is Evidence of Our Love for God

5

Scripture teaches that followers of Jesus are called to love their neighbor and that includes anyone we come into contact with. But Jesus also taught that loving our brothers and sisters in Christ has a unique significance. This is how all people will know that we are His disciples. They will recognize our love as being the same kind of love that Jesus had.

We have already looked at Jesus' analogy of the vine and its branches in John 15. The branches which abide in the vine will bear much fruit. To restate that last sentence, the believers who stay connected to Jesus and draw from Him will love abundantly. When Jesus came to this world and demonstrated the Father's love, He revealed a new kind of fruit—a spectacular new variety of grapes, to keep with the vine analogy. No one had ever seen grapes that looked or tasted quite like this before. When we abide in Jesus, we bear fruit that is characteristic of the vine. Our love will look just like the spectacular new love that Jesus revealed. And people will recognize it as the same variety. When onlookers see branches interacting with this unique variety of fruit, they will know where it came from. They will recognize the connection with Jesus.

Jesus said to love "just as I have loved you." While Jesus walked on this earth, His love was unique in that He actively loved outcasts, giving of Himself and expecting nothing in return. But His ultimate act of love, giving His life for us, is also a model for us to follow. This can take the form of a physical death in the most extreme situations, but it can also happen when a believer sets aside self-oriented life goals to promote the good of another. For example, Christian parents who spend much time and money investing in their own children in the areas of education, sports, and technology and yet ignore the seen needs of the children in the single-parent family in their church may not be loving "in deed and in truth." Including fatherless children in their father-led family activities can be a form of laying down their lives for another. Love gives to the point of self-sacrifice.

1 John 4 again connects the love that God has for us with the command that we ought to love one another. "No one has ever seen God" implies that the Father's love is not physically seen. But, when we love fellow believers as Jesus loved, we are putting God's love on display. Our love for God is manifested by the way we actively love brothers and sisters. The evidence that we have been impacted by God's love is that we love others sacrificially.

Action Step: Take stock of areas where God has given you plenty. Is it financially or regarding relationships? Do you have a spiritually and emotionally healthy family that is unbroken? A large home or piece of property? A large library of books or even season tickets to a sporting event? Now consider other families or individuals in your church. Can you think of anyone who is lacking in the very area that you have enjoyed plenty? Prayerfully consider whether there is a way you can sacrificially share from your plenty where another has a need.

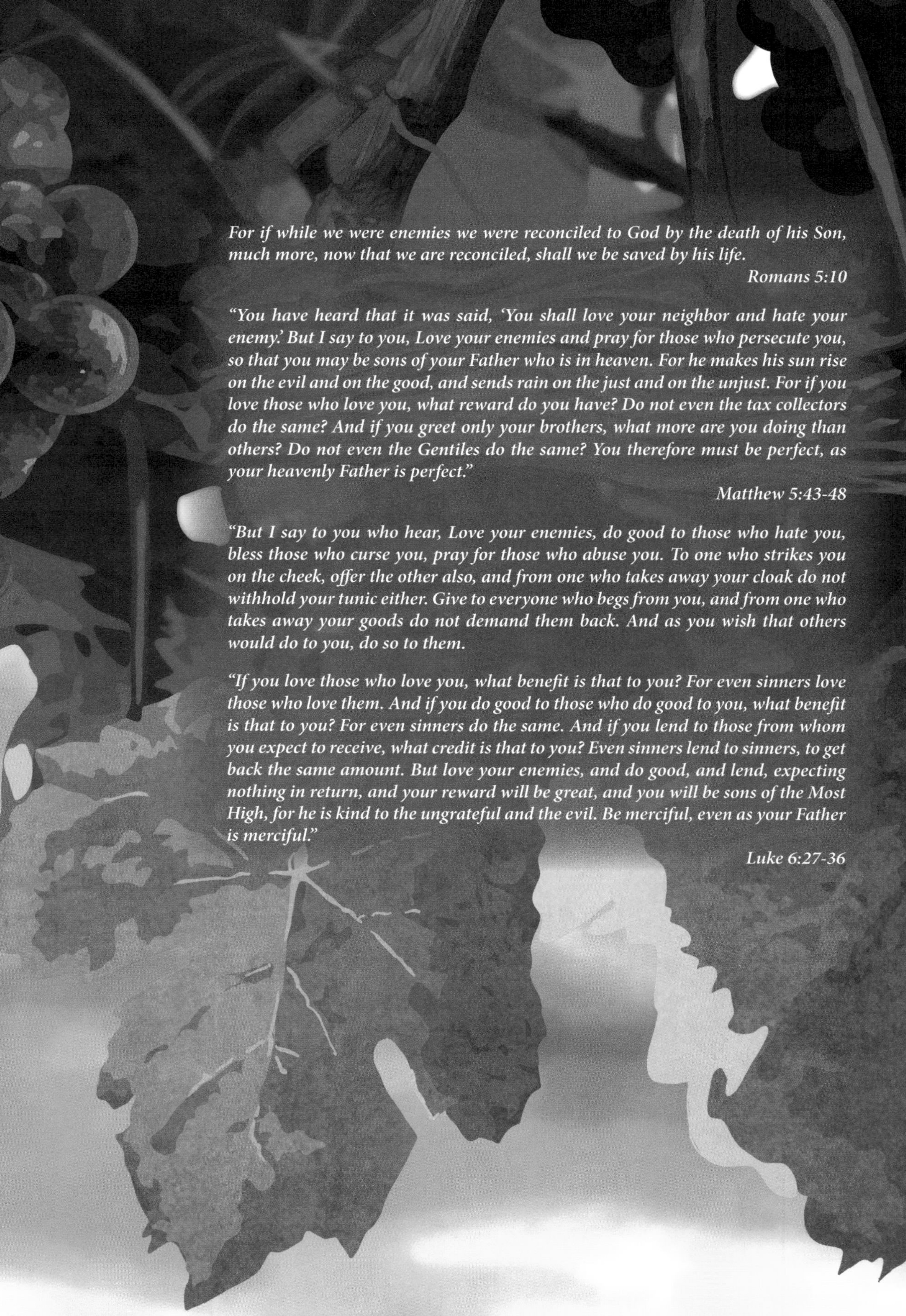

For if while we were enemies we were reconciled to God by the death of his Son, much more, now that we are reconciled, shall we be saved by his life.

Romans 5:10

"You have heard that it was said, 'You shall love your neighbor and hate your enemy.' But I say to you, Love your enemies and pray for those who persecute you, so that you may be sons of your Father who is in heaven. For he makes his sun rise on the evil and on the good, and sends rain on the just and on the unjust. For if you love those who love you, what reward do you have? Do not even the tax collectors do the same? And if you greet only your brothers, what more are you doing than others? Do not even the Gentiles do the same? You therefore must be perfect, as your heavenly Father is perfect."

Matthew 5:43-48

"But I say to you who hear, Love your enemies, do good to those who hate you, bless those who curse you, pray for those who abuse you. To one who strikes you on the cheek, offer the other also, and from one who takes away your cloak do not withhold your tunic either. Give to everyone who begs from you, and from one who takes away your goods do not demand them back. And as you wish that others would do to you, do so to them.

"If you love those who love you, what benefit is that to you? For even sinners love those who love them. And if you do good to those who do good to you, what benefit is that to you? For even sinners do the same. And if you lend to those from whom you expect to receive, what credit is that to you? Even sinners lend to sinners, to get back the same amount. But love your enemies, and do good, and lend, expecting nothing in return, and your reward will be great, and you will be sons of the Most High, for he is kind to the ungrateful and the evil. Be merciful, even as your Father is merciful."

Luke 6:27-36

Love

God's Love Includes Love for Enemies 6

The radical new self-giving love that Jesus displayed also includes loving one's enemies. God put enemy-love on display when He sent Jesus to die for sinners. Paul teaches in Romans that when we were sinners, we were actually enemies of God. Before finding new life in Christ, we were in opposition to God's work in the world. Yet, even as His enemies, He loved us. God did not love because people deserved it or earned it. He loved because it was His choice. He loved so much that He sent His Son to die for His enemies. Jesus showed this love on the cross when He prayed, "Father, forgive them, for they know not what they do" (Lk. 23:34). At the very moment that He was suffering excruciating physical pain for the sins of the world, He acknowledged that His death was offered for the benefit of the very people who crucified Him. His love was so spectacular that He prayed for the benefit of His executioners. If we ever find ourselves in a moment of questioning God's love for us because we are experiencing pain or trials in this life, we only need to look at the cross of Jesus Christ to see the extent of His great love for us.

In the Sermon on the Mount in Matthew, Jesus taught followers to "Love your enemies and pray for those who persecute you, so that you may be sons of your Father who is in heaven." God's goodness in maintaining the earth is extended to all people—good and evil, just and unjust. In the same way, His followers are called to extend love even to those who oppose them. In the Luke account of the Sermon, Jesus taught to bless those who curse and pray for those who abuse. That kind of love is definitely countercultural in our day, as it must have been in first-century Israel. Pray for those who abuse you? But abuse is evil! Does Jesus seriously expect us to love and bless and pray for abusers? His teaching makes it clear that He does. Those who crucified Christ were certainly abusive toward Him. In both the Matthew and Luke accounts, Jesus taught that there will be reward for followers who practice this kind of enemy-love. And in both accounts, Jesus taught that this kind of love is evidence that we are sons of God.

Once again, this is not a natural kind of love. This is not love that we can muster up in our own hearts. This is not an emotional kind of love. This is the *agape* love that is the fruit of abiding in Jesus Christ. It extends to neighbors, brothers, and sisters in Christ, and even to enemies. Not only does it not retaliate for wrongs done, it continues to actively love those who have wronged. It gives and expects nothing back. And it looks very different from the love the world offers.

Action Step: Make a list of several people who have hurt you where the sting of the hurt is still felt. Keep the list private between yourself and God. Next to each name, write some action that you feel able to do for that person. For some, prayer may be all you can choose because the relationship may feel too distant for anything else. For others, you may feel that you can speak blessings into their lives. Just a simple word of encouragement may be a start. And for others still, you might be able to do something practical for their good. Giving a small gift or going out of your way to do a favor for them are possibilities. You may find that these small steps make a difference in your relationships, but they will almost certainly make a difference in your own heart.

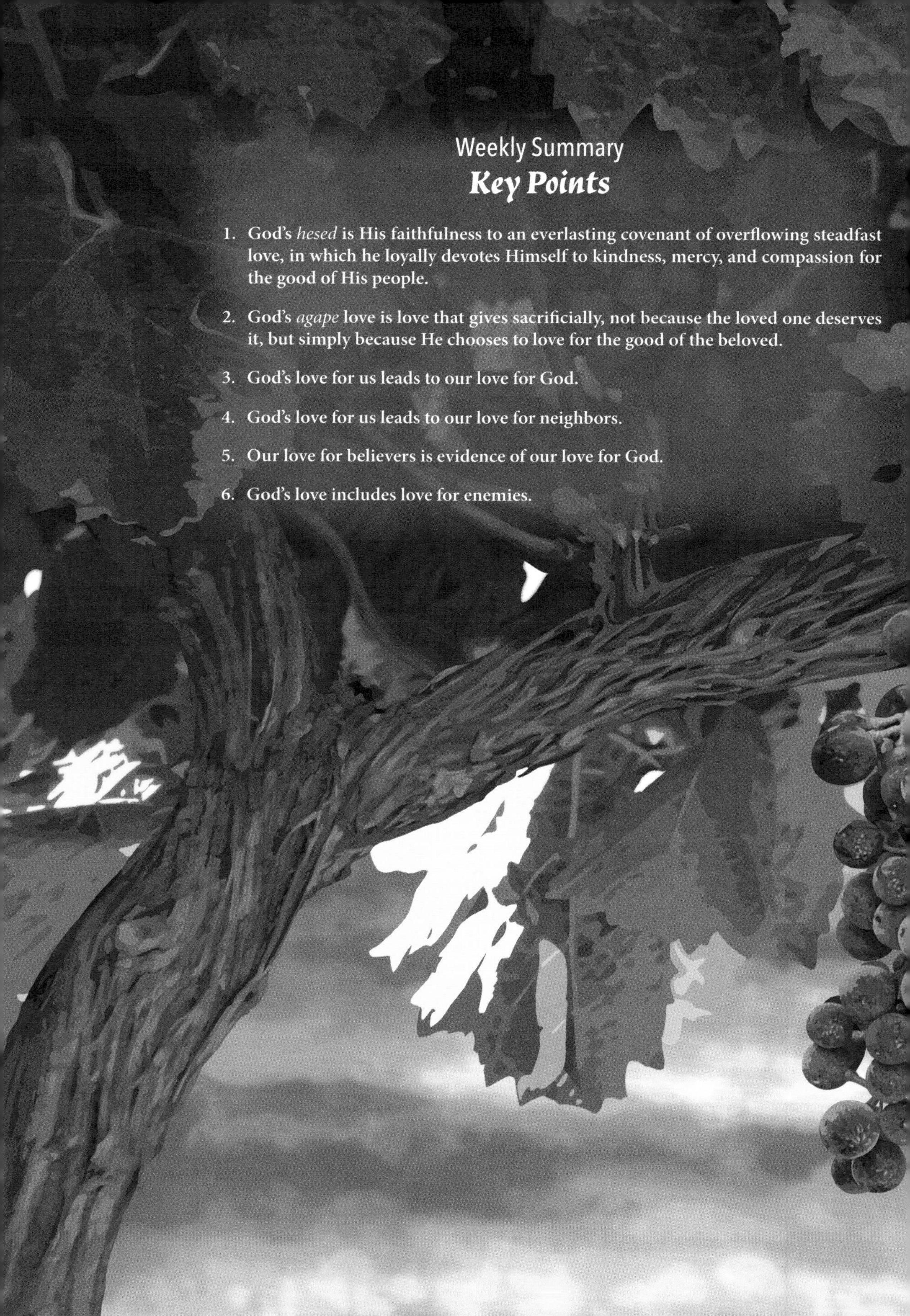

Weekly Summary
Key Points

1. God's *hesed* is His faithfulness to an everlasting covenant of overflowing steadfast love, in which he loyally devotes Himself to kindness, mercy, and compassion for the good of His people.

2. God's *agape* love is love that gives sacrificially, not because the loved one deserves it, but simply because He chooses to love for the good of the beloved.

3. God's love for us leads to our love for God.

4. God's love for us leads to our love for neighbors.

5. Our love for believers is evidence of our love for God.

6. God's love includes love for enemies.

Love

Action Steps

Go back through the action steps and complete any that you have not yet completed or repeat one that was meaningful:

1. Psalm 119:64 proclaims that the earth is full of God's *hesed*. His first act of love directed toward humanity was to create the world and all that is in it. He chose to reveal His nature by creating a place for us to live that cries out of His love. And He chose to create us to image His nature. Pray and praise God for including you in both the revelation and reflection of His abounding love.

2. Luke 15:11-32 tells the story of the Prodigal Son. There are many lessons in this parable, but read it with a particular focus on the father in the story and his love for both of his sons. Note that the father in this story is intended to represent God and His *agape* love for His children.

3. John 15 opens with a beautiful analogy described by Jesus with an image of Him as the vine, the Father as the gardener, and believers as the branches. The vine is the source of life for the branches. The branch can produce absolutely nothing in the way of godly love unless it is attached to—abiding in—the vine. Read John 15:1-11. Pray that God will help you learn to abide in the vine and draw love from its only true source.

4. Think of someone you encounter regularly in your life who may have a need for a little help. This might be as small as words of encouragement or as large as help with a home repair or a bag of groceries to feed their family. Make an arrangement today to sacrifice a bit of your time or finances and take action to be a neighbor to someone in need.

5. Take stock of areas where God has given you plenty. Is it financially or regarding relationships? Do you have a spiritually and emotionally healthy family that is unbroken? A large home or piece of property? A large library of books or even season tickets to a sporting event? Now consider other families or individuals in your church. Can you think of anyone who is lacking in the very area that you have enjoyed plenty? Prayerfully consider whether there is a way you can sacrificially share from your plenty where another has a need.

6. Make a list of several people who have hurt you where the sting of the hurt is still felt. Keep the list private between yourself and God. Next to each name, write some action that you feel able to do for that person. For some, prayer may be all you can choose because the relationship may feel too distant for anything else. For others, you may feel that you can speak blessings into their lives. Just a simple word of encouragement may be a start. And for others still, you might be able to do something practical for their good. Giving a small gift or going out of your way to do a favor for them are possibilities. You may find that these small steps make a difference in your relationships, but they will almost certainly make a difference in your own heart.

WEEK 13
Knowledge

God perfectly knows Himself and, being the source and author of all things, it follows that He knows all that can be known. And this He knows instantly and with a fullness of perfection that includes every possible item of knowledge concerning everything that exists or could have existed anywhere in the universe at any time in the past or that may exist in the centuries or ages yet unborn.

A.W. Tozer, *The Knowledge of the Holy*

"All things have been handed over to me by my Father, and no one knows the Son except the Father, and no one knows the Father except the Son and anyone to whom the Son chooses to reveal him."

Matthew 11:27

Great is our Lord, and abundant in power; his understanding is beyond measure.
Psalms 147:5

"Do you know the balancings of the clouds, the wondrous works of him who is perfect in knowledge?"

Job 37:16

Who has measured the Spirit of the LORD, or what man shows him his counsel? Whom did he consult, and who made him understand? Who taught him the path of justice, and taught him knowledge, and showed him the way of understanding?
Isaiah 40:13-14

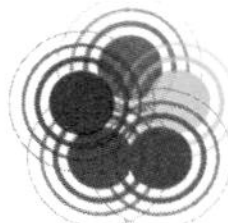

Knowledge
God's Knowledge of Himself

1

The more we study God's nature, the deeper knowledge we have of Him. But the more we study, the more we discover how much we *do not* know of Him. There is only one who can know God completely, and that is God Himself. As God is infinite in His essence, He is also infinite in His understanding and knowledge, which starts with His thorough knowledge and understanding of Himself. Each Person of the Trinity has a full knowledge of the other Persons. There are no questions in their understanding of each other.

Consider for a moment your knowledge of yourself. You know what you like and dislike. You know your life experiences, though it might start to get fuzzy if you try to recall the name of that girl you sat next to in first grade. But do you know all the details of what makes you *you*? Do you know *why* you have certain fears? Do you know *why* you love relaxing with country music, but you cringe when the TV is turned to sports…or the other way around? What is it about the way that you are wired that makes you passionate about that one thing, whatever it may be? You are a finite being, and you do not fully know yourself. God is an infinite being, and He completely knows everything there is to know about Himself.

The theological term for God's infinite knowledge is His *omniscience*. No one outside of God has given Him knowledge or shown Him how to understand. He has not been taught or informed by any man or woman. He does not accumulate knowledge bit by bit or reason out one fact from another. He never discovers anything because He has always known all. God is eternally and perfectly the One in possession of all knowledge. Every detail of every truth—past, present, and future—is immediately accessible to Him. In God there is never an "Aha!" moment where a lightbulb of understanding clicks on. All understanding is always present in Him.

We have studied multiple verses in Isaiah 40 throughout this book. This section of the book of Isaiah was written to comfort God's people who were in exile. Israel's sins had been pardoned, and God would fulfill His promises. Israel was assured of this because they were reminded in Isaiah 40 of God's power, gentleness, and knowledge. Because God is the source of all knowledge and had complete understanding of their situation, the Israelites could remain confident in delivery from their own brokenness and sin. In the same way, God's people today can be assured that He will use His power, gentle care, and knowledge to deliver us from our own brokenness.

Action Step: Psalm 147 is a hymn of praise for the God who heals the brokenhearted and restores the outcasts. He who has infinite knowledge of Himself also understands His people. Read all of Psalm 147, allowing it to lead you into praise for the all-knowing, all-powerful God of the brokenhearted.

For the word of God is living and active, sharper than any two-edged sword, piercing to the division of soul and of spirit, of joints and of marrow, and discerning the thoughts and intentions of the heart. And no creature is hidden from his sight, but all are naked and exposed to the eyes of him to whom we must give account.

Hebrews 4:12-13

You have set our iniquities before you, our secret sins in the light of your presence.

Psalms 90:8

O Lord, all my longing is before you; my sighing is not hidden from you.

Psalms 38:9

You have kept count of my tossings; put my tears in your bottle. Are they not in your book?

Psalms 56:8

"I the Lord search the heart and test the mind, to give every man according to his ways, according to the fruit of his deeds."

Jeremiah 17:10

If we had forgotten the name of our God or spread out our hands to a foreign god, would not God discover this? For he knows the secrets of the heart.

Psalms 44:20-21

By this we shall know that we are of the truth and reassure our heart before him; for whenever our heart condemns us, God is greater than our heart, and he knows everything.

1 John 3:19-20

Thus says the LORD, the King of Israel and his Redeemer, the LORD of hosts: "I am the first and I am the last; besides me there is no god. Who is like me? Let him proclaim it. Let him declare and set it before me, since I appointed an ancient people. Let them declare what is to come, and what will happen. Fear not, nor be afraid; have I not told you from of old and declared it? And you are my witnesses! Is there a God besides me? There is no Rock; I know not any."

Isaiah 44:6-8

Knowledge

God's Knowledge of His Creation

2

God's knowledge of His creation is perfect and complete. He knows every detail of every created thing because He knows Himself as its Creator. He does not need to observe our actions to gain new knowledge of who we are or what we are thinking. Before He even formed us in the womb, He already knew us (Jer. 1:5). He searches our hearts and understands every plan and thought (1 Chron. 28:9). He fashioned our hearts and observes all of our deeds (Ps. 33:15). He sees all of our steps (Job 34:21), and He even knows the exact number of hairs on our heads (Mt. 10:30).

Because God's knowledge of us penetrates and discerns the thoughts and intentions of the heart, there are no secret sins before God. If you have been wronged by another person and you are looking for opportunities to repay him, you may think you are not yet guilty of sin because you haven't taken action. But Jesus taught that we are responsible for our thoughts (Mt. 5), and you can be assured that He knows yours. If you gave a large gift to your church hoping it might be noticed by someone to earn you praise, know that God is fully aware of the intentions of your heart.

But the other side of God's knowledge of us is that He is fully aware of our pain and our needs. He never overlooks any of our requests before Him, even the silent longings of our hearts. He never forgets the pain we have suffered, including the pain of discipline from Him (Ps. 38). In Psalm 56, where David lamented over the attacks of his enemies, he continued to trust in God, who kept count of his "tossings" and put his tears in a bottle. The beauty of God's nature is that He loves His children no matter what inadequacies His omniscience sees in the depths of our hearts.

God's perfect knowledge leads to perfect judgment. There is no one more qualified to "give every man according to his ways, according to the fruit of his deeds" than the One who "knows the secrets of the heart." John reminds us in his first epistle that believers can be reassured that God is greater than our hearts because He knows everything. As people of faith, whenever we are convicted of sin, we can be comforted that God not only knows our sin, but He knows that He has forgiven our sin in Christ. God knows the depths of our hearts better than we do ourselves.

God's knowledge of all things future within His creation is so important that He used it in the book of Isaiah to prove His deity. God spoke much encouragement to His chosen people through the prophet Isaiah. He promised to restore them to their land and deliver them ultimately through a promised Messiah. He would use His people as a witness to all the nations. God would work through Israel to prove that He alone is God. In this context, Isaiah shared God's assurance that the gods of other nations cannot declare what is to come. These false gods cannot make promises for the future. Only God can perfectly declare what will happen. This is God's proof that there is no other God but Him.

Action Step: God's thorough knowledge of the secret sins of our hearts is humbling and should lead us to confession. His complete knowledge of our desire for Him and the pain we have suffered is tremendously comforting and worthy of praise. Spend time in prayer today praising and worshiping the God who knows the depths of our hearts.

When they came, he looked on Eliab and thought, "Surely the Lord*'s anointed is before him." But the* Lord *said to Samuel, "Do not look on his appearance or on the height of his stature, because I have rejected him. For the* Lord *sees not as man sees: man looks on the outward appearance, but the Lord looks on the heart."… And Jesse made seven of his sons pass before Samuel. And Samuel said to Jesse, "The* Lord *has not chosen these." Then Samuel said to Jesse, "Are all your sons here?" And he said, "There remains yet the youngest, but behold, he is keeping the sheep." And Samuel said to Jesse, "Send and get him, for we will not sit down till he comes here." And he sent and brought him in. Now he was ruddy and had beautiful eyes and was handsome. And the* Lord *said, "Arise, anoint him, for this is he." Then Samuel took the horn of oil and anointed him in the midst of his brothers. And the Spirit of the* Lord *rushed upon David from that day forward.*

1 Samuel 16:6-7, 10-13

O Lord*, you have searched me and known me! You know when I sit down and when I rise up; you discern my thoughts from afar. You search out my path and my lying down and are acquainted with all my ways. Even before a word is on my tongue, behold, O* Lord*, you know it altogether. You hem me in, behind and before, and lay your hand upon me. Such knowledge is too wonderful for me; it is high; I cannot attain it.*

Psalms 139:1-6

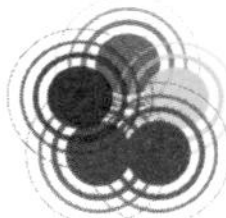

Knowledge

God's Knowledge of David

3

King David may have more pages of Scripture devoted to his life than any other person in the Bible besides Jesus Christ. The narrative of David's life begins in 1 Samuel, runs through 2 Samuel, and finishes early in 1 Kings. There is a shorter parallel account of his life in 1 Chronicles. And approximately half of the one hundred fifty psalms are attributed to David, giving a rich account of his personal thoughts and his worship. A thorough study of the life of David in these Scriptures reveals a man who grew intimately familiar with the character of God. Time after time in his psalms, David reminded himself of God's many perfect attributes. Pairing the narrative of his life alongside these psalms gives us a look at the life experiences that allowed David to see and to know God.

The account of David's life begins when he was anointed king of Israel by Samuel the prophet. A brief review of some early chapters of 1 Samuel can help provide understanding of the context of David's anointing. The people of Israel demanded a king like all the other nations had. The Lord saw their desire for a king as a rejection of Him as King. Still, He instructed Samuel to give them their king. The Lord led Samuel to Saul, who was very handsome and "from his shoulders upward he was taller than any of the people" (1 Sam. 9:2). The all-knowing God knew that this imposing physical figure would be the people's choice as king of Israel. The all-knowing God also knew that Saul would fail miserably as king. After King Saul disobeyed by offering an improper sacrifice, Samuel reprimanded Saul. "But now your kingdom shall not continue. The Lord has sought out a man after his own heart, and the Lord has commanded him to be prince over his people" (1 Sam. 13:14).

Saul continued to disappoint, and the Lord sent Samuel to the house of Jesse to anoint one of his sons as king. Samuel obeyed, but he was still looking at the outside appearance of Jesse's sons. Something in the appearance of Eliab, Jesse's oldest, made him think this must be the man. But the Lord corrected Samuel for looking at appearances and explained "the Lord looks on the heart." Seven of Jesse's sons passed before Samuel, and all were rejected by God before Jesse sent for the young shepherd boy that no man considered to be worthy of being king over Israel. The God, whose sight penetrates the depths of the human heart, had looked on David and had seen "a man after his own heart."

David was by no means perfect, and in later readings we will see his failures. But God, who saw all of David's past, present, and future thoughts and actions before Him continuously, knew David. God knew that this young man would have the obedient heart that could be shaped according to His purposes. God knew at David's anointing of all David's future sin, along with the man of faith David would become, and He chose David as king. At some point later in his life, as David grew in his knowledge of the Lord, the Holy Spirit inspired him to write the words of Psalm 139 to share his experience and deep understanding of the omniscience of God.

Action Step: David's role as a shepherd gets only passing mention in the account of his anointing as king in 1 Samuel 16. Yet the experience David gained as a shepherd would become important to the entire nation of Israel. Consider the humility of David. As the youngest of Jesse's sons, he had not been through any formal preparation for leading people. From his youngest days, he was likely very aware of his humble position in his family and among the people of Israel. Pray and consider how David's humble beginnings as a young shepherd may have influenced his humility before the Lord and his dependence on the Lord's knowledge of him.

On another Sabbath, he entered the synagogue and was teaching, and a man was there whose right hand was withered. And the scribes and the Pharisees watched him, to see whether he would heal on the Sabbath, so that they might find a reason to accuse him. But he knew their thoughts, and he said to the man with the withered hand, "Come and stand here." And he rose and stood there.

Luke 6:6-8

"It is the Spirit who gives life; the flesh is no help at all. The words that I have spoken to you are spirit and life. But there are some of you who do not believe." (For Jesus knew from the beginning who those were who did not believe, and who it was who would betray him.)

John 6:63-64

Then they seized him and led him away, bringing him into the high priest's house, and Peter was following at a distance. And when they had kindled a fire in the middle of the courtyard and sat down together, Peter sat down among them. Then a servant girl, seeing him as he sat in the light and looking closely at him, said, "This man also was with him." But he denied it, saying, "Woman, I do not know him." And a little later someone else saw him and said, "You also are one of them." But Peter said, "Man, I am not." And after an interval of about an hour still another insisted, saying, "Certainly this man also was with him, for he too is a Galilean." But Peter said, "Man, I do not know what you are talking about." And immediately, while he was still speaking, the rooster crowed. And the Lord turned and looked at Peter. And Peter remembered the saying of the Lord, how he had said to him, "Before the rooster crows today, you will deny me three times." And he went out and wept bitterly.

Luke 22:54-62

He said to him the third time, "Simon, son of John, do you love me?" Peter was grieved because he said to him the third time, "Do you love me?" and he said to him, "Lord, you know everything; you know that I love you." Jesus said to him, "Feed my sheep."

John 21:17

"I am the good shepherd. I know my own and my own know me, just as the Father knows me and I know the Father; and I lay down my life for the sheep."

John 10:14-15

Knowledge

Jesus and the Holy Spirit Are Omniscient 4

In Day 1 of this week, we touched on the fact that each Person of the Trinity has a full knowledge of the other Persons. The Father, the Son, and the Holy Spirit are one unified God in three Persons. Each Person is divine, and each shares the same attributes. Therefore, we should be able to find Scripture to support the omniscience of Jesus and the Holy Spirit.

Jesus was shown in many gospel accounts to have full knowledge of people's thoughts. He healed a man with a withered hand on the Sabbath while knowing the thoughts of the scribes and Pharisees that were sitting and waiting to judge Him for doing so. On another occasion, Jesus was teaching some spiritual truths to His followers, and He voiced His knowledge that some of them did not believe in Him. This was not mere intuition based on their reactions or body language. John clearly states that Jesus "knew from the beginning who those were who did not believe, and who it was who would betray him." Jesus' knowledge includes the same ability as the Father to deeply search our hearts in a way that is not limited to the present time.

One of the most detailed stories showing the omniscience of Jesus is the account of Peter's denial. Before His arrest, Jesus had told Peter that he would deny Him. Peter refused to believe Him and countered, "Lord, I am ready to go with you both to prison and to death." We might hope that Jesus' warning would prepare Peter's heart to do the right thing. But, even with this warning, later that same day Peter did deny knowing Jesus in exactly the way that Jesus had said he would—three times and right before the rooster crowed. Peter was brokenhearted by his failure. But after Jesus rose from the dead, he restored Peter by asking him three times if Peter loved Him and commanding Peter three times to feed His sheep. Peter was lovingly restored by Jesus and entrusted with a huge responsibility. Jesus, the Good Shepherd, having just laid down His life for His sheep, asked Peter to feed His flock with knowledge of their Shepherd and His teaching. But there is another subtle lesson in the passage. Peter communicated that he had learned his lesson: "Lord, you know everything." Peter had come to full realization of the omniscience of Jesus Christ.

In Paul's first letter to the Corinthians, he wrote that "the Spirit searches everything, even the depths of God" (1 Cor. 2:10). The Spirit of God can reveal to us the depths of God because He is of one mind with God. Only the omniscient Spirit can know the depths of the infinite God. The place where this gets very exciting for us as believers is that the all-knowing Spirit who searches the all-knowing God also gives *us* knowledge of the all-knowing Son and His gospel.

Action Step: Just a short time after Jesus asked Peter to feed His sheep, the Holy Spirit filled the disciples at Pentecost. Peter preached a powerful message filled with knowledge of God's plan in Jesus Christ. He made clear in his sermon that Jesus is the promised descendant of David that would inherit his throne forever, ruling as the perfect King. Three thousand people repented and were baptized that day. When Jesus asked Peter to feed His sheep, He had full knowledge of the abilities Peter would have to proclaim the gospel in the power of the Holy Spirit. God also has full knowledge of what you are capable of in the power of the Holy Spirit. Pray that He will guide you according to His knowledge of you.

Search me, O God, and know my heart! Try me and know my thoughts! And see if there be any grievous way in me, and lead me in the way everlasting!

Psalms 139:23-24

Indeed, I count everything as loss because of the surpassing worth of knowing Christ Jesus my Lord. For his sake I have suffered the loss of all things and count them as rubbish, in order that I may gain Christ

Philippians 3:8

But grow in the grace and knowledge of our Lord and Savior Jesus Christ. To him be the glory both now and to the day of eternity. Amen.

2 Peter 3:18

But thanks be to God, who in Christ always leads us in triumphal procession, and through us spreads the fragrance of the knowledge of him everywhere. For we are the aroma of Christ to God among those who are being saved and among those who are perishing, to one a fragrance from death to death, to the other a fragrance from life to life. Who is sufficient for these things?

2 Corinthians 2:14-16

I will remember the deeds of the LORD; yes, I will remember your wonders of old. I will ponder all your work, and meditate on your mighty deeds. Your way, O God, is holy. What god is great like our God?

Psalms 77:11-13

Knowledge
Human Knowledge of God 5

We began this book with a week of readings on why we should seek to know God followed by a week of study on how to know an incomprehensible God. A quick review of those Scriptures reminds us that God has chosen to reveal Himself to men and women who are designed in His image. We can increase in knowledge of God by studying Scripture with the guidance of the Holy Spirit. God's own omniscience is also a key part of our growth in Christ. We can agree with David's words in Psalm 139, and ask God to search our hearts and discover sin, then correct us and lead us in His way. Because He knows our hearts better than we do ourselves, He is able to guide the submitted heart to areas needing growth in knowledge and obedience. We know Him only because He first knew us (Gal. 4:8-9).

As Paul wrote in Philippians 3, there is no greater privilege than knowing Jesus Christ as Lord. Not only are we called to grow in knowledge of Him, we are also called to lead others to knowledge of Him. In his second letter to the Corinthians, Paul describes a vivid image—Christ leading us in a victory parade that "spreads the fragrance of the knowledge of him everywhere." Note from the following verses that this fragrant aroma is pleasing to some and a fragrance of death to others. We are not sufficient to determine where the aroma of knowledge of Christ will be attractive, but we are part of the "triumphal procession" called to spread it *everywhere*. We ourselves cannot cause the fragrance to bring life, but God has made us sufficient to share knowledge of Him.

One effective tool for spreading knowledge of God is our own personal testimony. In Christian circles, a personal testimony usually refers to one's own story of how they came to faith. There is Biblical evidence that we should think of a personal testimony in broader terms. One of the ways we can spread knowledge of Jesus Christ is to tell others what He continues to do for us. In fact, the act of remembering His ongoing work in our lives benefits our own faith as much as others. Psalm 77 is a great example of the transforming power of remembering what God has done. The psalm begins with the author crying out in desperation to God. In the midst of troubles and suffering, he wondered if he had been abandoned by the Lord. But in the middle of the psalm, he forced himself to remember what the Lord had done and meditated on the Lord's mighty deeds. He recalled all that God did in bringing His people out of Egypt. The way that the Lord rescued His people and led them like a flock caused the psalmist to say, "Your way, O God, is holy. What god is great like our God?" He found confidence and new hope in remembering the things God had done and what He can do. In days of trouble, we can remember the great things the Lord has done in our own lives to not lose sight of His character. When those around us have similar needs, we can spread this same knowledge of Him by sharing our own experiences. God can use the trials of our own lives to build our own faith and the faith of others.

Action Step: Read all of Psalm 77 and consider whether you have ever felt as if you were abandoned by God. Remember how He brought you through that time. Did that experience and God's work in it build your faith? Is there anyone in your life right now whose hope might be renewed by your knowledge of God gained through your own struggles?

For his invisible attributes, namely, his eternal power and divine nature, have been clearly perceived, ever since the creation of the world, in the things that have been made. So they are without excuse.

Romans 1:20

Now concerning food offered to idols: we know that "all of us possess knowledge." This "knowledge" puffs up, but love builds up. If anyone imagines that he knows something, he does not yet know as he ought to know. But if anyone loves God, he is known by God.

1 Corinthians 8:1-3

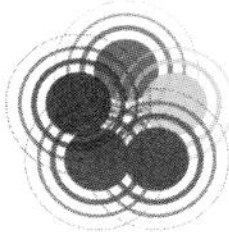

Knowledge

Human Knowledge of Creation 6

The human brain is an amazing organ. We are born with approximately one hundred billion brain cells. Each cell looks something like a starfish with a body and many thin, branching legs. Some of those thin legs can be very long, and those reach out to connect with other brain cells. That next brain cell connects with additional cells, and the resulting network of cells makes a pathway for electrical signals to travel, creating a many-branched, complex communication network. This network is always developing and changing. A newborn baby sees her father and hears his voice, and she is pleased. Her existing vision and hearing brain cell connections are strengthened. When the baby makes her first sound, and her father responds with a laugh and smile, other connections begin to strengthen as she learns that her sounds can cause a pleasant response from her father. All of these pathways continue to develop over the coming months until the infant learns to form actual words to communicate with her father. This continued development of pathways in the brain is the basic neuroscience of how we learn.

Over the next four to five years, this growing girl is exposed to reading by her parents. Learning to read requires additional reorganization of the connections between cells in the brain. Vision and speech areas of the brain are called on to make new connections as she sees letters and associates them with sounds. She isn't born with the pathways in place to read. In order to learn to read, complex new connections between regions of the brain need to be made and strengthened. The brain's ability to strengthen and restructure connections through adulthood is why we have the capacity to be life-long learners. This astounding capability to learn, which God has placed in the human brain, is how we acquire knowledge.

The ability that we have to acquire knowledge is a gift from God. Everything that exists falls into two categories—God, or that which is made by God. All knowledge that we gain of anything ultimately comes from God. He has chosen to reveal Himself to us, and He has given us the capacity to learn about His creation. Therefore, all knowledge should point us back to God in worship. As human beings, we often have the tendency to feel pride when we learn and accumulate knowledge. If we have a proper view of the source of our knowledge, all of our accumulated knowledge of our Creator and the world around us should instead lead us to praise. Rather than being impressed with ourselves over our understanding of the world, we should allow the understanding to point us to the God who has revealed His power and divine nature in the created world. Paul cautioned the Corinthians about letting their knowledge "puff" them up or give them pride. God alone is omniscient—no human is. We will never know all that there is to know about Him or about the world in which we live.

Action Step: Every field of study or work is ultimately a study of God or of what He has made. Science, math, and language are each a study of a different aspect of creation and man's role in it. Agriculture is clearly fulfilling the mandate to care for the earth and use it for food. An auto mechanic is relying on manufactured parts from the earth's elements and physical laws that allow him to fasten parts together and make an engine burn fuel to turn the vehicle's wheels. A mother who spends her entire day caring for children is a practical expert in human psychology and learning. How is your knowledge of your area of work tied to God and His creation? In what specific ways can you praise Him for His knowledge that He has shared with you?

Weekly Summary

Key Points

1. Though God is infinite in His essence, He is also infinite in His understanding and knowledge, which starts with His thorough knowledge and understanding of Himself.

2. God's knowledge of His creation is perfect and complete. He knows every detail of every created thing because He knows Himself as its Creator.

3. God, who saw all of David's past, present, and future thoughts and actions before Him continuously, knew David. God knew that this young man would have the obedient heart that could be shaped according to His purposes, and He called David to be king.

4. Jesus Christ and the Holy Spirit are omniscient.

5. God's knowledge of our hearts allows Him to lead us into growing knowledge of Him.

6. All human knowledge of God and of His creation ultimately comes from God and should lead us to praise Him.

7

Knowledge

Action Steps

Go back through the action steps and complete any that you have not yet completed or repeat one that was meaningful:

1. Psalm 147 is a hymn of praise for the God who heals the brokenhearted and restores the outcasts. He who has infinite knowledge of Himself also understands His people. Read all of Psalm 147, allowing it to lead you into praise for the all-knowing, all-powerful God of the brokenhearted.

2. God's thorough knowledge of the secret sins of our hearts is humbling and should lead us to confession. His complete knowledge of our desire for Him and the pain we have suffered is tremendously comforting and worthy of praise. Spend time in prayer today praising and worshiping the God who knows the depths of our hearts.

3. David's role as a shepherd gets only passing mention in the account of his anointing as king in 1 Samuel 16. Yet the experience David gained as a shepherd would become important to the entire nation of Israel. Consider the humility of David. As the youngest of Jesse's sons, he had not been through any formal preparation for leading people. From his youngest days, he was likely very aware of his humble position in his family and among the people of Israel. Pray and consider how David's humble beginnings as a young shepherd may have influenced his humility before the Lord and his dependence on the Lord's knowledge of him.

4. Just a short time after Jesus asked Peter to feed His sheep, the Holy Spirit filled the disciples at Pentecost. Peter preached a powerful message filled with knowledge of God's plan in Jesus Christ. He made clear in his sermon that Jesus is the promised descendant of David that would inherit his throne forever, ruling as the perfect King. Three thousand people repented and were baptized that day. When Jesus asked Peter to feed His sheep, He had full knowledge of the abilities Peter would have to proclaim the gospel in the power of the Holy Spirit. God also has full knowledge of what you are capable of in the power of the Holy Spirit. Pray that He will guide you according to His knowledge of you.

5. Read all of Psalm 77 and consider whether you have ever felt as if you were abandoned by God. Remember how He brought you through that time. Did that experience and God's work in it build your faith? Is there anyone in your life right now whose hope might be renewed by your knowledge of God gained through your own struggles?

6. Every field of study or work is ultimately a study of God or of what He has made. Science, math, and language are each a study of a different aspect of creation and man's role in it. Agriculture is clearly fulfilling the mandate to care for the earth and use it for food. An auto mechanic is relying on manufactured parts from the earth's elements and physical laws that allow him to fasten parts together and make an engine burn fuel to turn the vehicle's wheels. A mother who spends her entire day caring for children is a practical expert in human psychology and learning. How is your knowledge of your area of work tied to God and His creation? In what specific ways can you praise Him for His knowledge that He has shared with you?

WEEK 14
Power

When I have spoken all of Divine power that I can, when you have thought all that you can think of it, your souls will prompt you to conceive something more beyond what I have spoken, and what you have thought. His power shines in everything, and is beyond everything. There is infinitely more power lodged in his nature, not expressed to the world. The understanding of men and angels, centered in one creature, would fall short of the perception of the infiniteness of it. All that can be comprehended of it, are but little fringes of it, a small portion. No man ever discoursed, or can, of God's power, according to the magnificence of it. No creature can conceive it; God himself only comprehends it; God himself is only able to express it. Man's power being limited, his line is too short to measure the incomprehensible omnipotence of God.

Stephen Charnock, *The Existence and Attributes of God*

In the beginning, God created the heavens and the earth. The earth was without form and void, and darkness was over the face of the deep. And the Spirit of God was hovering over the face of the waters.

And God said, "Let there be light," and there was light. And God saw that the light was good. And God separated the light from the darkness. God called the light Day, and the darkness he called Night. And there was evening and there was morning, the first day.

Genesis 1:1-5

By faith we understand that the universe was created by the word of God, so that what is seen was not made out of things that are visible.

Hebrews 11:3

By the word of the LORD the heavens were made, and by the breath of his mouth all their host. He gathers the waters of the sea as a heap; he puts the deeps in storehouses.

Let all the earth fear the Lord; let all the inhabitants of the world stand in awe of him! For he spoke, and it came to be; he commanded, and it stood firm.

Psalms 33:6-9

For I know that the LORD is great, and that our Lord is above all gods. Whatever the LORD pleases, he does, in heaven and on earth, in the seas and all deeps.

Psalms 135:5-6

"Ah, Lord GOD! It is you who have made the heavens and the earth by your great power and by your outstretched arm! Nothing is too hard for you."

Jeremiah 32:17

Power

God's Power Revealed in Creation

1

I baked a cake today. I always bake cakes from scratch. By not using a package mix, I can prepare the freshest combination of ingredients, and I can control exactly what goes into the batter. I'm making the cake completely on my own, not relying on anyone else to do the preparation for me. Well, other than the farmers that grew the wheat and sugar cane and cocoa beans...and the food companies that processed the flour and sugar and cocoa...and the dairies that packaged the butter, milk, and eggs...and the grocery stores where I bought them all. By the time I had assembled ingredients, followed the recipe to mix the cake, and baked, cooled, and frosted the cake, three hours had passed. Along with all of my efforts to make the cake, there is science involved in turning a variety of uncake-like ingredients into cake, but I don't need to understand that if I simply follow the instructions. Given the proper time and all the raw materials, I can bake a pretty good cake.

God made the entire universe from nothing. He had no instructions to follow and no raw materials to work from. No one supplied Him with anything. There was no matter—no physical substance—until God spoke it into existence. He willed to create the heavens and the earth, and He breathed the word, and His desired result was achieved. What was conceived and commanded came to be. He brought order out of disorder, and it was good. He not only formed the matter, but He also designed and put in motion the scientific laws that govern matter from subatomic processes to the gravitational forces between planets, stars, and galaxies. Even on this grand scale, there was no loss of energy on His part in Creation, and He did not need the rest that He chose to take after the six days of Creation. He never grows tired (Is. 40:28). God chose to rest as an example to His new creation. His work required less effort for Him than breathing does for a healthy human being. This is the *omnipotence* of God—whatever He wills to do, He has the power to accomplish. He does not struggle or strive to see His purposes fulfilled but has the resources to easily complete anything He wills. God created all that there is, and He has infinite power over all that He made.

Revelation 4:11 says, "Worthy are you, our Lord and God, to receive glory and honor and power, for you created all things, and by your will they existed and were created." God receives glory and honor and power from our praises. He does not lack these things or grow greater in strength from our praise—His power is already infinite. He is the source of all glory and honor and power, and He shares these things with men and women made in His image. When we worship Him with our lives, we submit to His created order of directing glory and honor and power back to Him.

Action Step: Spend some time today worshiping God for His unlimited power. Meditate on the power that caused all matter to come into being from nothing. Consider a single leaf from a tree. When God created the trees in the garden of Eden and gave them as food for the animals, the leaves were equipped with every physical and chemical process to generate nutrients for themselves from sunlight and to produce oxygen to benefit animals as a by-product. Those trees and their descendants today also use capillary action, a physical force that depends in part on the chemical properties of water to cause the water to rise to the very tops of the tallest trees, even in opposition to the physical force of gravity. Not only was the physical substance of the tree created on the third day, but every physical and chemical force that the trees relied on for life was put in place. Every glimpse we see of His creation–from the exquisite detail of a single leaf to the spectacular variety of an entire forest–should remind us of His glory and power.

When Abram was ninety-nine years old the LORD appeared to Abram and said to him, "I am God Almighty; walk before me, and be blameless, that I may make my covenant between me and you, and may multiply you greatly."

Genesis 17:1-2

Now Abraham and Sarah were old, advanced in years. The way of women had ceased to be with Sarah. So Sarah laughed to herself, saying, "After I am worn out, and my lord is old, shall I have pleasure?" The LORD said to Abraham, "Why did Sarah laugh and say, 'Shall I indeed bear a child, now that I am old?' Is anything too hard for the LORD? At the appointed time I will return to you, about this time next year, and Sarah shall have a son."

Genesis 18:11-14

Then the LORD said to Moses, "Rise up early in the morning and present yourself before Pharaoh and say to him, 'Thus says the LORD, the God of the Hebrews, "Let my people go, that they may serve me. For this time I will send all my plagues on you yourself, and on your servants and your people, so that you may know that there is none like me in all the earth. For by now I could have put out my hand and struck you and your people with pestilence, and you would have been cut off from the earth. But for this purpose I have raised you up, to show you my power, so that my name may be proclaimed in all the earth."

Exodus 9:13-16

Power
God's Power Revealed to Israel 2

In Genesis 15, we read the account of the covenant that God made with Abram (soon to be Abraham), that his offspring would be as numerous as the stars. Although Abram had no children at that time, he believed God's promise. In Genesis 16, Abram and his wife, Sarai, had still not conceived a child, so they took matters into their own hands and carried out a plan to have Abram conceive a child through Sarai's servant, Hagar. The plan worked as far as producing a son, but Ishmael was not the son through whom God intended to fulfill the covenant. In Genesis 17, God reappeared to Abram, and He introduced Himself as *El Shaddai*, translated as God Almighty. The Creator of the universe has the power to deliver a son to Abram and Sarai, now renamed Abraham and Sarah. The human impossibility of the child being conceived is emphasized by some of the details in these chapters. Abraham was ninety-nine years old. Sarah was ninety. Sarah was no longer having the monthly cycles that bring fertility. Abraham and Sarah each laughed when they heard of God Almighty's promise to yet give them a son. God's response to Sarah emphasized His power again: "Is anything too hard for the Lord?" The God of infinite power, who made all of creation from nothing, certainly has power to conceive a life in the womb of a barren and aging woman.

The book of Genesis continues to follow the story of God working through Abraham, Isaac, and Jacob to grow and preserve a chosen people. God's power is on display throughout these stories, but His demonstration of power is most notable when He called the great nation of Israel out of Egypt in the Exodus. The Lord had heard the cries of His people being held in slavery in Egypt, and He remembered His covenant. It was time for the Lord to rescue His people. He chose Moses to confront Pharaoh, the leader of Egypt. The Lord gave Moses powerful signs to perform before Pharaoh, but Pharaoh's heart was hardened, and he would not let the people go. After six devastating plagues that God sent on the Egyptians, Pharaoh would still not release the Israelites. Before the seventh plague, God explained to Pharaoh why He had not simply struck down all of the Egyptians to let Israel freely leave the country: "But for this purpose I have raised you up, to show you my power, so that my name may be proclaimed in all the earth." Pharaoh had unquestioned power over the people of his nation. He was seen as a god on earth, given power by the numerous Egyptian gods. But the Lord demonstrated His complete power over Pharaoh and all of the gods of Egypt by defeating them with miraculous works. God wanted Pharaoh, all of Egypt, and the whole world to see His strength. God's power was clearly shown in the plagues, the parting of the Red Sea, the destruction of Pharaoh's army, His appearance in the pillars of clouds and fire, His arrival in thunder and lightning at Mt. Sinai, the preservation of the nation of Israel as they wandered in the wilderness, and the overwhelming defeat of Jericho when God Himself caused the city walls to collapse. The entire journey of Israel as told in the books of Exodus, Leviticus, Numbers, Deuteronomy, and Joshua is an account of the power of God to accomplish His will for Israel.

Action Step: Moses had a front-row seat to view the power of God on display throughout the period of the exodus from Egypt. The book of Deuteronomy is largely a review by Moses of all that God had done for Israel by His power in bringing them out of Egypt, through the wilderness, and into the Promised Land. Carefully read Deuteronomy 4:32-39 and allow yourself to imagine being a witness to these events that showed His great power.

"Your servant has struck down both lions and bears, and this uncircumcised Philistine shall be like one of them, for he has defied the armies of the living God." And David said, "The Lord who delivered me from the paw of the lion and from the paw of the bear will deliver me from the hand of this Philistine." And Saul said to David, "Go, and the Lord be with you!"

1 Samuel 17:36-37

Then David said to the Philistine, "You come to me with a sword and with a spear and with a javelin, but I come to you in the name of the Lord of hosts, the God of the armies of Israel, whom you have defied. This day the Lord will deliver you into my hand, and I will strike you down and cut off your head. And I will give the dead bodies of the host of the Philistines this day to the birds of the air and to the wild beasts of the earth, that all the earth may know that there is a God in Israel, and that all this assembly may know that the Lord saves not with sword and spear. For the battle is the Lord's, and he will give you into our hand."

1 Samuel 17:45-47

Ascribe power to God, whose majesty is over Israel, and whose power is in the skies. Awesome is God from his sanctuary; the God of Israel—he is the one who gives power and strength to his people. Blessed be God!

Psalms 68:34-35

"Both riches and honor come from you, and you rule over all. In your hand are power and might, and in your hand it is to make great and to give strength to all."

1 Chronicles 29:12

Power

God's Power Revealed in David

3

As we consider examples of power in the Bible, we cannot pass over the story of David and Goliath. Goliath was a Philistine who stood well over nine feet tall. He wore a bronze coat of mail that weighed 125 pounds. Combined with his helmet and the bronze on his legs, Goliath's *armor* likely weighed as much as David himself. His spear's head weighed fifteen pounds. Can you imagine lifting a spear with iron strapped to the end that weighs as much as a bowling ball? This was a powerful man, and he was defying the armies of Israel to send a man out to fight him. It is not surprising that they were "dismayed and greatly afraid."

Three of David's brothers were in the army facing Goliath and the Philistines. David's father sent David with supplies to his brothers, where he heard the challenge of Goliath. David understood Goliath to be defying the armies of the living God—in fact, defying God Himself. It wasn't long before David was volunteering to face Goliath. King Saul tried to warn David that he lacked the military experience needed to face this giant. But David had killed both lions and bears while protecting his sheep. He knew that the Lord had delivered him from these wild animals, and he had complete confidence in the Lord's power over Goliath. David knew that this battle was about defending the name of God. Saul tried to outfit David with armor, but David's confidence was in the Lord's strength not the protection of the armor or the strength of his weapons.

As they faced one another, Goliath cursed David by the Philistine gods. But David responded to Goliath that he was coming in the name of the Lord of hosts. David knew the Lord would have the victory, "that all the earth may know that there is a God in Israel, and that all this assembly may know that the Lord saves not with sword and spear." God would show His power to defend His name. With a simple sling and one smooth stone, David felled the giant Philistine. He finished the victory with Goliath's own sword. David, a simple youth with a simple weapon, defeated a massive, powerful, heavily armed, and well-trained soldier—not because of David's own strength or battle plan, but simply because the power of God stood with him. Once again, God showed that neither the false gods of other nations nor the physical or military strength of humans is any match for His power.

Because of a lifetime of experiences such as this, David wrote the words of Psalm 68 later in his life. It is a psalm celebrating the victory of the Lord over His enemies and for the benefit of His people. David ascribes power to God and declares that "He is the one who gives power and strength to his people." The hope of the psalm points toward a time when even the Gentiles would sing praise and ascribe power to God. Even near the end of his life, when David prayed over the offerings that Israel brought for the temple construction, David recognized that all power and might come from the Lord.

Action Step: Think of a time when you were overpowered or outmatched by someone. Maybe it was in an athletic contest or when you were competing for the same job as someone else. Maybe it was against your sibling who always got better grades than you. Although you may have been bested in one category, there is another physical or mental skill where you probably emerge on top. All strength and skills come from the Lord. He apportions them as He wills for His purposes. If you are submitted in obedience to God, He will give you the power to accomplish the tasks that He calls you to. How can you use this knowledge this week to do His work for the honor of His name?

And Mary said to the angel, "How will this be, since I am a virgin?"

And the angel answered her, "The Holy Spirit will come upon you, and the power of the Most High will overshadow you; therefore the child to be born will be called holy—the Son of God. And behold, your relative Elizabeth in her old age has also conceived a son, and this is the sixth month with her who was called barren. For nothing will be impossible with God."

Luke 1:34-37

In the beginning was the Word, and the Word was with God, and the Word was God. He was with God in the beginning. All things were created through him, and apart from him not one thing was created that has been created. In him was life, and that life was the light of men…

The Word became flesh and dwelt among us. We observed his glory, the glory as the one and only Son from the Father, full of grace and truth… No one has ever seen God. The one and only Son, who is himself God and is at the Father's side—he has revealed him.

John 1:1-4, 14, 18 (CSB)

Power

God's Power Revealed in the Incarnation 4

In the first chapter of Luke's gospel, the angel Gabriel announced to Mary that she had found favor with God and He had chosen her to bear a Son who would reign forever on the throne of David—a kingdom with no end. This had to have been overwhelming in so many ways for Mary. First, simply to have an angel appear to you and speak to you would be startling! And her Son would reign forever? How is it even possible that one man could be a king forever? And exactly why had *she* found favor with God? So many questions were introduced by this announcement! But the question that Mary posed, the most practical and direct question that was immediately apparent to her was, "How will this be, since I am a virgin?"

Mary knew that it was physically impossible for her to conceive a son at that time. She was engaged to Joseph, but she knew that she couldn't have a baby when she remained a virgin. Never before in mankind's history had a woman conceived a baby without a partner. Gabriel's answer, in short, was the power of God—"the power of the Most High will overshadow you." Gabriel even affirmed the human impossibility of this announcement by contrasting it with the reality that *nothing* is impossible with God. Again, this is the power of the God who created the entire universe from nothing. Not only does He have power to create life in a barren womb such as Sarah's, He has power to create life in a virgin womb.

But this is so much more spectacular than creating human life. This birth involved combining divine nature and human nature in one Person. This birth was the incarnation of the Son of God—the second Person of the Trinity taking on human flesh. The omnipotent God joined with the weakness of humanity. The God who has no need became dependent on others. The infinite in union with the finite. How can this be? When the Holy Spirit came upon Mary to conceive the child Jesus, the power displayed was beyond our comprehension. In a mysterious union, the very Son of God who was *with* God from all eternity and who *was* God from all eternity, the Son of God who created all things—this divine Person united Himself to human nature in one tiny person. The divine chose to contain Himself in a human womb for nine months. The Son of God chose to humble Himself to not only become human, but a human baby that would be totally dependent on parental care. The upside-down nature of God's kingdom is put on display when the omnipotent God calls on power beyond human understanding to experience powerlessness Himself. In one Person, at the same time the human nature of the infant Jesus was powerless over feeding Himself, the divine nature of the Lord Jesus continued to uphold "the universe by the word of his power" (Heb. 1:3).

Action Step: The idea of two natures in one Person is beyond our understanding. The coexistence of the human nature of Jesus that experienced weakness, hunger, and thirst, and the divine nature of Jesus that held power over all of creation, is not something that we ourselves have experienced in any way. In the description of this doctrine on page 97 of this book, we covered the reality that our finite minds cannot conceive of all that our infinite God can do. Faith includes believing some things that are beyond our understanding. Pray that God will give you faith to believe what is revealed in Scripture but beyond human understanding.

...and what is the immeasurable greatness of his power toward us who believe, according to the working of his great might that he worked in Christ when he raised him from the dead and seated him at his right hand in the heavenly places far above all rule and authority and power and dominion, and above every name that is named, not only in this age but also in the one to come.

Ephesians 1:19-21

Indeed, I count everything as loss because of the surpassing worth of knowing Christ Jesus my Lord. For his sake I have suffered the loss of all things and count them as rubbish, in order that I may gain Christ and be found in him, not having a righteousness of my own that comes from the law, but that which comes through faith in Christ, the righteousness from God that depends on faith—that I may know him and the power of his resurrection, and may share his sufferings, becoming like him in his death, that by any means possible I may attain the resurrection from the dead.

Philippians 3:8-11

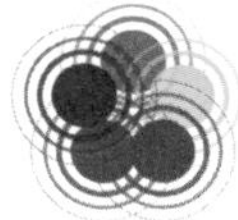

Power

God's Power Revealed in Jesus' Life and Resurrection

5

Just as the almighty power of God was demonstrated in the incarnation of Jesus Christ, Jesus displayed the same infinite power throughout His ministry on earth. In only one chapter of one gospel—Matthew 8—Jesus showed His power over leprosy, paralysis, fever, demon-possession, and the wind and sea. Jesus even demonstrated power over death when He called Lazarus out from the tomb. Jesus Christ shares all attributes of the Father, including omnipotence.

The power shown by Jesus Christ in His miracles was important to demonstrate His deity, but the power of His resurrection from the dead has direct impact on all believers for all time. Just as Jesus' birth showed more power than any human birth before it, His resurrection displayed more power and was more significant than Lazarus' return from the dead. Jesus rose from the dead, not to a broken and aging body that would eventually die again, but to a resurrected body that was glorified and imperishable (1 Cor. 15). In addition, the power that raised Him is at work in believers now, and it includes the power to walk in "newness of life" (Rom. 6:4). In His death and resurrection, Jesus has taken on our sin and has allowed us to become the righteousness of God (2 Cor. 5:21). Included in the resurrection of Jesus Christ is the power of the holy and righteous God to reconcile sinful humanity to Himself. The resurrection demonstrates unlimited power over both the physical and the spiritual worlds.

Ephesians 1 includes Paul's prayer for the Ephesians believers. In this prayer, Paul asked the Father to reveal wisdom and knowledge through the Holy Spirit. One of the blessings Paul wanted them to understand was the power God exercises toward those who believe. He wanted them to consciously experience the power that raised Jesus from the dead and seated Him at God's right hand in the heavenly places, where He exercises authority and power over all. It seems that Paul uses every word at his disposal to convey the greatness of God's power and might at work in the resurrection and ascension of Christ. This mighty victory has been completed in Christ and is ongoing in believers through Christ.

In Philippians 3, Paul expressed his own desire to know Christ and the power of His resurrection. In order to know Him and His power, it is necessary to humble ourselves to willingness to endure the same kind of suffering as Christ—suffering that we may not deserve. If we become like Him in His death, we can experience a resurrection like His, even to the level of being seated with Him in the heavenly places (Eph. 2:6).

Action Step: Jesus Christ definitely did not deserve the suffering that He endured on the cross. We also endure suffering in our lives that is not a direct result of our own sin or poor decisions on our part. Some translations of Philippians 3:10 refer to the "fellowship of his sufferings." Consider the hardships you are currently enduring. Are your trials deepening your fellowship with Jesus? How can appreciation for the power of His resurrection bring hope and comfort in your suffering?

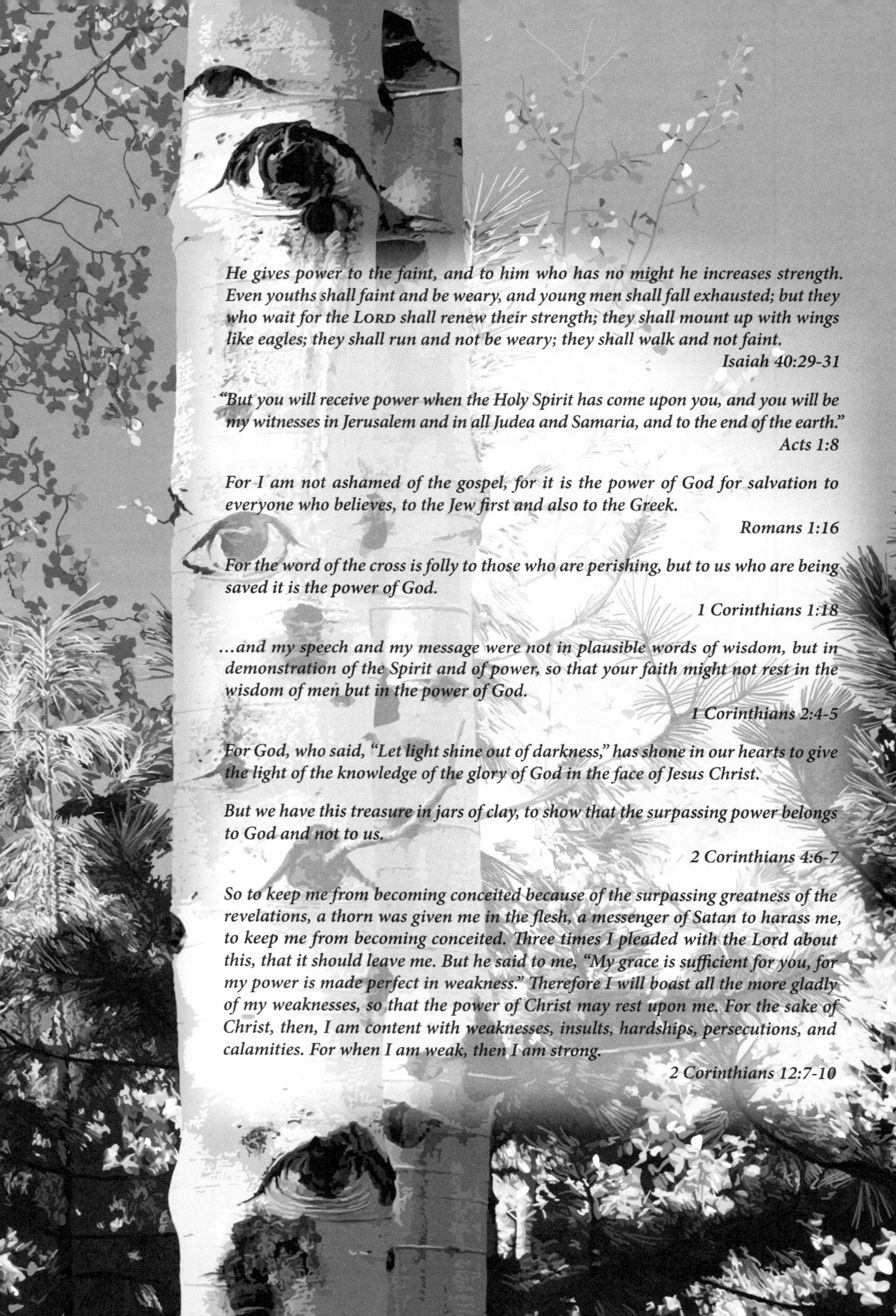

He gives power to the faint, and to him who has no might he increases strength. Even youths shall faint and be weary, and young men shall fall exhausted; but they who wait for the LORD shall renew their strength; they shall mount up with wings like eagles; they shall run and not be weary; they shall walk and not faint.

Isaiah 40:29-31

"But you will receive power when the Holy Spirit has come upon you, and you will be my witnesses in Jerusalem and in all Judea and Samaria, and to the end of the earth."

Acts 1:8

For I am not ashamed of the gospel, for it is the power of God for salvation to everyone who believes, to the Jew first and also to the Greek.

Romans 1:16

For the word of the cross is folly to those who are perishing, but to us who are being saved it is the power of God.

1 Corinthians 1:18

...and my speech and my message were not in plausible words of wisdom, but in demonstration of the Spirit and of power, so that your faith might not rest in the wisdom of men but in the power of God.

1 Corinthians 2:4-5

For God, who said, "Let light shine out of darkness," has shone in our hearts to give the light of the knowledge of the glory of God in the face of Jesus Christ.

But we have this treasure in jars of clay, to show that the surpassing power belongs to God and not to us.

2 Corinthians 4:6-7

So to keep me from becoming conceited because of the surpassing greatness of the revelations, a thorn was given me in the flesh, a messenger of Satan to harass me, to keep me from becoming conceited. Three times I pleaded with the Lord about this, that it should leave me. But he said to me, "My grace is sufficient for you, for my power is made perfect in weakness." Therefore I will boast all the more gladly of my weaknesses, so that the power of Christ may rest upon me. For the sake of Christ, then, I am content with weaknesses, insults, hardships, persecutions, and calamities. For when I am weak, then I am strong.

2 Corinthians 12:7-10

Power

God's Power Revealed in the Believer through the Holy Spirit

6

God delights in giving power to the weak. All of us are weak at times—even the young and strong will grow weary—but God is always an endless supply of strength to those who trust Him. We cannot enter into the Christian life apart from His power. We cannot walk in obedience to Him apart from His mighty work in us.

After Jesus' resurrection and ascension, the Holy Spirit was poured out on His disciples, bringing power to proclaim the gospel of Jesus Christ. The gospel message is the news of the life, death, and resurrection of Jesus bringing victory over sin and death in the life of the believer. When this message is preached, the power of God brings salvation. To some ears, the gospel is foolishness, but the same message results in salvation to those who are called to hear it. Impressive speeches are not what matters in preaching the gospel. It is not man's wisdom but the power of the Holy Spirit transforming hearts that brings people to trust in God's power. So the power of the Holy Spirit is essential in the heart of the speaker for sharing the message of the gospel, and the power of the Holy Spirit is essential in the heart of the hearer for being changed by the gospel. Paul preached by the power of God so that people would put faith in the power of God displayed in Jesus Christ.

Our human weakness—a jar of clay—holds invaluable treasure: knowledge of God in the gospel. He chooses to hold surpassing power in our unimpressive containers so that all will know that it is His power, not ours, that changes hearts. Paul described a thorn in his flesh that caused him weakness. You might even think of it as a crack in his clay jar. Though he pleaded in his prayers, he was told it would not be removed because it was an essential part of perfecting the display of Christ's power. The Lord's grace would be enough to carry him through the pain of the trial because Paul would focus on Christ's strength instead of his own. Again and again throughout the Bible, God used weak and broken people to do His work. His greatest works are contained, not in ornate golden urns, but in humble, insignificant pots. The treasure in the pot is what matters. The common pot will not damage the gospel message but enhance it. The power of the gospel includes the power to hold the cracked and weak clay pot together.

Why does God delight in giving His power to the weak? Because He wants us to come to Him. He is the never-ending source of power for His people. When we look for strength in ourselves to overcome specific sins, we are looking in exactly the wrong place. When we look to our friends or family or church leaders for hope in our trials, we are looking to the imperfect. But when we wait on the Lord for power for obedience and comfort, He will renew us because we are placing our trust right where He wants it to be.

Action Step: Read 1 Corinthians 1:18-30. God is glorified by using the weak and that which seems foolish in order to shame the strength and wisdom of this world. Our culture places high value on social position gained through the power of wealth, education, and celebrity. But God often chooses to work through the low and despised in this world so that it is clear that He is the source of the power. Evaluate your own attitude as to whether you routinely expect God to work through highly respected people or if you also anticipate His work among the lowly of your community. If you are in a humble position, are you prepared for God to show His strength in your weakness?

Weekly Summary

Key Points

1. God created all that there is, and He has infinite power over all that He made.
2. God's power was clearly shown in fulfilling His promise to give a son to Abraham and Sarah in their old age and in bringing Israel out of Egypt and into the Promised Land with spectacular miracles.
3. David's defeat of Goliath, a physically superior opponent, drew on God's power for the honor of His name.
4. The incarnation of Jesus Christ reveals power beyond human understanding.
5. The power of the resurrection of Jesus Christ has direct impact on all believers for all time.
6. God chooses to demonstrate His power in our weakness for His glory.

Power
Action Steps

Go back through the action steps and complete any that you have not yet completed or repeat one that was meaningful:

1. Spend some time today worshiping God for His unlimited power. Meditate on the power that caused all matter to come into being from nothing. Every glimpse we see of His creation—from the exquisite detail of a small flower to the most spectacular and colorful sunrise—should remind us of His glory and power.

2. Moses had a front-row seat to view the power of God on display throughout the period of the exodus from Egypt. The book of Deuteronomy is largely a review by Moses of all that God had done for Israel by His power in bringing them out of Egypt, through the wilderness, and into the Promised Land. Carefully read Deuteronomy 4:32-39 and allow yourself to imagine being a witness to these events that showed His great power.

3. Think of a time when you were overpowered or outmatched by someone. Maybe it was in an athletic contest or when you were competing for the same job as someone else. Maybe it was against your sibling who always got better grades than you. Although you may have been bested in one category, there is another physical or mental skill where you probably emerge on top. All strength and skills come from the Lord. He apportions them as He wills for His purposes. If you are submitted in obedience to God, He will give you the power to accomplish the tasks that He calls you to. How can you use this knowledge this week to do His work for the honor of His name?

4. The idea of two natures in one Person is beyond our understanding. The coexistence of the human nature of Jesus that experienced weakness, hunger, and thirst, and the divine nature of Jesus that held power over all of creation, is not something that we ourselves have experienced in any way. In the description of this doctrine on page 97 of this book, we covered the reality that our finite minds cannot conceive of all that our infinite God can do. Faith includes believing some things that are beyond our understanding. Pray that God will give you faith to believe what is revealed in Scripture but beyond human understanding.

5. Jesus Christ definitely did not deserve the suffering that He endured on the cross. We also endure suffering in our lives that is not a direct result of sin or poor decisions on our part. Some translations of Philippians 3:10 refer to the "fellowship of his sufferings." Consider the hardships you are currently enduring. Are your trials deepening your fellowship with Jesus? How can appreciation for the power of His resurrection bring hope and comfort in your suffering?

6. Read 1 Corinthians 1:18-30. God is glorified by using the weak and that which seems foolish in order to shame the strength and wisdom of this world. Our culture places high value on social position gained through the power of wealth, education, and celebrity. But God often chooses to work through the low and despised in this world so that it is clear that He is the source of the power. Evaluate your own attitude as to whether you routinely expect God to work through highly respected people or if you also anticipate His work among the lowly of your community. If you are in a humble position, are you prepared for God to show His strength in your weakness?

WEEK 15
Mercy

We've become so fearful and vengeful that we've thrown away children, discarded the disabled, and sanctioned the imprisonment of the sick and the weak—not because they are a threat to public safety or beyond rehabilitation but because we think it makes us seem tough, less broken... We've submitted to the harsh instinct to crush those among us whose brokenness is most visible.

But simply punishing the broken—walking away from them or hiding them from sight—only ensures that they remain broken and we do, too. There is no wholeness outside of our reciprocal humanity... In fact, there is a strength, a power even, in understanding brokenness, because embracing our brokenness creates a need and desire for mercy, and perhaps a corresponding need to show mercy. When you experience mercy, you learn things that are hard to learn otherwise. You see things you can't otherwise see; you hear things you can't otherwise hear. You begin to recognize the humanity that resides in each of us...

I began thinking about what would happen if we all just acknowledged our brokenness, if we owned up to our weaknesses, our deficits, our biases, our fears. Maybe if we did, we wouldn't want to kill the broken among us who have killed others. Maybe we would look harder for solutions to caring for the disabled, the abused, the neglected, and the traumatized. I had a notion that if we acknowledged our brokenness, we could no longer take pride in mass incarceration, in executing people, in our deliberate indifference to the most vulnerable...

The power of just mercy is that it belongs to the undeserving. It's when mercy is least expected that it's most potent—strong enough to break the cycle of victimization and victimhood, retribution and suffering. It has the power to heal the psychic harm and injuries that lead to aggression and violence, abuse of power, mass incarceration...

Mercy is just when it is rooted in hopefulness and freely given. Mercy is most empowering, liberating, and transformative when it is directed at the undeserving. The people who haven't earned it, who haven't even sought it, are the most meaningful recipients of our compassion.

Bryan Stevenson, *Just Mercy*

The LORD *passed before him and proclaimed, "The* LORD, *the* LORD, *a God merciful and gracious, slow to anger, and abounding in steadfast love and faithfulness, keeping steadfast love for thousands, forgiving iniquity and transgression and sin, but who will by no means clear the guilty, visiting the iniquity of the fathers on the children and the children's children, to the third and the fourth generation."*

Exodus 34:6-7

The LORD *is gracious and merciful, slow to anger and abounding in steadfast love. The* LORD *is good to all, and his mercy is over all that he has made.*

Psalms 145:8-9

"But I say to you, Love your enemies and pray for those who persecute you, so that you may be sons of your Father who is in heaven. For he makes his sun rise on the evil and on the good, and sends rain on the just and on the unjust."

Matthew 5:44-45

For he says to Moses, "I will have mercy on whom I have mercy, and I will have compassion on whom I have compassion." So then it depends not on human will or exertion, but on God, who has mercy.

Romans 9:15-16

Blessed be the God and Father of our Lord Jesus Christ, the Father of mercies and God of all comfort, who comforts us in all our affliction, so that we may be able to comfort those who are in any affliction, with the comfort with which we ourselves are comforted by God.

2 Corinthians 1:3-4

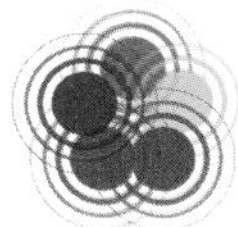

Mercy

God's Mercy and Patience

1

Mercy can be defined as compassion extended from one who has resources to those who have need. If the recipients had everything that they needed, there would be no need for mercy—anything given would simply be a gift. If the giver has no compassion, he or she might still give, but it would not be properly described as mercy. When a person with wealth recognizes the pain of hunger and buys food for the poor, mercy is displayed. When I demonstrate a lack of goodness by hurting a friend with damaging words, and the friend sees my regret and responds with ample goodness by forgiving me, there is mercy at work in our relationship. God's mercy is shown in His compassion extended to those in great need—people who are trapped in miserable conditions and are worthy of pity. For some, those miserable conditions may include poverty or sickness. The one misery that is common to all humanity is the despair of being trapped in sin and its painful consequences.

When the Lord revealed His name and character to Moses in Exodus 34, the first word He chose to describe Himself was "merciful." In fact, His mercy is over "all that he has made." The sun rising and the rain falling are evidence of God's compassion and goodness directed to all of His creation. His mercy is not just for those who deserve it. In fact, none of us deserve His mercy, and none of us can exert ourselves to grasp or earn it. Mercy simply exists in the heart of God and flows out of Him to all of His creation.

God's patience is closely tied to His mercy. Because He is perfect in justice, He would be well within His rights if He was to immediately punish us, even to the point of death, on any occasion of sin in our lives. But He chooses patience, restraining His anger and execution of justice to give the sinner time to repent. Because He is compassionate toward us in our need for redemption from sin, He gives time for us to turn to Jesus as our Savior from sin and death. This is why the Old Testament often describes God as "slow to anger." It is not that God does not get angry or completely forgoes justice. Justice and wrath toward sin will come, but God's patience and mercy cause Him to be slow to anger for the benefit of His beloved people.

The key to understanding the mercy of God is to truly appreciate our own need for it. If a poor family serves a meager dinner to their children and puts them to bed hungry every night, that is a miserable condition. If that same family refuses the food being generously passed out by a food bank across the street, they are either blind to their own need or too proud to let others help. When those parents stop and take notice of their children's desperate need, they may receive the mercy of food assistance. In the same way, if a sinner in need of redemption refuses to acknowledge his need for mercy from God, he is either blind to his own sin or so proud that he imagines himself able to lift himself out of his sinful condition. When that sinner stops and honestly evaluates his own brokenness, he is in a better position to trust the "Father of mercies" to meet his need. It is God's will to extend His mercy to all of creation, both by meeting physical needs and restraining His anger toward those who need salvation.

Action Step: The giver must recognize the need in order for the gift to properly be called mercy, but the recipient must also recognize their own need to receive the gift and properly appreciate the mercy. Do you appreciate your own need for mercy from God? In other words, do you have a proper view of the presence of sin in your life? Pray that God will help you understand His mercy and your need for it.

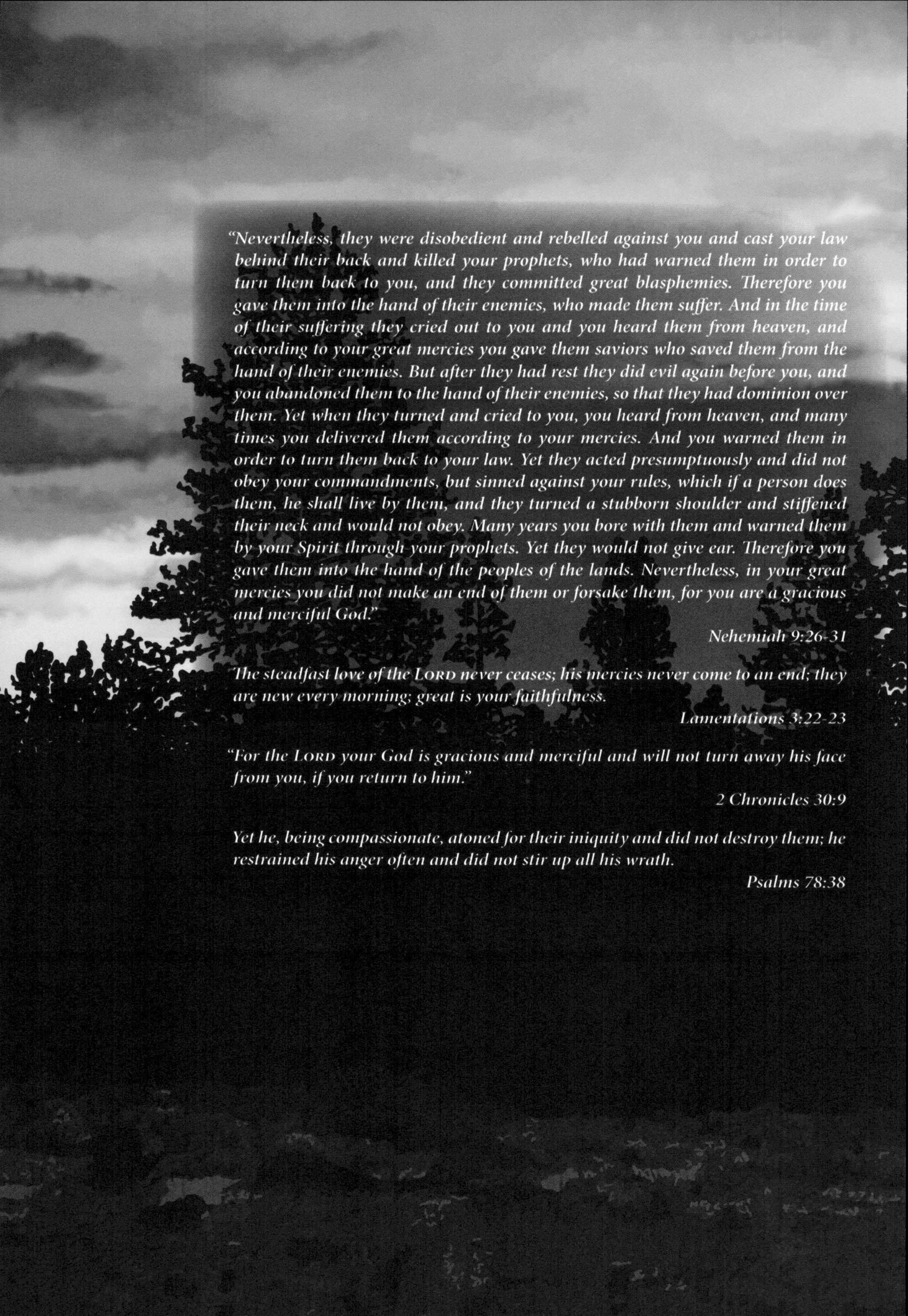

"Nevertheless, they were disobedient and rebelled against you and cast your law behind their back and killed your prophets, who had warned them in order to turn them back to you, and they committed great blasphemies. Therefore you gave them into the hand of their enemies, who made them suffer. And in the time of their suffering they cried out to you and you heard them from heaven, and according to your great mercies you gave them saviors who saved them from the hand of their enemies. But after they had rest they did evil again before you, and you abandoned them to the hand of their enemies, so that they had dominion over them. Yet when they turned and cried to you, you heard from heaven, and many times you delivered them according to your mercies. And you warned them in order to turn them back to your law. Yet they acted presumptuously and did not obey your commandments, but sinned against your rules, which if a person does them, he shall live by them, and they turned a stubborn shoulder and stiffened their neck and would not obey. Many years you bore with them and warned them by your Spirit through your prophets. Yet they would not give ear. Therefore you gave them into the hand of the peoples of the lands. Nevertheless, in your great mercies you did not make an end of them or forsake them, for you are a gracious and merciful God."

Nehemiah 9:26-31

The steadfast love of the LORD never ceases; his mercies never come to an end; they are new every morning; great is your faithfulness.

Lamentations 3:22-23

"For the LORD your God is gracious and merciful and will not turn away his face from you, if you return to him."

2 Chronicles 30:9

Yet he, being compassionate, atoned for their iniquity and did not destroy them; he restrained his anger often and did not stir up all his wrath.

Psalms 78:38

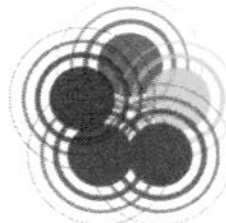

Mercy

God's Mercy toward Israel

2

Many would say that the Old Testament depicts an angry God who brings swift justice to all who disobey Him. This narrative would claim that the incarnation of Jesus Christ was when God revealed His mercy. While there is no doubt that Jesus' ministry was the ultimate revelation of God's mercy in human form, God very clearly revealed His heart of mercy throughout the Old Testament. The attributes that He revealed to Moses—"a God merciful and gracious, slow to anger, and abounding in steadfast love and faithfulness..."—were repeated many times throughout the Hebrew Scriptures. God's people were well aware that He should be described as merciful. But the Old Testament goes much further than just *calling* God merciful—His mercy is shown in action.

The book of Nehemiah is set at the end of a period of exile for the people of Israel. They had been exiled because of unfaithfulness to their covenant with the Lord. As the people were slowly returning to their homeland, Nehemiah returned to Jerusalem to oversee the rebuilding of the city's walls. After the walls were finished, the people of Israel were called to renew their covenant with God. Most of Nehemiah 9 is the prayer the Levites offered to God, recounting all He had done for the people of Israel. This review is a startling statement about God's mercy. God saw the affliction of His people in Egypt, He had compassion for them, and He brought them out of Egypt. But the people "refused to obey and were not mindful of the wonders that you performed among them." The prayer leaders recognized, "you are a God ready to forgive, gracious and merciful, slow to anger and abounding in steadfast love, and did not forsake them." Next, the people "made for themselves a golden calf" and "committed great blasphemies." Again, in His great mercy, God did not forsake them in the wilderness. The prayer next reminds the people of how God brought them into the land, and "they ate and were filled and became fat and delighted themselves in your great goodness." Still, the people were disobedient and killed God's prophets. God disciplined the people by giving them into the hands of their enemies. When the people cried out, God heard them and rescued them according to His great mercy. Yet again, the people did evil, God disciplined, they cried out, and He delivered them according to His mercies. And still one more cycle of disobedience, discipline, and restoration by God is recounted. Cycle after cycle of sin and disobedience on the part of the people of Israel was met with the mercy of God. At times, there was discipline to set them straight. But the historical account ends in verse 31: "Nevertheless, in your great mercies you did not make an end of them or forsake them, for you are a gracious and merciful God." Despite the persistent disobedience of God's people in the Old Testament, He remained the God of mercy and grace.

Action Step: Print out a copy of Nehemiah 9. Read the entire chapter. Using highlighters, mark all of the verses that tell of God's mercy with one color and all of the verses that tell of the people's failures with another color. You might even use a third color to highlight the verses that describe God's discipline used to correct the people. Note the number of times God's mercy covers His people. Every time the people rebelled, God responded with mercy. As the author of Lamentations proclaims, "His mercies never come to an end; they are new every morning." As you begin each day this week, thank God for His new mercy with every sunrise.

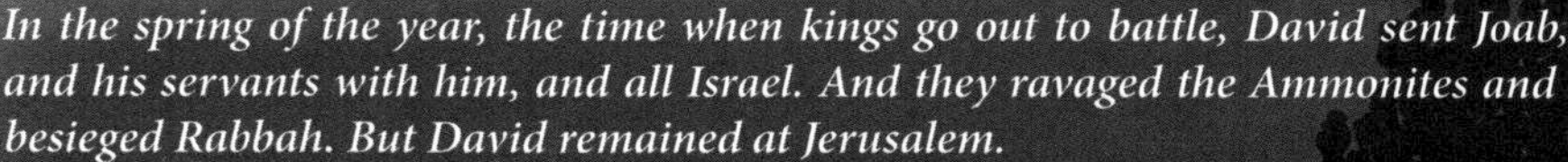

In the spring of the year, the time when kings go out to battle, David sent Joab, and his servants with him, and all Israel. And they ravaged the Ammonites and besieged Rabbah. But David remained at Jerusalem.

It happened, late one afternoon, when David arose from his couch and was walking on the roof of the king's house, that he saw from the roof a woman bathing; and the woman was very beautiful. And David sent and inquired about the woman. And one said, "Is not this Bathsheba, the daughter of Eliam, the wife of Uriah the Hittite?" So David sent messengers and took her, and she came to him, and he lay with her. (Now she had been purifying herself from her uncleanness.) Then she returned to her house. And the woman conceived, and she sent and told David, "I am pregnant."

2 Samuel 11:1-5

In the morning David wrote a letter to Joab and sent it by the hand of Uriah. In the letter he wrote, "Set Uriah in the forefront of the hardest fighting, and then draw back from him, that he may be struck down, and die." And as Joab was besieging the city, he assigned Uriah to the place where he knew there were valiant men. And the men of the city came out and fought with Joab, and some of the servants of David among the people fell. Uriah the Hittite also died.

2 Samuel 11:14-17

When the wife of Uriah heard that Uriah her husband was dead, she lamented over her husband. And when the mourning was over, David sent and brought her to his house, and she became his wife and bore him a son. But the thing that David had done displeased the LORD.

2 Samuel 11:26-27

"'Why have you despised the word of the LORD, to do what is evil in his sight? You have struck down Uriah the Hittite with the sword and have taken his wife to be your wife and have killed him with the sword of the Ammonites. Now therefore the sword shall never depart from your house, because you have despised me and have taken the wife of Uriah the Hittite to be your wife.' Thus says the LORD, 'Behold, I will raise up evil against you out of your own house. And I will take your wives before your eyes and give them to your neighbor, and he shall lie with your wives in the sight of this sun. For you did it secretly, but I will do this thing before all Israel and before the sun.'" David said to Nathan, "I have sinned against the LORD." And Nathan said to David, "The LORD also has put away your sin; you shall not die. Nevertheless, because by this deed you have utterly scorned the LORD, the child who is born to you shall die."

2 Samuel 12:9-14

Have mercy on me, O God, according to your steadfast love; according to your abundant mercy blot out my transgressions. Wash me thoroughly from my iniquity, and cleanse me from my sin!

Psalms 51:1-2

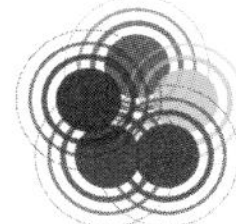

Mercy

God's Mercy toward David 3

As 2 Samuel 11 tells us, spring was the time when kings went out to battle. When King David should have been leading his men into battle, he was instead wandering into temptation. According to the law given to Moses by God—the law that David was accountable to—if a man commits adultery, he should be put to death (Lev. 20:10). David was aware of this consequence, so he sought to cover up his adultery by bringing Uriah, Bathsheba's husband, home from battle so Uriah would seem to be the one who had fathered the child that Bathsheba now carried. Uriah was an honorable man, and he refused to enjoy an intimate night with his wife while his fellow soldiers were off at battle. When David found out that Uriah had not even gone home to Bathsheba, David escalated the atrocity of his sin by sending him back to battle with a sealed note to the commander of the army that would ensure Uriah's death. David was responsible for the murder of Uriah, and the law of Moses was also clear that whoever takes a human life should also be put to death (Lev. 24:17). David's sins that year were worthy of two death sentences.

Considering David's intimate relationship with God, it is surprising he would think that these sins would escape God's notice. Nothing escapes His notice, and "the thing that David had done displeased the Lord." The Lord sent the prophet Nathan to confront David with a story that changed just enough details to help David see the injustice without seeing himself cast as the offender (2 Sam. 12:1-6). In fact, David pronounced a death sentence on the offender in Nathan's story, not realizing that he was judging his own sin. Through Nathan, God rebuked David's sin and promised very specific and severe consequences for David. David was convicted in his heart and confessed his sin. King David submitted to God and found forgiveness. The Lord promised that David would not die as a consequence for his sin, despite what God Himself had established as law *and* what David had judged himself worthy of. This was God's mercy in action.

Before David's sin with Bathsheba, God had made a covenant with him (2 Sam. 7). God promised to raise David's offspring as an heir to his kingdom. His steadfast love would not depart from David's offspring, and David's house, kingdom, and throne would be established forever. God had seen and known David's heart before he was anointed king (1 Sam. 16:7). God's mercy and His faithfulness to this covenant led Him to receive David's confession and refine his heart. David was so overwhelmed by God's mercy that he wrote Psalm 51 as a response to God's abundant mercy in this specific instance. Though the child conceived by their adultery would die, another son born to David and Bathsheba would be the promised offspring that would inherit David's throne. God's compassion for David's need for redemption moved Him to take a relationship that originated in adultery and remake it into the relationship that fulfilled the covenant, first with the birth of Solomon and ultimately by placing Bathsheba—"the wife of Uriah" — in the Matthew 1 genealogy of Jesus. Jesus is then the final fulfillment of the promise that an heir of David would reign forever.

Action Step: We tend to see the sins of others as worthy of judgment while we count on mercy for our own sins. Nathan wisely used this tendency in his story that convicted David of his sin. Read Psalm 51 and observe the balance struck by David between his cry for mercy from God and the weight of the burden of his sin and his need for cleansing. Are your own prayers of confession as humble as this one, recognizing your own unworthiness and God's great mercy and love as providing the only effective cleansing from sin?

The Lord is not slow to fulfill his promise as some count slowness, but is patient toward you, not wishing that any should perish, but that all should reach repentance.

2 Peter 3:9

"Seek the LORD while he may be found; call upon him while he is near; let the wicked forsake his way, and the unrighteous man his thoughts; let him return to the LORD, that he may have compassion on him, and to our God, for he will abundantly pardon."

Isaiah 55:6-7

"Say to them, As I live, declares the Lord GOD, I have no pleasure in the death of the wicked, but that the wicked turn from his way and live; turn back, turn back from your evil ways, for why will you die, O house of Israel?"

Ezekiel 33:11

Out of the depths I cry to you, O LORD! O Lord, hear my voice! Let your ears be attentive to the voice of my pleas for mercy! If you, O LORD, should mark iniquities, O Lord, who could stand? But with you there is forgiveness, that you may be feared.

Psalms 130:1-4

"Two men went up into the temple to pray, one a Pharisee and the other a tax collector. The Pharisee, standing by himself, prayed thus: 'God, I thank you that I am not like other men, extortioners, unjust, adulterers, or even like this tax collector. I fast twice a week; I give tithes of all that I get.' But the tax collector, standing far off, would not even lift up his eyes to heaven, but beat his breast, saying, 'God, be merciful to me, a sinner!' I tell you, this man went down to his house justified, rather than the other. For everyone who exalts himself will be humbled, but the one who humbles himself will be exalted."

Luke 18:10-14

The saying is trustworthy and deserving of full acceptance, that Christ Jesus came into the world to save sinners, of whom I am the foremost. But I received mercy for this reason, that in me, as the foremost, Jesus Christ might display his perfect patience as an example to those who were to believe in him for eternal life.

1 Timothy 1:15-16

Or do you presume on the riches of his kindness and forbearance and patience, not knowing that God's kindness is meant to lead you to repentance? But because of your hard and impenitent heart you are storing up wrath for yourself on the day of wrath when God's righteous judgment will be revealed.

Romans 2:4-5

Those whom I love, I reprove and discipline, so be zealous and repent.

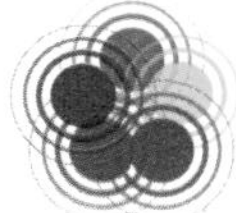

Mercy

Forgiveness Is Tied to God's Mercy 4

God extends mercy to His entire creation. But mercy only manifests as forgiveness toward people who place their faith in the one true God. The final intended result of His mercy and patience, for those who respond to it, is forgiveness of sins and restoration of relationship with Him. Mercy opens the door to walk into forgiveness.

The door itself—the thing that must be put into action to walk into forgiveness—is the repentance of coming to faith in Jesus Christ. The reason the Lord is patient toward us is that He is waiting for the repentance of all those that He has called. Simply put, repentance is turning to the Lord. The wicked and unrighteous may return to the Lord, and He will "abundantly pardon." God has "no pleasure in the death of the wicked." He desires that "the wicked turn from his way and live." But repentance is more than just a change of direction from walking away from God to walking toward Him. Repentance is a change of heart. Repentance includes being grieved over our sin. It is a humble cry to God, recognizing that He is the only rescue and our only hope. It is the cry of the psalmist, "Out of the depths I cry to you, O LORD! O Lord, hear my voice! Let your ears be attentive to the voice of my pleas for mercy!" It is the cry of the tax collector who beat his breast and felt unworthy to lift his eyes to heaven: "God, be merciful to me, a sinner!" And it is confidence that the finished work of Jesus Christ is enough to save us from our sins. The repentance that leads to forgiveness includes the recognition that Christ Jesus came into the world to save sinners and that those who believe in Him have eternal life. This repentance is a gift that flows out of God's mercy and grace (Acts 11:18; 2 Tim. 2:25).

Paul touched on repentance in Romans 2 within the context of a larger discussion on God's judgment. In chapter 1, Paul wrote about the wrath of God being revealed for the unrighteous. But in chapter 2, he pointed to the Jews in his audience who would judge others for their sins while they practice the very same things. The listeners were assuming that God's patience with their sin suggested that He was not going to judge them at all. However, Paul warned that God's patience with them was a kindness, allowing them time to repent of their sin by grieving and turning from it. Some have quoted Romans 2:4 to suggest that God always leads His people to repentance in a kind way. When the entire passage and all of Scripture are taken as context, it is clear that Paul is teaching that God's patience *is* a kindness. God may gently lead some to repentance, but He also may reprove and discipline people to lead them to repentance. Yet even hard circumstances are a kindness when they bring about repentance that activates God's forgiveness. When a sinner repents and turns to God in faith, His wrath and judgment are no longer stored up, and mercy leads to forgiveness.

Action Step: Much of this discussion on repentance is about the initial repentance of trusting Christ for salvation from sin. However, the believer is responsible for ongoing repentance of daily sin. Devote some time to prayer today to ask God to reveal any unconfessed sin in your life. Keep in mind that sin is not just wrong actions, but also wrong beliefs or motives. Every wrong action that we take can be traced to a wrong belief that we have about God or the gospel. There may even be times when we need to repent of doing the *right* thing for the *wrong* reason. As the Holy Spirit reveals sin, pray that He will guide you to a genuine repentance that includes confession, grief, and a change of heart to follow God. End your prayer with praise and worship to God for His mercy that allowed you time to repent of this sin.

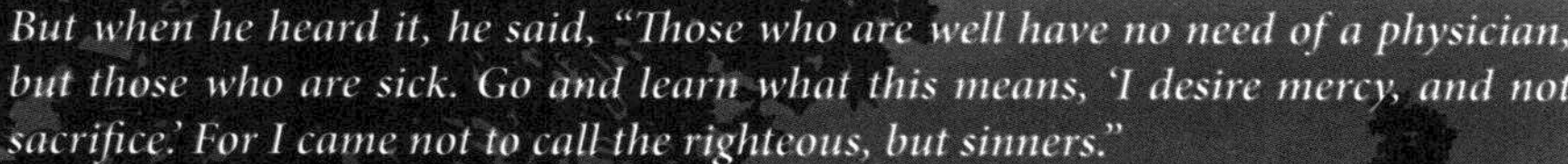

But when he heard it, he said, "Those who are well have no need of a physician, but those who are sick. Go and learn what this means, 'I desire mercy, and not sacrifice.' For I came not to call the righteous, but sinners."

Matthew 9:12-13

And Jesus went throughout all the cities and villages, teaching in their synagogues and proclaiming the gospel of the kingdom and healing every disease and every affliction. When he saw the crowds, he had compassion for them, because they were harassed and helpless, like sheep without a shepherd.

Matthew 9:35-36

Then Jesus called his disciples to him and said, "I have compassion on the crowd because they have been with me now three days and have nothing to eat. And I am unwilling to send them away hungry, lest they faint on the way."... And directing the crowd to sit down on the ground, he took the seven loaves and the fish, and having given thanks he broke them and gave them to the disciples, and the disciples gave them to the crowds. And they all ate and were satisfied. And they took up seven baskets full of the broken pieces left over.

Matthew 15:32, 35-37

And behold, there were two blind men sitting by the roadside, and when they heard that Jesus was passing by, they cried out, "Lord, have mercy on us, Son of David!" The crowd rebuked them, telling them to be silent, but they cried out all the more, "Lord, have mercy on us, Son of David!" And stopping, Jesus called them and said, "What do you want me to do for you?" They said to him, "Lord, let our eyes be opened." And Jesus in pity touched their eyes, and immediately they recovered their sight and followed him.

Matthew 20:30-34

For we ourselves were once foolish, disobedient, led astray, slaves to various passions and pleasures, passing our days in malice and envy, hated by others and hating one another. But when the goodness and loving kindness of God our Savior appeared, he saved us, not because of works done by us in righteousness, but according to his own mercy, by the washing of regeneration and renewal of the Holy Spirit,

Titus 3:3-5

Blessed be the God and Father of our Lord Jesus Christ! According to his great mercy, he has caused us to be born again to a living hope through the resurrection of Jesus Christ from the dead, to an inheritance that is imperishable, undefiled, and unfading, kept in heaven for you,

1 Peter 1:3-4

Mercy

Jesus and Mercy

5

Jesus Christ is the perfect living example of God's mercy. If we want to know what God's mercy looks like in human form, all we need to do is look at the gospel accounts of Jesus. Mercy was included in Jesus' own description of His reason for coming. After calling Matthew the tax collector to follow Him, Jesus gathered with tax collectors and sinners for a meal. The Pharisees wondered why a supposedly godly man would be in the company of such outcasts. When Jesus heard this, He responded, "Those who are well have no need of a physician, but those who are sick. Go and learn what this means, 'I desire mercy, and not sacrifice.' For I came not to call the righteous, but sinners" (Matt. 9:12-13). Jesus came to displace outward religious performances, such as sacrifices, and to demonstrate instead perfect mercy and compassion for sinners who needed a Savior.

Jesus showed compassion toward those who had physical needs such as healing and relieving them from hunger. As the Great Physician, He healed their diseases. As the Creator of all things, He miraculously fed thousands of hungry people with seven loaves of bread and a few small fish. Jesus also showed compassion toward those who were harassed and helpless. He brought the gospel of the kingdom to lost sheep without a shepherd. Time after time, Scripture records people crying out to Jesus for mercy and Jesus responding with pity and compassion. As the Son of God with infinite resources, He offered much to those who had great need.

The Son of God became man and affirmed the very real physical needs and suffering of this world. He had compassion for the helpless and met their needs with perfect mercy. But He also saw the spiritual needs of His people. He saw that we were slaves to sin and various passions. He saw our foolishness and disobedience and hate. And He came to save us from all of that. Not because we had done anything to deserve being saved, but according to His own mercy—His compassion for those who were in need of salvation—He came. By the great mercy of God, we have access to the regeneration of the Holy Spirit when we are born again by trusting in the resurrection of Jesus Christ for salvation from our sin. There has never been a greater human need than the need for rescue from our own sinful nature. So there has never been a greater act of mercy than the Father sending the Son for our redemption.

Action Step: How can you reflect the mercy that Jesus Christ has shown to you? While God can do great things, the miracles of Jesus are not daily at our disposal. However, we do not have to work miracles to meet the needs of those around us. Jesus also ate with outcasts and sinners. One group that is often avoided as outcasts today, even by those in the church, are prisoners. Yet Scripture calls us to remember those who are in prison as if we were there with them (Heb. 13:3). In Matthew 25, when Jesus separated the sheep from the goats, one of the indicators He used for those who were blessed by the Father was, "I was in prison and you came to me." Search prison ministry on the internet or make some phone calls to explore what you might be able to do to show mercy to those who are in prison. Remember that the mercy that God gives is always undeserved.

"Be merciful, even as your Father is merciful."

Luke 6:36

"Blessed are the merciful, for they shall receive mercy."

Matthew 5:7

"Therefore the kingdom of heaven may be compared to a king who wished to settle accounts with his servants. When he began to settle, one was brought to him who owed him ten thousand talents. And since he could not pay, his master ordered him to be sold, with his wife and children and all that he had, and payment to be made. So the servant fell on his knees, imploring him, 'Have patience with me, and I will pay you everything.' And out of pity for him, the master of that servant released him and forgave him the debt. But when that same servant went out, he found one of his fellow servants who owed him a hundred denarii, and seizing him, he began to choke him, saying, 'Pay what you owe.' So his fellow servant fell down and pleaded with him, 'Have patience with me, and I will pay you.' He refused and went and put him in prison until he should pay the debt. When his fellow servants saw what had taken place, they were greatly distressed, and they went and reported to their master all that had taken place. Then his master summoned him and said to him, 'You wicked servant! I forgave you all that debt because you pleaded with me. And should not you have had mercy on your fellow servant, as I had mercy on you?' And in anger his master delivered him to the jailers, until he should pay all his debt. So also my heavenly Father will do to every one of you, if you do not forgive your brother from your heart."

Matthew 18:23-35

Know this, my beloved brothers: let every person be quick to hear, slow to speak, slow to anger; for the anger of man does not produce the righteousness of God.

James 1:19-20

"Then the King will say to those on his right, 'Come, you who are blessed by my Father, inherit the kingdom prepared for you from the foundation of the world. For I was hungry and you gave me food, I was thirsty and you gave me drink, I was a stranger and you welcomed me, I was naked and you clothed me, I was sick and you visited me, I was in prison and you came to me.' Then the righteous will answer him, saying, 'Lord, when did we see you hungry and feed you, or thirsty and give you drink? And when did we see you a stranger and welcome you, or naked and clothe you? And when did we see you sick or in prison and visit you?' And the King will answer them, 'Truly, I say to you, as you did it to one of the least of these my brothers, you did it to me.'"

Matthew 25:34-40

Mercy

Mercy Among Us

6

All mercy has its source in God. His own nature overflows with mercy, and it is in Him that we obtain mercy. To the extent that He is our Father, we are responsible for reflecting that mercy. Because believers have been adopted into the family of God, we bear the family likeness. The Holy Spirit empowers us to look like Jesus. Therefore, we should be merciful, even as our Father is merciful.

Matthew 5-7 records Jesus' Sermon on the Mount, a guide for living life in the kingdom of God. The sermon opens with the Beatitudes, simple statements beginning with "Blessed are..." which describe the ideal follower of Jesus Christ and the spiritual rewards that result from their faithfulness. In one of these statements, Jesus said, "Blessed are the merciful, for they shall receive mercy" (Matt. 5:7). When we show mercy to others, we receive mercy from God. But remember that we can only give mercy because He has first shown us mercy. Mercy should be the natural outgrowth of a heart that has been moved by the mercy of God.

Jesus illustrates this with a parable in Matthew 18. A servant could not possibly repay a loan to his master. The debt was too great. The master ordered the servant and his family to be sold to pay off the debt. The servant begged for mercy. The master had pity and forgave the debt. An incredible burden had been lifted! This servant should have been overwhelmed with gratitude for the mercy shown to him! But he apparently was not. Another servant owed him a much smaller debt, and payment was demanded. The second servant pleaded for mercy and time to repay the debt. The first servant refused to show mercy and had his fellow servant thrown into prison. Not surprisingly, the master heard about this and was so angry that he had the first servant, whom he had previously forgiven, now thrown into prison, saying, "Should not you have had mercy on your fellow servant, as I had mercy on you?" Had the servant been deeply affected by the mercy shown by his master, he would have been moved to mercy for his fellow servant. Jesus warns that the full punishment for our sin is what we will face from our Father in heaven if we do not forgive our brother from the heart and thus demonstrate that we have been transformed by God's mercy. We are to show the same kind of patience and slowness to anger that the Father shows to us instead of hurrying to punish those who have hurt us.

Jesus' account of the Final Judgment in Matthew 25 gives some guidance as to others on whom our mercy should be focused. He lists the hungry, the thirsty, the stranger, the naked, the sick, and the prisoner. All of these people are disadvantaged outcasts—the "least of these." Our mercy is to be directed to those who are most in need of mercy. Showing mercy to strangers and sick people and poor people and prisoners can be uncomfortable. It puts us close to people that we might not otherwise choose to spend time with. But this is the kind of mercy that is most like the mercy that Jesus has shown to us. This is the kind of mercy that brings the kingdom of God to earth and demonstrates that we have been changed in our hearts by the mercy of God. Let us all be so moved by God's mercy that our hearts are positioned to show forgiveness and compassion to others in need.

Action Step: Consider a time recently when you have been wronged. What was your reaction? Did you cry for the justice that you felt you deserved? Or were you slow to anger, extending patience and mercy to the offender? Which attitude most represents God's disposition toward you?

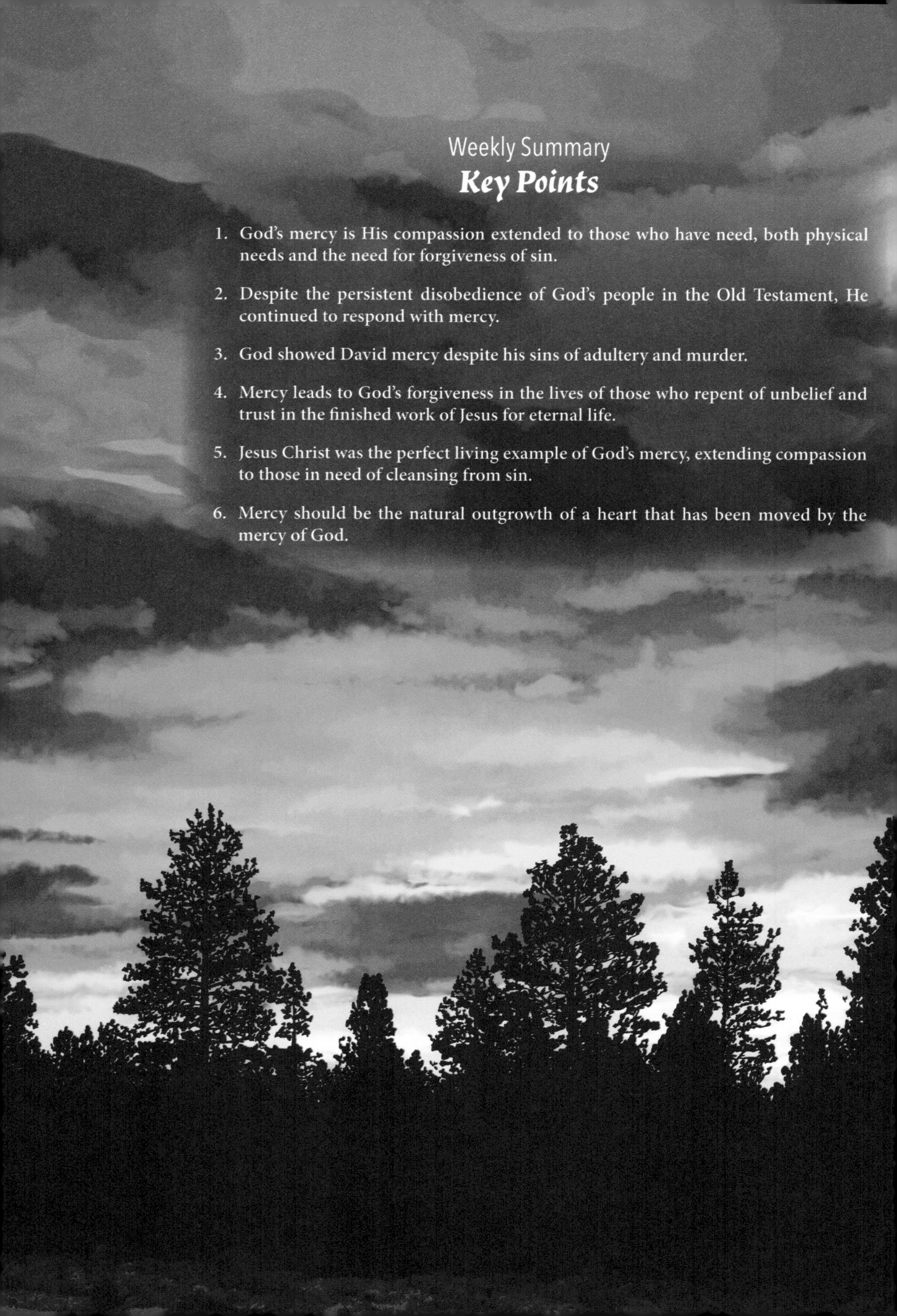

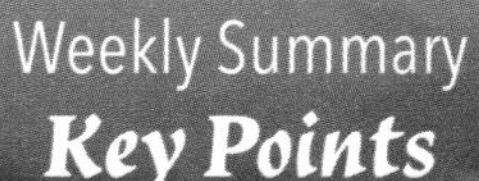

Weekly Summary
Key Points

1. God's mercy is His compassion extended to those who have need, both physical needs and the need for forgiveness of sin.

2. Despite the persistent disobedience of God's people in the Old Testament, He continued to respond with mercy.

3. God showed David mercy despite his sins of adultery and murder.

4. Mercy leads to God's forgiveness in the lives of those who repent of unbelief and trust in the finished work of Jesus for eternal life.

5. Jesus Christ was the perfect living example of God's mercy, extending compassion to those in need of cleansing from sin.

6. Mercy should be the natural outgrowth of a heart that has been moved by the mercy of God.

Mercy

Action Steps

Go back through the action steps and complete any that you have not yet completed or repeat one that was meaningful:

1. The giver must recognize the need in order for the gift to properly be called mercy, but the recipient must also recognize their own need to receive the gift and properly appreciate the mercy. Do you appreciate your own need for mercy from God? In other words, do you have a proper view of the presence of sin in your life? Pray that God will help you understand His mercy and your need for it.

2. Print out a copy of Nehemiah 9. Read the entire chapter. Using highlighters, mark all of the verses that tell of God's mercy with one color and all of the verses that tell of the people's failures with another color. You might even use a third color to highlight the verses that describe God's discipline used to correct the people. Note the number of times God's mercy covers His people. Every time the people rebelled, God responded with mercy. As the author of Lamentations proclaims, His "mercies never come to an end; they are new every morning." As you begin each day this week, thank God for His new mercy with every sunrise.

3. We tend to see the sins of others as worthy of judgment while we count on mercy for our own sins. Nathan wisely used this tendency in his story that convicted David of his sin. Read Psalm 51 and observe the balance struck by David between his cry for mercy from God and the weight of the burden of his sin and his need for cleansing. Are your own prayers of confession as humble as this one, recognizing your own unworthiness and God's great mercy and love as providing the only effective cleansing from sin?

4. Devote some time to prayer today to ask God to reveal any unconfessed sin in your life. Keep in mind that sin is not just wrong actions, but also wrong beliefs or motives. Every wrong action that we take can be traced to a wrong belief that we have about God or the gospel. There may even be times when we need to repent of doing the right thing for the wrong reason. As the Holy Spirit reveals sin, pray that He will guide you to a genuine repentance that includes confession, grief, and a change of heart to follow God. End your prayer with praise and worship to God for His mercy that allowed you time to repent of this sin.

5. How can you reflect the mercy that Jesus Christ has shown to you? We do not have to work miracles to meet the needs of those around us. Jesus also ate with outcasts and sinners. One group that is often avoided as outcasts today, even by those in the church, are prisoners. Yet Scripture calls us to remember those who are in prison as if we were there with them (Heb. 13:3). In Matthew 25, when Jesus separated the sheep from the goats, one of the indicators He used for those who were blessed by the Father was, "I was in prison and you came to me." Search prison ministry on the internet or make some phone calls to explore what you might be able to do to show mercy to those who are in prison. Remember that the mercy that God gives is always undeserved.

6. Consider a time recently when you have been wronged. What was your reaction? Did you cry for the justice that you felt you deserved? Or were you slow to anger, extending patience and mercy to the offender? Which attitude most represents

WEEK 16
Justice

In Genesis, we see that human beings were made "in the image of God." This means to say that humans were created to be God's representatives on earth and carry out His plan, abiding by the morals and concepts of justice that God himself abides by. According to the Biblical justice that God sets forth, all humans are equal, all humans are created in His image, and all humans deserve to be treated with fairness and justice.

Of course, as we all know, human beings do not always behave this way. Instead, even in the earliest parts of the Bible, we see humans rejecting God's principles of Biblical justice and instead begin defining good and evil for themselves in a way that gives them advantages over others. The strong take advantage of the vulnerable, both at an individual level and at a societal level. Throughout all of this, the justice that God intended for people to exhibit is nowhere to be found.

Out of this mess, though, God raises up a man named Abraham and positions him to start a new line of people with his family—one that is ruled by both righteousness and justice. So what does God mean when he tells Abraham and his people to live their lives with righteousness and justice? In the Bible, righteousness refers to a state of moral good in which you treat those around you with decency and fairness, recognizing that all of them are made in the image of God just like you.

While justice can be used to talk about retributive justice in which a person is punished for their wrongdoings, most of the time the Bible uses the word justice to refer to restorative justice, in which those who are unrightfully hurt or wronged are restored and given back what was taken from them. Taken this way, the combination of righteousness and justice that God dictates means a selfless way of life in which people do everything they can to ensure that others are treated well and injustices are fixed.

Tim Mackie and Jon Collins, *"Justice," The Bible Project* (website)

Clouds and thick darkness are all around him; righteousness and justice are the foundation of his throne.

Psalms 97:2

"but let him who boasts boast in this, that he understands and knows me, that I am the Lord who practices steadfast love, justice, and righteousness in the earth. For in these things I delight, declares the Lord."

Jeremiah 9:24

The King in his might loves justice. You have established equity; you have executed justice and righteousness in Jacob.

Psalms 99:4

"The Rock, his work is perfect, for all his ways are justice. A God of faithfulness and without iniquity, just and upright is he."

Deuteronomy 32:4

He loves righteousness and justice; the earth is full of the steadfast love of the Lord.

Psalms 33:5

Justice

Justice and Righteousness United in God 1

"The justice of God is what waits for those who do not pursue the righteousness of God." This is a summary of a simple understanding of justice and righteousness. But a careful study of Scripture reveals a relationship between justice and righteousness that is much more complex than that simple statement. In fact, to New Testament Greek writers, justice and righteousness are the same exact word.

The Greek word *dikaios* is an adjective that is translated in English Bibles as either *just* or *righteous*. The noun form *dikaiosune*, depending on the Bible version, is translated as either *justice* (*justification*) or *righteousness*. *Dikaioo*, the verb form, translates to *justify* or *declare righteous*.

These three different forms of this Greek word are seen in Romans 3:26: "It was to show his **righteousness** [*dikaiosune*] at the present time, so that he might be **just** [*dikaios*] and the **justifier** [*dikaioo*] of the one who has faith in Jesus" (ESV). But consider two other English translations:

"God presented him to demonstrate his **righteousness** at the present time, so that he would be **righteous** and **declare righteous** the one who has faith in Jesus." (CSB)

"God did this to demonstrate his **righteousness**, for he himself is **fair and just**, and he **makes sinners right** in his sight when they believe in Jesus." (NLT)

A comparison of these translations—"God is just," "God is righteous," and "God is fair and just"—reveals all are equivalent statements. Justice and righteousness are essentially the same attribute of God. Even in the Hebrew language of the Old Testament, the word *tsedeq* can be translated as justice or righteousness. This is further complicated by the Hebrew word *mishpat*, which is also translated as justice and is not easily distinguished from *tsedeq*. In fact, the two Hebrew words are quite often used in the same phrase in the Old Testament, especially when describing God. He delights in justice and righteousness. In English, we tend to favor the word justice when talking about the severe consequences of sin and the word righteousness when describing our right behavior and standing before God. But it is important to realize that, when we are talking about the perfect character of God, His justice and righteousness are one and the same. Being righteous, He will administer perfect justice to every person in His timing. As the standard for justice in all of creation, He is righteous in all that He does.

Action Step: The Psalms declare that "righteousness (*tsedeq*) and justice (*mishpat*) are the foundation of his throne." We can trust in His sovereign authority and rule because everything He does is based in His righteousness and justice. Spend some time in prayer today praising God that all of His ways are based in steadfast love, justice, and righteousness.

Father of the fatherless and protector of widows is God in his holy habitation. God settles the solitary in a home; he leads out the prisoners to prosperity, but the rebellious dwell in a parched land.

Psalms 68:5-6

...who executes justice for the oppressed, who gives food to the hungry. The LORD sets the prisoners free; the LORD opens the eyes of the blind. The LORD lifts up those who are bowed down; the LORD loves the righteous. The LORD watches over the sojourners; he upholds the widow and the fatherless, but the way of the wicked he brings to ruin.

Psalms 146:7-9

"Is not this the fast that I choose: to loose the bonds of wickedness, to undo the straps of the yoke, to let the oppressed go free, and to break every yoke?"

Isaiah 58:6

Therefore thus says the Lord GOD, "Behold, I am the one who has laid as a foundation in Zion, a stone, a tested stone, a precious cornerstone, of a sure foundation: 'Whoever believes will not be in haste.' And I will make justice the line, and righteousness the plumb line; and hail will sweep away the refuge of lies, and waters will overwhelm the shelter."

Isaiah 28:16-17

Justice

Biblical Justice

2

Psalm 68 is a song of praise to God. The people of Israel sang it to praise God for His care and protection. Before detailing the many ways that God has cared for all of Israel, the psalm recognizes the special care that He has for the most needy members of their community. He is praised for His special care for the fatherless, widows, those who are alone, and prisoners. Psalm 146 holds a similar list of those the Lord watches over, and it summarizes this care as executing justice for the oppressed. The Lord works righteousness and justice for all, but especially for those who are disadvantaged in society.

In Isaiah 58, the people asked God for righteous judgments and questioned why He did not recognize their fasts. God criticized their fasting, which was an outward show, while they continued to oppress others. This false religion was not acceptable to God. Instead, He described the justice that He wanted to see from His people—freeing people from oppression and injustice.

There is the justice presented in Scripture in which the wicked are held accountable for their sin and disobedience. But the overarching account of justice in Scripture is the story of God's work in restoring justice in this broken world by offering all people a right relationship with Him. Every human being is created in His image for a relationship with Him. His justice includes a standard by which all people have access to Him and opportunities to be valuable members of the people of God. Where there is inequity, equity should be restored so that all members of society can be His image-bearers and contribute to the community of His people. In God's system of justice, both the oppressor and the oppressed become equal contributing members of the community. Wrongs are righted, and the less privileged are lifted to places of value. Justice becomes a relational process when men and women treat all those around them with the value that they inherently have as people made in the image of God. A person who lives a life that consistently delivers justice to victims of injustice is considered righteous.

In Isaiah 28, the Lord described Himself as a builder laying a foundation. The tools at His disposal that keep the foundation straight and true are righteousness and justice. In the New Testament, both Paul and Peter cite this verse when they name the cornerstone of this foundation as Jesus. Righteousness and justice are inherent in the Father and in His Son. As God continues to build His kingdom, it will remain true to the righteousness and justice of the cornerstone, Jesus Christ.

Action Step: Social justice is a popular theme in today's culture. God is definitely concerned with justice in society, but the heart of Biblical justice is recognizing God's image in all people. If the goal of social justice is to elevate the oppressed above the oppressor, it is not Biblical justice. If the goal of criminal justice is to segregate all offenders into a permanent lower class that is stripped of social rights, it is not Biblical justice. Evaluate your own efforts toward social justice. As you lift victims of injustice, do you find yourself diminishing the image of God in another group of people?

"When you father children and children's children, and have grown old in the land, if you act corruptly by making a carved image in the form of anything, and by doing what is evil in the sight of the LORD your God, so as to provoke him to anger, I call heaven and earth to witness against you today, that you will soon utterly perish from the land that you are going over the Jordan to possess. You will not live long in it, but will be utterly destroyed. And the Lord will scatter you among the peoples, and you will be left few in number among the nations where the LORD will drive you. And there you will serve gods of wood and stone, the work of human hands, that neither see, nor hear, nor eat, nor smell. But from there you will seek the LORD your God and you will find him, if you search after him with all your heart and with all your soul. When you are in tribulation, and all these things come upon you in the latter days, you will return to the LORD your God and obey his voice. For the LORD your God is a merciful God. He will not leave you or destroy you or forget the covenant with your fathers that he swore to them."

Deuteronomy 4:25-31

"Yet you have been righteous in all that has come upon us, for you have dealt faithfully and we have acted wickedly."

Nehemiah 9:33

"Now therefore the sword shall never depart from your house, because you have despised me and have taken the wife of Uriah the Hittite to be your wife.' Thus says the LORD, 'Behold, I will raise up evil against you out of your own house. And I will take your wives before your eyes and give them to your neighbor, and he shall lie with your wives in the sight of this sun. For you did it secretly, but I will do this thing before all Israel and before the sun.'" David said to Nathan, "I have sinned against the LORD." And Nathan said to David, "The LORD also has put away your sin; you shall not die. Nevertheless, because by this deed you have utterly scorned the LORD, the child who is born to you shall die."

2 Samuel 12:10-14

The LORD is merciful and gracious, slow to anger and abounding in steadfast love. He will not always chide, nor will he keep his anger forever. He does not deal with us according to our sins, nor repay us according to our iniquities. For as high as the heavens are above the earth, so great is his steadfast love toward those who fear him; as far as the east is from the west, so far does he remove our transgressions from us. As a father shows compassion to his children, so the LORD shows compassion to those who fear him.

Psalms 103:8-13

Justice

Justice for Israel and David

3

"The justice of God is what waits for those who do not pursue the righteousness of God." As explained on Day 1, this is an over-simplified statement. Yet it is also a true statement. Those who continue to choose disobedience will at some point face God's justice. For the people of God, this might take the form of discipline. If God ignored all of the sin in this world, He would not be just. What does it look like in the Bible when God punishes sin in His people?

When God led the nation of Israel out of Egypt, through the Red Sea, and toward the new land that He had promised them, He made a covenant with them through Moses. He outlined what it would look like to worship Him and how to live in community with one another. He gave them laws, including the Ten Commandments. The first two commandments were to have no other gods before Him and not to worship carved images. Inheritance of the land that God had promised in the covenant that He made with Israel was conditional upon their obedience to His commands. In Deuteronomy 4, the people of Israel were standing on the threshold of their new land when Moses reminded them that there would be consequences for ignoring the Lord's commands. God specifically promised the people that if they worshiped carved images, they would be scattered from the land. God guided them into their land, and He lovingly led and cared for them for centuries there. Yet the people of Israel were repeatedly drawn to foreign gods and worshiped carved images. Some eight hundred years after the time of Moses, God fulfilled the promised discipline. The people of Israel were exiled from their land. When the people did not pursue Him, they faced the just consequences of the righteous God. But do not miss the rest of God's promise in Deuteronomy 4. When the people returned to God and obeyed His voice, He acted out of mercy and remembered His covenant. Israel returned to their land when they sought the Lord. In the book of Nehemiah, as the people were returning to Israel from this period of exile, they were able to recognize that God had been righteous in punishing His people. They acted wickedly, and He acted faithfully according to His promises, including painful consequences for their actions.

In our study on mercy, we read the story of David and Bathsheba. God did not punish David with the death sentence that his sin deserved. Although God extended mercy to David in that regard, there were just consequences for David's sin. Nathan confronted David with the Lord's sentence in 2 Samuel 12—the sword would never depart from David's house, David's wives would be taken from him before all of Israel, and the son born from David's sin with Bathsheba would die. In later years, David's son, Absalom, murdered his brother, Amnon. Absalom then rebelled against David, chased David from Jerusalem, and took the wives that David left behind. Eventually, Absalom was killed in a battle with David's men. God's mercy allowed David to continue to live and rule in Israel, but God's righteousness brought painful discipline for David's disobedience. Despite these consequences, David wrote Psalm 103, in which he focused on praise to God for His mercy and love. Those who disobey the Lord face just consequences, but when they return to Him, He meets them with mercy and love.

Action Step: The book of Hebrews includes teaching on discipline for believers who struggle against sin. Read Hebrews 12:3-11. The author teaches that God disciplines believers the same way that a father disciplines his sons—for their good. The discipline may be painful, but the result is "the peaceful fruit of righteousness to those who have been trained by it." When God brings discipline as a form of justice, it yields righteousness in people of faith. How have you experienced this discipline from God in your life?

But now the righteousness of God has been manifested apart from the law, although the Law and the Prophets bear witness to it—the righteousness of God through faith in Jesus Christ for all who believe. For there is no distinction: for all have sinned and fall short of the glory of God, and are justified by his grace as a gift, through the redemption that is in Christ Jesus, whom God put forward as a propitiation by his blood, to be received by faith. This was to show God's righteousness, because in his divine forbearance he had passed over former sins. It was to show his righteousness at the present time, so that he might be just and the justifier of the one who has faith in Jesus.

Romans 3:21-26

Therefore, as one trespass led to condemnation for all men, so one act of righteousness leads to justification and life for all men. For as by the one man's disobedience the many were made sinners, so by the one man's obedience the many will be made righteous.

Romans 5:18-19

For our sake he made him to be sin who knew no sin, so that in him we might become the righteousness of God.

2 Corinthians 5:21

He himself bore our sins in his body on the tree, that we might die to sin and live to righteousness. By his wounds you have been healed.

1 Peter 2:24

Behold my servant, whom I uphold, my chosen, in whom my soul delights; I have put my Spirit upon him; he will bring forth justice to the nations. He will not cry aloud or lift up his voice, or make it heard in the street; a bruised reed he will not break, and a faintly burning wick he will not quench; he will faithfully bring forth justice. He will not grow faint or be discouraged till he has established justice in the earth; and the coastlands wait for his law.

Isaiah 42:1-4

"In his days Judah will be saved, and Israel will dwell securely. And this is the name by which he will be called: 'The Lord is our righteousness.'"

Jeremiah 23:6

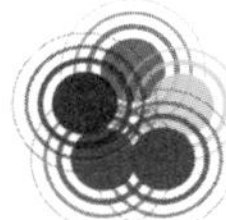

Justice

Justification by Faith 4

If God's perfect justice demands that sin deserves just punishment, how can He hand out mercy so easily to sinners who do not deserve it? How is it just on God's part that there are sinners who seem to have escaped any consequence for their offenses? Of course, the answers lie partly in our previous study on God's patience and mercy. But is God's mercy handed out arbitrarily for just certain people or certain sins? As previously stated, justice includes God's work in restoring this broken world by offering all people a right relationship with Him and equal standing as those who are all created in His image. How can He restore people when every sin demands just punishment? Who bears the punishment if a sinner gets to walk away with complete forgiveness? How is it just that a murderer does not die for his crime? On the other hand, if God's just punishment is for those who do not pursue the righteousness of God, then how do we pursue the righteousness of God?

The book of Romans includes the most complete explanation of the gospel of Jesus Christ in all of the Bible. Simply put, the Law shows us that we are all sinners who cannot be put right with God by our own behavior. Jesus Christ perfectly obeyed the Law in His life, and His act of obedience in dying on the cross bore the punishment for our sin. The righteousness of *God Himself* is freely given to those who have faith in Jesus Christ. The perfect obedience of Jesus Christ is credited as righteousness to people of faith. God's righteousness was shown and His justice verified when Jesus bore the punishment for our sins. Not only was it demonstrated that God is just in that there was punishment for sin, but it was shown that He is the One who justifies (declares righteous) those who have faith in Jesus. We pursue the righteousness of God by placing faith in Jesus Christ. The righteousness of God in the book of Romans refers to both our right position before God credited to us through faith, as well as the righteous moral character of God that is exhibited in ever-increasing measure in the life of believers living under the direction of the Holy Spirit.

Paul goes on to explain that this transaction even applied to people of faith in the time prior to Jesus—"in his divine forbearance he had passed over former sins." The sins of every person who had faith in God in Old Testament times were passed over in anticipation of the redemption that is achieved in Jesus Christ. This was God's plan all along, as conveyed through the prophets Isaiah and Jeremiah. Isaiah wrote of the Messiah who would "faithfully bring forth justice," including particular care for the weak ("bruised reed" and "faintly burning wick"). And Jeremiah spoke of the One who would save Judah and Israel as being called "The Lord is our righteousness." Jesus Christ brings justice to all of the nations when He conveys His righteousness to people all over the world who have faith in Him. At the end of time, justice will be perfectly established on earth under His reign, with all of His people being treated with perfect equity.

Action Step: The cross of Jesus Christ is where God's love and justice are seen to be in perfect harmony. Paul states in Romans 3 that God's righteousness is for all who believe. No matter how selfish or hurtful a person's past deeds are, if they come to faith in Christ, they receive the righteousness of God. If you struggle with guilt over past sins, know that you are righteous before God because of Jesus Christ. If another person has hurt you deeply with their sin and then repented of that sin and placed faith in Jesus, they are also clothed in Christ's righteousness. Is there anyone in your life, including yourself, whom you are actively opposing as being declared righteous before God?

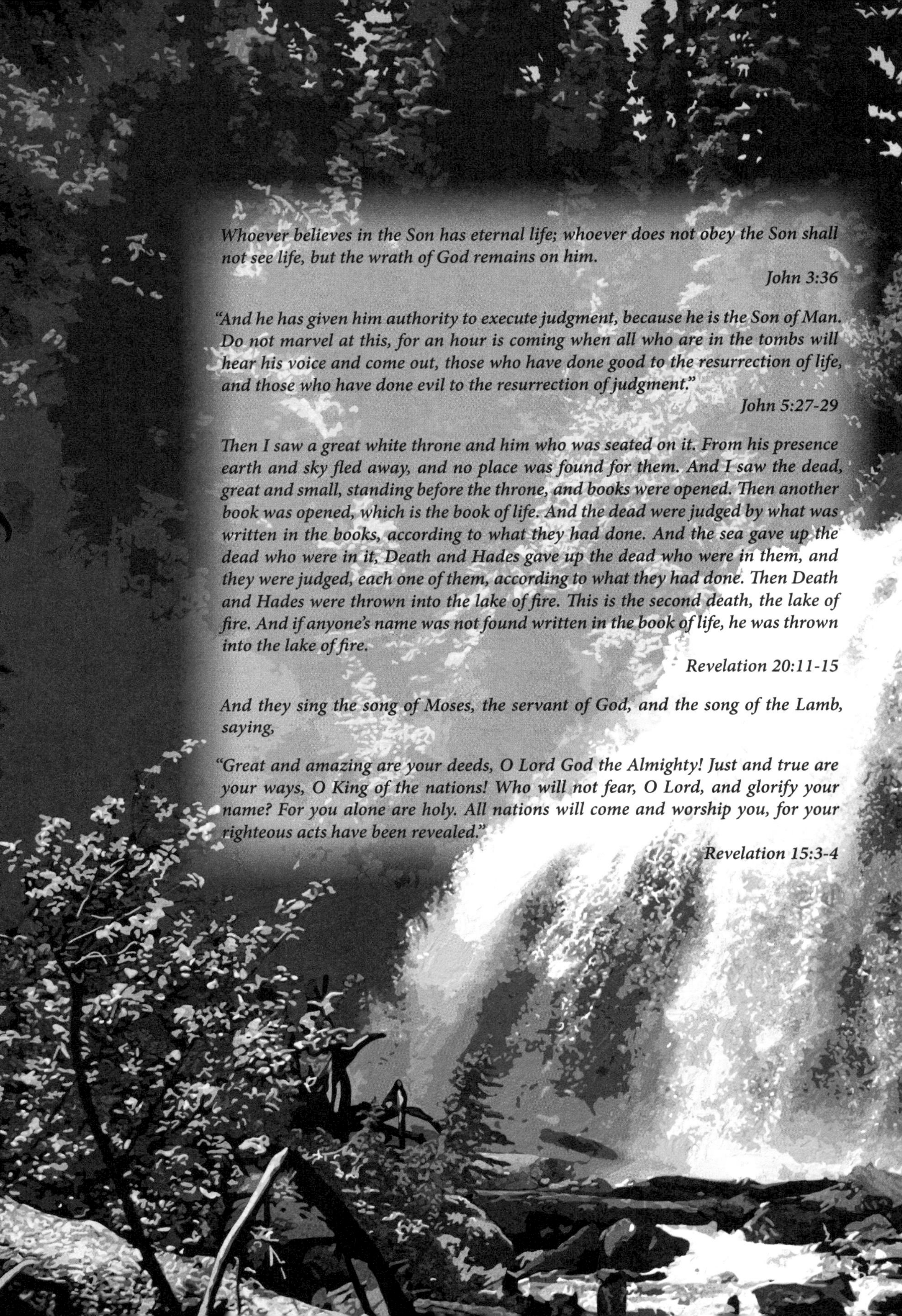

Whoever believes in the Son has eternal life; whoever does not obey the Son shall not see life, but the wrath of God remains on him.

John 3:36

"And he has given him authority to execute judgment, because he is the Son of Man. Do not marvel at this, for an hour is coming when all who are in the tombs will hear his voice and come out, those who have done good to the resurrection of life, and those who have done evil to the resurrection of judgment."

John 5:27-29

Then I saw a great white throne and him who was seated on it. From his presence earth and sky fled away, and no place was found for them. And I saw the dead, great and small, standing before the throne, and books were opened. Then another book was opened, which is the book of life. And the dead were judged by what was written in the books, according to what they had done. And the sea gave up the dead who were in it, Death and Hades gave up the dead who were in them, and they were judged, each one of them, according to what they had done. Then Death and Hades were thrown into the lake of fire. This is the second death, the lake of fire. And if anyone's name was not found written in the book of life, he was thrown into the lake of fire.

Revelation 20:11-15

And they sing the song of Moses, the servant of God, and the song of the Lamb, saying,

"Great and amazing are your deeds, O Lord God the Almighty! Just and true are your ways, O King of the nations! Who will not fear, O Lord, and glorify your name? For you alone are holy. All nations will come and worship you, for your righteous acts have been revealed."

Revelation 15:3-4

Justice

Final Justice

5

Believers are justified—declared righteous—by faith in Jesus Christ. The just penalty for all of a believer's sin is paid at the cross of Jesus. At the end of time, when the final judgment comes, the verdict is based on whether or not a person wears the righteousness of Christ, which is the free gift of grace for all who believe. Jesus is our advocate or intercessor before the Father. God is a righteous judge, and there is punishment for *all* sin. Those who do not pursue the righteousness of God by placing faith in Jesus Christ will face punishment on their own for their sins. There will be no advocate standing in on their behalf. They have chosen to live apart from pursuing God through Christ, and they will face justice apart from Christ. God's judgments are just, not arbitrary.

In John 3, John the Baptist is speaking of Jesus when he says that those who believe in the Son have eternal life, while those who do not obey the Son will bear the wrath of God. Notice the connection between believing and obeying. Those who do not obey the Son are disobedient first and foremost by not believing. And Scripture clearly teaches that those who believe will also obey in other areas. James teaches that faith without works is dead (Jms. 2:14-17). Good works are evidence of true faith. A life transformed by the righteousness of Jesus Christ will be a visibly changed life. So, when Jesus described the final resurrection and judgment by saying that those who have done good will experience the resurrection of life, He was not describing being saved by good works. He was affirming that believers who are given His righteousness will do good works for His glory and in His strength. Conversely, those who have done evil and have not been transformed by believing in His righteousness will experience the resurrection of judgment.

Revelation 20 is one Scripture that describes this resurrection of judgment. The book of Revelation, containing prophecies of the end of this age, is one of the more difficult-to-understand books of the Bible. Though there are differing interpretations of much of the text and the timing of these events, all are in agreement that there is a resurrection of the dead and a final judgment. The book of life records the names of those who believe the Son and have eternal life. When the dead are resurrected, those who do not have their names in the book of life will be punished for their sins. Scripture promises this final judgment when God will put all things right. The saints will proclaim that the Lord God's judgments are true and just. All of His judgments will affirm His righteousness, as He pours out judgment on those who have rejected Him and have persecuted believers. Those who have suffered injustices in this world can take comfort that our all-knowing God has seen every injustice, and He will judge accordingly.

Action Step: Many of us have suffered in this life because of the sins of others. We are called to not avenge ourselves (Rom. 12:19). Justice will roll down on every one of those offenses. In some cases, the offenders will face justice for their sins at the final judgment. In other cases, the punishment for those sins was borne at the cross by Jesus. But even when those offenders are forgiven of their sins, they may still face discipline by God. God's righteous work is not based in satisfying our selfish desire for revenge, but in achieving His perfect justice on earth. Victims of injustice can also know that offenders who come to the cross will face grief over their sin in the Spirit-led process of repentance (2 Cor. 7:10). Pray that God will help you to trust in His perfect justice.

"But let justice roll down like waters, and righteousness like an ever-flowing stream."
Amos 5:24

"But seek first the kingdom of God and his righteousness, and all these things will be added to you."

Matthew 6:33

"Blessed are those who hunger and thirst for righteousness, for they shall be satisfied."
Matthew 5:6

"Whoever believes in me, as the Scripture has said, 'Out of his heart will flow rivers of living water.'" Now this he said about the Spirit, whom those who believed in him were to receive, for as yet the Spirit had not been given, because Jesus was not yet glorified.

John 7:38-39

Religion that is pure and undefiled before God, the Father, is this: to visit orphans and widows in their affliction, and to keep oneself unstained from the world.
James 1:27

He has told you, O man, what is good; and what does the LORD require of you but to do justice, and to love kindness, and to walk humbly with your God?
Micah 6:8

"learn to do good; seek justice, correct oppression; bring justice to the fatherless, plead the widow's cause."

Isaiah 1:17

Open your mouth for the mute, for the rights of all who are destitute. Open your mouth, judge righteously, defend the rights of the poor and needy.
Proverbs 31:8-9

"Thus says the LORD of hosts, Render true judgments, show kindness and mercy to one another, do not oppress the widow, the fatherless, the sojourner, or the poor, and let none of you devise evil against another in your heart."
Zechariah 7:9-10

"Thus says the LORD: Do justice and righteousness, and deliver from the hand of the oppressor him who has been robbed. And do no wrong or violence to the resident alien, the fatherless, and the widow, nor shed innocent blood in this place."
Jeremiah 22:3

Justice

Do Justice, Be Righteous

6

Gravity causes water to flow downhill. That's some pretty basic science. But stop and think about that reality for a moment. There is never a time when the water resists gravity and stops flowing downhill. Water on a slope does not just stop, nor does it flow back uphill. When snowmelt cascades out of the mountains in a stream bed and reaches the lip of a rocky shelf above a thirty-foot drop off, the water will always crash down. It cannot stop at the edge of the rock. This is the image that the Lord gives to the prophet Amos to describe His desire for the flow of justice. Justice should "roll down like waters." It never stops flowing or retreats. Righteousness should be "an ever-flowing stream." The community that God created us for is one where justice and righteousness are as reliable as the flow of water obeying gravity. Jesus taught His followers "seek first the kingdom of God and his righteousness" and "Blessed are those who hunger and thirst for righteousness"; this is the unending flow of righteousness that Jesus has in mind. The kingdom of God overflows with justice.

There is a source for this unending, unstoppable flow of justice and righteousness. Jesus used the same image of flowing water in John 7. Whoever believes in Jesus will have rivers of living water flow out of their hearts. John makes it clear that this refers to the coming Holy Spirit. The Holy Spirit lives within believers in Jesus Christ. Because of the Spirit, we have rivers of living water flowing from our hearts. The Holy Spirit is the source for justice and righteousness flowing from our lives as reliably as water flows downhill. Submitted to God, we become instruments for God's righteousness (Rom. 6:13).

When a believer truly appreciates the gospel and understands that we have been given the righteousness of Christ, the transformation that comes should include the ability to see the image of God in others. The justice and righteousness flowing out of the heart of a person of faith will treat all people with the honor that God's image deserves. This transformed heart will agree with James' definition of pure religion: "visit orphans and widows in their affliction, and to keep oneself unstained from the world." This justice is what the prophet Micah describes as what is good and what the Lord requires of us. Doing justice involves correcting oppression, speaking for the powerless, and defending the rights of the poor and the needy. Although people of faith have a righteous standing before God because of Christ's righteousness, when we bring justice to those around us, we grow in practical righteousness. We can also bring justice to the world by being ambassadors for Christ, teaching the gospel, and exposing others to the justice of being declared righteous in Christ.

Action Step: Many times in Scripture we are commanded to minister to widows and orphans. What does this look like today, when those who meet the strict definition of widow and orphan may not be as prevalent as they were in Biblical times? One answer is that single parents and fatherless children can be seen as the widows and orphans of our day. Do you know a single parent or a child whose father or mother is not a part of his daily life? Contact the family and ask if there is anything you can do to help them financially or with a gift of your time. Even if there is no financial need, a fatherless child will almost always benefit from male mentors willing to show love.

Weekly Summary

Key Points

1. When we are talking about the perfect character of God, His justice and righteousness are essentially the same attribute.
2. The overarching account of justice in Scripture is the story of God's work in restoring justice in this broken world by offering all people a right relationship with Him.
3. Those who disobey the Lord face just consequences and discipline for their sin.
4. The righteousness of *God Himself* is freely given to those who have faith in Jesus Christ.
5. Those who have suffered injustices in this world can take comfort that our all-knowing God has seen every injustice, and He will judge accordingly.
6. The Holy Spirit is the source for justice and righteousness flowing from our lives.

Justice
Action Steps

7

Go back through the action steps and complete any that you have not yet completed or repeat one that was meaningful:

1. The Psalms declare that "righteousness (*tsedeq*) and justice (*mishpat*) are the foundation of his throne." We can trust in His sovereign authority and rule because everything He does is based in His righteousness and justice. Spend some time in prayer today praising God that all of His ways are based in steadfast love, justice, and righteousness.

2. Social justice is a popular theme in today's culture. God is definitely concerned with justice in society, but the heart of Biblical justice is recognizing God's image in all people. If the goal of social justice is to elevate the oppressed above the oppressor, it is not Biblical justice. If the goal of criminal justice is to segregate offenders into a permanent lower class that is stripped of social rights, it is not Biblical justice. Evaluate your own efforts toward social justice. As you lift victims of injustice, do you find yourself diminishing the image of God in another group of people?

3. The book of Hebrews includes teaching on discipline for believers who struggle against sin. Read Hebrews 12:3-11. The author teaches that God disciplines believers the same way that a father disciplines his sons—for their good. The discipline may be painful, but the result is "the peaceful fruit of righteousness to those who have been trained by it." When God brings discipline as a form of justice, it yields righteousness in people of faith. How have you experienced this discipline from God in your life?

4. The cross of Jesus Christ is where God's love and justice meet in perfect harmony. Paul states in Romans 3 that God's righteousness is for all who believe. No matter how selfish or hurtful a person's past deeds are, if they come to faith in Christ, they receive the righteousness of God. If you struggle with guilt over past sins, know that you are righteous before God because of Jesus Christ. If another person has hurt you deeply with their sin and then repented of that sin and placed faith in Jesus, they are also clothed in Christ's righteousness. Is there anyone in your life, including yourself, whom you are actively opposing as being declared righteous before God?

5. Many of us have suffered in this life because of the sins of others. We are called to not avenge ourselves (Rom. 12:19). Justice will roll down on every one of those offenses. In some cases, the offenders will face justice for their sins at the final judgment. In other cases, the punishment for those sins was borne at the cross by Jesus. But even when those offenders are forgiven of their sins, they may still face discipline by God. God's righteous work is not based in satisfying our selfish desire for revenge, but in achieving His perfect justice on earth. Victims of injustice can also know that offenders who come to the cross will face grief over their sin in the Spirit-led process of repentance (2 Cor. 7:10). Pray that God will help you to trust in His perfect justice.

6. Many times in Scripture we are commanded to minister to widows and orphans. What does this look like today, when those who meet the strict definition of widow and orphan may not be as prevalent as they were in Biblical times? One answer is that single parents and fatherless children can be seen as the widows and orphans of our day. Do you know a single parent or a child whose father or mother is not a part of his daily life? Contact the family and ask if there is anything you can do to help them financially or with a gift of your time. Even if there is no financial need, a fatherless child will almost always benefit from male mentors willing to show love.

WEEK 17

Faithful

That is the fact before us: God is faithful! He will remain faithful because He cannot change. He is perfectly faithful, because God is never partly anything. God is perfectly all that He is and never partly what He is. You can be sure that God will always be faithful. This faithful God, who never broke a promise and never violated a covenant, who never said one thing and meant another, who never overlooked anything or forgot anything, is the Father of our Lord Jesus and the God of the gospel. This is the God we adore and the God we preach.

A.W. Tozer, *The Attributes of God, Vol. 2*

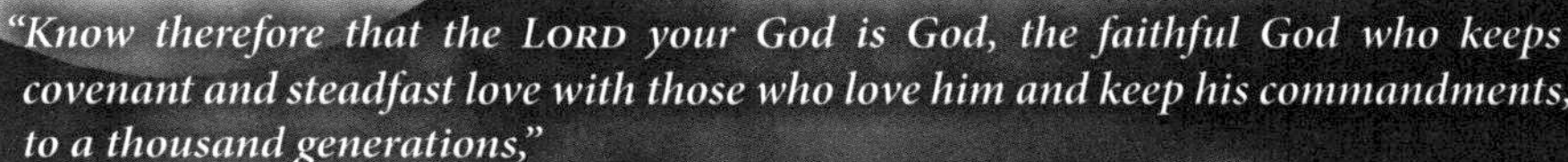

"Know therefore that the LORD your God is God, the faithful God who keeps covenant and steadfast love with those who love him and keep his commandments, to a thousand generations,"

Deuteronomy 7:9

For the word of the LORD is upright, and all his work is done in faithfulness.

Psalms 33:4

O LORD, you are my God; I will exalt you; I will praise your name, for you have done wonderful things, plans formed of old, faithful and sure.

Isaiah 25:1

"For a brief moment I deserted you, but with great compassion I will gather you. In overflowing anger for a moment I hid my face from you, but with everlasting love I will have compassion on you," says the LORD, your Redeemer. "This is like the days of Noah to me: as I swore that the waters of Noah should no more go over the earth, so I have sworn that I will not be angry with you, and will not rebuke you. For the mountains may depart and the hills be removed, but my steadfast love shall not depart from you, and my covenant of peace shall not be removed," says the LORD, who has compassion on you.

Isaiah 54:7-10

Not one word of all the good promises that the LORD had made to the house of Israel had failed; all came to pass.

Joshua 21:45

"Like the moon it shall be established forever, a faithful witness in the skies."

Psalms 89:37

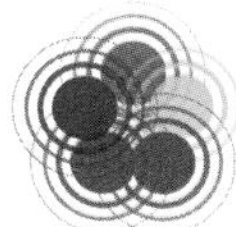

Faithful
God's Faithfulness Revealed

1

The dictionary defines faithful as steadfast, loyal, trustworthy, or staying true to promises made. Scripture presents God as the standard for this kind of faithfulness. God made a covenant with Abraham, promising that Abraham would have offspring as numerous as the stars and that He would give to them the land of Canaan. He also promised that He would extend His covenant to Abraham's offspring. God began fulfilling those promises when Abraham's wife, Sarah, miraculously gave birth to Isaac in her old age. Centuries later, the offspring of Abraham—the nation of Israel—took possession of the land of Canaan. As they journeyed to the land, God communicated to another chosen leader, Moses, His covenant with the offspring of Abraham. He promised them the land, but He also promised the nation would be removed from the land if they did not remain faithful to worshiping God alone. Moses reminded the Israelites that their part in the covenant was to love God and keep His commandments. When they did, their faithful God would keep His covenant and give steadfast love to a thousand generations. Again, God was faithful to His covenant. He gave the Israelites miraculous victories over other peoples as they entered the land. Approximately five hundred years later, when King Solomon dedicated the new temple in Jerusalem, he praised the Lord "who has given rest to his people Israel, according to all that he promised. Not one word has failed of all his good promise, which he spoke by Moses his servant" (1 Ki. 8:56). It was still another three hundred years (for Israel) and four hundred years (for Judah) before God's people were exiled from the land for worshiping idols and false gods. God remained faithful to His promised discipline.

The word of the Lord is upright—straight and consistent. Everything He does is faithful to His word and His character. He says what is true, and He does what He promises. Isaiah praised God for His plans to bring about justice and redemption—"plans formed of old, faithful and sure." Later in his book, Isaiah spoke of a future time for Israel—a time when God's anger would be past. In the New Covenant, the Lord will have compassion on His people—those who love Him—and His steadfast love will not depart. Even at the end of time when mountains and hills are moved, God will still be faithful to His covenant with His people.

Action Step: The length of the lunar cycle–the amount of time that it takes for the moon to transition through its different phases from new moon to full moon and back to new moon–is about 29.53 days. This number is not exact, and it varies because the moon orbits the earth in an ellipse rather than a perfect circle. For as long as mankind has observed the sky, every 29-30 days the moon has repeated this cycle. This may be why Psalm 89 describes the moon as "a faithful witness in the skies." Pay attention to the moon's cycle this month, and use the moon as a visible reminder to praise the faithfulness of its Creator. See also Jeremiah 31:35-36.

I will give thanks to you, O Lord, among the peoples; I will sing praises to you among the nations. For your steadfast love is great to the heavens, your faithfulness to the clouds.

Psalms 57:9-10

"Now therefore, O LORD, God of Israel, keep for your servant David my father what you have promised him, saying, 'You shall not lack a man to sit before me on the throne of Israel, if only your sons pay close attention to their way, to walk before me as you have walked before me.'"

1 Kings 8:25

And the LORD was angry with Solomon, because his heart had turned away from the LORD, the God of Israel, who had appeared to him twice and had commanded him concerning this thing, that he should not go after other gods. But he did not keep what the LORD commanded. Therefore the LORD said to Solomon, "Since this has been your practice and you have not kept my covenant and my statutes that I have commanded you, I will surely tear the kingdom from you and will give it to your servant. Yet for the sake of David your father I will not do it in your days, but I will tear it out of the hand of your son. However, I will not tear away all the kingdom, but I will give one tribe to your son, for the sake of David my servant and for the sake of Jerusalem that I have chosen."

1 Kings 11:9-13

Nevertheless, for David's sake the LORD his God gave him a lamp in Jerusalem, setting up his son after him, and establishing Jerusalem,

1 Kings 15:4

Jehoram the son of Jehoshaphat, king of Judah, began to reign… And he walked in the way of the kings of Israel, as the house of Ahab had done, for the daughter of Ahab was his wife. And he did what was evil in the sight of the LORD. Yet the LORD was not willing to destroy Judah, for the sake of David his servant, since he promised to give a lamp to him and to his sons forever.

2 Kings 8:16, 18-19

For the sake of your servant David, do not turn away the face of your anointed one. The LORD swore to David a sure oath from which he will not turn back: "One of the sons of your body I will set on your throne. If your sons keep my covenant and my testimonies that I shall teach them, their sons also forever shall sit on your throne."

Psalms 132:10-12

I will sing of the steadfast love of the LORD, forever; with my mouth I will make known your faithfulness to all generations. For I said, "Steadfast love will be built up forever; in the heavens you will establish your faithfulness."

Psalms 89:1-2

Faithful

God's Faithfulness to David

2

King David searched for words to convey the scope of God's love and faithfulness when he composed Psalm 57. Faithfulness reaching to the clouds is a picture of faithfulness that extends as far as the eye can see. The Lord made a covenant with David that is recorded for us in 2 Samuel 7. God promised to raise up David's offspring and establish the throne of his kingdom forever. His steadfast love would not depart from David's heirs. Though there would be discipline for sin, the bloodline of David would be the line of kings to rule Israel.

David's son, Solomon, was the first heir. He was aware of God's covenant with David, and he spoke of it at the dedication of the new temple (1 Ki. 8). He was even aware that he needed to walk with God the way that his father did. But Solomon's heart was not completely true to God. He took foreign wives, and he worshiped their foreign gods. The Lord was angry with Solomon, and He vowed to tear the kingdom from Solomon. But for the sake of David, to be faithful to His covenant, He promised to leave Solomon's son, Rehoboam, as ruler over one tribe (1 Ki. 11). Soon after Rehoboam was crowned king, there was a rebellion, and the kingdom split into Israel in the north and Judah in the south. The heirs of David still reigned in Judah.

Rehoboam was not a godly leader, and the people of Judah worshiped foreign gods. When he died, his son Abijam, the great-grandson of David, ruled in Judah. Abijam was no better than Rehoboam before him, but God remained faithful to His covenant with David, keeping David's heirs on the throne of Judah (1 Ki. 15). Skipping ahead three more generations was Jehoram, the great-grandson of Abijam, who also did what was evil before God. Still, Scripture records that God stayed faithful to His promise to David (2 Ki. 8). Time after time, God allowed the heirs of David to keep the throne in Judah for the sake of His promise to David. God remained faithful even when the kings of His people were not. The people of Israel were aware of God's covenant with David, and they also proclaimed confidence in His promise as they worshiped with songs such as Psalm 89 and Psalm 132. Even in the midst of a crisis such as the exile to Babylon, when no king ruled in Israel or Judah, the faithful of Israel would sing these psalms and trust in the faithfulness of God to return an heir of David to the throne in Jerusalem.

The confidence of the people of Israel was not misplaced. Although no descendant of David ruled in Jerusalem for approximately six hundred years after the Babylonian exile, Jesus Christ was born from the line of David. Jesus was always the promised heir of David that would reign on the throne of David forever. God's faithfulness was revealed to Judah as they saw generation after generation of David's descendants continuing to reign. In the same way, we can see the fulfillment of His promises in the coming of Jesus Christ and know that Jesus will rule completely and eternally when He comes again.

Action Step: Read all of Psalm 89. This psalm celebrates God's faithful character at the same time that it mourns the difficult situation the people were then experiencing. As you read, look carefully for themes of God's faithfulness. The beginning of the psalm overflows with confidence in His faithfulness, but near the end it asks where this faithfulness is now. Can you relate to this tension between confidence and questioning in your own life? Psalm 89 may be a great place for you to bookmark in your Bible, returning to it as a way to lay your questions before the Lord when it *feels* like God is not faithful.

Now the LORD said to Abram, "Go from your country and your kindred and your father's house to the land that I will show you. And I will make of you a great nation, and I will bless you and make your name great, so that you will be a blessing. I will bless those who bless you, and him who dishonors you I will curse, and in you all the families of the earth shall be blessed."

Genesis 12:1-3

"Now therefore, if you will indeed obey my voice and keep my covenant, you shall be my treasured possession among all peoples, for all the earth is mine; and you shall be to me a kingdom of priests and a holy nation. These are the words that you shall speak to the people of Israel."

Exodus 19:5-6

"When your days are fulfilled and you lie down with your fathers, I will raise up your offspring after you, who shall come from your body, and I will establish his kingdom. He shall build a house for my name, and I will establish the throne of his kingdom forever. I will be to him a father, and he shall be to me a son. When he commits iniquity, I will discipline him with the rod of men, with the stripes of the sons of men, but my steadfast love will not depart from him, as I took it from Saul, whom I put away from before you. And your house and your kingdom shall be made sure forever before me. Your throne shall be established forever."

2 Samuel 7:12-16

But as it is, Christ has obtained a ministry that is as much more excellent than the old as the covenant he mediates is better, since it is enacted on better promises. For if that first covenant had been faultless, there would have been no occasion to look for a second. For he finds fault with them when he says:

"Behold, the days are coming, declares the Lord, when I will establish a new covenant with the house of Israel and with the house of Judah, not like the covenant that I made with their fathers on the day when I took them by the hand to bring them out of the land of Egypt. For they did not continue in my covenant, and so I showed no concern for them, declares the Lord. For this is the covenant that I will make with the house of Israel after those days, declares the Lord: I will put my laws into their minds, and write them on their hearts, and I will be their God, and they shall be my people. And they shall not teach, each one his neighbor and each one his brother, saying, 'Know the Lord,' for they shall all know me, from the least of them to the greatest. For I will be merciful toward their iniquities, and I will remember their sins no more."

Hebrews 8:6-12 (verses 8-12 are cited from Jeremiah 31:31-34)

For I tell you that Christ became a servant to the circumcised to show God's truthfulness, in order to confirm the promises given to the patriarchs, and in order that the Gentiles might glorify God for his mercy. As it is written,

"Therefore I will praise you among the Gentiles, and sing to your name."

Romans 15:8-9

Therefore, holy brothers, you who share in a heavenly calling, consider Jesus, the apostle and high priest of our confession, who was faithful to him who appointed him, just as Moses also was faithful in all God's house.

Hebrews 3:1-2

Faithful

God's Faithfulness Revealed in the New Covenant

3

Throughout the Old Testament, God revealed His faithfulness by keeping promises that He made to Abraham, Isaac, Jacob, Moses, the nation of Israel, and King David. Throughout the Old Testament, the people of God proved very unfaithful by not being able to obey God's commandments. All of those covenants were laying the groundwork for God's ultimate promise to re-establish the relationship that He had with men and women that had been broken by Adam and Eve's sin. In hints and shadows all throughout the Old Testament, God points the way to a New Covenant. Every Old Testament covenant promise that was made is completely fulfilled in Jesus Christ.

When God promised Abraham that he would be the father of many nations and all the families of the earth would be blessed through him, that is fulfilled as the gospel of Jesus, Abraham's offspring, is delivered to all nations. When God promised the Israelites that they would be His treasured possession if they obeyed His commandments, Jesus Christ became the perfect Israelite and obeyed the law perfectly to redeem them from their failure to obey it themselves. As a result, people of faith from all nations can be "a chosen race, a royal priesthood, a holy nation, a people for his own possession" (1 Pet. 2:9). When God promised David an heir whose throne would be established forever, Jesus Christ came to establish His kingdom, which will finally and completely fulfill that promise when He returns to reign eternally.

The faithfulness of the Father is most completely revealed in the ministry of the faithful Son of God. Paul teaches in Romans 15 that Christ came to the nation of Israel to demonstrate God's truthfulness by confirming the promises given to the patriarchs—Abraham, Isaac, and Jacob. In this faithfulness of Jesus Christ to the nation of Israel, the rest of the world can also look on and glorify God for His mercy. All nations are blessed in the New Covenant. The book of Hebrews says that it is a better covenant, enacted on better promises. Previous covenants that required obedience from human participants had faults because men and women were not able to obey. But the author of Hebrews cites the Old Testament prophet Jeremiah, pointing out that this New Covenant would include God writing His laws in minds and hearts and not just on tablets of stone. This New Covenant would actually transform the hearts of the people who enter into it through faith, causing them to love God and His commandments. This covenant is the culmination of all of the promises of God in all previous covenants. For those who enter into this covenant in faith, He has promised "I will be their God, and they shall be my people… and I will remember their sins no more." People of Israel—and now all nations of the world—can rest with the knowledge that He will remain faithful to this covenant forever.

Action Step: Jesus Christ was the perfectly faithful man by fulfilling the entire law and obeying the Father, even to the point of dying on the cross. As the Son of God, Jesus displayed the perfect faithfulness of God by fulfilling God's covenant promises. In both His human nature and in His divine nature, Jesus Christ is faithful forever. Pray that God will strengthen you with His Spirit to become more like Christ in faithfulness.

FORGIVE AND CLEANSE
If we confess our sins, he is faithful and just to forgive us our sins and to cleanse us from all unrighteousness.

1 John 1:9

SANCTIFY
Now may the God of peace himself sanctify you completely, and may your whole spirit and soul and body be kept blameless at the coming of our Lord Jesus Christ. He who calls you is faithful; he will surely do it.

1 Thessalonians 5:23-24

And I am sure of this, that he who began a good work in you will bring it to completion at the day of Jesus Christ.

Philippians 1:6

COMFORT, RESTORE, AND STRENGTHEN
Therefore let those who suffer according to God's will entrust their souls to a faithful Creator while doing good.

1 Peter 4:19

And after you have suffered a little while, the God of all grace, who has called you to his eternal glory in Christ, will himself restore, confirm, strengthen, and establish you.

1 Peter 5:10

PROTECT FROM TEMPTATION AND EVIL
No temptation has overtaken you that is not common to man. God is faithful, and he will not let you be tempted beyond your ability, but with the temptation he will also provide the way of escape, that you may be able to endure it.

1 Corinthians 10:13

But the Lord is faithful. He will establish you and guard you against the evil one.

2 Thessalonians 3:3

REMAIN FAITHFUL
if we are faithless, he remains faithful—for he cannot deny himself.

2 Timothy 2:13

Let us hold fast the confession of our hope without wavering, for he who promised is faithful.

Hebrews 10:23

Faithful
God's Promises in the New Covenant 4

The New Testament lists many promises to which God will be faithful in the New Covenant through the gospel of Jesus Christ. First, He is faithful to *forgive*. As soon as we recognize our need for forgiveness from God and confess our need for redemption from Him, He is faithful to forgive and cleanse us. He is also just in doing so because Jesus paid the penalty for our sins on the cross. This is not just for "small" sins. This is not just for "invisible" sins. If we confess our big, damaging, hurtful, ugly sins, He is faithful to forgive and cleanse.

Next, He is faithful to *sanctify*. Sanctification is the process of becoming holy. We are declared righteous by faith in Jesus. We become more righteous in practice as we become more like Jesus through the work of the Holy Spirit in our hearts. This is sanctification. And God will "surely do it" for those who love Him. Note that it is *He* who will sanctify us completely, not we ourselves. We are responsible for taking steps of obedience, but only He can complete the process. Once He has begun the process in the life of a believer, it will certainly be completed.

He also promises to "*restore, confirm, strengthen, and establish*" believers who have suffered. It is just as He promised in the Psalms: "The Lord is near to the brokenhearted and saves the crushed in spirit. Many are the afflictions of the righteous, but the Lord delivers him out of them all" (Ps. 34:18-19). Suffering is not evidence that God is not caring for us. It is actually within God's will for us to suffer and to trust Him to faithfully care for us through the suffering. It is in the midst of suffering that one can most clearly see the comfort and strength that comes from God. Whatever length of time we suffer is short when contrasted to the eternal glory we will enjoy in Christ.

God also promises to *not let us be tempted beyond our ability to endure.* He will provide a way of escape if we look to Him for strength. The way out may be an actual escape from the presence of the temptation, but it may also be the strength to endure a situation that cannot be escaped. Likewise, He is faithful to *guard us against the evil one.* Satan is the tempter. Just as he tried to entice Jesus to sin in the desert, he works on believers to tempt them into sin and disobedience. The Lord will guard us by strengthening us to resist such temptation.

God promises to *remain faithful, even when we are not.* No matter how hard we try, we will fail. Our trust in God may falter for a moment, and sin will result. But God's faithfulness does not depend on our faithfulness. He cannot go against His character and behave unfaithfully. God will remain true to His promises, and we can always hold on to our hope because of His faithfulness.

Action Step: When one deeply considers the promises of the New Covenant, one can easily see they are truly astounding. All of this culminates in what the author of Hebrews calls "a better hope… through which we draw near to God" (Heb. 7:19). There is simply no greater promise available to mankind than the promise to draw near to God. Every physical or relational blessing pales in comparison to the opportunity to have a relationship with the infinite, eternal, loving God of all creation. Meditate on God's covenants and praise Him for His faithfulness to keep covenant with His people.

"Do not think that I have come to bring peace to the earth. I have not come to bring peace, but a sword. For I have come to set a man against his father, and a daughter against her mother, and a daughter-in-law against her mother-in- law. And a person's enemies will be those of his own household. Whoever loves father or mother more than me is not worthy of me, and whoever loves son or daughter more than me is not worthy of me. And whoever does not take his cross and follow me is not worthy of me. Whoever finds his life will lose it, and whoever loses his life for my sake will find it."

Matthew 10:34-39

Beloved, do not be surprised at the fiery trial when it comes upon you to test you, as though something strange were happening to you. But rejoice insofar as you share Christ's sufferings, that you may also rejoice and be glad when his glory is revealed. If you are insulted for the name of Christ, you are blessed, because the Spirit of glory and of God rests upon you.

1 Peter 4:12-14

Who shall separate us from the love of Christ? Shall tribulation, or distress, or persecution, or famine, or nakedness, or danger, or sword? As it is written, "For your sake we are being killed all the day long; we are regarded as sheep to be slaughtered." No, in all these things we are more than conquerors through him who loved us.

Romans 8:35-37

"Behold, the hour is coming, indeed it has come, when you will be scattered, each to his own home, and will leave me alone. Yet I am not alone, for the Father is with me. I have said these things to you, that in me you may have peace. In the world you will have tribulation. But take heart; I have overcome the world."

John 16:32-33

We are afflicted in every way, but not crushed; perplexed, but not driven to despair; persecuted, but not forsaken; struck down, but not destroyed; always carrying in the body the death of Jesus, so that the life of Jesus may also be manifested in our bodies. For we who live are always being given over to death for Jesus' sake, so that the life of Jesus also may be manifested in our mortal flesh.

2 Corinthians 4:8-11

Not only that, but we rejoice in our sufferings, knowing that suffering produces endurance, and endurance produces character, and character produces hope, and hope does not put us to shame, because God's love has been poured into our hearts through the Holy Spirit who has been given to us.

Romans 5:3-5

Faithful

When We Think God Is Unfaithful 5

Americans believe hard work leads to success. A 2012 Pew Research Center study showed that 77% of Americans surveyed believed that most people can succeed if they are willing to work hard. In other words, we believe prosperity and a comfortable lifestyle are a natural result of good work ethic. Unfortunately, we seem to have allowed this cultural view to blend in with our expectations of the Christian faith. Whether conscious or not, American Christians often operate out of a belief system that if we work hard at our faith, trust God and obey, our lives will be blessed with physical comfort and material success. That is not a belief system that is supported by Scripture.

Jesus promised suffering: "And whoever does not take his cross and follow me is not worthy of me" (Mt. 10:38); "In the world you will have tribulation" (Jn. 16:33). These words of our Savior do not agree with a belief system that faithful Christians should not suffer. There are many Old Testament promises for material prosperity in Israel, but we must be careful not to claim covenant promises for Israel as promises for believers in the New Covenant today. God will give His people prosperity of every kind in the age to come. But for this church age, Jesus and the New Testament writers promised suffering. It is right for those suffering to cry out in grief to God—even to question why we suffer, though we may not get a clear answer. What Jesus has not left us room for is to be surprised by suffering or to believe that God is not being faithful when we suffer.

There are times in the Christian life when it may *feel* like God is unfaithful. You may pray and seek the guidance of Scripture before making significant life choices, but the choices made may still end in disappointment. You may be filled with faith and determined to serve Him, but tragedy could then strike. You may make a choice to do the hard thing that aligns with Scripture, but your friends and family could turn against you. You may marry a Christian, but still your spouse may cheat on you. Does this mean that God is not being faithful to His promises?

Because God is faithful and He keeps every one of His promises, when it seems that He is being unfaithful, it is likely because we are believing in the wrong promises. God is faithful because He has promised to be *with* us in these trials. He has not promised us a life free from trials.

Action Step: Spend some time in prayer asking God to help you uncover your own attitudes about trials. It *is* possible to have a knowledge of Jesus' promise of sufferings and *still* be surprised when trials come in our own lives. When you face trials, do you tend to feel God has abandoned you, or do you anticipate His presence and work in the midst of your suffering? It is so easy to slip into having expectations of God that are outside of the promises of Scripture.

But the fruit of the Spirit is love, joy, peace, patience, kindness, goodness, faithfulness, gentleness, self-control; against such things there is no law.

Galatians 5:22-23

"Now therefore fear the LORD and serve him in sincerity and in faithfulness. Put away the gods that your fathers served beyond the River and in Egypt, and serve the LORD."

Joshua 24:14

Let not steadfast love and faithfulness forsake you; bind them around your neck; write them on the tablet of your heart.

Proverbs 3:3

"His master said to him, 'Well done, good and faithful servant. You have been faithful over a little; I will set you over much. Enter into the joy of your master.'"

Matthew 25:21

"Woe to you, scribes and Pharisees, hypocrites! For you tithe mint and dill and cumin, and have neglected the weightier matters of the law: justice and mercy and faithfulness. These you ought to have done, without neglecting the others. You blind guides, straining out a gnat and swallowing a camel!"

Matthew 23:23-24

But above all, my brothers, do not swear, either by heaven or by earth or by any other oath, but let your "yes" be yes and your "no" be no, so that you may not fall under condemnation.

James 5:12

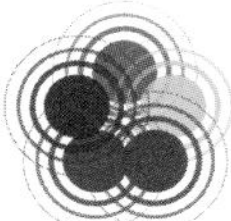

Faithful

Called to Be Faithful

6

Faithfulness is listed in Galatians 5 as a fruit of the Spirit. Paul's description of the fruit of the Spirit is one of the most powerful and concise statements in all of Scripture describing what it looks like to reflect the character of God. A New Covenant believer with a heart that has been transformed by God's love and the work of the Holy Spirit will grow fruit. This fruit will develop over time into maturity simply by being nourished by the Spirit of God. This fruit, including faithfulness, is both expected and commanded of children of God who bear the family image.

Above all else, the faithfulness the Spirit enables in believers' lives is faithfulness to worship God alone. We are to put away any other gods—anything that we value above Him—and "serve Him in sincerity and in faithfulness." Steadfast love and faithfulness should never depart from us as we serve Him out of love for Him, not just because we are commanded to. Jesus told a parable illustrating the rewards of faithful service to God. A man entrusted three servants with various property amounts as he went on an extended journey. When he returned, he checked in with his servants to find that two of them had wisely invested what was entrusted to them. Even though the amounts they were given and the amounts earned on their investments were different, each servant was given the same reward for faithfulness—responsibility over even more of the master's property. The third servant acted out of fear and buried what he was given, earning only rebuke from his master. Using all that God has given us in faithful service to Him is rewarded with increasing opportunities to serve, both in this life and in eternity.

Faithful character should be evident in our relationships with each other as well. This faithfulness is synonymous with trustworthiness. Children of God should be people who value keeping promises. In the same way that God keeps His promises, believers should be faithful to their words. While humans do not have all the power needed to overcome unforeseen obstacles, we can exercise wisdom in only making promises that we have the ability to keep. Failing to keep a promise does not reflect the character of the faithful God.

Action Step: Our own faithfulness should mirror the faithfulness of Jesus Christ. He was faithful in His obedience to the Father. Jesus taught that our obedience matters also: "If you love me, you will keep my commandments" (Jn. 14:15). The radical difference in the New Covenant is that our obedience–our faithfulness to the covenant–is a *result* of faith in Jesus. Faith in Jesus leads to a heart transformed by His love and the Holy Spirit within us, which yields a desire to keep His commandments. What action can you take today toward another person in your life that would reflect the faithful and loving character of Jesus?

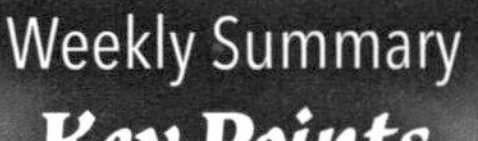

Weekly Summary

Key Points

1. Everything the Lord does is faithful to His Word and His character. He says what is true, and He does what He promises.

2. God's faithfulness was revealed to Judah as they saw generation after generation of David's descendants continuing to reign in fulfillment of God's promise to David.

3. Every Old Testament covenant promise that was made is completely fulfilled in Jesus Christ.

4. God will remain true to His promises in the New Covenant, and we can always hold on to our hope because of His faithfulness.

5. Jesus promised suffering. Because God is faithful and He keeps every one of His promises, when it seems that He is being unfaithful, it is likely because we are believing in the wrong promises.

6. Faithful character should be evident in our relationship with God and with each other as well.

Faithful

Action Steps

Go back through the action steps and complete any that you have not yet completed or repeat one that was meaningful:

1. The length of the lunar cycle—the amount of time that it takes for the moon to transition through its different phases from new moon to full moon and back to new moon—is about 29.53 days. For as long as mankind has observed the sky, every 29-30 days the moon has repeated this cycle. This may be why Psalm 89 describes the moon as "a faithful witness in the skies." Pay attention to the moon's cycle this month, and use the moon as a visible reminder to praise the faithfulness of its Creator. See also Jeremiah 31:35-36.

2. Read all of Psalm 89. This psalm celebrates God's faithful character at the same time that it mourns the difficult situation the people were then experiencing. As you read, look carefully for themes of God's faithfulness. The beginning of the psalm overflows with confidence in His faithfulness, but near the end it asks where this faithfulness is now. Can you relate to this tension between confidence and questioning in your own life? Psalm 89 may be a great place for you to bookmark in your Bible, returning to it as a way to lay your questions before the Lord when it *feels* like God is not faithful.

3. Jesus Christ was the perfectly faithful man by fulfilling the entire law and obeying the Father, even to the point of dying on the cross. As the Son of God, Jesus displayed the perfect faithfulness of God by fulfilling God's covenant promises. In both His human nature and in His divine nature, Jesus Christ is faithful forever. Pray that God will strengthen you with His Spirit to become more like Christ in faithfulness.

4. When one deeply considers the promises of the New Covenant, one can easily see they are truly astounding. All of this culminates in what the author of Hebrews calls "a better hope… through which we draw near to God" (Heb. 7:19). There is simply no greater promise available to mankind than the promise to draw near to God. Every physical or relational blessing pales in comparison to the opportunity to have a relationship with the infinite, eternal, loving God of all creation. Meditate on God's covenants and praise Him for His faithfulness to keep covenant with His people.

5. Spend some time in prayer asking God to help you uncover your own attitudes about trials. It *is* possible to have a knowledge of Jesus' promise of sufferings and *still* be surprised when trials come in our own lives. When you face trials, do you tend to feel God has abandoned you, or do you anticipate His presence and work in the midst of your suffering? It is so easy to slip into having expectations of God that are outside of the promises of Scripture.

6. Our own faithfulness should mirror the faithfulness of Jesus Christ. He was faithful in His obedience to the Father. Jesus taught that our obedience matters also: "If you love me, you will keep my commandments" (Jn. 14:15). The radical difference in the New Covenant is that our obedience—our faithfulness to the covenant—is a *result* of faith in Jesus. Faith in Jesus leads to a heart transformed by His love and the Holy Spirit within us, which yields a desire to keep His commandments. What action can you take today toward another person in your life that would reflect the faithful and loving character of Jesus?

WEEK 18
Grace

Your worst days are never so bad that you are beyond the reach of God's grace. And your best days are never so good that you are beyond the need of God's grace.
Jerry Bridges, *The Discipline of Grace*

"You have heard that it was said to those of old, 'You shall not murder; and whoever murders will be liable to judgment.' But I say to you that everyone who is angry with his brother will be liable to judgment; whoever insults his brother will be liable to the council; and whoever says, 'You fool!' will be liable to the hell of fire."

Matthew 5:21-22

"You have heard that it was said, 'You shall not commit adultery.' But I say to you that everyone who looks at a woman with lustful intent has already committed adultery with her in his heart."

Matthew 5:27-28

And he said, "What comes out of a person is what defiles him. For from within, out of the heart of man, come evil thoughts, sexual immorality, theft, murder, adultery, coveting, wickedness, deceit, sensuality, envy, slander, pride, foolishness. All these evil things come from within, and they defile a person."

Mark 7:20-23

So whoever knows the right thing to do and fails to do it, for him it is sin.

James 4:17

…as it is written: "None is righteous, no, not one; no one understands; no one seeks for God. All have turned aside; together they have become worthless; no one does good, not even one."

Romans 3:10-12

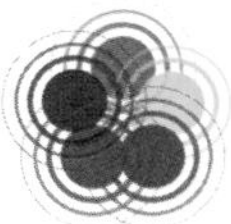

Grace

Our Need for Grace

1

When was the last time that you murdered someone? Or cheated on your spouse? Most people would never consider such behavior. But Jesus said that if you are angry with your brother, you are just as liable to judgment as a murderer. He also said that anyone who lusts has already committed adultery in his heart. His point was not to just extend the Ten Commandments to a longer list. His point was that our sin goes deeper than just actions into the sinful condition of our hearts.

Sin is not just the wrong things that we do or think, but it is the very condition of our hearts. Apart from Christ, our sin has made us enemies of God (Rom. 5:10). As believers, we have died to the reign of sin in our lives, but as long as we live in this world, there is a tension between our new Spirit-led hearts and our own sinful tendencies that continue to tempt us. In our own strength, we still gravitate toward self-rule and rebellion against God's rule. A heart that is naturally inclined toward sin is the reason why every single human being needs God's grace.

Most people have an understanding of grace as the characteristic of God that leads Him to forgive His people for sin. This is a good place to start, but even this first step in defining grace cannot be fully appreciated unless we have a full Biblical understanding of our own sinful condition. Jesus taught that we are defiled by things that come from our hearts as common as deceit, envy, and pride. Have you ever stretched the truth when telling a story for a bigger reaction? I have. That's deceit, and it has defiled us. Have you ever said or done something to win the praise of others? I have. That's pride, and it has defiled us. Have you ever wished that you could have someone else's job or car or house? I have. That's envy, and it has defiled us. To be defiled is to be polluted, spoiled, or made unholy. Not one single person that has ever lived, other than Jesus Christ, has lived a truly righteous life. James wrote that even when we fail to do the good that we ought to do, it is sin. Both the murderer and the one who is sinfully angry are defiled sinners in need of God's grace.

Grace and mercy seem to almost be interchangeable words, both in the Bible and as used by Christians. But there are subtle differences. Regarding our sin, God's mercy is His *withholding* of just punishment while He patiently waits for repentance. In contrast, regarding our sin, God's grace is a positive *giving* of what is needed to resolve our sinful condition. Just as we saw that mercy goes further than God's patience to also include compassion toward victims of injustice, we will also see that God's grace is a much broader concept than just salvation from sin.

Action Step: Are you grieved by your sin? Has the commonness of evil coming from your own heart dulled your senses to the polluting effect of sin? Are we so surrounded by evil in this world that our own sin seems inconsequential in comparison? Picture yourself standing before Jesus while you are dripping with deceit, envy, and pride. Would your stains seem inconsequential then? If we are not genuinely grieved by the sins of our hearts, but only grieved by the social consequences when our sin is discovered by others, then we are not seriously evaluating our own sin and practicing true repentance. Pray and ask God to help you see your sin as He sees it.

And he said, "I will make all my goodness pass before you and will proclaim before you my name 'The Lord.' And I will be gracious to whom I will be gracious, and will show mercy on whom I will show mercy."

Exodus 33:19

Turn to me and be gracious to me, as is your way with those who love your name.

Psalms 119:132

"For if you return to the Lord, your brothers and your children will find compassion with their captors and return to this land. For the Lord your God is gracious and merciful and will not turn away his face from you, if you return to him."

2 Chronicles 30:9

The Lord is merciful and gracious, slow to anger and abounding in steadfast love. He will not always chide, nor will he keep his anger forever. He does not deal with us according to our sins, nor repay us according to our iniquities. For as high as the heavens are above the earth, so great is his steadfast love toward those who fear him; as far as the east is from the west, so far does he remove our transgressions from us.

Psalms 103:8-12

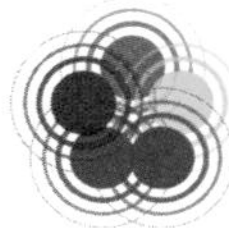

Grace

Old Testament Grace

2

Suppose you are in a job where you work closely with someone you really like. You have similar goals and personalities and almost never clash. When this agreeable coworker shows up late to a scheduled meeting, you find it easy to brush off the tardiness and jump right into the meeting when they arrive. One might say that you are favorably inclined toward your coworker. To be favorable toward someone is to approve or express enthusiasm. To be inclined is to bend or lean. To be favorably inclined, then, is to lean toward approving someone. In other words, you are more likely to give the friendly coworker grace.

God's grace is the part of His goodness that leans toward favoring people who do not deserve His favor. In one limited sense, His grace is for all people because He continues to faithfully sustain creation. But the most vital aspects of God's grace are for specific people according to His sovereign will—"I will be gracious to whom I will be gracious." God was gracious to Israel in the Old Testament by choosing to come near to them so that other nations would notice this nation and glorify their God (Deut. 4:6-8). But if we look carefully at Israel's own Scriptures—the Old Testament—we can see that there are certain qualifiers to be recipients of grace and favor. Unlike the example of the fictitious coworker, God's favor is not based on personality or likability.

In Psalm 119 we learn it is God's way to be gracious toward those who love His name. The implication seems to be that this is a unique grace that doesn't apply to all people. 2 Chronicles 30 is part of the story of Hezekiah, king of Judah. Hezekiah was reigning in the southern kingdom of Judah when the northern kingdom of Israel was exiled to Assyria for disobedience. Hezekiah led the people of Judah and a remaining remnant in Israel back to the Lord. He cleansed the temple in Jerusalem, and he called the people to celebrate the Passover, which they had not been observing according to the Lord's commands. Hezekiah sent word to all of Israel and Judah, calling them to return to the Lord. It was in this call that the king said, "For the Lord your God is gracious and merciful and will not turn away his face from you, if you return to him." There was a condition applied to receive this grace and mercy—"if you return to him." David, in Psalm 103, assured his people that God maintains steadfast love toward and removes the transgressions from those who fear Him. In all of these Scriptures we see that God's grace is directed toward those who love His name, return to Him, and fear Him. In summary, God is favorably inclined toward those who choose to be in a covenant relationship with Him. We can find grace throughout the Old Testament as we notice God's willingness to forgive His people of sin.

Action Step: Find a globe of the earth, or at least a ball that can represent the globe. Place your finger on a spot on the globe that represents your current location. Begin to trace your finger straight north on the globe, and note at which point your finger is no longer traveling north but changes to a southern direction. Because the earth rotates on a north/south axis, you only get as far as the North Pole before you are headed south. The distance from the North Pole to the South Pole can be measured. Now return your finger to your current location and start tracing your finger straight east. At what point is your finger no longer going east? The answer is never! You can go around the globe hundreds of times in that same direction, and your finger will still be traveling to the east. It never changes to west! The distance from the east to the west cannot be measured. That's how far God removes the sins of those who fear Him! That is amazing grace!

What then shall we say was gained by Abraham, our forefather according to the flesh? For if Abraham was justified by works, he has something to boast about, but not before God. For what does the Scripture say? "Abraham believed God, and it was counted to him as righteousness,"

Now to the one who works, his wages are not counted as a gift but as his due. And to the one who does not work but believes in him who justifies the ungodly, his faith is counted as righteousness... Therefore, since we have been justified by faith, we have peace with God through our Lord Jesus Christ. Through him we have also obtained access by faith into this grace in which we stand, and we rejoice in hope of the glory of God...

But the free gift is not like the trespass. For if many died through one man's trespass, much more have the grace of God and the free gift by the grace of that one man Jesus Christ abounded for many. And the free gift is not like the result of that one man's sin. For the judgment following one trespass brought condemnation, but the free gift following many trespasses brought justification.

Romans 4:1-5; 5:1-2, 15-16

...for all have sinned and fall short of the glory of God, and are justified by his grace as a gift, through the redemption that is in Christ Jesus,

Romans 3:23-24

...so that in the coming ages he might show the immeasurable riches of his grace in kindness toward us in Christ Jesus. For by grace you have been saved through faith. And this is not your own doing; it is the gift of God, not a result of works, so that no one may boast.

Ephesians 2:7-9

For you know the grace of our Lord Jesus Christ, that though he was rich, yet for your sake he became poor, so that you by his poverty might become rich.

2 Corinthians 8:9

So too at the present time there is a remnant, chosen by grace. But if it is by grace, it is no longer on the basis of works; otherwise grace would no longer be grace.

Romans 11:5-6

Now the law came in to increase the trespass, but where sin increased, grace abounded all the more, so that, as sin reigned in death, grace also might reign through righteousness leading to eternal life through Jesus Christ our Lord.

Romans 5:20-21

Grace

Saving Grace

3

I work for a small newspaper where I receive an hourly wage. There is an expectation that when I work a certain number of hours in a month, I will be paid the agreed-upon wages. In a sense, my employer owes me a debt for the hours that I have worked until I have received my pay. In contrast, a gift is something that is given with no work done to earn it. When I choose a birthday gift for one of my children, I don't choose based on what that child has done to deserve the gift. I choose based on my love for my child. This is how the Apostle Paul describes the free gift of grace by which we are saved from our sin. God loves us, and He chooses to gift us with His favor.

There is no kind or amount of work we can do to earn God's extravagant grace. It is a free gift that brings us eternal life through the work of Jesus Christ. Saving grace is the favor of God leaning toward us, even though we all fall short of being able to earn His favor. What we have earned in our sin is death and eternal separation from God. But out of the richness of His grace, Jesus chose to become poor, setting aside His heavenly privileges and becoming a man. The Son of God did this for us so that He could gift us with the riches of eternal life and acceptance with God. The grace in which we stand—the undeserved favor of God—is only available to us through faith in Jesus Christ. Even that ability to have faith is a gift from God. If we attempt to stand in our own righteousness to please God, we are depriving ourselves of the benefits of grace. Paul goes so far as to say that grace would not even be grace if our salvation came through our own works. The gospel is the good news that our salvation is a gift of God's grace through faith—trusting in God's work for our salvation—which is contradictory to relying on our own works for salvation. The more we study Scripture and understand how far short of God's holiness our own lives fall, the more we can appreciate how incredibly indebted we are to God's grace.

God's grace that saves is a gift given to those who enter into a covenant relationship with Him through faith. Whether a faithful follower of God in Old-Testament times or a follower of Jesus in the New Covenant, a person is saved only by grace through faith. All believers for all time enter into a covenant relationship with God by faith—believing His promises, trusting Him, and loving Him. Paul points out in Romans 4 that Abraham was declared righteous by faith. In fact, no one in the past, present, or future can ever be declared righteous apart from grace through faith. Believers in the time before Christ had faith in the promises of God, including the promised Messiah. Both the Old Testament believer living two thousand years before Christ looking ahead to the promise of God's salvation and a present believer living two thousand years after Christ looking back to the cross are saved by grace through faith.

Action Step: When you receive a gift from someone, a proper response is to express thanks to the giver, often in the form of a written note. Write a note of thanks today to God for the gift of the immeasurable riches of His grace in Christ Jesus.

For the grace of God has appeared, bringing salvation for all people, training us to renounce ungodliness and worldly passions, and to live self-controlled, upright, and godly lives in the present age, waiting for our blessed hope, the appearing of the glory of our great God and Savior Jesus Christ, who gave himself for us to redeem us from all lawlessness and to purify for himself a people for his own possession who are zealous for good works.

Titus 2:11-14

For I am the least of the apostles, unworthy to be called an apostle, because I persecuted the church of God. But by the grace of God I am what I am, and his grace toward me was not in vain. On the contrary, I worked harder than any of them, though it was not I, but the grace of God that is with me.

1 Corinthians 15:9-10

May grace and peace be multiplied to you in the knowledge of God and of Jesus our Lord.

2 Peter 1:2

But grow in the grace and knowledge of our Lord and Savior Jesus Christ. To him be the glory both now and to the day of eternity. Amen.

2 Peter 3:18

"And I will give you a new heart, and a new spirit I will put within you. And I will remove the heart of stone from your flesh and give you a heart of flesh. And I will put my Spirit within you, and cause you to walk in my statutes and be careful to obey my rules."

Ezekiel 36:26-27

For we do not have a high priest who is unable to sympathize with our weaknesses, but one who in every respect has been tempted as we are, yet without sin. Let us then with confidence draw near to the throne of grace, that we may receive mercy and find grace to help in time of need.

Hebrews 4:15-16

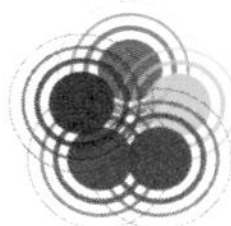

Grace

Sanctifying Grace

4

God's grace brings us salvation through faith in Jesus Christ. But His grace is so much more. God's grace also trains us how we should live today, even as we anticipate the future reign of Christ. Grace works within us to build us up and strengthen us in the process of sanctification—being made holy. Our ability to pursue holiness is not by our own strength, but by the grace of God.

Paul wrote in his letter to Titus that, along with bringing salvation, grace actually trains us to put off ungodliness and to live godly lives. Through God's grace we are being purified for Jesus, progressing toward becoming people who are passionate about doing good. In his first letter to the Corinthians, Paul again describes multiple applications of grace. God's saving grace toward Paul was not in vain. God's grace also called him to be an apostle, and grace equipped Paul to work hard in his apostolic ministry.

One way God's grace can move us toward holiness is when we focus on the extravagance of God's saving grace. In his second epistle, Peter ties knowledge of the Lord Jesus Christ together with grace to both start and end his letter. The more knowledge that we gain as we understand who Jesus is and the grace He has brought, the more we can appreciate His grace and grow in love for Him. A deep love for Jesus leads to a greater passion to serve Him with good works, and this growing obedience is the process of sanctification. As a believer understands the grace that has brought salvation and the promises that God has fulfilled in that salvation, he or she grows to trust the future eternal promises of God. Hope in the promises of God and love for God—both rooted in God's saving grace—can drive a desire for obedience.

As fallen human beings, *wanting* to obey is not always enough to bring about obedience. The most significant way that grace leads to obedience is through the presence of the Holy Spirit. Paul's prayer for the Ephesian church was that they be "strengthened with power through his Spirit in your inner being" (Eph. 3:16) to be "filled with all the fullness of God" (Eph. 3:19). God's favor leans toward us to such an extent that He sends His Spirit to give believers the strength to do His will. Hundreds of years before the birth of Jesus, God spoke through the prophet Ezekiel to promise a time when He would send His Spirit to cause people to obey Him, turning hearts of stone into hearts of flesh. The presence of the Holy Spirit—the Spirit of grace (Heb. 10:29)—in the heart of a believer is a grace that sanctifies us. Even in the hardest and rockiest times of our lives, God can bring about growth, "for it is good for the heart to be strengthened by grace" (Heb. 13:9).

Action Step: Hebrews 4 gives us the confidence to draw near to the "throne of grace." The awesome privilege granted to us in Jesus Christ is access to a loving relationship with the Ruler of all creation. Not only are we given permission to enter His throne room, we are also promised "mercy and grace in time of need." Whether your need is forgiveness from sin or power to obey or strength to bear trials, God's mercy and grace are available to those who seek Him. Enter before His throne of grace today in prayer to seek His mercy and grace.

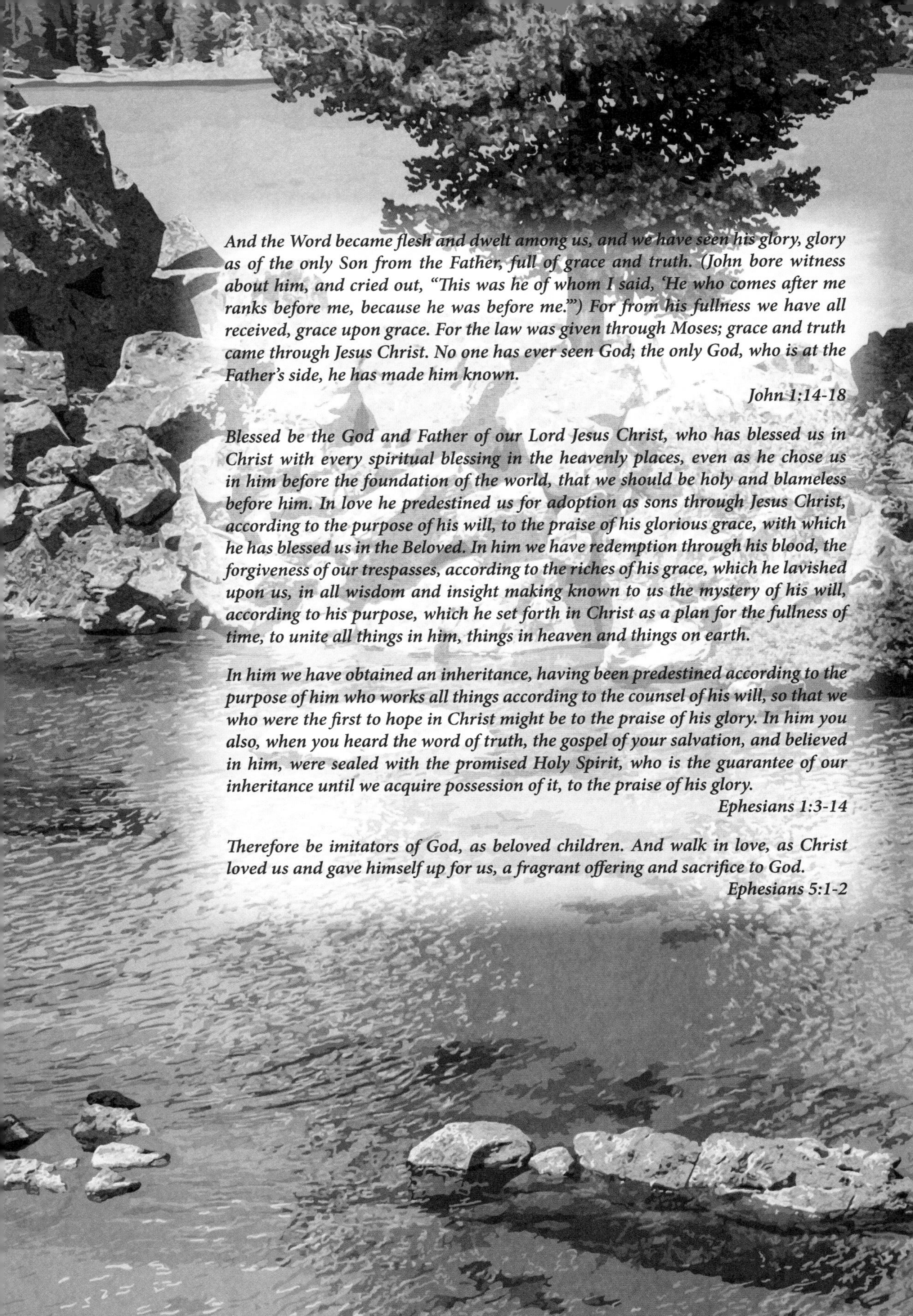

And the Word became flesh and dwelt among us, and we have seen his glory, glory as of the only Son from the Father, full of grace and truth. (John bore witness about him, and cried out, "This was he of whom I said, 'He who comes after me ranks before me, because he was before me.'") For from his fullness we have all received, grace upon grace. For the law was given through Moses; grace and truth came through Jesus Christ. No one has ever seen God; the only God, who is at the Father's side, he has made him known.

John 1:14-18

Blessed be the God and Father of our Lord Jesus Christ, who has blessed us in Christ with every spiritual blessing in the heavenly places, even as he chose us in him before the foundation of the world, that we should be holy and blameless before him. In love he predestined us for adoption as sons through Jesus Christ, according to the purpose of his will, to the praise of his glorious grace, with which he has blessed us in the Beloved. In him we have redemption through his blood, the forgiveness of our trespasses, according to the riches of his grace, which he lavished upon us, in all wisdom and insight making known to us the mystery of his will, according to his purpose, which he set forth in Christ as a plan for the fullness of time, to unite all things in him, things in heaven and things on earth.

In him we have obtained an inheritance, having been predestined according to the purpose of him who works all things according to the counsel of his will, so that we who were the first to hope in Christ might be to the praise of his glory. In him you also, when you heard the word of truth, the gospel of your salvation, and believed in him, were sealed with the promised Holy Spirit, who is the guarantee of our inheritance until we acquire possession of it, to the praise of his glory.

Ephesians 1:3-14

Therefore be imitators of God, as beloved children. And walk in love, as Christ loved us and gave himself up for us, a fragrant offering and sacrifice to God.

Ephesians 5:1-2

Grace

Grace as God Giving Himself

5

If grace is the undeserved favor of God leaning toward us, then we cannot limit His grace to that which saves us and sanctifies us. In fact, God bends so much toward our favor that He actually gives us Himself. The fullest revelation of God's grace came in the sending of "the only Son from the Father, full of grace and truth." We have seen that the Old Testament reveals God's grace, but in the life, death, and resurrection of Jesus Christ, the fullness of God's grace was revealed. In the gospel, grace is piled on top of grace.

Paul opens his letter to the Ephesians with praise to God for our spiritual blessings in Christ. The Father has blessed us with "every spiritual blessing" in Jesus Christ. All of these blessings are given "according to the purpose of his will" and "according to the riches of his grace." The vast stores of His grace lead to believers being chosen, holy, loved, adopted, redeemed, forgiven, united in Him, and sealed with the Holy Spirit. All Persons of the Trinity work together to bring these spiritual blessings according to grace. The Father has blessed us and chosen us, the Son has redeemed us with His blood, and the Holy Spirit has sealed us and guaranteed our inheritance. God has lavished His undeserved favor upon us out of love to adopt believers into His family. The end goal is the "praise of his glory"—a glory that gathers all creation back to being united in Him and under His authority.

But we cannot forget that all of this came at a great cost. While grace is a free gift for us to accept, a gift always costs the giver something. The Son of God paid His own life to purchase our redemption. The sinless Son of God felt excruciating physical pain as He was tortured on the cross and spiritual agony as He bore the burden of our sin and the weight of our shame. He gave Himself up as a sacrifice for us. God made the gift of His grace available to us at great cost to Himself. The Father sent the Son, full of grace and truth, to reveal Himself and to reconcile us to Himself. The Father sent the Spirit to dwell within us so that we might know Him and obey Him. Out of the overflow of His love, in the midst of our desperate need for restoration to Him, God chooses to grace us with Himself.

Action Step: We have already seen that Peter begins and ends his second letter with words of grace. Paul begins and ends *every one* of his New Testament letters with greetings of grace.

> "Grace to you and peace from God our Father and the Lord Jesus Christ." 1 Corinthians 1:3

> "The grace of the Lord Jesus Christ and the love of God and the fellowship of the Holy Spirit be with you all." 2 Corinthians 13:14

John ends the book of Revelation with a grace message, giving us the last verse of the Bible:

> "The grace of the Lord Jesus be with all. Amen." Revelation 22:21

These apostles were not using these words as mere salutations, the way we begin a letter with "Dear..." or sign off with "Sincerely..." These authors recognized that the grace of God, along with bringing us into relationship with Him, is the characteristic of God that we cannot live without. His grace keeps us alive, growing, and free from condemnation every single day of our lives. Without His favor, we would be unable to walk in a relationship with Him, and we would be eternally lost. Look for these messages of grace near the beginning and end of each of Paul's epistles in the New Testament, and mark them as reminders of the grace that sustains you.

Walk in wisdom toward outsiders, making the best use of the time. Let your speech always be gracious, seasoned with salt, so that you may know how you ought to answer each person.

Colossians 4:5-6

Let no corrupting talk come out of your mouths, but only such as is good for building up, as fits the occasion, that it may give grace to those who hear. And do not grieve the Holy Spirit of God, by whom you were sealed for the day of redemption. Let all bitterness and wrath and anger and clamor and slander be put away from you, along with all malice. Be kind to one another, tenderhearted, forgiving one another, as God in Christ forgave you.

Ephesians 4:29-32

As each has received a gift, use it to serve one another, as good stewards of God's varied grace: whoever speaks, as one who speaks oracles of God; whoever serves, as one who serves by the strength that God supplies—in order that in everything God may be glorified through Jesus Christ. To him belong glory and dominion forever and ever. Amen.

1 Peter 4:10-11

We want you to know, brothers, about the grace of God that has been given among the churches of Macedonia, for in a severe test of affliction, their abundance of joy and their extreme poverty have overflowed in a wealth of generosity on their part. For they gave according to their means, as I can testify, and beyond their means, of their own accord… But as you excel in everything—in faith, in speech, in knowledge, in all earnestness, and in our love for you—see that you excel in this act of grace also.

2 Corinthians 8:1-3,7

For this is a gracious thing, when, mindful of God, one endures sorrows while suffering unjustly. For what credit is it if, when you sin and are beaten for it, you endure? But if when you do good and suffer for it you endure, this is a gracious thing in the sight of God. For to this you have been called, because Christ also suffered for you, leaving you an example, so that you might follow in his steps.

1 Peter 2:19-21

Grace

Stewards of Grace

6

The Greek word *charis*, which is most often translated to grace in English Bibles, is used over one hundred fifty times in the New Testament. In most occasions it is used to describe grace that flows from God to people. God's way of leaning toward favoring sinners who are undeserving of His favor is certainly worthy of much discussion and praise. There are also a handful of times that grace is used to describe behavior that flows from one person or group to another. These are the ways that we are called to reflect God's grace.

Several of these verses apply grace to the words we speak. Speech that is gracious and seasoned with salt, when brought to those outside the church, are words that are attractive, flavorful, and have a lasting impression. It seems that a proper Christian response to those outside the church who question our faith is a kind and gracious answer, not a harsh argument. In Ephesians 4, the context is a discussion of life within the body of Christ. Our words to brothers and sisters in Christ should not corrupt, but they should build up and encourage others, giving them grace. We have seen that the Holy Spirit strengthening us is a grace from God. By the same Spirit, we can speak words to one another that strengthen with grace. The passage goes on to call believers to be "kind to one another, tenderhearted, forgiving one another, as God in Christ forgave you." Although we cannot give grace that saves another person, we are called to follow the example of God's forgiveness and forgive others according to His grace given to us. If we are unwilling to forgive someone, we may not have a proper understanding of God's grace toward us.

Another way that we can steward God's grace is to use the spiritual gifts that He has given us to serve one another. Spiritual gifts are a grace that God gives to all believers, and we manage the gift well when we use it to build one another up. Those with speaking gifts, such as prophecy-telling and teaching, should use the gifts to speak the words that God has given in Scripture. Those with service gifts, such as giving or serving others, should use their gifts in the strength—grace—that the Holy Spirit gives. Paul wrote in 2 Corinthians that financial giving is an act of grace. The Macedonian believers, saturated in the grace of God, wanted to give freely out of their meager resources to benefit others.

Peter describes it as a gracious thing when believers maintain focus on God to find strength to endure suffering. Just as Jesus suffered unjustly in an act of grace, God sees our actions as gracious when we do good and suffer for it, following Christ's example with His power.

We cannot give grace that saves or sanctifies another person. But we can show favor to others with kind and encouraging words, forgiveness, the benefit of our spiritual gifts, financial gifts, and advice to endure trials with faith. For these actions to truly be acts of grace, this favor should be shown to even those who are unworthy of our grace and cannot repay us. Just as God's grace is His leaning to favor those who do not deserve His favor, our grace should also extend to the undeserving. Our offer of grace cannot be based on what others have done for us. Otherwise grace would no longer be grace.

Action Step: Is there someone in your life that you can deliver grace to today? Every one of us is surrounded by others in need of encouragement, forgiveness, or financial help. Find a way to be a steward of God's grace today.

Key Points

1. Human sin goes deeper than just actions into the sinful condition of our hearts. This is why every single person needs God's grace.
2. It is God's way to be gracious toward those who choose to be in a covenant relationship with Him.
3. There is no kind or amount of work we can do to earn God's extravagant grace. It is a free gift that brings us eternal life through the work of Jesus Christ. The grace in which we stand—the undeserved favor of God—is only available to us through faith in Jesus Christ.
4. God's grace also trains us how we should live today. God's favor leans toward us to such an extent that He sends His Spirit to give believers the strength to do His will.
5. Out of the overflow of His love, in the midst of our desperate need for restoration to Him, God chooses to grace us with Himself by sending Jesus Christ and the Holy Spirit.
6. Just as God's grace is His leaning to favor those who do not deserve His favor, our grace in the form of kindness, forgiveness, and encouragement should also extend to the undeserving.

Grace

Action Steps

7

Go back through the action steps and complete any that you have not yet completed or repeat one that was meaningful:

1. Are you grieved by your sin? Has the commonness of evil coming from your own heart dulled your senses to the polluting effect of sin? Are we so surrounded by evil in this world that our own sin seems inconsequential in comparison? Picture yourself standing before Jesus while you are dripping with deceit, envy, and pride. Would your stains seem inconsequential then? If we are not genuinely grieved by the sins of our hearts, but only grieved by the social consequences when our sin is discovered by others, then we are not seriously evaluating our own sin and practicing true repentance. Pray and ask God to help you see your sin as He sees it.

2. Find a globe of the earth or at least a ball that can represent the globe. Place your finger on a spot on the globe that represents your current location. Begin to trace your finger straight north on the globe, and note at which point your finger is no longer traveling north but changes to a southern direction. Because the earth rotates on a north/south axis, you only get as far as the North Pole before you are headed south. The distance from the North Pole to the South Pole can be measured. Now return your finger to your current location and start tracing your finger straight east. At what point is your finger no longer going east? The answer is never! You can go around the globe hundreds of times in that same direction, and your finger will still be traveling to the east. It never changes to west! The distance from the east to the west cannot be measured. That's how far God removes the sins of those who fear Him! That is amazing grace!

3. When you receive a gift from someone, a proper response is to express thanks to the giver, often in the form of a written note. Write a note of thanks today to God for the gift of the immeasurable riches of His grace in Christ Jesus.

4. Hebrews 4 gives us the confidence to draw near to the "throne of grace." The awesome privilege granted to us in Jesus Christ is access to a loving relationship with the Ruler of all creation. Not only are we given permission to enter His throne room, we are also promised "mercy and grace in time of need." Whether your need is forgiveness from sin or power to obey or strength to bear trials, God's mercy and grace are available to those who seek Him. Enter before His throne of grace today in prayer to seek His mercy and grace.

5. We have already seen that Peter begins and ends his second letter with words of grace. Paul begins and ends *every one* of his New Testament letters with greetings of grace. These authors recognized that the grace of God, along with bringing us into relationship with Him, is the characteristic of God that we cannot live without. His grace keeps us alive, growing, and free from condemnation every single day of our lives. Without His favor, we would be unable to walk in a relationship with Him, and we would be eternally lost. Look for these messages of grace near the beginning and end of each of Paul's epistles in the New Testament, and mark them as reminders of the grace that sustains you.

6. Is there someone in your life that you can deliver grace to today? Every one of us is surrounded by others in need of encouragement, forgiveness, or financial help. Find a way to be a steward of God's grace today.

WEEK 19
Holy

God's holiness is not simply the best we know infinitely bettered. We know nothing like the divine holiness. It stands apart, unique, unapproachable, incomprehensible, and unattainable. The natural man is blind to it. He may fear God's power and admire His wisdom, but His holiness he cannot even imagine. Only the Spirit of the Holy One can impart to the human spirit the knowledge of the holy....

God is holy with an absolute holiness that knows no degrees, and this He cannot impart to His creatures. But there is a relative and contingent holiness which He shares with angels and seraphim in heaven and with redeemed men on earth as their preparation for heaven. This holiness God can and does impart to His children. He shares it with them by imputation and by importation, and because He has made it available to them through the blood of the Lamb, He requires it of them.

A. W. Tozer, *The Knowledge of the Holy*

This is the message we have heard from him and proclaim to you, that God is light, and in him is no darkness at all. If we say we have fellowship with him while we walk in darkness, we lie and do not practice the truth. But if we walk in the light, as he is in the light, we have fellowship with one another, and the blood of Jesus his Son cleanses us from all sin. If we say we have no sin, we deceive ourselves, and the truth is not in us. If we confess our sins, he is faithful and just to forgive us our sins and to cleanse us from all unrighteousness.

1 John 1:5-9

...who alone has immortality, who dwells in unapproachable light, whom no one has ever seen or can see. To him be honor and eternal dominion. Amen.

1 Timothy 6:16

Bless the LORD, O my soul! O LORD my God, you are very great! You are clothed with splendor and majesty, covering yourself with light as with a garment, stretching out the heavens like a tent.

Psalms 104:1-2

And the city has no need of sun or moon to shine on it, for the glory of God gives it light, and its lamp is the Lamb.

Revelation 21:23

The sun shall be no more your light by day, nor for brightness shall the moon give you light; but the LORD will be your everlasting light, and your God will be your glory. Your sun shall no more go down, nor your moon withdraw itself; for the LORD will be your everlasting light, and your days of mourning shall be ended.

Isaiah 60:19-20

And the glory of the LORD went up from the cherub to the threshold of the house, and the house was filled with the cloud, and the court was filled with the brightness of the glory of the LORD.

Ezekiel 10:4

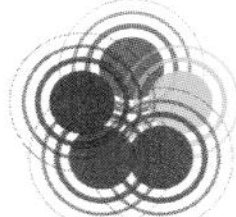

Holy

God Is Light

1

On August 21, 2017, the United States experienced a total solar eclipse. The sixty to seventy-mile-wide path of the eclipse stretched from the Pacific coast of Oregon across the entire width of the continent to the Atlantic coast of South Carolina. The outer edge of this path of totality ran right through our backyard. Because we were watching near the edge of the path of totality, the total eclipse lasted less than one minute. But what a spectacular minute it was! Once the moon completely obscured the breadth of the sun, we were able to safely remove our protective glasses and view with our naked eyes the spectacular corona radiating from behind the moon. It was the most breathtaking sight my eyes have ever seen.

What makes a total solar eclipse possible? The sun is four hundred times the diameter of the moon. How could the relatively tiny sphere of the moon obscure something that dwarfs it in size? God has designed our solar system so that the moon is almost exactly four hundred times closer to the earth than the sun is. The sun and the moon are so perfectly set in the sky that when they line up with each other, the moon just barely covers the sun. If the moon was much larger, it would cover up the sun's corona so an eclipse would mean just darkness. If the moon was much farther from the earth, it would appear small enough that it would not cover the full width of the sun. The only reason that a total solar eclipse is such a sensational sight is because God designed it for us to experience awe. In fact, one might say He designed it to reveal something about Himself. "The heavens declare the glory of God, and the sky above proclaims his handiwork" (Ps. 19:1).

Light is often used in Scripture to represent God's holiness. There is no darkness, meaning unseen evil, in God. He is without sin, without imperfection, and completely transcendent in His holiness. His light is "unapproachable" in that unholy creatures cannot behold the full perfection of His holiness. Yet the miraculous truth is that through the cleansing blood of Jesus we can walk in fellowship with God in His light, which continues to reveal our sin.

Ezekiel had a vision of the throne room of God, and he wrote, "the court was filled with the brightness of the glory of the Lord." John Piper defines God's glory as "the manifest beauty of his holiness. It is the going public of his holiness." The glory of the Lord is the means by which He shows His holiness, sometimes through a visible manifestation such as light. When the people of God see a manifestation of the glory of God, Scripture often describes it as brilliant light.

God's holiness is His complete purity and separation from sin. His holiness is closely tied to His transcendence, as discussed earlier in this book under the section "Far above Creation." His holiness is transcendent—beyond the limits of all possible experience and knowledge. We can neither approach His holiness nor completely appreciate it. But to help us in our understanding, on the first day of Creation, God created light, then He used the imagery of light in Scripture to begin to reveal His holiness and glory. And He designed the total solar eclipse to give us an occasional glimpse into the spectacular beauty of light.

Action Step: The imagery of light as a manifestation of God's holiness is made literal at the end of time in the holy city of New Jerusalem. "The city has no need of sun or moon to shine on it, for the glory of God gives it light, and its lamp is the Lamb" (Rev. 21:23). Praise and worship the God whose glory will light His eternal city for His people.

Now Moses was keeping the flock of his father-in-law, Jethro, the priest of Midian, and he led his flock to the west side of the wilderness and came to Horeb, the mountain of God. And the angel of the Lord *appeared to him in a flame of fire out of the midst of a bush. He looked, and behold, the bush was burning, yet it was not consumed. And Moses said, "I will turn aside to see this great sight, why the bush is not burned." When the* Lord *saw that he turned aside to see, God called to him out of the bush, "Moses, Moses!" And he said, "Here I am." Then he said, "Do not come near; take your sandals off your feet, for the place on which you are standing is holy ground." And he said, "I am the God of your father, the God of Abraham, the God of Isaac, and the God of Jacob." And Moses hid his face, for he was afraid to look at God.*

Exodus 3:1-6

And above the expanse over their heads there was the likeness of a throne, in appearance like sapphire; and seated above the likeness of a throne was a likeness with a human appearance. And upward from what had the appearance of his waist I saw as it were gleaming metal, like the appearance of fire enclosed all around. And downward from what had the appearance of his waist I saw as it were the appearance of fire, and there was brightness around him. Like the appearance of the bow that is in the cloud on the day of rain, so was the appearance of the brightness all around.

Such was the appearance of the likeness of the glory of the Lord. *And when I saw it, I fell on my face, and I heard the voice of one speaking.*

Ezekiel 1:26-28

"Therefore say to the house of Israel, Thus says the Lord God: *It is not for your sake, O house of Israel, that I am about to act, but for the sake of my holy name, which you have profaned among the nations to which you came. And I will vindicate the holiness of my great name, which has been profaned among the nations, and which you have profaned among them. And the nations will know that I am the* Lord, *declares the Lord* God, *when through you I vindicate my holiness before their eyes. I will take you from the nations and gather you from all the countries and bring you into your own land. I will sprinkle clean water on you, and you shall be clean from all your uncleannesses, and from all your idols I will cleanse you. And I will give you a new heart, and a new spirit I will put within you. And I will remove the heart of stone from your flesh and give you a heart of flesh. And I will put my Spirit within you, and cause you to walk in my statutes and be careful to obey my rules."*

Ezekiel 36:22-27

When the day of Pentecost arrived, they were all together in one place. And suddenly there came from heaven a sound like a mighty rushing wind, and it filled the entire house where they were sitting. And divided tongues as of fire appeared to them and rested on each one of them. And they were all filled with the Holy Spirit and began to speak in other tongues as the Spirit gave them utterance.

Acts 2:1-4

Holy

God Is a Consuming Fire

2

Along with light, another image from creation that God has used to reveal His holiness is fire. When the Lord first appeared to Moses in the wilderness to call him to lead Israel, He appeared "in a flame of fire out of the midst of a bush." Moses looked to see this bush that was burning yet not being consumed. The first thing the Lord said to Moses, after calling his name, was, "Do not come near; take your sandals off your feet, for the place on which you are standing is holy ground." God manifested in fire in a common bush on a mountain and transformed what was common into a sacred place. Everyday dirt was transformed to holy ground because of the presence of the holy God.

As Moses led the Israelites out of Egypt, God demonstrated His holy presence with them each night in a pillar of fire to light their way (Ex. 13:21). And when He met His people at Mt. Sinai, He descended in fire, causing the mountain to tremble, and He warned Moses to keep the people from coming up the mountain lest they perish by looking on His holiness and glory (Ex. 19:16-25).

Isaiah wrote of the dilemma of God's people as sinners unfit to dwell in the presence of God: "The sinners in Zion are afraid; trembling has seized the godless: 'Who among us can dwell with the consuming fire? Who among us can dwell with everlasting burnings?'" (Is. 33:14). Even the author of Hebrews—after spending most of his letter detailing how Jesus has opened up access to God so we may approach Him with confidence—warns that our God is a consuming fire (Heb. 12:29). God's holiness is so transcendent over our sinfulness that this fire of holiness can consume the unholy sinner that does not approach Him with reverence and awe through faith in Jesus Christ.

The prophet Ezekiel was called to minister to the people of Judah during their exile to Babylon. The focus of Ezekiel's call was to defend the holiness of God's name. The Lord first came to Ezekiel in a vision, which the prophet describes in detail at the beginning of his book. Ezekiel appeared to have difficulty describing what he saw, using metaphors throughout his description. But images of "the appearance of fire" and "brightness" are words that he uses repeatedly to describe his vision of a likeness of the glory of the Lord. The images seared into Ezekiel's memory from that vision equipped him to speak to God's people of His holiness. In the short term, God planned to show His holiness to the nations by restoring His people to their land. The way that God would ultimately vindicate His holiness and proclaim His glory, as prophesied through Ezekiel, would be to put His Spirit within them to cause them to obey.

This promise saw its fulfillment when, after Jesus ascended to heaven, the Holy Spirit was poured out to believers in "divided tongues as of fire." In this case, the holy presence of God's Spirit came to dwell with common men and women in the appearance of fire to make the common holy, rather than to consume the unholy.

Action Step: Light and fire in Scripture are used in both figurative and literal ways to reveal the holy character of God. There is also much imagery in Scripture about God using "fire" in the form of trials to refine our faith. Read 1 Peter 1:6-7 and consider how God has used trials to prove to you the genuineness of your faith that has been tested by fire.

"You are to distinguish between the holy and the common, and between the unclean and the clean, and you are to teach the people of Israel all the statutes that the LORD has spoken to them by Moses."

Leviticus 10:10-11

The LORD spoke to Moses after the death of the two sons of Aaron, when they drew near before the LORD and died, and the LORD said to Moses, "Tell Aaron your brother not to come at any time into the Holy Place inside the veil, before the mercy seat that is on the ark, so that he may not die. For I will appear in the cloud over the mercy seat. But in this way Aaron shall come into the Holy Place: with a bull from the herd for a sin offering and a ram for a burnt offering. He shall put on the holy linen coat and shall have the linen undergarment on his body, and he shall tie the linen sash around his waist, and wear the linen turban; these are the holy garments. He shall bathe his body in water and then put them on. And he shall take from the congregation of the people of Israel two male goats for a sin offering, and one ram for a burnt offering."

Leviticus 16:1-5

Now even the first covenant had regulations for worship and an earthly place of holiness. For a tent was prepared, the first section, in which were the lampstand and the table and the bread of the Presence. It is called the Holy Place. Behind the second curtain was a second section called the Most Holy Place, having the golden altar of incense and the ark of the covenant covered on all sides with gold, in which was a golden urn holding the manna, and Aaron's staff that budded, and the tablets of the covenant. Above it were the cherubim of glory overshadowing the mercy seat. Of these things we cannot now speak in detail.

These preparations having thus been made, the priests go regularly into the first section, performing their ritual duties, but into the second only the high priest goes, and he but once a year, and not without taking blood, which he offers for himself and for the unintentional sins of the people.

Hebrews 9:1-7

Now Nadab and Abihu, the sons of Aaron, each took his censer and put fire in it and laid incense on it and offered unauthorized fire before the LORD, which he had not commanded them. And fire came out from before the LORD and consumed them, and they died before the LORD. Then Moses said to Aaron, "This is what the LORD has said: 'Among those who are near me I will be sanctified, and before all the people I will be glorified.'" And Aaron held his peace.

Leviticus 10:1-3

Holy

The Most Holy Place

3

In the books of Exodus and Leviticus, God gave Moses very specific and detailed instructions for the construction and use of the tabernacle where God would dwell with His people. "Exactly as I show you concerning the pattern of the tabernacle, and of all its furniture, so you shall make it" (Ex. 25:9). All of the instructions were to be followed exactly because the pattern being followed was the design of the heavenly sanctuary (Heb. 8:5). Nothing about this tabernacle or the worship within was to be taken lightly. All of the objects within the tabernacle were set apart for holy use—"You shall consecrate them, that they may be most holy. Whatever touches them will become holy" (Ex. 30:29). The clothing that the priests wore also had specific descriptions given by God Himself because even these garments were holy (Ex. 28). The basic design of the tabernacle was an outer rectangular court walled with linen hanging from bronze pillars. Within this court was the rectangular tent of meeting or the Holy Place, walled with curtains and a tent of goats' hair over the top. Only priests could enter into the Holy Place. Daily sacrifices were offered at the entrance to the tent of meeting to atone for the people's sins, and the Lord promised, "There I will meet with the people of Israel, and it shall be sanctified by my glory" (Ex. 29:43).

Already we can begin to appreciate the respect and reverence commanded of the priests of Israel in the presence of God in the tabernacle. But inside the Holy Place, behind a thick veil, was the Most Holy Place. Only the high priest could enter through this veil, and he could only come one time each year on the Day of Atonement. Inside the Most Holy Place, the golden mercy seat rested on the ark of the covenant. This place was exceedingly holy because the Lord Himself appeared in a cloud over the mercy seat. The high priest had to be very careful about the way he prepared to enter behind the veil, preparing offerings and wearing holy garments, and he had to come *only* on the designated day, "so that he may not die." It was a dangerous thing to approach the holy God in *any* other way than the way that He provided. This was demonstrated by the death of two of Aaron's sons who offered "unauthorized fire" before the Lord and were consumed by fire themselves. We are not told in Scripture exactly what their offense was, but they went outside the guidelines of what God had commanded for the offering, thus introducing the common or profane into the holy.

The design of the tabernacle, with veils and walls separating the people from the Lord, along with the sacrifices to atone for sin, were a daily reminder of the people's uncleanness before the holy God. These barriers were not to be crossed by common people. Great care was taken in the construction and worship at the tabernacle because these holy things were set apart for a holy use—approaching the perfectly holy God.

Action Step: We will see in later readings this week why there is no need for physical barriers in our places of worship any longer. Yet it is still important to our spiritual lives to daily be reminded of God's holiness. Jesus provided for us a model for revering God's holiness daily in the Lord's Prayer: "Our Father in heaven, hallowed be your name" (Matt. 6:9). Set a goal of praying daily and incorporating worship of His holiness in your prayer.

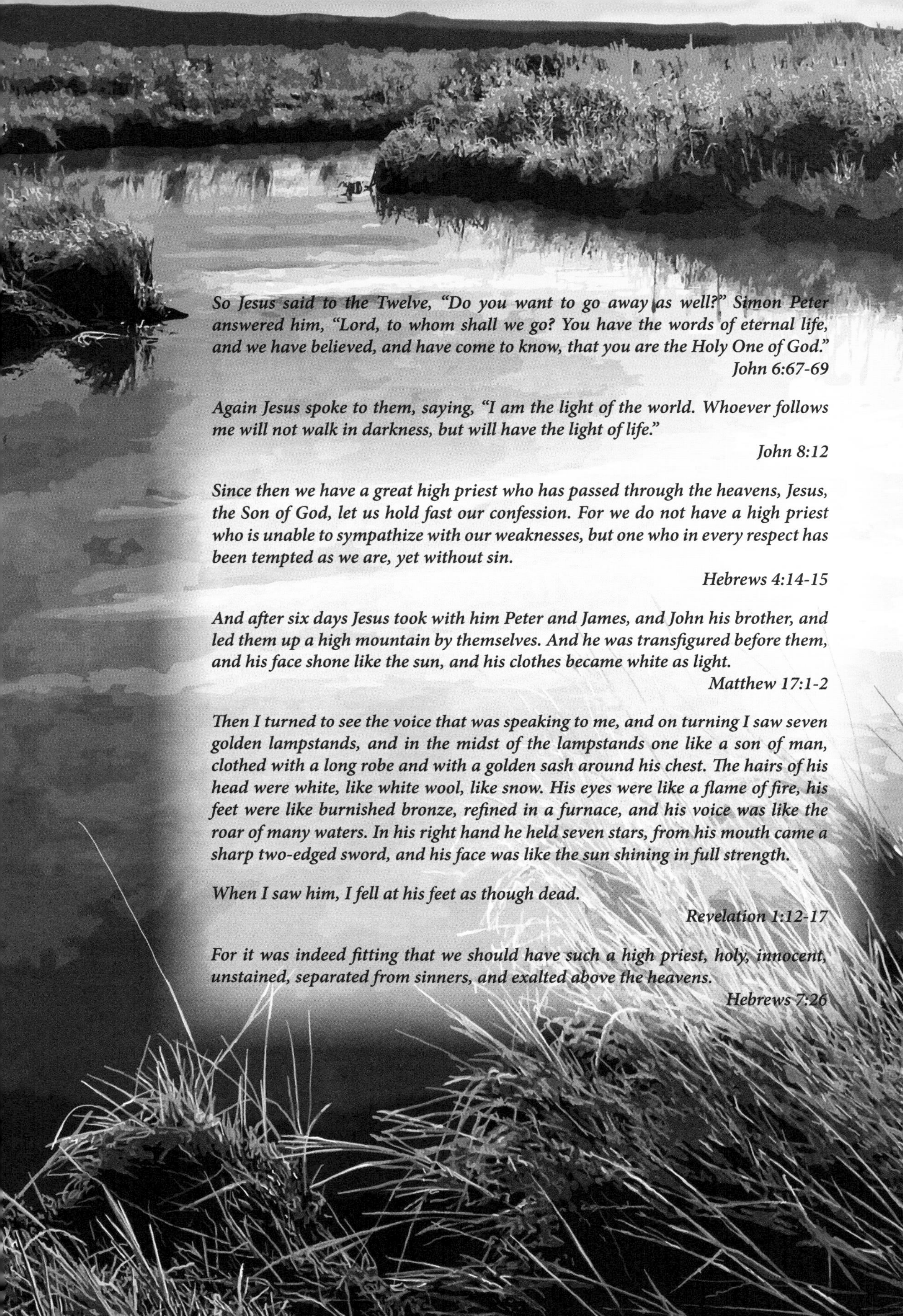

So Jesus said to the Twelve, "Do you want to go away as well?" Simon Peter answered him, "Lord, to whom shall we go? You have the words of eternal life, and we have believed, and have come to know, that you are the Holy One of God."

John 6:67-69

Again Jesus spoke to them, saying, "I am the light of the world. Whoever follows me will not walk in darkness, but will have the light of life."

John 8:12

Since then we have a great high priest who has passed through the heavens, Jesus, the Son of God, let us hold fast our confession. For we do not have a high priest who is unable to sympathize with our weaknesses, but one who in every respect has been tempted as we are, yet without sin.

Hebrews 4:14-15

And after six days Jesus took with him Peter and James, and John his brother, and led them up a high mountain by themselves. And he was transfigured before them, and his face shone like the sun, and his clothes became white as light.

Matthew 17:1-2

Then I turned to see the voice that was speaking to me, and on turning I saw seven golden lampstands, and in the midst of the lampstands one like a son of man, clothed with a long robe and with a golden sash around his chest. The hairs of his head were white, like white wool, like snow. His eyes were like a flame of fire, his feet were like burnished bronze, refined in a furnace, and his voice was like the roar of many waters. In his right hand he held seven stars, from his mouth came a sharp two-edged sword, and his face was like the sun shining in full strength.

When I saw him, I fell at his feet as though dead.

Revelation 1:12-17

For it was indeed fitting that we should have such a high priest, holy, innocent, unstained, separated from sinners, and exalted above the heavens.

Hebrews 7:26

Holy

The Holiness of Jesus Christ

4

Jesus Christ, the Son of God, shares in the full holiness of God. When the angel announced His birth to Mary, he said, "The Holy Spirit will come upon you, and the power of the Most High will overshadow you; therefore the child to be born will be called holy—the Son of God" (Lk. 1:35). Even before His birth, Jesus was proclaimed holy because his humanity would be conceived by the Holy Spirit through the power of God. After beginning His ministry, Jesus was referred to by Peter as "the Holy One of God." And Jesus described Himself as one "whom the Father consecrated and sent into the world" (Jn. 10:36). The word "consecrated" here is translated as set apart, sanctified, or made holy in other Bible versions. In fact, this Greek word, *hagiazo*, is an action word that is translated in different verses and different English translations as hallowed, made sacred, consecrated, sanctified, made holy, set apart, and purified.

Jesus described Himself as "the light of the world." Acting as light, Jesus revealed the holiness and knowledge of God to His followers. This imagery also recalls the Exodus, where God led the nation of Israel out of Egypt by manifesting as a pillar of fire to light their way at night. It is clear that the "light of the world" has "no darkness at all" in Him when the author of Hebrews states that Jesus is one "who in every respect has been tempted as we are, yet without sin."

For most of His life on earth, Jesus' appearance was that of any other man, not showing any visible manifestation of the glory of God. Peter, James, and John had the privilege of witnessing a moment on the mountain when Jesus was transfigured to show a glimpse of His divine glory. Jesus' face shone like the sun, and his clothes became as white as light. The disciples were terrified by even this brief look at Jesus' holiness. John, having already witnessed this transfiguration, was even more astonished by Jesus' glorified appearance in his Revelation vision. In that case, his description of Jesus is even more awe-inspiring, and John "fell at his feet as though dead." This was the risen and glorified Christ, displaying His divine holiness in a way that John had never seen on earth.

The book of Hebrews provides the most emphatic description of Jesus' holiness, describing His sinlessness in multiple ways: holy, innocent, unstained, and separated from sinners. The holiness of the Father does not diminish in the Son, but the divine glory was veiled during His time on earth. Jesus was set apart by the Father to be sent into the world, but now Jesus has ascended into heaven, glorified by the Father according to Jesus' prayer in John 17:5—"And now, Father, glorify me in your own presence with the glory that I had with you before the world existed."

Action Step: As we read through the New Testament, it is easy to be attracted to the humanity of Jesus. We are permitted to see His hunger, His fatigue, and His sorrow. Read Revelation 1:12-17 on the opposite page carefully. This is a description of Jesus Christ in all of His heavenly glory. Reflect on this spectacular description of Christ, and "Worship the Lord in the splendor of holiness; tremble before him, all the earth!" (Ps. 96:9).

Now the point in what we are saying is this: we have such a high priest, one who is seated at the right hand of the throne of the Majesty in heaven, a minister in the holy places, in the true tent that the Lord set up, not man.

Hebrews 8:1-2

But when Christ appeared as a high priest of the good things that have come, then through the greater and more perfect tent (not made with hands, that is, not of this creation) he entered once for all into the holy places, not by means of the blood of goats and calves but by means of his own blood, thus securing an eternal redemption. For if the blood of goats and bulls, and the sprinkling of defiled persons with the ashes of a heifer, sanctify for the purification of the flesh, how much more will the blood of Christ, who through the eternal Spirit offered himself without blemish to God, purify our conscience from dead works to serve the living God.

Hebrews 9:11-14

For Christ has entered, not into holy places made with hands, which are copies of the true things, but into heaven itself, now to appear in the presence of God on our behalf. Nor was it to offer himself repeatedly, as the high priest enters the holy places every year with blood not his own, for then he would have had to suffer repeatedly since the foundation of the world. But as it is, he has appeared once for all at the end of the ages to put away sin by the sacrifice of himself.

Hebrews 9:24-26

For since the law has but a shadow of the good things to come instead of the true form of these realities, it can never, by the same sacrifices that are continually offered every year, make perfect those who draw near.

Hebrews 10:1

And by that will we have been sanctified through the offering of the body of Jesus Christ once for all.

And every priest stands daily at his service, offering repeatedly the same sacrifices, which can never take away sins. But when Christ had offered for all time a single sacrifice for sins, he sat down at the right hand of God, waiting from that time until his enemies should be made a footstool for his feet. For by a single offering he has perfected for all time those who are being sanctified.

Hebrews 10:10-14

Therefore, brothers, since we have confidence to enter the holy places by the blood of Jesus, by the new and living way that he opened for us through the curtain, that is, through his flesh, and since we have a great priest over the house of God, let us draw near with a true heart in full assurance of faith, with our hearts sprinkled clean from an evil conscience and our bodies washed with pure water.

Hebrews 10:19-22

Holy

Made Holy in Christ

5

Followers of Jesus are called to be holy—"you also be holy in all your conduct, since it is written, 'You shall be holy, for I am holy'" (1 Pet. 1:16). Jesus told His followers, "You are the light of the world" (Mt. 5:14). Jesus calls us to bear the family image of holiness and shine the light of knowledge of Him throughout the world. But if holiness is defined as pure, separated from sin, and set apart for holy purpose, how can we obey this command? Can we *will* ourselves to be holy? Is it within our power to be separated from sin? After all, "all have sinned and fall short of the glory of God" (Rom. 3:23). If God's glory is His holiness put on display, we are *all* falling short of holiness.

To understand God's solution to the problem, we can follow the author of Hebrews back to the holiness of the tabernacle. The book of Hebrews is written to a Jewish audience and contrasts the Old Covenant with the better New Covenant. The author describes how everything about the Old Covenant pointed toward a fulfillment in Jesus Christ. The tabernacle and its separate rooms are referred to as "holy places made with hands, which are copies of the true things." But Christ, with His death, resurrection, and ascension, has entered "into heaven itself, now to appear in the presence of God on our behalf." The old sacrifices were just a reminder of the people's sin, and they never had the power to make them holy. Therefore, the walls and barriers of the tabernacle separating the people from their holy God remained day after day, year after year, and the priests continued to maintain the ritual offerings and sacrifices just to be able to come close to the barriers. Christ's sacrifice was infinitely greater. His blood, offered once for all, has secured an eternal redemption. By offering a perfect sacrifice without blemish, Jesus was able to purify us, separating us from our sin. Those who place their faith in the sacrifice of Jesus are made holy in His death. Our holiness *has* been secured already. In Christ we have been set apart and purified from sin.

When Jesus died on the cross, the curtain in the temple which separated the Holy Place from the Most Holy Place was torn in two from top to bottom. The author of Hebrews explains that the curtain was the flesh of Jesus, torn to open up a way for us to enter into the holy places—not just into the Holy Place, but into the Most Holy Place, into the very presence of God. We have been purified from the inside, not just received a ritual washing on the outside. The blood of Jesus Christ, when applied in faith, makes us holy so that we can draw near to God's throne with confidence that we will not be consumed by His holiness. He is every bit as holy as He was in the wilderness tabernacle. It remains true that sinful humans may only approach the holy God in exactly the way that He provides. But now God has provided Jesus as the way and fulfilled all of His promises for relationship with us by making us holy in Christ. There are many astounding truths in the gospel. One of the most astounding is that any part of the brilliant fiery holiness of God can be applied to sinful humanity through the blood of Jesus Christ.

Action Step: The sacrificial work of Christ is completed, and He is seated at the right hand of God. There is no need for additional sacrifices and no need for the special layout of the tabernacle that Israel had in the wilderness. The church is now God's temple and where His Spirit dwells (1 Cor. 3:16-17). Just as the tabernacle was made holy by God, so we as the body of Christ are made holy by His presence within us. Celebrate that truth with someone from your local church body this week. In doing so, you are helping to build up a church that honors the holiness of God.

Beloved, we are God's children now, and what we will be has not yet appeared; but we know that when he appears we shall be like him, because we shall see him as he is. And everyone who thus hopes in him purifies himself as he is pure.

1 John 3:2-3

And we all, with unveiled face, beholding the glory of the Lord, are being transformed into the same image from one degree of glory to another. For this comes from the Lord who is the Spirit.

2 Corinthians 3:18

"By this my Father is glorified, that you bear much fruit and so prove to be my disciples."

John 15:8

Therefore, preparing your minds for action, and being sober-minded, set your hope fully on the grace that will be brought to you at the revelation of Jesus Christ. As obedient children, do not be conformed to the passions of your former ignorance, but as he who called you is holy, you also be holy in all your conduct, since it is written, "You shall be holy, for I am holy."

1 Peter 1:13-16

Since we have these promises, beloved, let us cleanse ourselves from every defilement of body and spirit, bringing holiness to completion in the fear of God.

2 Corinthians 7:1

Strive for peace with everyone, and for the holiness without which no one will see the Lord.

Hebrews 12:14

But that is not the way you learned Christ!—assuming that you have heard about him and were taught in him, as the truth is in Jesus, to put off your old self, which belongs to your former manner of life and is corrupt through deceitful desires, and to be renewed in the spirit of your minds, and to put on the new self, created after the likeness of God in true righteousness and holiness.

Ephesians 4:20-24

Holy

Continuing Holiness in the Holy Spirit

6

Scripture promises that believers *have been* made holy in Christ: "But you were washed, you were sanctified, you were justified in the name of the Lord Jesus Christ and by the Spirit of our God" (1 Cor. 6:11). In terms of being able to draw near to the holy God, sanctification is complete in the once-for-all death of Jesus Christ. However, we are definitely not holy in terms of being without sin in our daily experience. There is another aspect of sanctification in which we are continuing to be made holy.

John, in his first epistle, wrote that we are God's children now, but we do not yet see what we will be. In other words, we aren't holy in practice. When Jesus Christ returns, we will see Him as He is, and we will be like Him, conformed to His image and without sin. Our hope in this future completion of sanctification in Christ should drive our ongoing growth in holiness now. As we set our hope fully in Christ and behold the glory of the Lord, soaking in His holiness, we are transformed into His image more and more by the work of the Holy Spirit in our lives. The goal of this progressive sanctification is to become more like Christ, which is to restore the family image of God that was given to men and women at creation but then broken by sin. The astounding truth that Jesus taught is that the fruit of our good works glorifies God. God's holiness is made known to the world when disciples of Jesus Christ bear the family image!

This continuing sanctification is not possible apart from the Spirit's work in our lives. However, it is also necessary for us to cooperate with His work. Setting our hope fully on the future promises of God is part of what Peter describes as "preparing your minds for action." Then Peter goes on to say that obedience is the result of prepared minds. Because we are children of God, we willfully choose not to follow ignorant or worldly passions, but instead, we choose obedience to God, which leads to holiness. We are commanded to be holy because as children of God we are not only declared holy, but we have the Spirit and the Scriptures to assist us in holy living. The inner transformation in our hearts accomplished by God leads to increasing outward expressions of holiness. Because we have the promises of being reconciled with God and adopted into His family, let us put off the sin that defiles us physically and spiritually and cooperate with the Holy Spirit in completing our holiness. The author of Hebrews urges us to strive for holiness, reminding us that without the holiness that Christ has already accomplished and our continued pursuit of holiness powered by the grace of God, we will not see Him. If we are not striving for holiness—if sanctification is not important to us—it calls into question whether we have really been transformed by the gospel.

Action Step: One of the ways that the Spirit works to grow our holiness is through discipline. Hebrews 12:10 says, "he disciplines us for our good, that we may share his holiness." God is treating us just like any good father would treat his children–by disciplining us with love to train us in holiness. If you are facing a difficult trial right now, whether it was brought on by your own sin or not, bring it in prayer to God. Submit your will to His so that He can discipline you to share His holiness.

Weekly Summary

Key Points

1. Light is often used in Scripture to represent God's holiness. There is no darkness, meaning unseen evil, in God. He is without sin, without imperfection, and completely transcendent in His holiness. When the people of God see a manifestation of the glory of God, Scripture often describes it as brilliant light.

2. God's holiness is so transcendent over our sinfulness that the fire of His holiness can consume the unholy sinner that does not approach Him with reverence and awe through faith in Jesus Christ.

3. The design of the tabernacle, with veils and walls separating the people from the Lord, along with the sacrifices to atone for sin, were a daily reminder of the people's uncleanness before the holy God.

4. Jesus Christ, the Son of God, shares in the full holiness of God. As "the light of the world," Jesus revealed the holiness and knowledge of God to His followers.

5. Those who place their faith in the sacrifice of Jesus are made holy in His death. In Christ we have been set apart and purified from sin.

6. As we set our hope fully in Christ and behold the glory of the Lord, soaking in His holiness, we are continually being made holy by the work of the Holy Spirit in our lives.

Holy
Action Steps

Go back through the action steps and complete any that you have not yet completed or repeat one that was meaningful:

1. The imagery of light as a manifestation of God's holiness is made literal at the end of time in the holy city of New Jerusalem. "The city has no need of sun or moon to shine on it, for the glory of God gives it light, and its lamp is the Lamb" (Rev. 21:23). Praise and worship the God whose glory will light His eternal city for His people.

2. Light and fire in Scripture are used in both figurative and literal ways to reveal the holy character of God. There is also much imagery in Scripture about God using "fire" in the form of trials to refine our faith. Read 1 Peter 1:6-7 and consider how God has used trials to prove to you the genuineness of your faith that has been tested by fire.

3. We will see in later readings this week why there is no need for physical barriers in our places of worship any longer. Yet it is still important to our spiritual lives to daily be reminded of God's holiness. Jesus provided for us a model for revering God's holiness daily in the Lord's Prayer: "Our Father in heaven, hallowed be your name" (Matt. 6:9). Set a goal of praying daily and incorporating worship of His holiness in your prayer.

4. As we read through the New Testament, it is easy to be attracted to the humanity of Jesus. We are permitted to see His hunger, His fatigue, and His sorrow. Read Revelation 1:12-17 on page 304 carefully. This is a description of Jesus Christ in all of His heavenly glory. Reflect on this spectacular description of Christ, and "Worship the Lord in the splendor of holiness; tremble before him, all the earth!" (Ps. 96:9).

5. The sacrificial work of Christ is completed, and He is seated at the right hand of God. There is no need for additional sacrifices and no need for the special layout of the tabernacle that Israel had in the wilderness. The church is now God's temple and where His Spirit dwells (1 Cor. 3:16-17). Just as the tabernacle was made holy by God, so we as the body of Christ are made holy by His presence within us. Celebrate that truth with someone from your local church body this week. In doing so, you are helping to build up a church that honors the holiness of God.

6. One of the ways that the Spirit works to grow our holiness is through discipline. Hebrews 12:10 says, "he disciplines us for our good, that we may share his holiness." God is treating us just like any good father would treat his children—by disciplining us with love to train us in holiness. If you are facing a difficult trial right now, whether it was brought on by your own sin or not, bring it in prayer to God. Submit your will to His so that He can discipline you to share His holiness.

WEEK 20
Wise

For the truth is that God in his wisdom, to make and keep us humble and to teach us to walk by faith, has hidden from us almost everything that we should like to know about the providential purposes which he is working out in the churches and in our own lives....

This is the way of wisdom. Clearly, it is just one facet of the life of faith. For what underlies and sustains it? Why, the conviction that the inscrutable God of providence is the wise and gracious God of creation and redemption.... We can trust him and rejoice in him, even when we cannot discern his path....

For what is this wisdom that he gives? As we have seen, it is not a sharing in all his knowledge, but a disposition to confess that he is wise, and to cleave to him and live for him in the light of his Word through thick and thin.

J. I. Packer, *Knowing God*

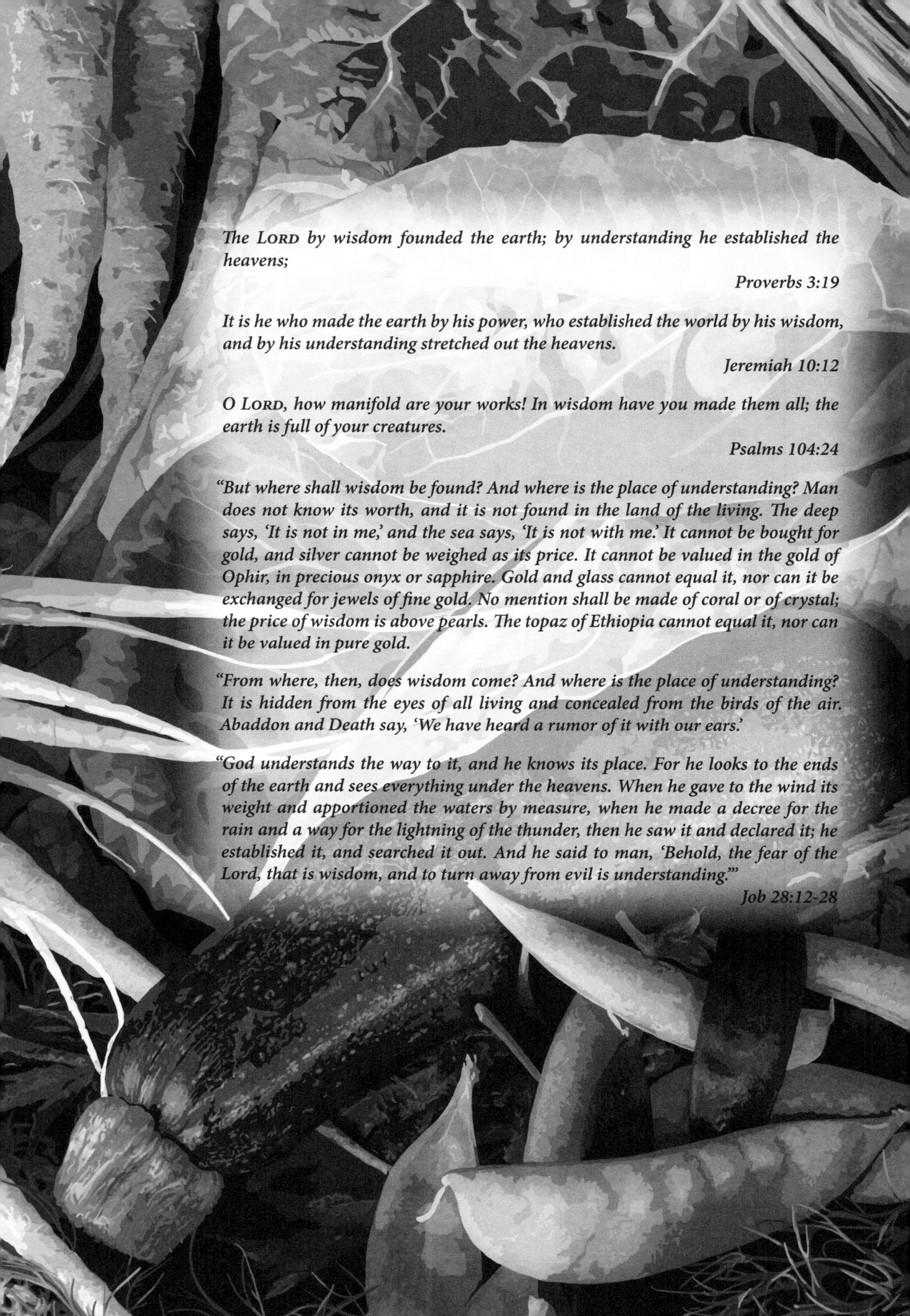

The LORD *by wisdom founded the earth; by understanding he established the heavens;*

Proverbs 3:19

It is he who made the earth by his power, who established the world by his wisdom, and by his understanding stretched out the heavens.

Jeremiah 10:12

O LORD, *how manifold are your works! In wisdom have you made them all; the earth is full of your creatures.*

Psalms 104:24

"But where shall wisdom be found? And where is the place of understanding? Man does not know its worth, and it is not found in the land of the living. The deep says, 'It is not in me,' and the sea says, 'It is not with me.' It cannot be bought for gold, and silver cannot be weighed as its price. It cannot be valued in the gold of Ophir, in precious onyx or sapphire. Gold and glass cannot equal it, nor can it be exchanged for jewels of fine gold. No mention shall be made of coral or of crystal; the price of wisdom is above pearls. The topaz of Ethiopia cannot equal it, nor can it be valued in pure gold.

"From where, then, does wisdom come? And where is the place of understanding? It is hidden from the eyes of all living and concealed from the birds of the air. Abaddon and Death say, 'We have heard a rumor of it with our ears.'

"God understands the way to it, and he knows its place. For he looks to the ends of the earth and sees everything under the heavens. When he gave to the wind its weight and apportioned the waters by measure, when he made a decree for the rain and a way for the lightning of the thunder, then he saw it and declared it; he established it, and searched it out. And he said to man, 'Behold, the fear of the Lord, that is wisdom, and to turn away from evil is understanding.'"

Job 28:12-28

Wise

God's Wisdom Revealed in Creation

1

Wisdom and knowledge are mentioned in the same breath in Scripture. Both wisdom and knowledge are attributes of God and therefore intertwined within His nature. But they are not the same thing. Whereas knowledge is a body of facts, wisdom is the ability to discern well how to apply the knowledge. God is the source of all wisdom *and* knowledge, and He is limitless in both. God's perfect wisdom is based on a foundation of infinite knowledge. As we will see in this study of wisdom, it is possible for human beings to have knowledge without wisdom, but it is not possible for us to have wisdom without knowledge. For us to hope to reflect God's wisdom, we must first soak in knowledge of Him.

As with all of God's attributes, His wisdom is not completely revealed to us and must ultimately be accepted in faith. Isaiah wrote that God "is wonderful in counsel and excellent in wisdom" (Is. 28:29). Paul teaches that He is "the only wise God" (Rom. 16:27). Beyond believing these promises, we can look to Scripture to see glimpses of God's wisdom on display. God's wisdom was first revealed in Creation. The earth was founded and established by His wisdom. The huge variety of amazing things He created have all been made in wisdom, including an incredible assortment of creatures and the food that sustains them.

Job expounded on God's wisdom in response to the errant counsel that he received from his friends. Eliphaz, Bildad, and Zophar all had their say. Job had heard all that he could handle, and he responded with a speech that spans six chapters. Within this speech, as Job longed for God to answer his pleas, he spoke of the value of wisdom, more precious than gold and the finest jewels. Man cannot even know the full value of godly wisdom. It is priceless. In Job's experience, God's wisdom was inaccessible to man, hidden from the eyes of all living creatures. But Job acknowledged that God knows the place of wisdom. Things that are too mysterious for man to understand and too powerful for man to control—the wind, the waters, the rain, and lightning—were all established in God's wisdom. Only God understands this kind of wisdom. The fact that Job used the wind as a picture of God's wisdom and understanding was a *huge* statement of faith for him. It was a great wind from the wilderness that struck the house and caused it to collapse, killing all of his children inside. Job acknowledged God's wisdom as displayed in creation. His lament was that he needed to find divine wisdom in his suffering and his counselors were not offering it.

Even as mankind grows in scientific knowledge of this world, there is still so much that we don't understand about it. God understands every detail of everything that He has created. His wisdom conceived and set in motion the earth and heavens, with principles scientists barely understand. He oversees and sustains the creation in ways that we do not comprehend. This is God's wisdom revealed in creation—having full knowledge of all that He has created and applying that knowledge to the benefit of all creation and to His own glory.

Action Step: Job's faith allowed him to praise God for His wisdom, even in the midst of his suffering. Job proclaimed, "with God are wisdom and might; he has counsel and understanding" (Job 12:13). Is your faith strong enough to praise and trust God's wisdom even when you are suffering intensely? Pray and ask God to increase your faith. Remember that though Job was desperate to have a full understanding of his suffering, God did not grant Job this kind of wisdom. What God did grant Job was faith to trust in God's wisdom.

Oh, the depth of the riches and wisdom and knowledge of God! How unsearchable are his judgments and how inscrutable his ways!

"For who has known the mind of the Lord, or who has been his counselor?"

Romans 11:33-34

In him we have redemption through his blood, the forgiveness of our trespasses, according to the riches of his grace, which he lavished upon us, in all wisdom and insight making known to us the mystery of his will, according to his purpose, which he set forth in Christ as a plan for the fullness of time, to unite all things in him, things in heaven and things on earth.

Ephesians 1:7-10

Of this gospel I was made a minister according to the gift of God's grace, which was given me by the working of his power. To me, though I am the very least of all the saints, this grace was given, to preach to the Gentiles the unsearchable riches of Christ, and to bring to light for everyone what is the plan of the mystery hidden for ages in God who created all things, so that through the church the manifold wisdom of God might now be made known to the rulers and authorities in the heavenly places.

Ephesians 3:7-10

Wise

God's Wisdom Revealed in Redemption 2

Even more than the wisdom displayed in creation, God's wisdom is revealed in the redemption of His children. When we studied God's incomprehensible nature, we learned the wisdom of God is beyond our abilities to fully comprehend, which led us to praise (page 33). The verses from Romans 11 that we considered then were written by Paul to praise God's wisdom. The place where Paul saw God's wisdom displayed was in the gospel. The gospel is God's eternal plan to redeem His people from sin, and this redemption plan demonstrates the infinite depth of God's wisdom.

Paul deeply connects the gospel with God's wisdom in the book of Ephesians. Paul begins his letter by describing our many spiritual blessings in Christ. Among these blessings is our redemption—our forgiveness from sin—a product of God's grace which He poured out on us in all wisdom and insight. The gospel unites all things to Christ, and none of this could be accomplished without the amazing richness of God's wisdom. This wisdom that conceived the gospel plan is filled with paradoxes that human wisdom would not foresee. *The death of Jesus Christ is used by God to defeat death. The human suffering of Jesus gives way to the divine power of the resurrection. The shame of the cross leads to His glory and ours. The One who demands justice is the One who justifies. The emptying of the Son of God leads to believers being filled with all the fullness of God.* In the wisdom of God's kingdom, *the last is made first, to save your life you must lose it, and to be rich in this kingdom one must be poor in spirit.* This wisdom of God is so far beyond our understanding that it seems foolish to the world.

God's wisdom is so spectacular that it is a work of art. The Greek word that Paul uses to describe God's wisdom—*polypoikilos*—means multi-faceted, many-sided, or marked with a great variety of colors. In Ephesians 3:10, it is translated as *manifold.* The wisdom of God must be viewed from many perspectives to be appreciated. Like viewing the texture of every brushstroke in a master's painting or rotating a gem to view its sparkle from every side, the gospel must be contemplated deeply for one to begin to appreciate its beauty and the wisdom underlying its plan. This creative work of wisdom is exhibited before the rulers and authorities in the heavenly places. Even these angelic beings who are closest to God's presence in heaven find new revelation of His wisdom in the gospel's plan of redemption, which has united a people in Christ in one body—the church.

Action Step: On a blank piece of letter-sized paper, write the eight paradoxes listed in italics on this page. Look up the following Scriptures and match each with the paradox in the list that it supports: Matthew 10:39; Philippians 3:10; Matthew 5:3; Romans 3:26; Hebrews 2:14; Hebrews 12:2; Philippians 2:5-8 with Ephesians 3:19; Matthew 20:16. Consider how the wisdom of God displayed in this gospel plan is in opposition to the wisdom of this world.

For the word of the cross is folly to those who are perishing, but to us who are being saved it is the power of God. For it is written,

"I will destroy the wisdom of the wise, and the discernment of the discerning I will thwart."

Where is the one who is wise? Where is the scribe? Where is the debater of this age? Has not God made foolish the wisdom of the world? For since, in the wisdom of God, the world did not know God through wisdom, it pleased God through the folly of what we preach to save those who believe. For Jews demand signs and Greeks seek wisdom, but we preach Christ crucified, a stumbling block to Jews and folly to Gentiles, but to those who are called, both Jews and Greeks, Christ the power of God and the wisdom of God. For the foolishness of God is wiser than men, and the weakness of God is stronger than men.

For consider your calling, brothers: not many of you were wise according to worldly standards, not many were powerful, not many were of noble birth. But God chose what is foolish in the world to shame the wise; God chose what is weak in the world to shame the strong; God chose what is low and despised in the world, even things that are not, to bring to nothing things that are, so that no human being might boast in the presence of God. And because of him you are in Christ Jesus, who became to us wisdom from God, righteousness and sanctification and redemption, so that, as it is written, "Let the one who boasts, boast in the Lord."

1 Corinthians 1:18-31

...that their hearts may be encouraged, being knit together in love, to reach all the riches of full assurance of understanding and the knowledge of God's mystery, which is Christ, in whom are hidden all the treasures of wisdom and knowledge.

Colossians 2:2-3

Wise

God's Wisdom Revealed in Christ

3

While the wisdom of God is revealed in the gospel plan of salvation, perhaps the more accurate statement is that the wisdom of God is revealed in Jesus Christ. Paul also wrote about God's wisdom in 1 Corinthians, beginning his discussion by quoting Isaiah. God had spoken through Isaiah that the people honored Him with their lips only, but not with their hearts. Therefore, God said He would upend the wisdom of those who called themselves wise and discerning. Human wisdom does not "get" the gospel. God has made the wisdom of this world into foolishness through the person and work of Jesus Christ. Paul explains that as he preached Christ crucified, it tripped up both Jews and Gentiles. A crucified Messiah showing human weakness did not meet any of their expectations. But for the Jews and Gentiles who were called, Christ was seen as both the power and wisdom of God.

Paul goes on to explain that the foolishness of God is wiser than men. Of course, there is nothing foolish about God at all, but God's wisdom cannot even be measured by the wisdom of this world. It is not that there is a continuum of wisdom with men and women at one end and God at the other and a bit of overlap in between. God's wisdom is of a kind that is completely inaccessible to those who measure wisdom by the world's standards. His wisdom is on another scale altogether. To those operating on the worldly wisdom scale, God's wisdom appears to be foolishness. Anyone who imagines that they can out-think God in matters of life and purpose and eternity will find that God destroys their human wisdom. And the way that He has destroyed the world's wisdom is in Christ Jesus, "who became to us wisdom from God, righteousness and sanctification and redemption." Throughout His teaching ministry, Jesus demonstrated wisdom from God. As Matthew recorded, "the crowds were astonished at his teaching, for he was teaching them as one who had authority, and not as their scribes" (Mt. 7:28-29). Jesus never referenced human teachers to support His teaching because He taught from the wisdom and knowledge of God. And beyond the wisdom Jesus displayed in His life on earth, His death and His resurrection demonstrate God's wisdom in achieving righteousness, sanctification, and redemption in the lives of those who believe.

The gospel that Paul preached appeared foolish to the world because God chose people who were weak, despised, and of low social status to shame those who the Jewish and Greek culture lifted up as important and influential. The point of this wise plan is God's glory—that those who boast can only boast in the Lord, not in any wisdom of their own. It is not the wise of this world who are saved, but those who rely on God's wisdom. Paul speaks of this in his letter to the Colossians as a mystery—something that was once hidden but has now been disclosed. Jesus Christ, the Son of God, is the one in whom all the treasures of wisdom and knowledge are hidden. Only when the Son of God became flesh was this wisdom uncovered. Only those who are in Christ can begin to understand the wisdom of God. Jesus Christ is God's wisdom in human form.

Action Step: In Proverbs 8, wisdom is personified as the speaker of the proverb. Those of us with the benefit of New Testament revelation can see that as wisdom speaks, the poetic voice at times anticipates the ultimate personification of wisdom in Jesus Christ. Read Proverbs 8 with a focus on thinking of the speaker as wisdom, but also as a foreshadower of Christ. This is particularly evident in that wisdom was with God prior to creation (v. 23-26) as Jesus was (Jn. 17:5), and wisdom was part of the act of creating (v. 27-31) as Jesus was (Jn. 1:1-3).

Daniel answered and said:

"Blessed be the name of God forever and ever, to whom belong wisdom and might. He changes times and seasons; he removes kings and sets up kings; he gives wisdom to the wise and knowledge to those who have understanding; he reveals deep and hidden things; he knows what is in the darkness, and the light dwells with him."

Daniel 2:20-22

"To you, O king, as you lay in bed came thoughts of what would be after this, and he who reveals mysteries made known to you what is to be. But as for me, this mystery has been revealed to me, not because of any wisdom that I have more than all the living, but in order that the interpretation may be made known to the king, and that you may know the thoughts of your mind."

Daniel 2:29-30

"The secret things belong to the LORD our God, but the things that are revealed belong to us and to our children forever, that we may do all the words of this law."

Deuteronomy 29:29

And we know that for those who love God all things work together for good, for those who are called according to his purpose. For those whom he foreknew he also predestined to be conformed to the image of his Son, in order that he might be the firstborn among many brothers. And those whom he predestined he also called, and those whom he called he also justified, and those whom he justified he also glorified.

Romans 8:28-30

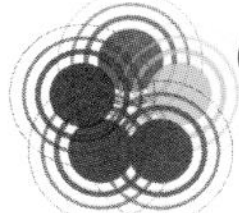

Wise

God's Wisdom Revealed in His Activity in the Lives of the Faithful

4

Daniel was a young man when he was taken from his home in Judah by the Babylonians. Nebuchadnezzar, the king of Babylon, had defeated the king of Judah and removed many of God's people to Babylon. This was an exile that God had warned the people about through several prophets, making clear to His people that this exile was under His direction as a consequence for the people's rebellion. Among the first wave of people taken to Babylon were some young men who remained faithful to God, including Daniel. God equipped Daniel and his friends with wisdom and skills to honor Him in this foreign land. The king even tested them and was impressed by their wisdom and understanding, finding them "ten times better than all the magicians and enchanters that were in all his kingdom" (Dan. 1:20).

Not long after, Nebuchadnezzar had a troubling dream. The king summoned all those magicians and enchanters of his kingdom and made a rather surprising request. He asked them to not only tell what the dream meant, but also describe what he had actually dreamed! If they didn't tell him both the dream and its interpretation, they would be killed. These men with the wisdom of the world recognized that no one on earth could tell the king what he had dreamed, but only the gods could. In reality, even their false gods were not able to provide them with information about the dream. Not only were the Babylonian wise men to be killed, but also Daniel and his friends. Daniel sought wisdom and mercy from God, who then revealed the king's dream to Daniel in a vision. Daniel praised God in response with the words from Daniel 2:20-22. Daniel acknowledged that wisdom can only come from God and that His wisdom determines the affairs of men. He sets up kings, and He removes them. God gives wisdom where He wills, and He reveals deep and hidden things. The mystery that God revealed to Daniel allowed him to appear before the king and describe both the dream and its interpretation. Daniel did not credit his own wisdom before the king; instead, he gave glory to God alone for revealing the mystery.

God's wisdom belongs to Him alone. He chooses to reveal some of the mysteries of His wisdom to His faithful people for us to know Him and obey Him. The law revealed to Moses for the people of Israel is an example of God's wisdom revealed. The incarnation, teaching, and gospel plan of redemption accomplished in Jesus Christ were a greater revelation of God's wisdom. At times we can see God's wise plan unfolding in our own individual lives as Daniel did. But sometimes we cannot see God's wise plan because His wisdom is beyond our understanding. There is much that He has not revealed to us. This is where we need to have faith and humility and trust that, for those who love God, He is working all things for our good according to His wisdom and purposes—that we will be like Christ and bear the family image. If we truly believe that God's wisdom is unmeasurable and that He has all power and sovereignty to accomplish everything He wills for those He loves, we should be *thankful* that He is not working all of His plans within the range of our limited wisdom and understanding.

Action Step: God's wisdom, power, and knowledge are revealed to us in a huge way when we consider the promise that He is using *all things* for good for those who love Him. Every minute of every day, God is aware of everything that impacts the lives of all people, and He has the wisdom and power to use those events for the spiritual growth of every believer involved. Pray and worship God for His infinite wisdom.

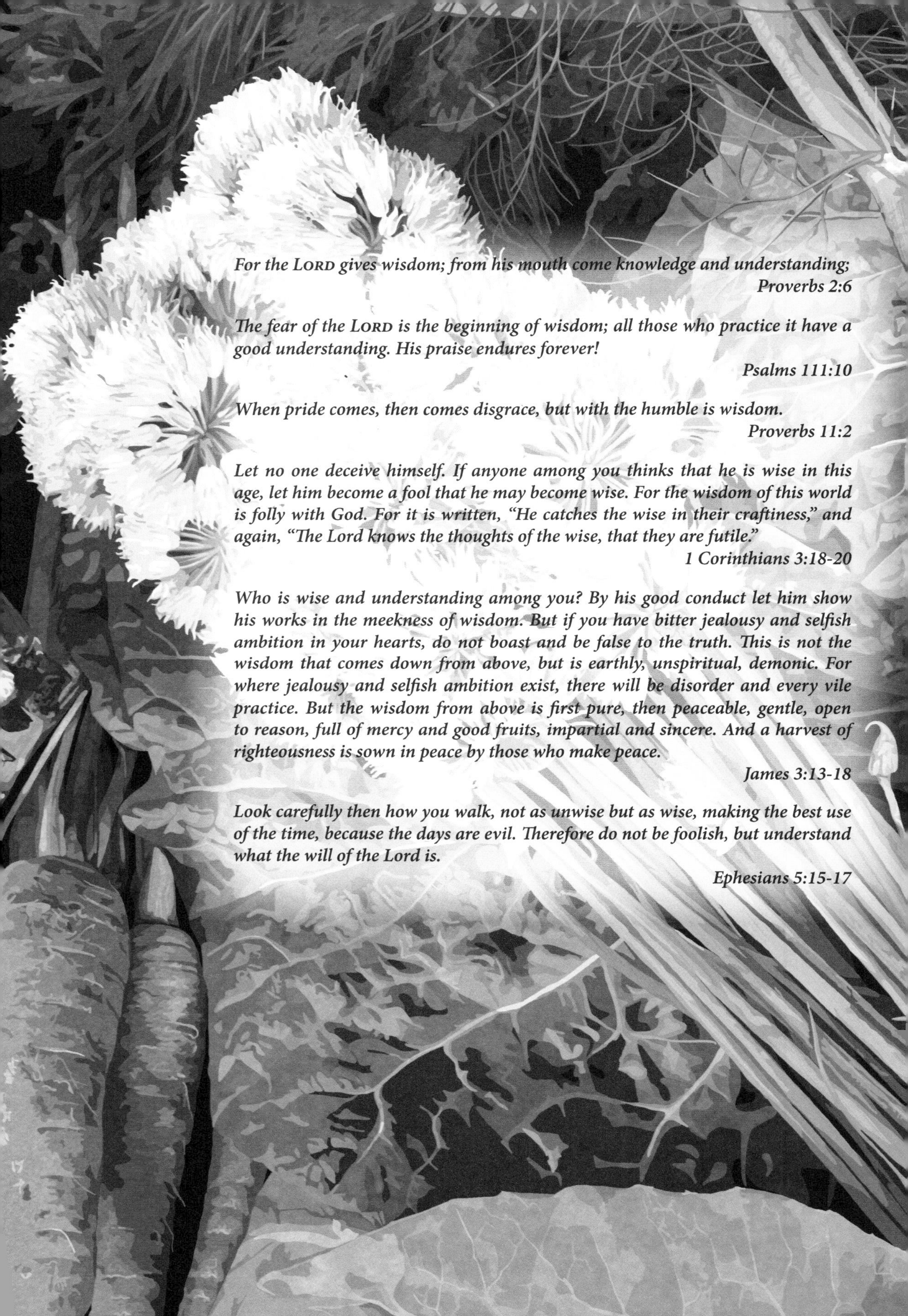

For the Lord gives wisdom; from his mouth come knowledge and understanding;
Proverbs 2:6

The fear of the Lord is the beginning of wisdom; all those who practice it have a good understanding. His praise endures forever!
Psalms 111:10

When pride comes, then comes disgrace, but with the humble is wisdom.
Proverbs 11:2

Let no one deceive himself. If anyone among you thinks that he is wise in this age, let him become a fool that he may become wise. For the wisdom of this world is folly with God. For it is written, "He catches the wise in their craftiness," and again, "The Lord knows the thoughts of the wise, that they are futile."
1 Corinthians 3:18-20

Who is wise and understanding among you? By his good conduct let him show his works in the meekness of wisdom. But if you have bitter jealousy and selfish ambition in your hearts, do not boast and be false to the truth. This is not the wisdom that comes down from above, but is earthly, unspiritual, demonic. For where jealousy and selfish ambition exist, there will be disorder and every vile practice. But the wisdom from above is first pure, then peaceable, gentle, open to reason, full of mercy and good fruits, impartial and sincere. And a harvest of righteousness is sown in peace by those who make peace.
James 3:13-18

Look carefully then how you walk, not as unwise but as wise, making the best use of the time, because the days are evil. Therefore do not be foolish, but understand what the will of the Lord is.
Ephesians 5:15-17

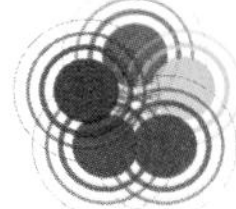

Wise

Godly Wisdom Gained through Fear of the Lord

5

In the very first week of this study, on page 15, we saw in Proverbs 2 that all wisdom, knowledge, and understanding come from the Lord. The fear of the Lord is the beginning of wisdom. Proverbs 11 adds the information that wisdom is with the humble. These ideas are very closely related in that a significant part of fearing the Lord is humbling ourselves before Him and recognizing His exalted position over us. To kneel before God with a heart that is free from all attempts at gaining wisdom through human effort and to seek His wisdom is progress toward fearing the Lord. The one who thinks that he is wise must become a fool—acknowledge a complete lack of godly wisdom and reject earthly wisdom—before being filled with God's wisdom. James instructs his readers, "If any of you lacks wisdom, let him ask God, who gives generously to all without reproach, and it will be given him" (Jms. 1:5). The first step is recognizing that we lack wisdom in ourselves. Asking God from a posture of insufficiency brings His generous gift of wisdom.

James returns to a fuller explanation of the differences between worldly wisdom gained through human thinking and godly wisdom given by the Lord in chapter 3 of his letter. In his definition, earthly wisdom is closely tied to jealousy and selfish ambition. In contrast, there is wisdom that does not originate in the heart of man, but from the heart of God. This is the wisdom that we are called to walk in. Godly wisdom is untainted by sin, and it brings rest and harmony rather than conflict or disorder. This wisdom exhibits mildness, reasonably adjusting to work with others and obey God. When we walk in God's wisdom, we extend kindness toward those in need and bring positive results to their lives and our own. Finally, wisdom from above seeks the good of all kinds of people without favoritism or hypocrisy.

The difference between God's wisdom and man's wisdom can be seen in our actions. The ambitious businessman who seeks to build his company primarily to advance his own wealth is operating out of selfish ambition, demonstrating that his wisdom is earthly. A woman who seeks to gain knowledge to shame someone that she disagrees with or dislikes exhibits wisdom that is not pure and therefore not from above. Anyone who would apply their knowledge in a way that advances their own agenda at the expense of others or in a way that creates disorder is operating out of foolishness, not godly wisdom. Every single one of us is guilty of this at one time or another. The important thing is to grow in our ability to recognize this in ourselves so that we can humbly repent of earthly wisdom, resume a posture of fear of the Lord, and ask Him to give us His wisdom from above. The humility of godly wisdom will always walk carefully and listen to others with godly wisdom, understanding the need for continued growth in wisdom.

Action Step: Pay attention to your actions throughout the day today with a goal of evaluating the wisdom displayed in your own life. Stop periodically for a five-minute break from your daily activities to consider whether your actions are creating harmony or conflict, whether they are exhibiting kindness toward others or trying to advance yourself. Are your actions consistent with your beliefs? Are you exhibiting godly wisdom? Pray and ask God to give you His wisdom. For an even better evaluation, ask another trusted believer to watch for the same evidences of wisdom in your life.

Your commandment makes me wiser than my enemies, for it is ever with me. I have more understanding than all my teachers, for your testimonies are my meditation. I understand more than the aged, for I keep your precepts.

Psalms 119:98-100

Let the word of Christ dwell in you richly, teaching and admonishing one another in all wisdom, singing psalms and hymns and spiritual songs, with thankfulness in your hearts to God.

Colossians 3:16

But as for you, continue in what you have learned and have firmly believed, knowing from whom you learned it and how from childhood you have been acquainted with the sacred writings, which are able to make you wise for salvation through faith in Christ Jesus. All Scripture is breathed out by God and profitable for teaching, for reproof, for correction, and for training in righteousness, that the man of God may be complete, equipped for every good work.

2 Timothy 3:14-17

Yet among the mature we do impart wisdom, although it is not a wisdom of this age or of the rulers of this age, who are doomed to pass away. But we impart a secret and hidden wisdom of God, which God decreed before the ages for our glory. None of the rulers of this age understood this, for if they had, they would not have crucified the Lord of glory. But, as it is written,

"What no eye has seen, nor ear heard, nor the heart of man imagined, what God has prepared for those who love him"—

these things God has revealed to us through the Spirit. For the Spirit searches everything, even the depths of God. For who knows a person's thoughts except the spirit of that person, which is in him? So also no one comprehends the thoughts of God except the Spirit of God. Now we have received not the spirit of the world, but the Spirit who is from God, that we might understand the things freely given us by God. And we impart this in words not taught by human wisdom but taught by the Spirit, interpreting spiritual truths to those who are spiritual.

The natural person does not accept the things of the Spirit of God, for they are folly to him, and he is not able to understand them because they are spiritually discerned. The spiritual person judges all things, but is himself to be judged by no one. "For who has understood the mind of the Lord so as to instruct him?" But we have the mind of Christ.

1 Corinthians 2:6-16

Wise

Godly Wisdom Gained from the Word 6

The fear of the Lord is the beginning of wisdom. God will give His wisdom to those who humbly seek it. Still, all wisdom must have a foundation of knowledge, and godly wisdom is grounded in knowledge of the Lord as revealed in His Word. David recognized this when he wrote Psalm 19, saying, "The law of the Lord is perfect, reviving the soul; the testimony of the Lord is sure, making wise the simple" (Ps. 19:7). Again, in Psalm 119, a poetic tribute to the gift of God's Word, the writer was inspired by the Holy Spirit to affirm that God's commandments made him wiser than his enemies who did not follow God's Word. In his letter to the Colossians, Paul encourages his readers to "let the word of Christ dwell in you richly, teaching and admonishing one another in all wisdom." The word of Christ recorded in the Bible includes all of Scripture, since all Scripture is breathed out by God and culminates in the ministry of Jesus Christ. The words of Scripture, recorded in their original writings, are the very words of God. As we read, memorize, and mediate on the Bible, we are letting God's Word dwell in us. As we interact with other believers in wisely studying and discussing the Word, we are teaching and admonishing one another. The result is growth in godly knowledge and wisdom. Paul also wrote to Timothy that the sacred writings—Scripture—were able to make him "wise for salvation through faith in Christ Jesus." Scripture has the power to bring people to faith and to strengthen faith because the writing of Scripture was inspired by the same Holy Spirit that transforms hearts. Guided by the Holy Spirit and informed by Scripture, believers grow in knowledge and wisdom.

We have already seen that Paul includes teachings about wisdom in the first few chapters of his first letter to the Corinthians. After introducing God's wisdom and contrasting it with the wisdom of men, Paul moves into an explanation that the teaching he was called to—the gospel—was the wisdom of God as revealed to Paul by the Holy Spirit, who searches the depths of God. His readers then and now can understand these spiritual truths by the same Holy Spirit. The gospel message that Paul preached to the first-century church is the gospel message that we have recorded for us in the Bible. The end goal of the teaching is to understand more of God and His plan for salvation. In this confusing world where we are distracted and enticed by sin, we cannot grow in godly wisdom without being firmly grounded in knowledge of God's character, will, and commands as revealed in the Bible.

Action Step: Do you love God's Word? Do you have a passion for seeking more understanding of God's ways and His nature as revealed in Scripture? The author of Psalm 119 also wrote, "In the way of your testimonies I delight as much as in all riches. I will meditate on your precepts and fix my eyes on your ways. I will delight in your statutes; I will not forget your word" (Ps. 119:14-16). Pray and ask God to increase your desire for His Word so that you may grow in knowledge and wisdom.

Weekly Summary

Key Points

1. God's wisdom was first revealed in Creation. The earth was founded and established by His wisdom.
2. The wisdom of God revealed in our redemption from sin is so far beyond our human understanding that it seems foolish to the world.
3. Jesus Christ is God's wisdom in human form.
4. God's wisdom works all things for good, but sometimes we cannot see God's wise plan because His wisdom is beyond our understanding.
5. The one who thinks that he is wise must fear God and humble himself before being filled with God's wisdom.
6. All wisdom must have a foundation of knowledge, and godly wisdom is grounded in knowledge of the Lord as revealed in His Word.

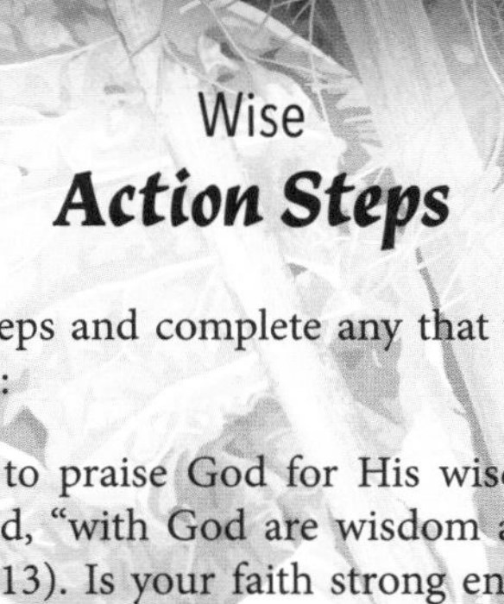

Wise
Action Steps

Go back through the action steps and complete any that you have not yet completed or repeat one that was meaningful:

1. Job's faith allowed him to praise God for His wisdom, even in the midst of his suffering. Job proclaimed, "with God are wisdom and might; he has counsel and understanding" (Job 12:13). Is your faith strong enough to praise and trust God's wisdom even when you are suffering intensely? Pray and ask God to increase your faith. Remember that though Job was desperate to have a full understanding of his suffering, God did not grant Job this kind of wisdom. What God did grant Job was faith to trust in God's wisdom.

2. On a blank piece of letter-sized paper, write the eight paradoxes listed in italics on page 317. Look up the following Scriptures and match each with the paradox in the list that it supports: Matthew 10:39; Philippians 3:10; Matthew 5:3; Romans 3:26; Hebrews 2:14; Hebrews 12:2; Philippians 2:5-8 with Ephesians 3:19; Matthew 20:16. Consider how the wisdom of God displayed in this gospel plan is in opposition to the wisdom of this world.

3. In Proverbs 8, wisdom is personified as the speaker of the proverb. Those of us with the benefit of New Testament revelation can see that as wisdom speaks, the poetic voice at times anticipates the ultimate personification of wisdom in Jesus Christ. Read Proverbs 8 with a focus on thinking of the speaker as wisdom, but also as a foreshadower of Christ. This is particularly evident in that wisdom was with God prior to creation (v. 23-26) as Jesus was (Jn. 17:5), and wisdom was part of the act of creating (v. 27-31) as Jesus was (Jn. 1:1-3).

4. God's wisdom, power, and knowledge are revealed to us in a huge way when we consider the promise that He is using *all things* for good for those who love Him. Every minute of every day, God is aware of everything that impacts the lives of all people, and He has the wisdom and power to use those events for the spiritual growth of every believer involved. Pray and worship God for His infinite wisdom.

5. Pay attention to your actions throughout the day today with a goal of evaluating the wisdom displayed in your own life. Stop periodically for a five-minute break from your daily activities to consider whether your actions are creating harmony or conflict, or whether they are exhibiting kindness toward others or trying to advance yourself. Are your actions consistent with your beliefs? Are you exhibiting godly wisdom? Pray and ask God to give you His wisdom. For an even better evaluation, ask another trusted believer to watch for the same evidences of wisdom in your life.

6. Do you love God's Word? Do you have a passion for seeking more understanding of God's ways and His nature as revealed in Scripture? The author of Psalm 119 also wrote, "In the way of your testimonies I delight as much as in all riches. I will meditate on your precepts and fix my eyes on your ways. I will delight in your statutes; I will not forget your word" (Ps. 119:14-16). Pray and ask God to increase your desire for His Word so that you may grow in knowledge and wisdom.

WEEK 21
Presence

…God fills heaven and earth just as the ocean fills a bucket which has been submerged in it a mile down. The bucket is full of the ocean, but the ocean surrounds the bucket in all directions. So when God says He fills heaven and earth, He does. But heaven and earth are submerged in God, and all space is too…. God is not contained; God contains.

A.W. Tozer, *The Attributes of God, Vol. 1*

"Am I a God at hand, declares the LORD, and not a God far away? Can a man hide himself in secret places so that I cannot see him? declares the LORD. Do I not fill heaven and earth? declares the LORD."

Jeremiah 23:23-24

"Yet he is actually not far from each one of us, for 'In him we live and move and have our being'; as even some of your own poets have said, 'For we are indeed his offspring.'"

Acts 17:27-28

Where shall I go from your Spirit? Or where shall I flee from your presence? If I ascend to heaven, you are there! If I make my bed in Sheol, you are there! If I take the wings of the morning and dwell in the uttermost parts of the sea, even there your hand shall lead me, and your right hand shall hold me.

Psalms 139:7-10

"But will God indeed dwell on the earth? Behold, heaven and the highest heaven cannot contain you; how much less this house that I have built!"

1 Kings 8:27

"Have I not commanded you? Be strong and courageous. Do not be frightened, and do not be dismayed, for the LORD your God is with you wherever you go."

Joshua 1:9

Draw near to God, and he will draw near to you. Cleanse your hands, you sinners, and purify your hearts, you double-minded.

James 4:8

Behold, the LORD's hand is not shortened, that it cannot save, or his ear dull, that it cannot hear; but your iniquities have made a separation between you and your God, and your sins have hidden his face from you so that he does not hear.

Isaiah 59:1-2

...one God and Father of all, who is over all and through all and in all.

Ephesians 4:6

Presence

Omnipresence

1

At this moment, as you read this page, your body is occupying space. Whether you are seated or standing or lying down, you are in a defined space. You cannot be in another space at the same time. You might be on the phone with someone in another location or dreaming of a beach far away, but your physical body is finite and limited to one location at a time.

God is present everywhere. His entire being is in every location at all times and not limited by space. He is aware of spatial limitations, as He has created the heavens and the earth for created beings to occupy, but He is not constrained by that space. The Creator cannot be contained or held captive by His creation. As you occupy space at this moment, God surrounds you—and everything else in creation—with His presence. These descriptions may sound vaguely familiar to you because I used some of the same language to describe God's eternal nature. In the same way that God created time for His creation to inhabit, He created space for us as well. But in both realities—time and space—He is everywhere present in all times and all places at once. God spoke through the prophet Jeremiah, "Do I not fill heaven and earth?" He fills all created spaces and goes even beyond them. As Paul addressed the crowd in Athens, he quoted one of their own poets who wrote something that he imagined to be true of their gods, but Paul claimed it as indeed true of the One True God—"In him we live and move and have our being." Regardless of how far we travel in our lives or in human history, our existence is always within God.

This aspect of God's nature is referred to as *omnipresence*. David was aware of it as he wrote Psalm 139, exclaiming that whether he went to the extreme of heaven or to the opposite extreme of Sheol—the place of death—God would be there. Solomon, David's son, was aware of God's omnipresence as he dedicated the new temple and acknowledged that neither the temple, nor earth, nor heaven—not even the highest heaven—could contain God.

If God is present *everywhere*, then what hope is offered by Scripture when God promises to be near? When the Lord encouraged Joshua with the promise that He would be "with you wherever you go," how was that comforting to Joshua if the Lord is equally present with Joshua's enemies? When James wrote that sinners should draw near to God so that He would draw near to them, wasn't God already near to them in His omnipresence? The answer, found throughout Scripture, is that God makes His presence specially known in certain places, times, and people. Though He is present everywhere, He may choose to manifest His presence in more significant ways. There are also times when God may withdraw His special presence as a form of judgment, as when He spoke through Isaiah to the people of Judah that their "iniquities have made a separation between you and your God, and your sins have hidden his face from you so that he does not hear." The people were separated from God not spatially, but relationally, because of their sin. But most often in Scripture, God's presence is manifest for certain people in certain locations to make Him known to His covenant people. God's specially manifested presence is most often promised as a relational blessing.

Action Step: As you spend time in prayer today, consider God's very real presence with you. Now consider that His omnipresence places Him in and over and through every one of the 7.7 billion people currently living on this planet, leaving "no creature...hidden from his sight" (Heb. 4:13). Worship God for the awesome wonder of His omnipresence.

...then the Lord God formed the man of dust from the ground and breathed into his nostrils the breath of life, and the man became a living creature. And the Lord God planted a garden in Eden, in the east, and there he put the man whom he had formed.

Genesis 2:7-8

The Lord God took the man and put him in the garden of Eden to work it and keep it. And the Lord God commanded the man, saying, "You may surely eat of every tree of the garden, but of the tree of the knowledge of good and evil you shall not eat, for in the day that you eat of it you shall surely die."

Then the Lord God said, "It is not good that the man should be alone; I will make him a helper fit for him." Now out of the ground the Lord God had formed every beast of the field and every bird of the heavens and brought them to the man to see what he would call them. And whatever the man called every living creature, that was its name. The man gave names to all livestock and to the birds of the heavens and to every beast of the field. But for Adam there was not found a helper fit for him. So the Lord God caused a deep sleep to fall upon the man, and while he slept took one of his ribs and closed up its place with flesh. And the rib that the Lord God had taken from the man he made into a woman and brought her to the man.

Genesis 2:15-22

So when the woman saw that the tree was good for food, and that it was a delight to the eyes, and that the tree was to be desired to make one wise, she took of its fruit and ate, and she also gave some to her husband who was with her, and he ate. Then the eyes of both were opened, and they knew that they were naked. And they sewed fig leaves together and made themselves loincloths.

And they heard the sound of the Lord God walking in the garden in the cool of the day, and the man and his wife hid themselves from the presence of the Lord God among the trees of the garden. But the Lord God called to the man and said to him, "Where are you?" And he said, "I heard the sound of you in the garden, and I was afraid, because I was naked, and I hid myself."

Genesis 3:6-10

Presence

God's Presence in the Garden

2

From the moment God formed Adam from the dust of the ground, He was present with man in a special way. God did not speak a word from a distance to create the man, but He molded his body, implying a "hands-on" technique. When Eve was created, the Lord began His work with a rib taken from Adam's side. Again, this was a more intimate act than when God simply spoke to create light or dry land or seas. God was present in a personal way with Adam and Eve even as He created them.

"The LORD God took the man and put him in the garden of Eden to work it and keep it." This suggests a special presence of God with Adam as well. "Took" implies that God somehow transported or carried Adam to the garden. God's omnipresence was over and through and in all that He created, but God's presence manifested to Adam in a relationship of care, possibly even touch. In the same way, when God created Eve, He "brought her to the man." God did not *send* her to the man, he *brought* her, implying interaction between God and the people bearing His image.

After Adam and Eve disobeyed God and ate of the fruit, we see another special manifestation of God's presence. "And they heard the sound of the LORD God walking in the garden in the cool of the day, and the man and his wife hid themselves from the presence of the LORD God among the trees of the garden." The first thing that we can note is that the sound they heard was identifiable to them as the sound of God approaching. They must have heard this sound before in order to identify it as the approach of God. He walked among them in a way that we do not experience today. And what sound did God make as He came near? The sound of God "walking" suggests footsteps or possibly rustling bushes. The phrase translated as "in the cool of the day" in Hebrew is literally "in the wind of the day." God appeared to Job in a whirlwind (Job 38:1). When the Holy Spirit came at Pentecost, there was a "sound like a mighty rushing wind" (Acts 2:2). Was the sound of God approaching in the garden like the sound of wind moving through the trees? We can't know for certain, but we can know that Adam and Eve experienced God in the garden of Eden in some physical ways that we do not sense Him.

But we also have to wonder whether they lacked some knowledge of God that we do have access to. Adam and Eve attempted to hide themselves from God's presence among the trees. Did they really believe they could hide from the omnipresent God? This brings to mind the typical toddler who, while standing in plain sight in the middle of a room, covers her eyes and expects that no one can see her because she cannot see them! God was as present crouched under the trees with Adam and Eve as He was anywhere else in all of creation and beyond. Had God not revealed this about Himself? Or in their fear were they simply choosing not to let the truth apply to their lives at that moment? There is no doubt from these first few chapters of Genesis that God, though omnipresent, has a heart to manifest His presence in a special way among His people.

Action Step: Scripture has clearly revealed the truth of God's omnipresence. We cannot plead ignorance in this regard. But does this truth affect your daily life? If Jesus Christ was physically walking beside you throughout the day today, would His physical presence change your actions or words? Should the reality of God's spiritual presence with you have any less impact?

King Nebuchadnezzar made an image of gold, whose height was sixty cubits and its breadth six cubits. He set it up on the plain of Dura, in the province of Babylon. Then King Nebuchadnezzar sent to gather the satraps, the prefects, and the governors, the counselors, the treasurers, the justices, the magistrates, and all the officials of the provinces to come to the dedication of the image that King Nebuchadnezzar had set up. Then the satraps, the prefects, and the governors, the counselors, the treasurers, the justices, the magistrates, and all the officials of the provinces gathered for the dedication of the image that King Nebuchadnezzar had set up. And they stood before the image that Nebuchadnezzar had set up. And the herald proclaimed aloud, "You are commanded, O peoples, nations, and languages, that when you hear the sound of the horn, pipe, lyre, trigon, harp, bagpipe, and every kind of music, you are to fall down and worship the golden image that King Nebuchadnezzar has set up. And whoever does not fall down and worship shall immediately be cast into a burning fiery furnace." Therefore, as soon as all the peoples heard the sound of the horn, pipe, lyre, trigon, harp, bagpipe, and every kind of music, all the peoples, nations, and languages fell down and worshiped the golden image that King Nebuchadnezzar had set up...

...Shadrach, Meshach, and Abednego answered and said to the king, "O Nebuchadnezzar, we have no need to answer you in this matter. If this be so, our God whom we serve is able to deliver us from the burning fiery furnace, and he will deliver us out of your hand, O king. But if not, be it known to you, O king, that we will not serve your gods or worship the golden image that you have set up."

Then Nebuchadnezzar was filled with fury, and the expression of his face was changed against Shadrach, Meshach, and Abednego. He ordered the furnace heated seven times more than it was usually heated. And he ordered some of the mighty men of his army to bind Shadrach, Meshach, and Abednego, and to cast them into the burning fiery furnace. Then these men were bound in their cloaks, their tunics, their hats, and their other garments, and they were thrown into the burning fiery furnace. Because the king's order was urgent and the furnace overheated, the flame of the fire killed those men who took up Shadrach, Meshach, and Abednego. And these three men, Shadrach, Meshach, and Abednego, fell bound into the burning fiery furnace.

Then King Nebuchadnezzar was astonished and rose up in haste. He declared to his counselors, "Did we not cast three men bound into the fire?" They answered and said to the king, "True, O king." He answered and said, "But I see four men unbound, walking in the midst of the fire, and they are not hurt; and the appearance of the fourth is like a son of the gods."

Then Nebuchadnezzar came near to the door of the burning fiery furnace; he declared, "Shadrach, Meshach, and Abednego, servants of the Most High God, come out, and come here!" Then Shadrach, Meshach, and Abednego came out from the fire. And the satraps, the prefects, the governors, and the king's counselors gathered together and saw that the fire had not had any power over the bodies of those men. The hair of their heads was not singed, their cloaks were not harmed, and no smell of fire had come upon them.

Daniel 3:1-7, 16-27

Presence

God's Presence with Israel

3

Throughout this book we have seen many ways that God uniquely made His presence known to the nation of Israel. He appeared in a pillar of fire and a pillar of smoke as His people made their way out of Egypt. His presence was shown at Mt. Sinai when the mountain was wrapped in thick smoke, thunder, and lightning. He appeared in a cloud over the mercy seat in the Most Holy Place of the tabernacle, and His glory filled Solomon's temple in the form of a cloud. God promised the people of Israel that if they obeyed His law and kept their covenant with Him, He would make His dwelling among them and in relationship with them and make His presence known in ways that were not seen in other nations.

But Israel did not keep their covenant. They disobeyed God. The prophet Ezekiel described God's special presence departing from the temple in Jerusalem (Ezek. 10). The people were exiled to Babylon. But God was not done showing His presence to bless those who were faithful to Him. At nearly the same time that Ezekiel wrote of God's departure from the temple, Daniel wrote the account of Shadrach, Meshach, and Abednego, three men who continued to have faith in God even when they had been removed from their homeland.

King Nebuchadnezzar of Babylon had a giant golden statue erected, and everyone present was commanded to worship the image whenever they heard the music playing. The consequences for failure to worship the image were made clear from the start—you would be thrown into a fiery furnace. Shadrach, Meshach, and Abednego were known to Nebuchadnezzar. They had been appointed by the king to positions of leadership at Daniel's request. But the king did not understand that God's command to not worship any other gods was vastly more important to these three men than any command from the king of Babylon. They were turned in to the king for their refusal to bow down, and the king went into a furious rage. He asked them once again to worship the image, and he suggested that no god would be able to deliver them from his punishment. The faith of these three Jews was incredible. They firmly believed in God's power to save them from the furnace, but *even if He did not deliver them*, they would not disobey God. The king ordered the furnace to be heated to seven times its normal strength, and the king's men cast them into the furnace. The power of the flames was so great that even the soldiers that threw them in were consumed by the flames. But Shadrach, Meshach, and Abednego were not consumed. Nebuchadnezzar observed, "I see four men unbound, walking in the midst of the fire, and they are not hurt; and the appearance of the fourth is like a son of the gods." God manifest His presence in a special way to bless His faithful people. God chose to enter into the furnace of affliction with His faithful to save them, leaving them untouched by the fire. The omnipresent God could have saved them in many unseen ways, but instead He chose to make His presence known, not only to the three Jews, but also to the king of Babylon.

Action Step: The prophet Isaiah wrote to the people of Judah before they were exiled to Babylon to warn them of coming judgment and to promise that God would restore them: "When you pass through the waters, I will be with you; and through the rivers, they shall not overwhelm you; when you walk through fire you shall not be burned, and the flame shall not consume you." God fulfilled this promise to Shadrach, Meshach, and Abednego in a literal and very spectacular way. Still, a mature faith realizes that even if God does not deliver us from harm, He has promised to be with us in a personal way. Will you trust that He is relationally present with you in trials regardless of the immediate outcome?

And the Word became flesh and dwelt among us, and we have seen his glory, glory as of the only Son from the Father, full of grace and truth.

John 1:14

Therefore, if anyone is in Christ, he is a new creation. The old has passed away; behold, the new has come.

2 Corinthians 5:17

"Abide in me, and I in you. As the branch cannot bear fruit by itself, unless it abides in the vine, neither can you, unless you abide in me. I am the vine; you are the branches. Whoever abides in me and I in him, he it is that bears much fruit, for apart from me you can do nothing."

John 15:4-5

Therefore, as you received Christ Jesus the Lord, so walk in him, rooted and built up in him and established in the faith, just as you were taught, abounding in thanksgiving.

Colossians 2:6-7

If then you have been raised with Christ, seek the things that are above, where Christ is, seated at the right hand of God. Set your minds on things that are above, not on things that are on earth. For you have died, and your life is hidden with Christ in God.

Colossians 3:1-3

I have been crucified with Christ. It is no longer I who live, but Christ who lives in me. And the life I now live in the flesh I live by faith in the Son of God, who loved me and gave himself for me.

Galatians 2:20

Jesus answered him, "If anyone loves me, he will keep my word, and my Father will love him, and we will come to him and make our home with him."

John 14:23

You, however, are not in the flesh but in the Spirit, if in fact the Spirit of God dwells in you. Anyone who does not have the Spirit of Christ does not belong to him. But if Christ is in you, although the body is dead because of sin, the Spirit is life because of righteousness. If the Spirit of him who raised Jesus from the dead dwells in you, he who raised Christ Jesus from the dead will also give life to your mortal bodies through his Spirit who dwells in you.

Romans 8:9-11

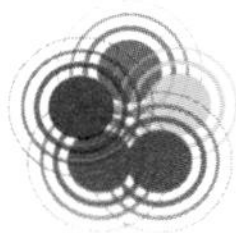

Presence

Christ in Us

4

The four gospels open the New Testament with the greatest news in all of human history. The Son of God came down to dwell with His people on earth. The divine wrapped Himself in human flesh and dwelt among us. The word *dwelt* means that He set up his tabernacle. No longer would God's presence among His people be hidden behind barriers in a man-made tabernacle or temple. In the incarnation, the Son descended to earth to walk among the people He loved. Jesus' life on earth was lived in perfect obedience to the Father. He was crucified for our sins and resurrected to defeat death, and He ascended to the Father to reign and intercede for us. Scripture teaches that people with faith in Christ receive His obedience as our righteousness (Rom. 5:19), that we are crucified with Him (Rom. 6:6), and that we are raised with Him and seated with Him in heavenly places (Eph. 2:6). All of these accomplishments are achieved only by Christ, but the resulting spiritual blessings are ours because we have a miraculous union with Jesus Christ. Though Christ has ascended and is no longer present bodily on earth, He is spiritually present with believers.

The Apostle Paul refers to this union as being "in Christ." The Apostle John refers to it as abiding in Christ as a branch abides in the vine. When a person comes to faith in Christ, the Holy Spirit does a supernatural work to unite that person to the person of Christ. This bond cannot be broken. Through this bond, our lives are hidden with Christ in God, meaning we are securely held in fellowship with the triune God. Everything that Christ is worthy of through His perfect life is gifted to believers by grace because of our union with Christ. *In Christ* you are a new creation. *In Christ* you are able to bear abundant fruit. *In Christ* you are rooted, built up, and established in the faith. Scripture also describes the relationship as Christ living in us or the Holy Spirit dwelling in us. Jesus taught that He and the Father would make their home with those who love Him. In the New Covenant, the entire Godhead is present in intimate fellowship with people of faith.

If we place our faith in Jesus Christ, He dwells *within us* by His Spirit. At the same time, the Holy Spirit unites us to Christ so we can say that we are *in Him*. This is God's special presence with His faithful people in the age of the church, between the ascension of Jesus Christ and His coming return. God's presence is actually in His people. We can have communion with God only through our union with Christ. We have power to obey like Christ because Christ is in us.

Action Step: Because our union with Christ is a spiritual reality and not something we can easily see, it is so hard to grasp and take hold of. At its most basic level, it may help to think about how being *in Christ* impacts our relationship with God. When God looks at you, He sees you as being in Christ, having accomplished everything that Christ accomplished in His life, death, resurrection, and ascension. You are covered by a blanket of Christ. You can think of *Christ in you* as how you have the power to obey God and bear the family image. In your daily walk on this earth, you can look like Jesus in your behavior because He is in you. As you walk through your day today, prayerfully consider how your relationship with God is impacted by the reality of being *in Christ* and how your thoughts, words, and actions are affected by the reality that *Christ is in you*.

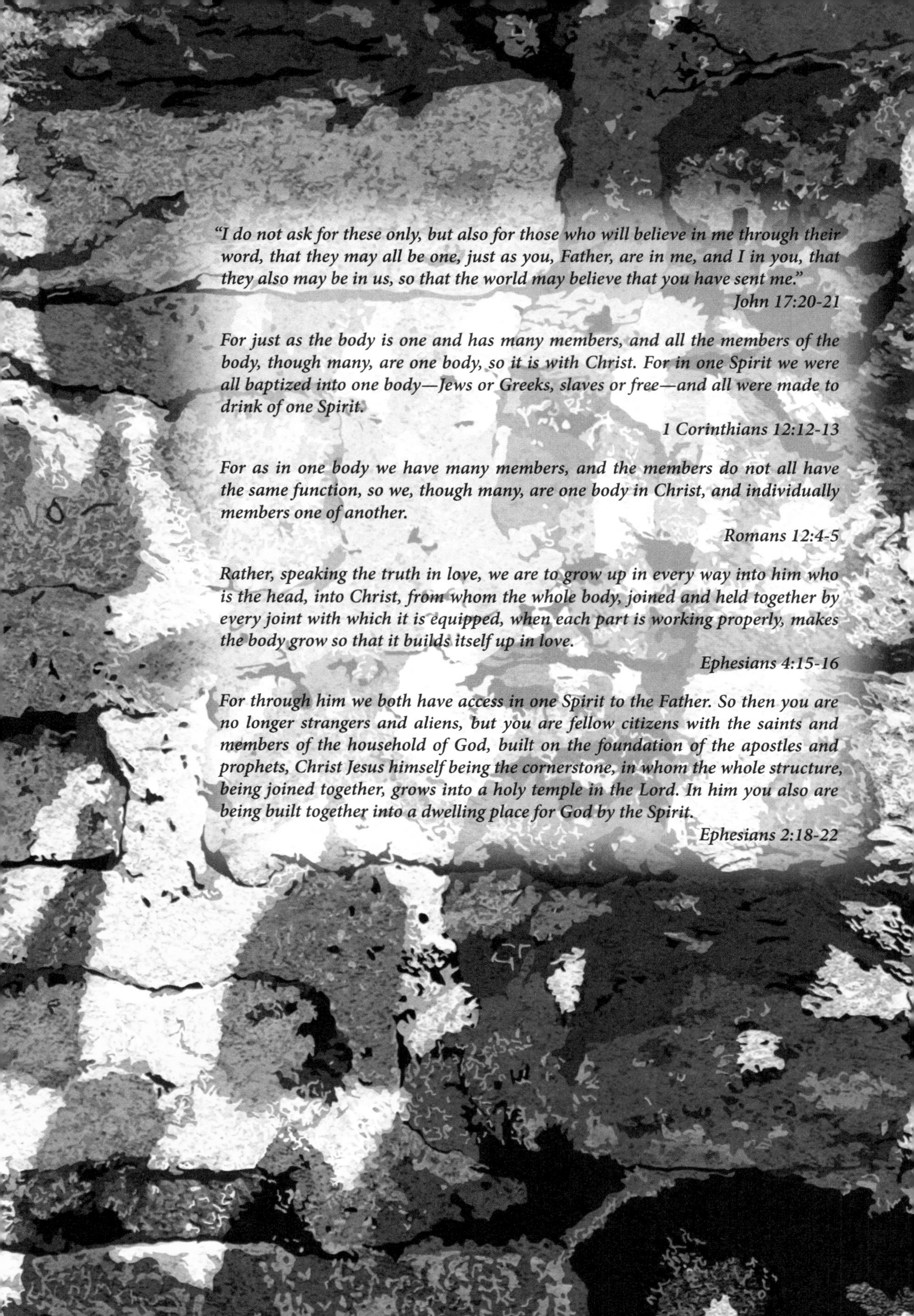

"I do not ask for these only, but also for those who will believe in me through their word, that they may all be one, just as you, Father, are in me, and I in you, that they also may be in us, so that the world may believe that you have sent me."

John 17:20-21

For just as the body is one and has many members, and all the members of the body, though many, are one body, so it is with Christ. For in one Spirit we were all baptized into one body—Jews or Greeks, slaves or free—and all were made to drink of one Spirit.

1 Corinthians 12:12-13

For as in one body we have many members, and the members do not all have the same function, so we, though many, are one body in Christ, and individually members one of another.

Romans 12:4-5

Rather, speaking the truth in love, we are to grow up in every way into him who is the head, into Christ, from whom the whole body, joined and held together by every joint with which it is equipped, when each part is working properly, makes the body grow so that it builds itself up in love.

Ephesians 4:15-16

For through him we both have access in one Spirit to the Father. So then you are no longer strangers and aliens, but you are fellow citizens with the saints and members of the household of God, built on the foundation of the apostles and prophets, Christ Jesus himself being the cornerstone, in whom the whole structure, being joined together, grows into a holy temple in the Lord. In him you also are being built together into a dwelling place for God by the Spirit.

Ephesians 2:18-22

Presence

God's Presence in the Church 5

On the night He was arrested, Jesus prayed for His disciples and for all those who would believe through His disciples. In other words, His prayer was even for believers in this day. The prayer is recorded in John 17. Jesus referred to our spiritual union with Him when He prayed "that they also may be in us." He prayed that believers would be in the Father and Son just as the Son is in the Father and the Father is in the Son. He prayed that we would be one. Because we are in Christ, we have communion with God, and we also have communion with every other believer across all time and in every place—they are also in Christ! Our union with Christ leads to unity among all believers. This unity is spiritual, but it should also be visible to the world "so that the world may believe."

Every believer is in Christ from the moment of salvation. That common union gives us a common purpose. Paul uses several different analogies in teaching about this unity of believers. The one he seems to draw on most frequently in his letters is the image of a body. Every person who believes in Christ as Lord and Savior is united to Christ by the Holy Spirit and connected to the one body with Christ as the head. Each believer remains an individual with their own function, but the members work together to serve the entire body. When the body is working properly, the whole body grows and matures, as each member is contributing in the way that God has designed.

The human body requires food for survival. The empty stomach sends hunger signals to the brain. The brain acts to coordinate an effort from all parts of the body to satisfy its needs. The eyes see the food. Signals travel from the brain by nerves to the muscles of the feet and legs to move the body into position. In the same manner, the brain signals the arms and hands to pick up the food. The mouth bites, the nose and tongue coordinate to experience taste, the esophagus contracts to move the food, and the stomach and intestines draw nourishment. Every part has to work properly under the coordination of the head to achieve the goal. So it is in Christ. We are all parts of one body, and He gives the members diverse tasks according to the purposes for which He designed us with the goal of serving Him.

Another image that Paul uses to describe believers collectively is that of a building. Most important to the whole structure is Jesus Christ as the cornerstone. The foundation was built by aligning the leaders of the early church to Jesus Christ. The whole structure continues to be built, stone by stone, believer by believer. We are stones forming the same building and members of the same household. The structure is being built to be a temple—a holy place for God to dwell. The community of all believers—the Church—is where God meets with His people for fellowship. This temple built with living stones is holy because of God's presence. Christ is present in the body as its head. The Father is present in the temple of living stones. The Church is activated as one functioning unit by the Holy Spirit. There would be no unity in the body of Christ without our union with Christ holding us together.

Action Step: From the moment of salvation, we have been connected to a body of believers in Christ. What can you change in your commitments to become more connected to a local part of the larger body of believers? Even when church relationships are difficult, if we choose to love and stay connected with each other because of our common union (communion) with Christ, there can be significant growth. As Christ is present in us, we need to be present with one another. Choose someone from the body of Christ to be present with this week.

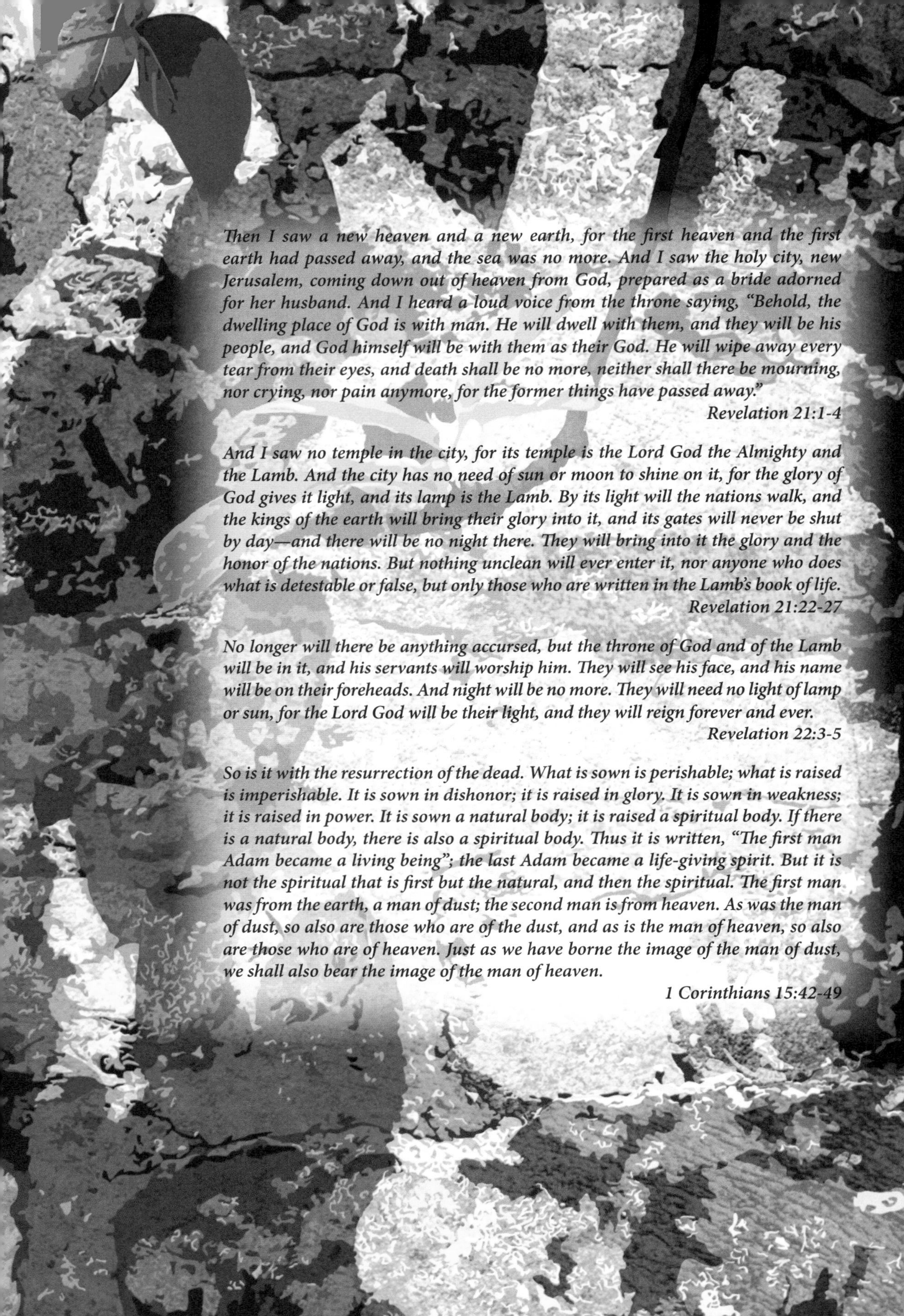

Then I saw a new heaven and a new earth, for the first heaven and the first earth had passed away, and the sea was no more. And I saw the holy city, new Jerusalem, coming down out of heaven from God, prepared as a bride adorned for her husband. And I heard a loud voice from the throne saying, "Behold, the dwelling place of God is with man. He will dwell with them, and they will be his people, and God himself will be with them as their God. He will wipe away every tear from their eyes, and death shall be no more, neither shall there be mourning, nor crying, nor pain anymore, for the former things have passed away."

Revelation 21:1-4

And I saw no temple in the city, for its temple is the Lord God the Almighty and the Lamb. And the city has no need of sun or moon to shine on it, for the glory of God gives it light, and its lamp is the Lamb. By its light will the nations walk, and the kings of the earth will bring their glory into it, and its gates will never be shut by day—and there will be no night there. They will bring into it the glory and the honor of the nations. But nothing unclean will ever enter it, nor anyone who does what is detestable or false, but only those who are written in the Lamb's book of life.

Revelation 21:22-27

No longer will there be anything accursed, but the throne of God and of the Lamb will be in it, and his servants will worship him. They will see his face, and his name will be on their foreheads. And night will be no more. They will need no light of lamp or sun, for the Lord God will be their light, and they will reign forever and ever.

Revelation 22:3-5

So is it with the resurrection of the dead. What is sown is perishable; what is raised is imperishable. It is sown in dishonor; it is raised in glory. It is sown in weakness; it is raised in power. It is sown a natural body; it is raised a spiritual body. If there is a natural body, there is also a spiritual body. Thus it is written, "The first man Adam became a living being"; the last Adam became a life-giving spirit. But it is not the spiritual that is first but the natural, and then the spiritual. The first man was from the earth, a man of dust; the second man is from heaven. As was the man of dust, so also are those who are of the dust, and as is the man of heaven, so also are those who are of heaven. Just as we have borne the image of the man of dust, we shall also bear the image of the man of heaven.

1 Corinthians 15:42-49

Presence

God's Presence in the Heavenly City

6

From Genesis to Revelation, God has made clear His desire to dwell with men and women. In addition to the reality that all creation lives and moves in God (His omnipresence), His will is to make His relational presence known to those who seek Him and have faith in Him. In fact, one major theme of the entire Bible is the revelation of the glory of God in redeeming a people that are fit to dwell in His presence. God is incomprehensible, and His eternal plan for His people is also beyond our comprehension. But He has revealed in Scripture glimpses of what it will look like when He dwells with us eternally.

The book of Revelation describes a new heaven and a new earth. There will be a holy city, New Jerusalem, where God will dwell with people. "He will wipe away every tear from their eyes" is a promise that recalls some of the personal, intimate language of Genesis 2 when God formed Adam and Eve. If the wiping of tears is literal, physical touch is implied. At the culmination of history, after Jesus returns and all things are made new, God will make His presence known among His people in ways that we perceive with our senses—ways that we do not now experience. God Himself will be the temple where we worship. The glory of God and the Lamb will give all the light that we need, and there will be no night. There will be no sinful people needing to be protected from the holy light of the glory of God; those who hope in Jesus Christ and have their names written in the Lamb's book of life will bask eternally in the light of God's glory wherever they go. The omnipresence of God will no longer be an unseen promise, but it will be more apparent to us when all of the new heaven and new earth is illuminated by God's glory. Our present faith in what is not seen will be rewarded by seeing His face. Several times in Revelation the people are referred to as "a great multitude." This is no small group of people who will be living in the presence of God and the Lamb and in community with one another. The community of all believers from all time will live in sin-free communion with the triune God.

Note that this is not just a restoration of the garden of Eden, though there are features that are similar to Eden before the fall. This is an entirely remade creation—a new heaven and a new earth. We will live in a beautiful city constructed from precious metals and fine jewels. And nothing unclean, detestable, or false will ever enter this city! Our bodies will not be just like what we live in now, they will be completely changed. Our resurrection bodies will be raised imperishable, in glory and power, and in the heavenly image of Christ rather than the earthly image of Adam. Our bodies will be spiritual in the sense that they will be glorified and completely transformed by the Holy Spirit into the image of Jesus Christ. God's plan to dwell with man is not a throwback to the garden of Eden, it is even better! The God who promises to dwell with us in this new creation is worthy of our faith and hope. And we will experience His presence in a fullness never before experienced by people—a presence that is unhindered by the sins of mankind.

Action Step: David wrote Psalm 16 to express confidence in God's care and His presence. He closes the psalm with a sure hope that God would "make known to me the path of life; in your presence there is fullness of joy; at your right hand are pleasures forevermore" (Ps. 16:11). Peter quoted this psalm in Acts 2, applying its truth to the resurrection of Christ. Because Christ completed His work on earth and ascended to the Father, He opened the way for His followers to find fullness of joy in God's presence now and forevermore. Even when life is difficult, how can you continue to find hope in His presence?

Weekly Summary

Key Points

1. God is present everywhere. His entire being is in every location at all times and not limited by space. Though He is present everywhere, He may choose to manifest His presence in more significant ways.
2. Adam and Eve experienced God in the garden of Eden in some physical ways that we do not sense Him. Though omnipresent, God has a heart to manifest His presence in a special way among His people.
3. Throughout the Old Testament, God uniquely made His presence known to the nation of Israel.
4. God's special presence with His faithful people in the age of the church is actually in His people. We can have communion with God only through our union with Christ.
5. Because we are in Christ, we have communion with God and we also have communion with every other believer across all time and in every place.
6. In the heavenly city, the community of all believers from all time will live in sin-free communion with the triune God.

Presence
Action Steps

Go back through the action steps and complete any that you have not yet completed or repeat one that was meaningful:

1. As you spend time in prayer today, consider God's very real presence with you. Now consider that His omnipresence places Him in and over and through every one of the 7.7 billion people currently living on this planet, leaving "no creature…hidden from his sight" (Heb. 4:13). Worship God for the awesome wonder of His omnipresence.

2. Scripture has clearly revealed the truth of God's omnipresence. We cannot plead ignorance in this regard. But does this truth affect your daily life? If Jesus Christ was physically walking beside you throughout the day today, would His physical presence change your actions or words? Should the reality of God's spiritual presence with you have any less impact?

3. The prophet Isaiah wrote to the people of Judah before they were exiled to Babylon to warn them of coming judgment and to promise that God would restore them: "When you pass through the waters, I will be with you; and through the rivers, they shall not overwhelm you; when you walk through fire you shall not be burned, and the flame shall not consume you." God fulfilled this promise to Shadrach, Meshach, and Abednego in a literal and very spectacular way. Still, a mature faith realizes that even if God does not deliver us from harm, He has promised to be with us in a personal way. Will you trust that He is relationally present with you in trials regardless of the immediate outcome?

4. Because our union with Christ is a spiritual reality and not something we can easily see, it is so hard to grasp and take hold of. At its most basic level, it may help to think about how being *in Christ* impacts our relationship with God. When God looks at you, He sees you as being in Christ, having accomplished everything that Christ accomplished in His life, death, resurrection, and ascension. You are covered by a blanket of Christ. You can think of *Christ in you* as how you have the power to obey God and bear the family image. In your daily walk on this earth, you can look like Jesus in your behavior because He is in you. As you walk through your day today, prayerfully consider how your relationship with God is impacted by the reality of being *in Christ* and how your thoughts, words, and actions are affected by the reality that *Christ is in you*.

5. From the moment of salvation, we have been connected to a body of believers in Christ. What can you change in your commitments to become more connected to a local part of the larger body of believers? Even when church relationships are difficult, if we choose to love and stay connected with each other because of our common union (communion) with Christ, there can be significant growth. As Christ is present in us, we need to be present with one another. Choose someone from the body of Christ to be present with this week.

6. David wrote Psalm 16 to express confidence in God's care and His presence. He closes the psalm with a sure hope that God would "make known to me the path of life; in your presence there is fullness of joy; at your right hand are pleasures forevermore" (Ps. 16:11). Peter quoted this psalm in Acts 2, applying its truth to the resurrection of Christ. Because Christ completed His work on earth and ascended to the Father, He opened the way for His followers to find fullness of joy in God's presence now and forevermore. Even when life is difficult, how can you continue to find hope in His presence?

WEEK 22
Good

Ultimately, God isn't good because he does good things for us. And God isn't good because of something in us. God is good because of something in him. He can be nothing else.

Chip Ingram, *The Real God*, 75.

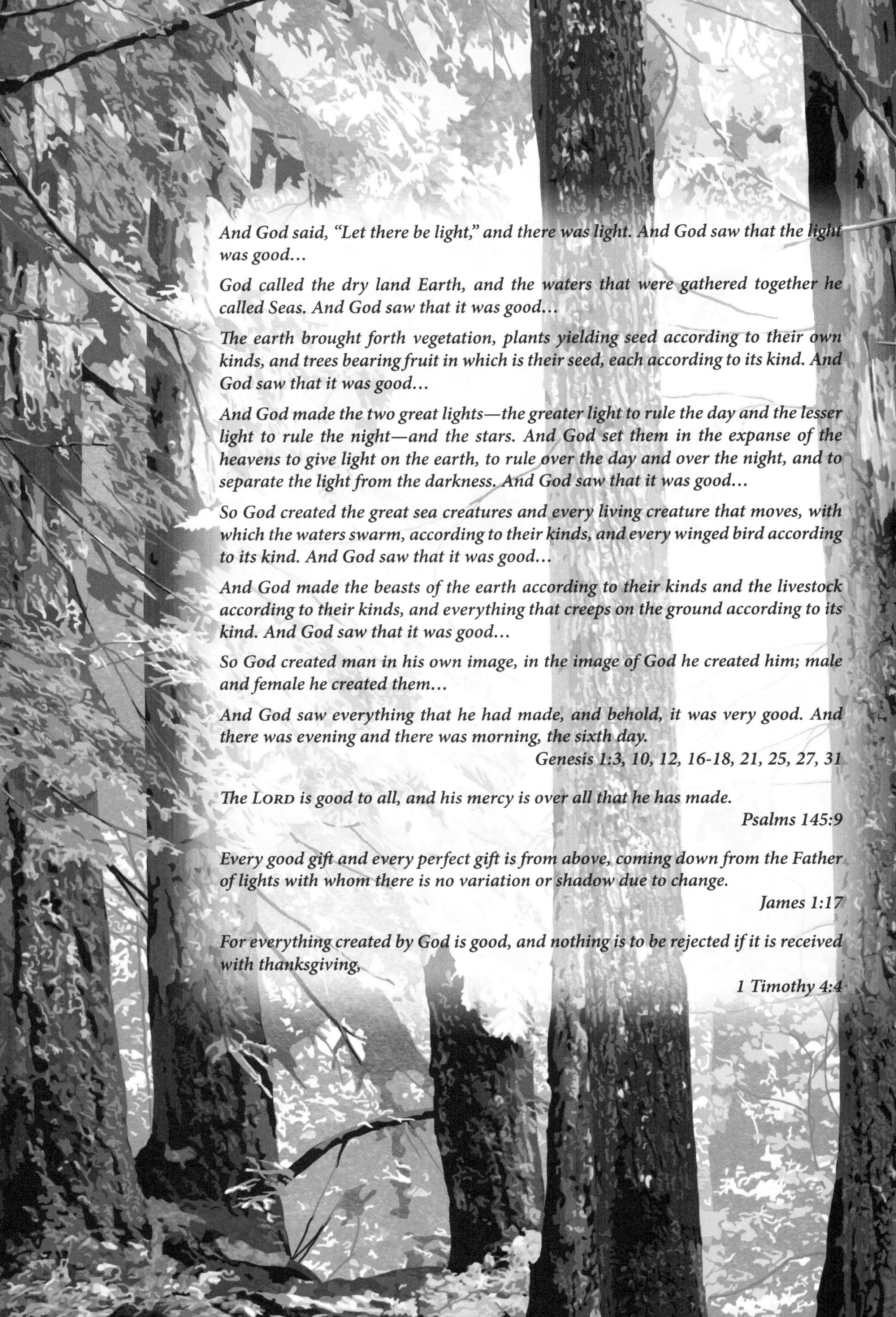

And God said, "Let there be light," and there was light. And God saw that the light was good…

God called the dry land Earth, and the waters that were gathered together he called Seas. And God saw that it was good…

The earth brought forth vegetation, plants yielding seed according to their own kinds, and trees bearing fruit in which is their seed, each according to its kind. And God saw that it was good…

And God made the two great lights—the greater light to rule the day and the lesser light to rule the night—and the stars. And God set them in the expanse of the heavens to give light on the earth, to rule over the day and over the night, and to separate the light from the darkness. And God saw that it was good…

So God created the great sea creatures and every living creature that moves, with which the waters swarm, according to their kinds, and every winged bird according to its kind. And God saw that it was good…

And God made the beasts of the earth according to their kinds and the livestock according to their kinds, and everything that creeps on the ground according to its kind. And God saw that it was good…

So God created man in his own image, in the image of God he created him; male and female he created them…

And God saw everything that he had made, and behold, it was very good. And there was evening and there was morning, the sixth day.

Genesis 1:3, 10, 12, 16-18, 21, 25, 27, 31

The LORD is good to all, and his mercy is over all that he has made.

Psalms 145:9

Every good gift and every perfect gift is from above, coming down from the Father of lights with whom there is no variation or shadow due to change.

James 1:17

For everything created by God is good, and nothing is to be rejected if it is received with thanksgiving,

1 Timothy 4:4

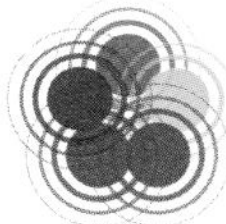

Good

God's Goodness in Creation

1

To begin a study of the goodness of God, we don't have to go any further than the first chapter of the first book of the Bible, Genesis 1. The Creation account is a description of how God, who is overflowing with goodness, reached out to display His goodness outside of Himself. Each day of Creation begins with God speaking, "And God said..." Nearly every day ends with the same approval: "And God saw that it was good." God, being the source of all that is good, declares something He has made good when it reflects something of the good that is inherent in Him.

It is God's design that the world He created reflects His goodness and that His creation provides much of the language that God uses to reveal Himself and His kingdom throughout Scripture. On the first day, God spoke and created light...and it was good. The Scriptures describe God as light (1 Jn. 1:5), and Jesus said that He is the light of the world (Jn. 8:12). Light is a good metaphor for God's holiness and revelation of His knowledge. On the third day, God spoke and created vegetation—plants, seeds, and trees. Plants are good, and Jesus used imagery of seeds (Mt. 13:3-9), the harvest (Mt. 13:24-30), and trees (Mt. 13:31-32) to explain the kingdom of God. On the sixth day, God spoke and made the beasts of the earth and livestock, then He deemed it good for Jesus to be revealed as the Lamb of God (Is. 53:7; Jn. 1:29). Also on the sixth day, God made man—in His own image, male and female. Being made in the image of God, men and women were created with the capacity to uniquely reflect God's character and participate in a relationship with Him. Along with the image of God came the honor and responsibility of ruling over creation (Ps. 8:5-6). As He completed Creation, God declared it very good.

In Creation, God showed that He is good—kind, generous, benevolent, beautiful, pleasant, and favorable—to all that He made. Everything that is good originates in God, and everything created by God is good. His desire is to bless what He has created and dwell with men and women on the earth, continuing to share His goodness. On the seventh day, God rested because He was satisfied with the reflection of His goodness in what He had made.

Action Step: Print a copy of Genesis 1 or use your Bible for highlighting. You will need five different colors for highlighting. With one color, highlight every instance of "And [or Then] God said." Use a second color to highlight all the words that God spoke in the chapter. With the third color, highlight the descriptions of what was created. Then use the fourth color to highlight every occurrence of "good" or "very good." Use the last color to highlight each day of Creation ("the first day," etc.). Review what you have highlighted to see the pattern of Creation–God speaks, matter takes shape, the result is declared good, and the day is completed. The culmination of this rhythm of creativity is a world that is good and fit to reveal God's character and to provide a place for God to dwell with men and women.

The LORD God took the man and put him in the garden of Eden to work it and keep it. And the LORD God commanded the man, saying, "You may surely eat of every tree of the garden, but of the tree of the knowledge of good and evil you shall not eat, for in the day that you eat of it you shall surely die."

Genesis 2:15-17

Now the serpent was more crafty than any other beast of the field that the Lord God had made.

He said to the woman, "Did God actually say, 'You shall not eat of any tree in the garden'?" And the woman said to the serpent, "We may eat of the fruit of the trees in the garden, but God said, 'You shall not eat of the fruit of the tree that is in the midst of the garden, neither shall you touch it, lest you die.'" But the serpent said to the woman, "You will not surely die. For God knows that when you eat of it your eyes will be opened, and you will be like God, knowing good and evil." So when the woman saw that the tree was good for food, and that it was a delight to the eyes, and that the tree was to be desired to make one wise, she took of its fruit and ate, and she also gave some to her husband who was with her, and he ate.

Genesis 3:1-6

Good

Adam and Eve Define Good

2

In Genesis 2, a more detailed description of the sixth day of Creation, we learn that God prepared a garden in Eden and settled man into the garden to work and keep it. Food was plentiful, as God caused every beautiful tree that is good for food to spring up from the ground. Also growing in the garden were two unique trees—the tree of life and the tree of the knowledge of good and evil. One clear command is recorded that God gave to Adam in the garden: "You may surely eat of every tree of the garden, but of the tree of the knowledge of good and evil you shall not eat, for in the day that you eat of it you shall surely die." Then the Lord God made Eve to help Adam—a companion fit for him. This was paradise—a place where God would walk with Adam and Eve in the garden. This was God's creation that was described as "very good" at the close of Genesis 1.

Tragically, this paradise did not last long. Into this scene entered the serpent, who began to question Eve about God's command to Adam. In fact, the serpent was questioning not just the command, but the very character of God. The serpent implied to Eve that God might not be seeking that which was best for Adam and Eve. The evil serpent went so far as to suggest that God, who is infinitely good, might be withholding something good from them. Satan, in the form of the serpent, accused God of lying. As evil as this serpent's suggestions were, we should take careful notice of Eve's conclusion: "The woman saw that the tree was good for food." God had declared His creation very good. But by commanding that they not eat from this tree of the knowledge of good and evil, God had declared this tree *not* good for eating. Eve had decided to become her own judge of what was good.

This is the very meaning behind not eating of the tree of the knowledge of good and evil. God's desire for men and women was that they rely on His wisdom to determine what is good and evil. The decision that the fruit was good for eating was a decision to not submit to God's definition of good. This was a sin of disobedience, but, even deeper, it was a sin of rebellion against God's goodness. Adam and Eve were offered the opportunity to experience the goodness of God by walking with Him in the garden in obedience to His command. Instead, they chose to experience evil first-hand by disobedience. Rather than believing God's definition of goodness, they followed their own.

This is an ongoing way that we descendants of Adam and Eve continue to sin. We continue to live under our own definition of good. This is seen most clearly in defiant acts of disobedience against God's commands—lying, stealing, or gossiping to advance our own "good" interests. Even those of us who love Jesus and seek to follow Him slip into our own comfortable definitions of goodness. We seek what is pleasant and free of pain. We assume that something that is difficult to bear could not be from God.

Action Step: Consider your own life and any ways that you may have questioned God's goodness. Is it possible that in those circumstances you were trying to be the judge of what is good in your life and not submitting to God's greater good? Pray and ask for the Holy Spirit's guidance in this evaluation of yourself.

But for me it is good to be near God; I have made the Lord God my refuge, that I may tell of all your works.

Psalms 73:28

"Yet he did not leave himself without witness, for he did good by giving you rains from heaven and fruitful seasons, satisfying your hearts with food and gladness."

Acts 14:17

Oh give thanks to the Lord, for he is good, for his steadfast love endures forever!

Psalms 107:1

We know that all things work together for the good of those who love God, who are called according to his purpose. For those he foreknew he also predestined to be conformed to the image of his Son, so that he would be the firstborn among many brothers and sisters. And those he predestined, he also called; and those he called, he also justified; and those he justified, he also glorified.

Romans 8:28-30 (CSB)

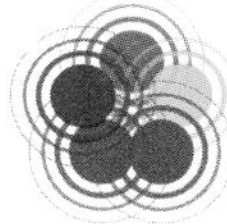

Good

Scripture Defines Good 3

Adam and Eve's future was tragically changed by their attempts to define good for themselves. Death was introduced into paradise. They were driven from the garden. Our evaluation of what is good must be based in what God says, not in what seems good to us. Psalm 73 states, "But it is good for me to be near to God." One thing God defines as good is having people near to Him in a relationship. In the book of Acts, we read, "He did good by giving you rains from heaven and fruitful seasons, satisfying your hearts with food and gladness." What is good in this passage? The Lord's provision for all of the people on earth is good. These gifts should point us back to Him as the giver of all good things.

The central topic of Psalm 107 is the way that God delivers His children from distress when they cry out to Him, and the psalm opens with a declaration of His goodness and love. The words "because" and "for" may be used interchangeably. So a paraphrase of Psalm 107:1 might be, "Oh give thanks to the Lord, *because* he is good, *because* his steadfast love endures forever." This helps us to see *how* we know that the Lord is good—*because* we see that His steadfast love endures forever. Likewise, Romans 8:28-29 can be paraphrased, "We know that all things work together for the good of those who love God, who are called according to his purpose. *Because* those he foreknew he also predestined to be conformed to the image of his Son, so that he would be the firstborn among many brothers and sisters." The *because* in this passage introduces the purpose that is good. We know that all things work together for the good of those who love God, but *how* do we know? *Because* those He foreknew He also predestined to be conformed to the image of His Son. There is an unbreakable sequence of promises in these verses. Those whom God foreknew as His children He also predestined. All of those who are predestined, He also called, then justified, and He also will glorify. This glorifying will be the completion of our sanctification, when God will finish the process of conforming us to the image of His Son. Once God has foreknown and predestined, the process is so assured that "glorified" is in past tense, as if it has already been completed. Please notice that this entire paragraph in Romans 8 is about the work that God is doing, and therefore, it cannot fail. But notice also that this work is not completed until future glory. All the things that God is working toward now will not be finished until Jesus returns. The final good purpose of God here is the completion of our being conformed to the image of Christ, when we are glorified.

Those who love God can rest assured that He will use every painful and difficult circumstance in their lives for good, but not necessarily good as we would like to define it. This is not a promise that believers will be healed of every disease or rescued from every tragedy. This is not a promise that we will see good purpose *in this life* for every painful thing that happens to us. God has much higher intentions for us than just happiness in this world. Sometimes God delivers us from troubles by transforming us more and more into the image of Jesus Christ so that we are fully equipped to face our troubles the way that Christ faced the cross. The challenge is to find hope in the goodness of future glory.

Action Step: Since an ultimate goal of God's goodness is to conform you to the image of His Son, are you willing to grow toward that goal now in this life? Are you willing to be transformed by trials? Do you see trials as a time when God has withdrawn from you, or do you draw near to Him and embrace the goodness of being made to look like Jesus? Pray and ask the Holy Spirit to help you trust God and His process.

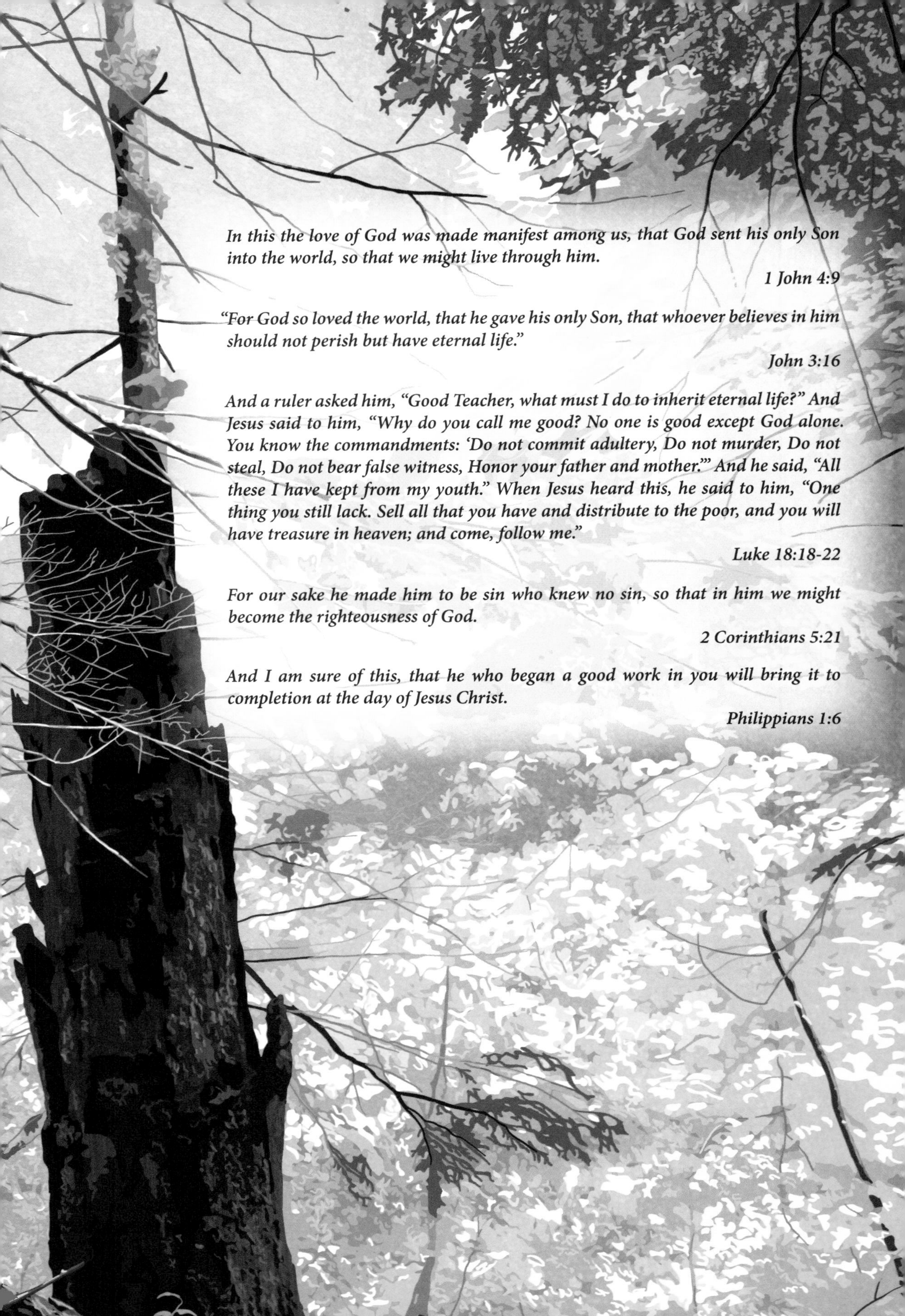

In this the love of God was made manifest among us, that God sent his only Son into the world, so that we might live through him.

1 John 4:9

"For God so loved the world, that he gave his only Son, that whoever believes in him should not perish but have eternal life."

John 3:16

And a ruler asked him, "Good Teacher, what must I do to inherit eternal life?" And Jesus said to him, "Why do you call me good? No one is good except God alone. You know the commandments: 'Do not commit adultery, Do not murder, Do not steal, Do not bear false witness, Honor your father and mother.'" And he said, "All these I have kept from my youth." When Jesus heard this, he said to him, "One thing you still lack. Sell all that you have and distribute to the poor, and you will have treasure in heaven; and come, follow me."

Luke 18:18-22

For our sake he made him to be sin who knew no sin, so that in him we might become the righteousness of God.

2 Corinthians 5:21

And I am sure of this, that he who began a good work in you will bring it to completion at the day of Jesus Christ.

Philippians 1:6

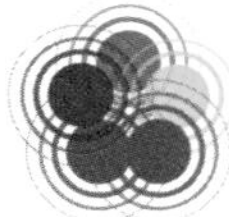

Good
God's Goodness in Redemption 4

God's inherent goodness is expressed outwardly in many of His attributes. His goodness expressed in giving sinners time to repent of their sins is His patience. His goodness expressed as compassion for those in need is His mercy. God's grace is His goodness extended to those who have earned eternal death for their sins. When God offers, out of His goodness, the gift of Himself, this is God's love.

> *God's love is an exercise of his goodness toward individual sinners whereby, having identified himself with their welfare, he has given his Son to be their Savior, and now brings them to know and enjoy him in a covenant relation.*
>
> J. I. Packer, *Knowing God*

God willed to redeem us simply because of His goodness, not because of anything worthy in us. When Adam and Eve fell and tarnished the good image of God that He had placed in them, God's own goodness did not waver. The goodness that caused God to create men and women in His image persevered to rescue mankind from the fall. The goodness of God offered His own Son in a gift of love to redeem us from our sin. Stephen Charnock summed this up in *The Existence and Attributes of God* well over one hundred years ago: "Divine justice laid 'upon him the iniquity of us all,' but Divine goodness intended it for our rescue."

The life of Jesus on earth was a tangible display of the goodness of God. In His encounter with the rich young ruler in Luke 18, the young man called Jesus, "good teacher." Jesus' response was, "Why do you call me good? No one is good except God alone." This response was not a denial of His own goodness by Jesus. He said Himself, "I and the Father are one" (Jn. 10:30). Jesus Christ is "the radiance of the glory of God and the exact imprint of his nature" (Heb. 1:3). Jesus' question was actually a challenge to the young ruler in which He may well have been saying, "If you are willing to call me good, are you willing to call me God?" Jesus also pointed out to the young man that following Him was the greatest of all good. No amount of "good" that any person does will earn us eternal life. Only Jesus, the Son of God, was a perfectly good man. Only by believing in Jesus Christ and placing our trust in His righteousness can we be made righteous ourselves. Only God's "good work" of redemption in us can bring us to eternal life in Him.

Action Step: God has shown His goodness in creating us. He has shown His goodness in redeeming us. And He continues to show His goodness in making us like Christ. There is absolutely nothing in us that qualifies us for receiving any of this goodness from Him. Praise and worship God for the good work He is doing in your life.

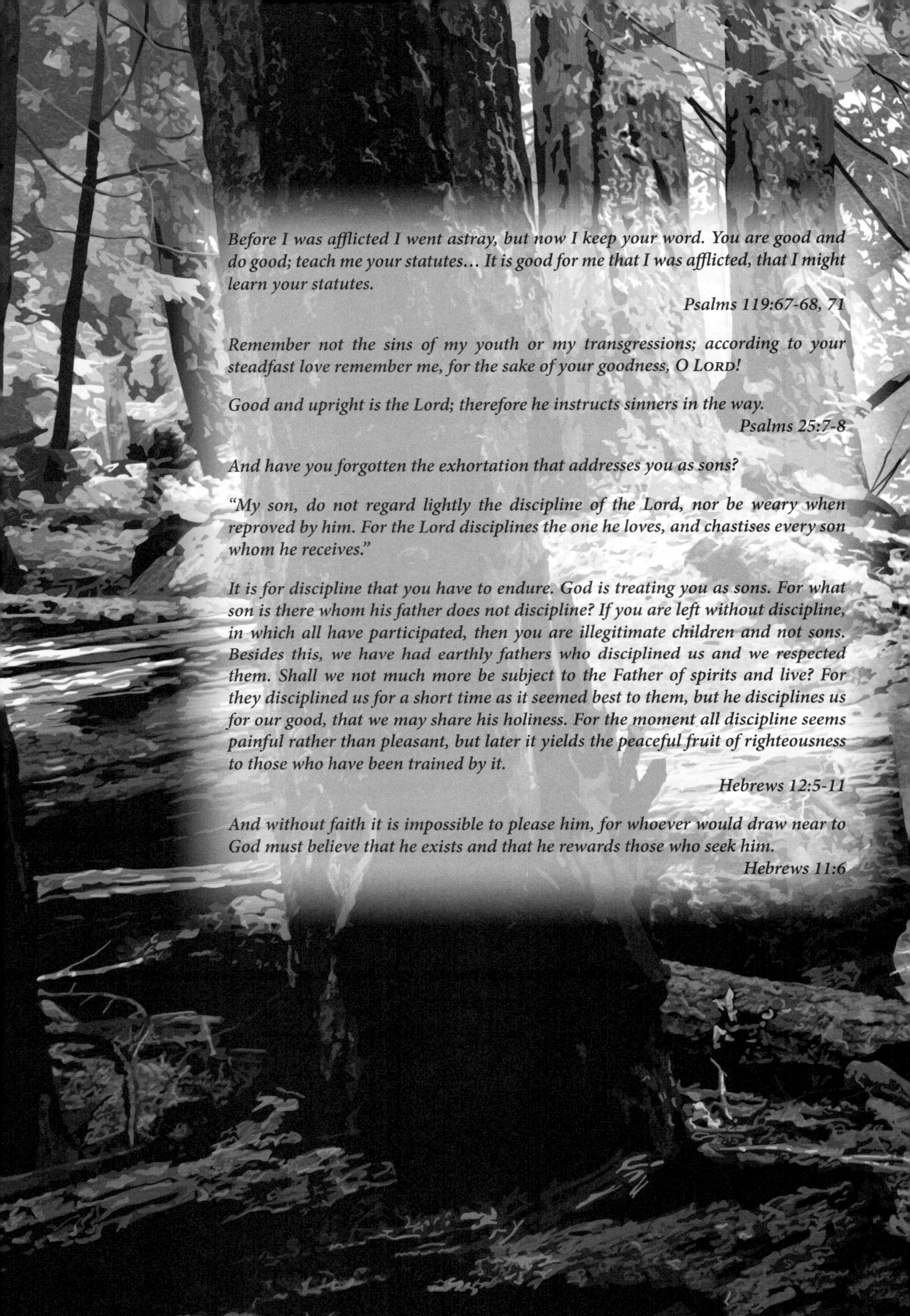

Before I was afflicted I went astray, but now I keep your word. You are good and do good; teach me your statutes… It is good for me that I was afflicted, that I might learn your statutes.

Psalms 119:67-68, 71

Remember not the sins of my youth or my transgressions; according to your steadfast love remember me, for the sake of your goodness, O Lord!

Good and upright is the Lord; therefore he instructs sinners in the way.

Psalms 25:7-8

And have you forgotten the exhortation that addresses you as sons?

"My son, do not regard lightly the discipline of the Lord, nor be weary when reproved by him. For the Lord disciplines the one he loves, and chastises every son whom he receives."

It is for discipline that you have to endure. God is treating you as sons. For what son is there whom his father does not discipline? If you are left without discipline, in which all have participated, then you are illegitimate children and not sons. Besides this, we have had earthly fathers who disciplined us and we respected them. Shall we not much more be subject to the Father of spirits and live? For they disciplined us for a short time as it seemed best to them, but he disciplines us for our good, that we may share his holiness. For the moment all discipline seems painful rather than pleasant, but later it yields the peaceful fruit of righteousness to those who have been trained by it.

Hebrews 12:5-11

And without faith it is impossible to please him, for whoever would draw near to God must believe that he exists and that he rewards those who seek him.

Hebrews 11:6

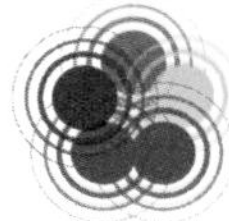

Good

God's Discipline Is Good

5

Part of God's work in redeeming and sanctifying believers is carrying out discipline. Because God is the source of all good and being near to Him is good, it is good for God to train us away from our attempts to settle for the good we find in anything less than Him. Every good gift that He gives us in this world is intended to direct our focus to Him as the giver, yet we so often find ourselves satisfied in focusing on the good gifts themselves. The psalmist declares of God, "You are good and do good." But he follows that with a request: "teach me your statutes," in other words, His law. According to this author, one of the ways God teaches obedience is through affliction. David wrote in Psalm 25 that one of the ways that God shows His goodness is by instructing sinners in the way, meaning the way of following Him. We are saved by faith in Christ and not through the law, but God's desire is to perfect those who have been saved, so He disciplines His sons and daughters.

In Hebrews 12, the author quoted Proverbs 3:11-12, which urges readers not to take the Lord's discipline lightly, but also not to grow weary of the discipline and give up hope. Expanding on that teaching, Hebrews compares the Lord's discipline to that of earthly fathers. If earthly fathers know the importance of discipline, how much more does our perfect Heavenly Father know? Earthly fathers operate out of limited knowledge and experience. But God has perfect knowledge and wisdom to discipline His sons and daughters for our good to bring about holiness and righteousness. The discipline of the Lord actually proves that we are His children and that He loves us. The end result is to teach us what it looks like to bear the image of God. The author of Hebrews admits that it seems painful. It is not pleasant to be disciplined. But the fruit is worth the pain if we allow ourselves to be trained by it. Not all of our trials in this life are because of our own sin, but all of our trials can be used by God to train us in godliness.

Our responsibility is to trust God in this process. Even when our circumstances in life may suggest differently, we need to trust that God can use them for good. Satan may attempt to bring about our destruction with trials and temptations, but he is under God's authority. God will not allow us to be tempted beyond what we can endure (1 Cor. 10:13), and He will take every difficulty that Satan intends for evil and use it for our good. We cannot let our circumstances, as difficult and painful as they may be, damage our trust in the goodness of God. This is what faith is—"the assurance of things hoped for, the conviction of things not seen" (Heb. 11:1). Faith looks past what we see before us and trusts in the promises of God. God has promised that He is good. God has promised that He works all things for the good of those who love Him to conform them to the image of Christ. And God has promised that He rewards those who seek Him. Do not be weary when being disciplined by your Father, but focus on His love for you and the good work that He is doing in you.

Action Step: An earthly father builds the trust of his child over time. He helps feed the hungry toddler, carries the preschooler in his arms, and stops the small child from running into the street. He won't let the girl eat so much candy that she feels sick, he sets a curfew for his sixteen-year-old driver and disciplines her when she comes home late. When these things are done in love for the good of the child, that earthly father is an imperfect example of the way that God disciplines us for our good. Write a letter to your Heavenly Father that addresses some of the ways that He has disciplined you. Be sure to cover whether the discipline felt painful and what you may have learned from it. Has it increased your trust in Him?

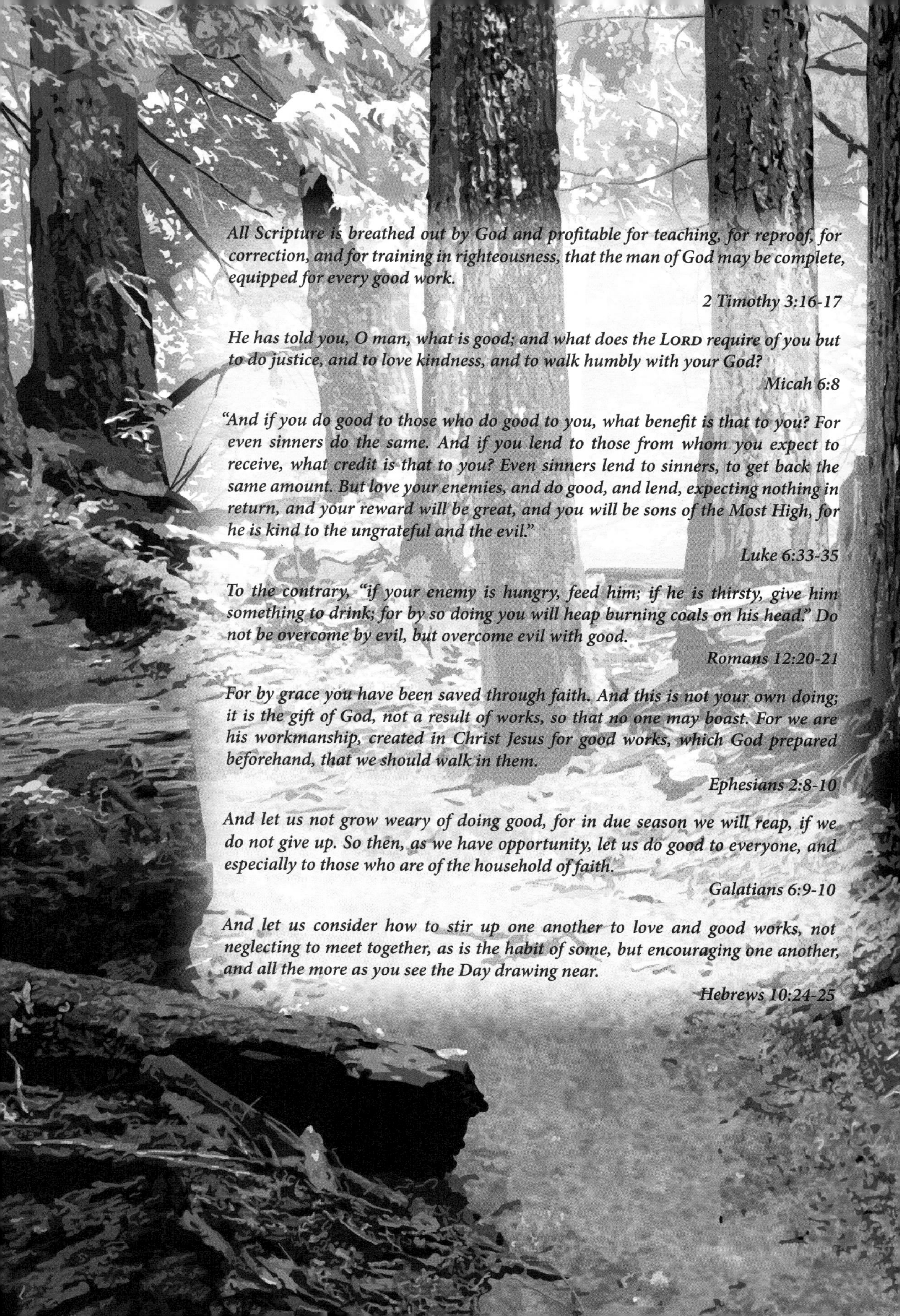

All Scripture is breathed out by God and profitable for teaching, for reproof, for correction, and for training in righteousness, that the man of God may be complete, equipped for every good work.

2 Timothy 3:16-17

He has told you, O man, what is good; and what does the LORD require of you but to do justice, and to love kindness, and to walk humbly with your God?

Micah 6:8

"And if you do good to those who do good to you, what benefit is that to you? For even sinners do the same. And if you lend to those from whom you expect to receive, what credit is that to you? Even sinners lend to sinners, to get back the same amount. But love your enemies, and do good, and lend, expecting nothing in return, and your reward will be great, and you will be sons of the Most High, for he is kind to the ungrateful and the evil."

Luke 6:33-35

To the contrary, "if your enemy is hungry, feed him; if he is thirsty, give him something to drink; for by so doing you will heap burning coals on his head." Do not be overcome by evil, but overcome evil with good.

Romans 12:20-21

For by grace you have been saved through faith. And this is not your own doing; it is the gift of God, not a result of works, so that no one may boast. For we are his workmanship, created in Christ Jesus for good works, which God prepared beforehand, that we should walk in them.

Ephesians 2:8-10

And let us not grow weary of doing good, for in due season we will reap, if we do not give up. So then, as we have opportunity, let us do good to everyone, and especially to those who are of the household of faith.

Galatians 6:9-10

And let us consider how to stir up one another to love and good works, not neglecting to meet together, as is the habit of some, but encouraging one another, and all the more as you see the Day drawing near.

Hebrews 10:24-25

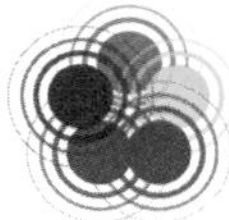

Good

Do Good to Everyone 6

Scripture makes clear that we are to do good. But how do we know what is good? Who should we do good for? Again, we have to be guided by the Bible, not just our own ideas. Paul wrote in his second letter to Timothy that one goal of teaching and training from Scripture is to be "equipped for every good work." All of Scripture provides a lifetime of reference material for how to do good works.

The prophet Micah wrote to the nation of Israel that they had been told what was good—doing justice and loving kindness and walking humbly with God. We have covered this verse before in this book because justice and loving kindness (*hesed*) are attributes of God. Walking humbly with God and reflecting His nature is good. It is how we show a fallen world His attributes. Jesus taught that our good deeds are not just for those who do good to us. That is easy for anyone to do. Only sons of the Most High are good to their enemies as well. Not only are we to love our enemies, but we are called to show that love by seeking their good. In fact, we can actually *overcome* evil with good. Our kindness toward an enemy can actually cause him to feel shame and repent.

There is certainly a spiritual component empowering our good works. Goodness is included in the fruit of the Spirit in Galatians 5. As the Holy Spirit molds God's character in us, we mirror His goodness in our lives. We are saved by faith, not by good works, but good works are an outgrowth of saving faith. God created us for good works, and He has prepared them in advance for us to walk in them. God uses believers to accomplish some of His work. We have spiritual guidance and strength to equip us for doing good, but there is effort on our part as well. It is possible to "grow weary of doing good," but we are urged to look to the future harvest and not give up. Being part of an encouraging community of faith is also important so that we can "stir up one another to love and good works." We are called to do good for everyone, but especially for other believers because we are all part of the family of God.

The guidance of God's Word is our first measure of what good works should look like in our lives. The work of the Holy Spirit is necessary to give us power and discernment to walk in good works. A local church body provides both the encouragement and the first place to accomplish good works. In addition, there is a powerful role for our good works to play in overcoming evil. The good works that we walk in by the power of the Spirit begin to restore the image of God in us that He proclaimed as "very good."

Action Step: What does it look like to "stir up one another to love and good works"? Have a conversation with another member of your local church to talk about how you can encourage one another in good works.

Weekly Summary

Key Points

1. In Creation, God showed that He is good—kind, generous, benevolent, beautiful, pleasant, and favorable—to all that He made. Everything that is good originates in God, and everything created by God is good.

2. Adam and Eve were offered the opportunity to experience the goodness of God by walking with Him in the garden in obedience to His command. Rather than believing God's definition of goodness, they followed their own.

3. Our evaluation of what is good must be based in what God says in Scripture, not in what seems good to us.

4. God willed to redeem us simply because of His goodness, not because of anything worthy in us.

5. Because God is the source of all good and being near to Him is good, it is good for God to train us away from our attempts to settle for the good we find in anything less than Him.

6. The guidance of God's Word is our first measure of what good works should look like in our lives. The work of the Holy Spirit is necessary to give us power and discernment to walk in good works.

Good

Action Steps

Go back through the action steps and complete any that you have not yet completed or repeat one that was meaningful:

1. Print a copy of Genesis 1 or use your Bible for highlighting. You will need five different colors for highlighting. With one color, highlight every instance of "And [or Then] God said." Use a second color to highlight all the words that God spoke in the chapter. With the third color, highlight the descriptions of what was created. Then use the fourth color to highlight every occurrence of "good" or "very good." Use the last color to highlight each day of Creation ("the first day," etc.). Review what you have highlighted to see the pattern of Creation—God speaks, matter takes shape, the result is declared good, and the day is completed. The culmination of this rhythm of creativity is a world that is good and fit to reveal God's character and to provide a place for God to dwell with men and women.

2. Consider your own life and any ways that you may have questioned God's goodness. Is it possible that in those circumstances you were trying to be the judge of what is good in your life and not submitting to God's greater good? Pray and ask for the Holy Spirit's guidance in this evaluation of yourself.

3. Since an ultimate goal of God's goodness is to conform you to the image of His Son, are you willing to grow toward that goal now in this life? Are you willing to be transformed by trials? Do you see trials as a time when God has withdrawn from you, or do you draw near to Him and embrace the goodness of being made to look like Jesus? Pray and ask the Holy Spirit to help you trust God and His process.

4. God has shown His goodness in creating us. He has shown His goodness in redeeming us. And He continues to show His goodness in making us like Christ. There is absolutely nothing in us that qualifies us for receiving any of this goodness from Him. Praise and worship God for the good work He is doing in your life.

5. An earthly father builds the trust of his child over time. He helps feed the hungry toddler, carries the preschooler in his arms, and stops the small child from running into the street. He won't let the girl eat so much candy that she feels sick, he sets a curfew for his sixteen-year-old driver and disciplines her when she comes home late. When these things are done in love for the good of the child, that earthly father is an imperfect example of the way that God disciplines us for our good. Write a letter to your Heavenly Father that addresses some of the ways that He has disciplined you. Be sure to cover whether the discipline felt painful and what you may have learned from it. Has it increased your trust in Him?

6. What does it look like to "stir up one another to love and good works"? Have a conversation with another member of your local church to talk about how you can encourage one another in good works.

WEEK 23
The God Who Suffers with Us

According to Christian theology, suffering is not meaningless—neither in general nor in particular instances. For God has purposed to defeat evil so exhaustively on the cross that all the ravages of evil will someday be undone and we, despite participating in it so deeply, will be saved. God is accomplishing this not in spite of suffering, agony, and loss but through it—it is through the suffering of God that the suffering of humankind will eventually be overcome and undone. While it is impossible not to wonder whether God could have done all this some other way—without allowing all the misery and grief—the cross assures us that, whatever the unfathomable counsels and purposes behind the course of history, they are motivated by love for us and absolute commitment to our joy and glory.

So suffering is at the very heart of the Christian faith. It is not only the way Christ became like and redeemed us, but it is one of the main ways we become like him and experience his redemption.

Timothy Keller, *Walking with God through Pain and Suffering*

The LORD God said to the serpent, "Because you have done this, cursed are you above all livestock and above all beasts of the field; on your belly you shall go, and dust you shall eat all the days of your life. I will put enmity between you and the woman, and between your offspring and her offspring; he shall bruise your head, and you shall bruise his heel."

To the woman he said, "I will surely multiply your pain in childbearing; in pain you shall bring forth children. Your desire shall be contrary to your husband, but he shall rule over you."

And to Adam he said, "Because you have listened to the voice of your wife and have eaten of the tree of which I commanded you, 'You shall not eat of it,' cursed is the ground because of you; in pain you shall eat of it all the days of your life;"

Genesis 3:14-17

Yet it was the will of the LORD to crush him; he has put him to grief;

Isaiah 53:10

"And now, brothers, I know that you acted in ignorance, as did also your rulers. But what God foretold by the mouth of all the prophets, that his Christ would suffer, he thus fulfilled."

Acts 3:17-18

"The Son of Man must suffer many things and be rejected by the elders and chief priests and scribes, and be killed, and on the third day be raised."

Luke 9:22

"Was it not necessary that the Christ should suffer these things and enter into his glory?"

Luke 24:26

...explaining and proving that it was necessary for the Christ to suffer and to rise from the dead, and saying, "This Jesus, whom I proclaim to you, is the Christ."

Acts 17:3

For it was fitting that he, for whom and by whom all things exist, in bringing many sons to glory, should make the founder of their salvation perfect through suffering.

Hebrews 2:10

For we do not have a high priest who is unable to sympathize with our weaknesses.

Hebrews 4:15

Therefore he had to be made like his brothers in every respect, so that he might become a merciful and faithful high priest in the service of God, to make propitiation for the sins of the people. For because he himself has suffered when tempted, he is able to help those who are being tempted.

Hebrews 2:17-18

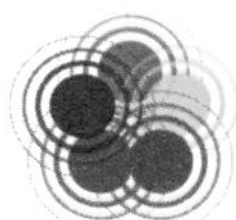

The God Who Suffers with Us
Why Did Jesus Have to Suffer?

1

In this book we have studied more than twenty attributes of God that are revealed in Scripture, all with a look at how the character of God may transform us, especially in the midst of suffering. Grounded in what we have learned about the nature of God, we will finish this study with a direct look at human suffering. We can't even begin to wrestle with a Biblical understanding of suffering without a deep consideration of the cross of Jesus Christ. The question posed here is not, "Why did Jesus have to die?" Multiple answers to that question have been covered previously in this study—to show His love for us, to pay the penalty for our sins and give us His righteousness, to enable us to draw near to God, and to give us eternal life. The question posed here is, "Why did Jesus have to *suffer* when He died for us?" Why was it not God's will that Jesus quickly die from the slash of a Roman sword? In light of God's nature, we have to conclude that the brutality of the crucifixion was completely within God's will because He is sovereign, and also that it was consistent with God's goodness and love—in fact, that it was consistent with all of His character.

Suffering entered the world with human sin. God pronounced a curse on the serpent who had deceived Eve: "on your belly you shall go, and dust you shall eat all the days of your life." He pronounced a curse on Eve: "in pain you shall bring forth children." And He pronounced a curse on Adam: "cursed is the ground because of you; in pain you shall eat of it all the days of your life." All of these curses share the consequence of suffering. At the same time, God announced that another would suffer when He spoke to the serpent: "he shall bruise your head, and you shall bruise his heel." The one who would bruise the serpent's head—in other words, overcome Satan as the ruler of this world—was Jesus Christ. Even as early as Genesis 3, there is a revelation that Jesus would suffer—the serpent would bruise His heel. It was necessary for Jesus to suffer to fulfill this promise and all other Old Testament prophecies of a suffering Messiah. But this still doesn't answer why God could not have designed another way from the very beginning for Christ to redeem the world that didn't involve horrible suffering. Is there a deeper meaning to the statement that it was *necessary* for the Christ to suffer?

The author of Hebrews gave more insight into the suffering of Jesus when he wrote that it was "fitting" that God "should make the founder of their salvation perfect through suffering." It was fitting that Jesus would experience obedience to the Father through intense suffering as a human so that He would be the perfect sacrifice for sins. Jesus was already perfect in being without sin, but He was made into a perfectly appropriate sacrifice by obedience through the suffering that is common to humanity. The human condition after the Fall includes suffering. God has declared it fitting that the redemption from the Fall would come through suffering as well. Before the creation of the world, all three Persons of the Trinity were in agreement that the best way to accomplish human redemption was for the Son of God to unite His divine nature to a human nature so that He could experience, not sin, but the suffering and death that are the human consequences of sin. The Son of God Himself has suffered with us, thus He can identify completely with the human condition. Because Jesus has suffered as a human, He can help those who are suffering.

Action Step: Jesus sympathizes with our suffering and our temptations (Heb. 4:15). He has experienced every type of trial that you might encounter in your life (Heb. 2:17). Pray and ask God to help you better understand and trust the sympathy and mercy that Jesus has for you in your suffering.

Surely he has borne our griefs and carried our sorrows; yet we esteemed him stricken, smitten by God, and afflicted. But he was pierced for our transgressions; he was crushed for our iniquities; upon him was the chastisement that brought us peace, and with his wounds we are healed. All we like sheep have gone astray; we have turned—every one—to his own way; and the Lord *has laid on him the iniquity of us all.*

Isaiah 53:4-6

Now from the sixth hour there was darkness over all the land until the ninth hour. And about the ninth hour Jesus cried out with a loud voice, saying, "Eli, Eli, lema sabachthani?" that is, "My God, my God, why have you forsaken me?"

Matthew 27:45-46

My God, my God, why have you forsaken me? Why are you so far from saving me, from the words of my groaning? O my God, I cry by day, but you do not answer, and by night, but I find no rest.

Yet you are holy, enthroned on the praises of Israel. In you our fathers trusted; they trusted, and you delivered them. To you they cried and were rescued; in you they trusted and were not put to shame...

For he has not despised or abhorred the affliction of the afflicted, and he has not hidden his face from him, but has heard, when he cried to him.

Psalms 22:1-5, 24

Christ redeemed us from the curse of the law by becoming a curse for us—for it is written, "Cursed is everyone who is hanged on a tree"—

Galatians 3:13

He is the propitiation for our sins, and not for ours only but also for the sins of the whole world.

1 John 2:2

2

The God Who Suffers with Us

My God, My God Why Have You Forsaken Me?

The consideration of the cross of Jesus Christ includes not only the question of why He suffered, but also a view of *how much* He suffered. The physical torture alone almost defies description. Before He was even arrested, He agonized over the impending suffering such that "his sweat became like great drops of blood falling down to the ground" (Lk. 22:44). After the arrest, He was spit on, struck, and slapped before Caiaphas and scourged by Pilate's men. He had a crown of thorns pressed onto His head and was struck on the head with a reed by the soldiers. He was stripped naked, and then the soldiers pounded nails through His hands and feet and suspended Him on the wooden beams. His emotional suffering included His closest disciples being unable to stay awake to support Him in His time of need. He was betrayed by another disciple and denied by one who had slept. People testified falsely against Him, the crowds demanded His crucifixion, and those who passed by the scene of the crucifixion insulted Him. The spiritual leaders of Israel mocked Him on the cross. He was even reviled by both of the thieves who hung beside Him until one turned to Him in faith.

Jesus endured all this, and still the most intense suffering was ahead of him. By noon (the sixth hour in the Jewish day), the skies had grown dark. For the next three hours, the dark skies pictured the judgment that was being carried out on Jesus while He was being held accountable for our sin. The curse and wrath of God for every single sin ever committed by all believers for all time was borne by Jesus Christ in that time. His suffering was great because the magnitude of our sin is so great. Even more so, His suffering was great because He endured it separated in some way from the Father. The cry of Jesus from the cross, "My God, my God, why have you forsaken me?" came at the end of the three hours of darkness. The Persons of the Godhead could never be disconnected from one another, but the spiritual anguish faced by Jesus was that the perfect intimate fellowship that He had experienced with the Father for eternity was somehow diminished. The holy Father determined not to rescue the sin-bearing Son. In the same way that we cannot fully understand with our finite minds the communion that exists eternally in the Trinity, we cannot comprehend what Jesus experienced in the way of disruption of communion on the cross. Yet the reality that we must grasp is that *we don't ever have to experience this forsakenness because Christ has experienced it for us!*

The words that Jesus cried out were originally written by David in Psalm 22. David's circumstances suggested to him that God was far from him. However, by the end of Psalm 22, David proclaimed praise to God, who had *not* hidden His face. Just as David trusted the holy God of Israel for eventual rescue, Jesus knew that any separation from His Father would not last. Jesus trusted the Father to restore fellowship with His Son and finish the work of redemption so that Jesus would be "the firstborn among many brothers" (Rom. 8:29).

Action Step: Jesus Christ has experienced every kind of human suffering. Whatever your trial is–abandonment by family members, physical abuse, excruciating pain, humiliation at the hands of those who disagree with you, shame from those in power over you, anticipation of a death, betrayal by friends, false accusations, hunger, thirst–He has faced the same trial that you are facing. During His life, Jesus even experienced homelessness (Mt. 8:20) and the temptation to take shortcuts to satisfy His human desires (Mt. 4:3). Cry out to Him in prayer and ask Him to help bear the burden you are carrying.

"I form light and create darkness, I make well-being and create calamity, I am the LORD*, who does all these things."*

Isaiah 45:7

"For my name's sake I defer my anger, for the sake of my praise I restrain it for you, that I may not cut you off. Behold, I have refined you, but not as silver; I have tried you in the furnace of affliction. For my own sake, for my own sake, I do it, for how should my name be profaned? My glory I will not give to another."

Isaiah 48:9-11

For the Lord will not cast off forever, but, though he cause grief, he will have compassion according to the abundance of his steadfast love; for he does not afflict from his heart or grieve the children of men.

Lamentations 3:31-33

"Come, let us return to the LORD*; for he has torn us, that he may heal us; he has struck us down, and he will bind us up."*

Hosea 6:1

For we do not want you to be unaware, brothers, of the affliction we experienced in Asia. For we were so utterly burdened beyond our strength that we despaired of life itself. Indeed, we felt that we had received the sentence of death. But that was to make us rely not on ourselves but on God who raises the dead. He delivered us from such a deadly peril, and he will deliver us. On him we have set our hope that he will deliver us again.

2 Corinthians 1:8-10

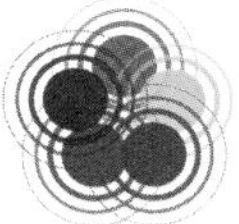

The God Who Suffers with Us

Does God Cause or Allow Suffering?

3

Is God ever the active cause of suffering, or does He merely *allow* suffering for His good purposes? The Bible is clear that all people will suffer. Jesus Himself promised, "In the world you will have tribulation" (Jn. 16:33). There are multiple reasons for our suffering, all attributable to the sin that has marred humanity and this world.

Let's first consider suffering as a consequence of our own sin. Isaiah told the people of coming judgment. They had been disobedient to God's covenant, and there was discipline coming in the form of exile and suffering. Isaiah spoke the words of the Lord saying, "I form light and create darkness, I make well-being and create calamity, I am the Lord, who does all these things." This calamity or disaster that the Lord was bringing had a specific purpose of bringing God's people back to obedience. The people were being "tried in the furnace of affliction." God's will was to preserve a people for the sake of His own praise and glory. When His people continue in disobedience, God will bring suffering in the form of discipline to bring about repentance. Even in this discipline, the fullness of all of God's attributes are seen—"though he cause grief, he will have compassion according to the abundance of his steadfast love." But not all suffering is a consequence of our own sin. That simplistic thinking was the misunderstanding of Job's friends who insisted wrongly that he was suffering because of great sin in his life. Suffering can also result in our lives because of the sins of those around us or the brokenness of a creation that is corrupted by sin (Rom. 8:18-22).

In 2 Corinthians Paul tells of the affliction that he experienced in Asia. He gives the good reason for the suffering—"that was to make us rely not on ourselves but on God who raises the dead." Neither Satan nor any people who may have sought harm for Paul would have had a good intent. Only God would bring affliction with good intentions, including spiritual growth and hope for delivery from the suffering. There are strong arguments in Scripture that God is not merely standing by *allowing* this suffering of His apostles, but that He may actually play an active role in *bringing* the suffering to cause growth. We don't seem to have the right vocabulary to describe God's role in human suffering. If we say that He causes suffering, we must be very careful to note that God is neither tempted with evil, nor does He tempt anyone (Jms. 1:13). Though God does not do evil, we have to ask ourselves if everything that brings discomfort into our lives is indeed evil. On the other hand, if we say that God only allows suffering, we must not remove Him too far from any situation, because He is intimately present in every believer's life and sovereign over every detail of all life. "Allowing" would still have to include God intentionally choosing this event for this believer. Suffering is not dictated by random chance, but it is limited by our infinite, wise, and good God. What matters in the end is that His will is done in both our joys and our sorrows. Difficult circumstances directed by God accomplish His purposes—purposes that are always consistent with His character, His glory, and the good of His people.

Action Step: The important thing to remember about God's role in our suffering is that He is always present in it. Jesus suffered separation from the Father as He bore the consequences for our sin so that those who place their faith in this work of Jesus on the cross will never be forsaken by the Father for their sin. Just as Jesus cried out to the Father in pain and lament on the cross, He expects us to cry out to Him. But our cries should be cries of faith, trusting that God will deliver us from suffering in His time. Prayerfully consider how your own trials might help you to rely on God rather than your own strength.

But we have this treasure in jars of clay, to show that the surpassing power belongs to God and not to us. We are afflicted in every way, but not crushed; perplexed, but not driven to despair; persecuted, but not forsaken; struck down, but not destroyed; always carrying in the body the death of Jesus, so that the life of Jesus may also be manifested in our bodies. For we who live are always being given over to death for Jesus' sake, so that the life of Jesus also may be manifested in our mortal flesh. So death is at work in us, but life in you.

2 Corinthians 4:7-12

Now I rejoice in my sufferings for your sake, and in my flesh I am filling up what is lacking in Christ's afflictions for the sake of his body, that is, the church, of which I became a minister according to the stewardship from God that was given to me for you, to make the word of God fully known, the mystery hidden for ages and generations but now revealed to his saints. To them God chose to make known how great among the Gentiles are the riches of the glory of this mystery, which is Christ in you, the hope of glory.

Colossians 1:24-27

The Spirit himself bears witness with our spirit that we are children of God, and if children, then heirs—heirs of God and fellow heirs with Christ, provided we suffer with him in order that we may also be glorified with him.

Romans 8:16-17

...that I may know him and the power of his resurrection, and may share his sufferings, becoming like him in his death, that by any means possible I may attain the resurrection from the dead.

Philippians 3:10-11

Blessed be the God and Father of our Lord Jesus Christ, the Father of mercies and God of all comfort, who comforts us in all our affliction, so that we may be able to comfort those who are in any affliction, with the comfort with which we ourselves are comforted by God. For as we share abundantly in Christ's sufferings, so through Christ we share abundantly in comfort too. If we are afflicted, it is for your comfort and salvation; and if we are comforted, it is for your comfort, which you experience when you patiently endure the same sufferings that we suffer. Our hope for you is unshaken, for we know that as you share in our sufferings, you will also share in our comfort.

2 Corinthians 1:3-7

For what credit is it if, when you sin and are beaten for it, you endure? But if when you do good and suffer for it you endure, this is a gracious thing in the sight of God. For to this you have been called, because Christ also suffered for you, leaving you an example, so that you might follow in his steps. He committed no sin, neither was deceit found in his mouth. When he was reviled, he did not revile in return; when he suffered, he did not threaten, but continued entrusting himself to him who judges justly.

1 Peter 2:20-23

The God Who Suffers with Us

Christ in You, the Hope of Glory 4

As we studied God's presence, we explored the Biblical teaching that believers are "in Christ." We are spiritually united with Jesus Christ so that we are in Him and He is in us. Our union with Christ—God's presence with us—is our most desperate need as we face suffering. Paul wrote in 2 Corinthians of his own afflictions as connected to the death of Christ. Christ's death on the cross is the ultimate example of God using human weakness to bring victory. Jesus offered His weak and human flesh as a sacrificial death to gain spiritual victory for all who believe. Paul uses this analogy to teach that God's surpassing power that was displayed in Jesus' resurrection gave Paul strength to find victory in his own suffering and afflictions. Paul's human weaknesses were an opportunity for God to show His strength, not only to Paul, but also to others watching Paul.

In his letter to the Colossians, Paul refers to this as "filling up what is lacking in Christ's afflictions for the sake of his body, that is, the church." Christ's death and resurrection are lacking nothing when it comes to victory over sin and death. The only thing lacking in Christ's afflictions is the ongoing demonstration—in endurance through suffering—of God's power for those who believe. When believers suffer, Christ suffers with us and gives us the grace to persevere. This can be accomplished only because Christ is in us—present in our lives to endure our trials with us and give us the hope that we will be glorified with Him. Paul points out in his letter to the Romans that our willingness to endure suffering for Christ is evidence that we are children of God. Paul was able to endure all of his suffering because he shared it with Christ, and he looked forward to a resurrection like Jesus Christ's (Phil. 3:10-11).

When we are united with Christ, both our own faith and the faith of those around us can be strengthened in our afflictions. In addition, there is comfort found in Christ. When we rest in the God and Father of our Lord Jesus Christ, we are leaning on the God of all comfort. He personally comforts those who are suffering in Christ. In turn, as we experience God's comfort, we are able to comfort those around us who also suffer. We can patiently endure suffering knowing that God's comfort is present with us and this trial will enable us to share His comfort with others.

For those who are in Christ, our suffering is united with Christ's suffering. His suffering was unique in bearing our sin, but we remain united with the One who has endured every kind of affliction and temptation known to humanity. We are strengthened by Him and called to follow His example of patient endurance, not striking back or threatening anyone, but entrusting ourselves to God and His justice. In all these ways, the suffering that we endure is a gift and privilege for those who are in Christ (Phil. 1:29-30).

Action Step: Everyone who suffers has a choice. The afflicted can run to God in Christ to draw comfort from the Father of mercies and the Son who Himself endured every kind of suffering. Or, the afflicted can choose to be angry at God for their suffering. He is, after all, sovereign over all of our circumstances. Jesus warned that "many will fall away" in the midst of great tribulation (Mt. 24:9-10). Spend time in prayer today asking the Holy Spirit to help you evaluate your own attitude toward your hardships. What can you do to draw near to God in your trials instead of harboring anger toward Him?

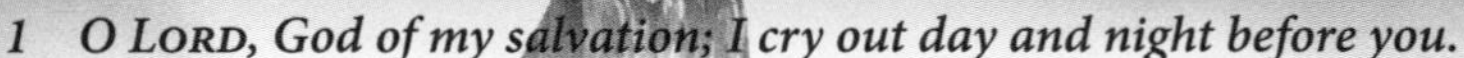

1 O Lord, God of my salvation; I cry out day and night before you.
2 Let my prayer come before you; incline your ear to my cry!
3 For my soul is full of troubles, and my life draws near to Sheol.
4 I am counted among those who go down to the pit; I am a man who has no strength,
5 like one set loose among the dead, like the slain that lie in the grave, like those whom you remember no more, for they are cut off from your hand.
6 You have put me in the depths of the pit, in the regions dark and deep.
7 Your wrath lies heavy upon me, and you overwhelm me with all your waves. Selah
8 You have caused my companions to shun me; you have made me a horror to them. I am shut in so that I cannot escape;
9 my eye grows dim through sorrow. Every day I call upon you, O Lord; I spread out my hands to you.
10 Do you work wonders for the dead? Do the departed rise up to praise you? Selah
11 Is your steadfast love declared in the grave, or your faithfulness in Abaddon?
12 Are your wonders known in the darkness, or your righteousness in the land of forgetfulness?
13 But I, O Lord, cry to you; in the morning my prayer comes before you.
14 O Lord, why do you cast my soul away? Why do you hide your face from me?
15 Afflicted and close to death from my youth up, I suffer your terrors; I am helpless.
16 Your wrath has swept over me; your dreadful assaults destroy me.
17 They surround me like a flood all day long; they close in on me together.
18 You have caused my beloved and my friend to shun me; my companions have become darkness.

Psalms 88:1-18

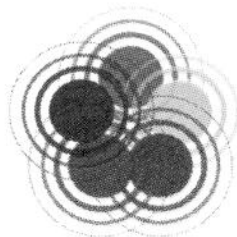

The God Who Suffers with Us
Biblical Lament

5

God is present in our suffering to comfort us. We will consider in tomorrow's reading that we are called to rejoice when we suffer. However, before we can talk about rejoicing in our trials, we have to recognize that suffering is heart-wrenching. Scripture affirms that a proper response to our afflictions is lament. Not only does God *not* correct people for expressing distress through lament, but the Holy Spirit has inspired the writers of Scripture to include expressions of lament for us to pattern our own after.

The psalms are full of the emotions of their authors, including lament. Psalm 88 is perhaps the most brokenhearted cry of them all. Much lament in the psalms is followed by praise and expressions of faith in the Lord. However, the author of this psalm remains downcast throughout his cry to God. But he did cry *to God*, "O Lord, God of my salvation; I cry out day and night before you." That in itself is what makes this psalm an appropriate expression to guide us into our own lament. Although he felt that the Lord had cast his soul away and hidden His face, the author still cried out to Him. At the same time that he felt that God abandoned him, he continued to trust that God would hear him. Even the most pained and broken cries that we call out can still be expressions of faith when we bring these cries to God. A cry from the pit of despair is a cry of faith when one acknowledges that God is the only One who can help. This is the inward groaning that Paul wrote we all experience as we wait for the redemption of our bodies (Rom. 8:23).

And God will redeem His own. He will save us from the pit of despair. He will right all wrongs and heal all the sick and resurrect the dead. But the complete realization of God's justice and power to save will not come until Jesus' return. In the meantime, God came to live with us in the pit of suffering in the persons of Jesus Christ and the Holy Spirit dwelling in us. And Jesus joins us in our grief.

The prophet Isaiah described the coming Messiah as "a man of sorrows, and acquainted with grief." Jesus grieved over the hardness of hearts of the Pharisees (Mk. 3:5). He grieved over the sins of Jerusalem (Mt. 23:37-39). He "was deeply moved in his spirit and greatly troubled" when He saw Mary grieving over the death of her brother, Lazarus, and Jesus wept alongside her (Jn. 11:33). As Jesus anticipated His own death in the garden, He told His disciples, "My soul is very sorrowful, even to death" (Mt. 26:38). And we have already considered His cry of lament on the cross when He was separated from the Father so that we who believe would never be forsaken. Not only is lament tolerated by God, but Jesus showed us that it is the proper human response to our suffering. The garden of Eden, at the completion of Creation, did not include sin, suffering, and death. It is fitting that men and women created in the image of God should mourn the devastating consequences of sin.

Action Step: Set aside some quiet reflective time alone to write out your own lament to God using Psalm 88 as a guide. Pour out all of your fears and frustrations and hurts before Him, recognizing that He is the only One with resources to save you, whether that is by lifting you out of your circumstances or walking with you through them. The contents of your lament should be the honest cries of your heart, but the recipient of your deepest lament should always be God. Remember, "the Lord is near to the brokenhearted and saves the crushed in spirit" (Ps. 34:18).

Count it all joy, my brothers, when you meet trials of various kinds, for you know that the testing of your faith produces steadfastness. And let steadfastness have its full effect, that you may be perfect and complete, lacking in nothing.

James 1:2-4

Therefore, since we have been justified by faith, we have peace with God through our Lord Jesus Christ. Through him we have also obtained access by faith into this grace in which we stand, and we rejoice in hope of the glory of God. Not only that, but we rejoice in our sufferings, knowing that suffering produces endurance, and endurance produces character, and character produces hope, and hope does not put us to shame, because God's love has been poured into our hearts through the Holy Spirit who has been given to us.

Romans 5:1-5

Therefore, since we are surrounded by so great a cloud of witnesses, let us also lay aside every weight, and sin which clings so closely, and let us run with endurance the race that is set before us, looking to Jesus, the founder and perfecter of our faith, who for the joy that was set before him endured the cross, despising the shame, and is seated at the right hand of the throne of God.

Hebrews 12:1-2

So we do not lose heart. Though our outer self is wasting away, our inner self is being renewed day by day. For this light momentary affliction is preparing for us an eternal weight of glory beyond all comparison, as we look not to the things that are seen but to the things that are unseen. For the things that are seen are transient, but the things that are unseen are eternal.

2 Corinthians 4:16-18

For I consider that the sufferings of this present time are not worth comparing with the glory that is to be revealed to us. For the creation waits with eager longing for the revealing of the sons of God. For the creation was subjected to futility, not willingly, but because of him who subjected it, in hope that the creation itself will be set free from its bondage to corruption and obtain the freedom of the glory of the children of God. For we know that the whole creation has been groaning together in the pains of childbirth until now. And not only the creation, but we ourselves, who have the firstfruits of the Spirit, groan inwardly as we wait eagerly for adoption as sons, the redemption of our bodies. For in this hope we were saved. Now hope that is seen is not hope. For who hopes for what he sees? But if we hope for what we do not see, we wait for it with patience.

Romans 8:18-25

In this you rejoice, though now for a little while, if necessary, you have been grieved by various trials, so that the tested genuineness of your faith—more precious than gold that perishes though it is tested by fire—may be found to result in praise and glory and honor at the revelation of Jesus Christ.

1 Peter 1:6-7

The God Who Suffers with Us

Count it All Joy

6

The challenge to the sufferer who is in Christ is that at the same time that the heart is crying out in lament to God, there is a Biblical command for our minds to focus on joy. How can this be? How can a shattered heart ever coincide with a mind set on joy? James teaches that believers should count it all joy when they encounter trials, and he gives a specific line of reasoning—"know that the testing of your faith produces steadfastness." To *know* is an action of the mind. *Know* that the trial is a test of faith and *know* that when you push through the test, the result will be steadfastness. Steadfastness is patient enduring or perseverance. In the end, *know* that the full effect of the perseverance is completeness so you will lack nothing. Counting it all joy requires setting the mind on God's promises.

Paul follows the same line of reasoning in Romans 5. Rejoice in your suffering because it produces endurance, which leads to character, which produces hope. Hope does not disappoint us because of what we are hoping in—God's love poured into our hearts through the Holy Spirit. The key to joy in suffering is knowing that God has taken us through a process where we are learning to trust, *by experience*, that His love—the love that has reconciled us to Him through the death of Christ—is our greatest treasure. There are many things in this world that bring us satisfaction, and many of them are *good* things. Everything that we find satisfaction in outside of God will eventually disappoint us. The joy is that finding fulfillment in God will *never* disappoint us. This joy is not happiness that a devastating thing happened in our lives but a joy of growing into closer fellowship with God and a closer resemblance to the image of Jesus Christ *through* that horrible experience. And these things can never be taken away! This kind of growth in trials completes our faith, so we lack nothing in the way of trust for God.

This is the way that Jesus endured the cross—"for the joy that was set before him." The joy that He anticipated on the cross that allowed Him to endure its suffering included enjoying the redemption of humanity. Despite the physical, emotional, and spiritual agony that He endured, He set His mind on the joy of what was being accomplished. Jesus knew that fellowship between God and believers was secured through His suffering, and He considered that joy. God's love, which poured into our hearts through the Holy Spirit, was the joy set before Jesus in His suffering, and we are called to find joy in the midst of our suffering with our hope set on the very same secure promise. Paul had experienced intense persecution when he wrote, "this light momentary affliction is preparing for us an eternal weight of glory beyond all comparison." What we see and feel and lament is intense suffering. What we cannot see, but we *know* in faith, is a glory so great that it makes the affliction seem small. We must set our minds on unseen eternal glory—a resurrection like Christ's into everlasting fellowship with the triune God. In this way the joy of our future hope can coexist with the grief of our trials.

Action Step: Turn to the Table of Contents of this book and review the attributes of God that we have studied. This list represents the nature of the God who is sovereign over and present in our suffering. Have you learned enough about Him that you can trust Him in your suffering? Have you learned enough about Him that you are confident that He is more precious to you than anything this earth offers? Pray and ask the Holy Spirit to help you evaluate areas where you need to grow toward completion.

Weekly Summary

Key Points

1. The Son of God Himself has suffered with us, thus He can identify completely with the human condition. Because Jesus has suffered as a human, He can help those who are suffering.

2. The suffering of Jesus Christ was great because the magnitude of our sin is so great. We don't ever have to experience forsakenness because Christ has experienced it for us!

3. There are strong arguments in Scripture that God is not merely standing by *allowing* this suffering of His apostles, but that He may actually play an active role in *bringing* the suffering to cause growth. What matters in the end is that His will is done in both our joys and our sorrows.

4. When believers suffer, Christ suffers with us and gives us the grace to persevere.

5. Scripture affirms that a proper response to our afflictions is lament. Not only is lament tolerated by God, but it is modeled for us by Jesus.

6. Counting it all joy requires setting the mind on God's promises in faith.

The God Who Suffers with Us

Action Steps

7

Go back through the action steps and complete any that you have not yet completed or repeat one that was meaningful:

1. Jesus sympathizes with our suffering and our temptations (Heb. 4:15). He has experienced every type of trial that you might encounter in your life (Heb. 2:17). Pray and ask God to help you better understand and trust the sympathy and mercy that Jesus has for you in your suffering.

2. Jesus Christ has experienced every kind of human suffering. Whatever your trial is—abandonment by family members, physical abuse, excruciating pain, humiliation at the hands of those who disagree with you, shame from those in power over you, anticipation of a death, betrayal by friends, false accusations, hunger, thirst—He has faced the same trial that you are facing. During His life, Jesus even experienced homelessness (Mt. 8:20) and the temptation to take shortcuts to satisfy His human desires (Mt. 4:3). Cry out to Him in prayer and ask Him to help bear the burden you are carrying.

3. The important thing to remember about God's role in our suffering is that He is always present in it. Jesus suffered separation from the Father as He bore the consequences for our sin so that those who place their faith in this work of Jesus on the cross will never be forsaken by the Father for their sin. Just as Jesus cried out to the Father in pain and lament on the cross, He expects us to cry out to Him. But our cries should be cries of faith, trusting that God will deliver us from suffering in His time. Prayerfully consider how your own trials might help you to rely on God rather than your own strength.

4. Everyone who suffers has a choice. The afflicted can run to God in Christ to draw comfort from the Father of mercies and the Son who Himself endured every kind of suffering. Or, the afflicted can choose to be angry at God for their suffering. He is, after all, sovereign over all of our circumstances. Jesus warned that "many will fall away" in the midst of great tribulation (Mt. 24:9-10). Spend time in prayer today asking the Holy Spirit to help you evaluate your own attitude toward your hardships. What can you do to draw near to God in your trials instead of harboring anger toward Him?

5. Set aside some quiet reflective time alone to write out your own lament to God using Psalm 88 as a guide. Pour out all of your fears and frustrations and hurts before Him, recognizing that He is the only One with resources to save you, whether that is by lifting you out of your circumstances or walking with you through them. The contents of your lament should be the honest cries of your heart, but the recipient of your deepest lament should always be God. Remember, "the Lord is near to the brokenhearted and saves the crushed in spirit" (Ps. 34:18).

6. Turn to the Table of Contents of this book and review the attributes of God that we have studied. This list represents the nature of the God who is sovereign over and present in our suffering. Have you learned enough about Him that you can trust Him in your suffering? Have you learned enough about Him that you are confident that He is more precious to you than anything this earth offers? Pray and ask the Holy Spirit to help you evaluate areas where you need to grow toward completion.

They shall not hurt or destroy in all my holy mountain; for the earth shall be full of the knowledge of the LORD as the waters cover the sea.

Isaiah 11:9

His divine power has granted to us all things that pertain to life and godliness, through the knowledge of him who called us to his own glory and excellence, by which he has granted to us his precious and very great promises, so that through them you may become partakers of the divine nature, having escaped from the corruption that is in the world because of sinful desire.

2 Peter 1:3-4

Conclusion

Many people question God's character or purposes when they suffer. If God is all-powerful, why didn't He stop this? If God is good, why does He let bad things happen to me? If God loves me, shouldn't He rescue me from this pain? I don't deserve this!

Rather than allowing ourselves to be shaped by a culture that would have us believe that God's purpose is to make us happy and comfortable in this world or that there is no God and everything that happens is just random chance, we must look to God's Word to trust in who He has revealed Himself to be. When random chance is perceived as in control, suffering appears meaningless. When we realize that God is in control and consider the fullness of all of His character, suffering has purpose. When you think you are suffering unjustly, consider the cross, where the sinless Son of God suffered to bring justice to the world. Remember that the Father who watches over the suffering in our lives is the God who loves us enough to redeem us through His own suffering. He is the God who knows our hearts and has both wisdom and power to use all things in our lives for good. His ways are incomprehensible to us, but He is faithful to all of His children to finish His work in them. He is unchanging, but He is sovereign over all circumstances in our lives to change us into His image. He is present with us, bringing mercy and grace in our times of need. This infinite God has reasons for us to endure suffering that we cannot fully comprehend. A Biblical view of God's nature is life-transforming for all believers, but especially when we suffer.

Acknowledgments

This book is the result of more than a decade of crying out to God for understanding in the midst of suffering. Before any person, I direct my thanks to God for His patience, goodness and love as He has guided me through His Word to know and trust Him more deeply. This book would have never made it past the concept stage apart from the grace of God. For that matter, even the concept was a gift of His grace.

Thank you to the friends that have encouraged me and prayed for this project from its early stages. Anne, Phyllis, Karen, Cheri, Lisa, Melissa, Katie, Mikee, Debbie, Julie, Ryan, Stu, Jessica, Todd & Karen and many more—your encouragement has sustained me along the way. Thank you to my friend Jess for design suggestions to make the text and images work together on the page.

I am grateful to John Fox of BookFox (www.thejohnfox.com) for copy editing services and additional encouragement that this project was worthy of publication. Thanks also to Alexis J. Miller for helping me to put together the bibliography and marketing copy. Chris Gilbert (www.studiogearbox.com) is an incredibly talented designer who created a fantastic cover for this project and I am deeply grateful for the gift of his time.

Thank you to my family members for your patience over 3 years as I worked on this project. From building me a writing desk to bearing with me as I drew on my iPad during family movie nights to shivering in the snowy wilderness while shooting promotional videos, you never questioned my sanity. Thank you to Kelsey, Jared, and Jackie for each supplying me with photos to use as reference for my art. And to my husband, John, for countless hours of discussion on Scripture and theology, always encouraging me to remain true to God's Word.

The highest thanks and all praise go to God, who reveals Himself to men and women created in His image. The story of Him choosing a people to redeem and conform to the image of Jesus Christ is the greatest story that can ever be told.

For ongoing updates on *Transformed by God's Nature* and associated projects, please visit our website at www.logbridgebooks.com.

Find us on Facebook at www.facebook.com/logbridgebooks.

Bibliography

I would not have been able to even begin to write this book without the guidance of the following resources. Studying the teaching of Spirit-led men and women who have written throughout the history of the church has been invaluable in understanding God's revelation of Himself. The Biblical insight and ideas communicated by these authors are well worth further study.

Books on God's Attributes

Alcorn, Nanci, Beth Crosby, Barbara Dewing, Peri Layton, Rakel Thurman, and Devonne Wolf. *How Great Is Our God* (Bible study curriculum). Boring, OR: Good Shepherd Community Church, 2015.

Bavinck, Herman. *God and Creation.* Vol. 2 of *Reformed Dogmatics*, edited by John Bolt. Translated by John Vriend. Grand Rapids, MI: Baker Academic, 2004.

Charnock, Stephen, and William Symington. *The Existence and Attributes of God.* Grand Rapids, MI: Baker Books, 1996. Project Gutenberg. First published 1853 by Pennsylvania State University.

Ingram, Chip. *The Real God: How He Longs for You to See Him.* Grand Rapids, MI: Baker Books, 2016.

Packer, J. I. *Knowing God.* Downers Grove, IL: InterVarsity Press, 1973.

Pink, Arthur W. *The Attributes of God.* Grand Rapids, MI: Baker Books, 1975.

Tozer, A. W., and David E. Fessenden. *The Attributes of God. Vol. 1 and 2.* Chicago, IL: Wing Spread Publishers, 2007.

Tozer, A. W. *The Knowledge of the Holy.* New York, NY: Harper One, 1961.

Reference

Brand, Chad, Charles Draper, Archie England, Steve Bond, E. Ray Clendenen, Trent C. Butler, and Bill Latta, eds. *Holman Illustrated Bible Dictionary.* Nashville, TN: Holman Reference, 2003.

Burge, Gary M., and Andrew E. Hill, eds. *The Baker Illustrated Bible Commentary.* Grand Rapids, MI: Baker Books, 2012.

Elwell, Walter A., ed. *Evangelical Dictionary of Theology.* Grand Rapids, MI: Baker BookHouse, 2001.

Enns, Paul P. *The Moody Handbook of Theology.* Chicago, IL: Moody Publishers, 2008.

ESV Study Bible: English Standard Version. Wheaton, IL: Crossway, 2008.

Grudem, Wayne. *Systematic Theology: An Introduction to Biblical Doctrine.* Grand Rapids, MI: Zondervan, 1994.

Rydelnik, Michael, and Michael G. Vanlaningham, eds. *The Moody Bible Commentary.* Chicago, IL: Moody Publishers, 2014.

Ryrie, Charles Caldwell, ed. *Ryrie Study Bible*, New American Standard Bible. Chicago, IL: Moody Publishers, 2012.

Sproul, R. C., ed. *The Reformation Study Bible*, English Standard Version. Orlando, FL: Reformation Trust, 2015.

Walvoord, John F., and Roy B. Zuck, eds. *The Bible Knowledge Commentary: New Testament*. Colorado Springs, CO: Victor, 1983.

Walvoord, John F., and Roy B. Zuck, eds. *The Bible Knowledge Commentary: Old Testament*. Colorado Springs, CO: Victor, 1983.

Wiersbe, Warren W., ed. *The Transformation Study Bible*, New Living Translation. Colorado Springs, CO: David C. Cook, 2009.

Wiersbe, Warren W. *The Wiersbe Bible Commentary: New Testament*. Colorado Springs, CO: David C. Cook, 2007.

Wiersbe, Warren W. *The Wiersbe Bible Commentary: Old Testament*. Colorado Springs, CO: David C. Cook, 2007.

Why Study God's Nature?

Spurgeon, Charles Haddon. "The Immutability of God." The Spurgeon Center. https://www.spurgeon.org/resource-library/sermons/the-immutability-of-god#flipbook/.

Incomprehensible

Howell, Elizabeth. "How Many Stars Are in the Milky Way?" Space.com. March 30, 2018. https://www.space.com/25959-how-many-stars-are-in-the-milky-way.html.

Siegel, Ethan. "This Is How We Know There Are Two Trillion Galaxies In The Universe." Forbes. October 18, 2018. https://www.forbes.com/sites/startswithabang/2018/10/18/this-is-how-we-know-there-are-two-trillion-galaxies-in-the-universe/#66cc6d795a67.

Triune

Lewis, C. S. *Mere Christianity*. New York, NY: Macmillan Publishing, 1952.

Sanders, Fred. *The Deep Things of God: How the Trinity Changes Everything*. Wheaton, IL: Crossway Books, 2010.

Sanders, Fred. *The Triune God*. Grand Rapids, MI: Zondervan, 2016.

Sproul, R. C. "The Athanasian Creed." Ligonier Ministries. August 1, 2007. http://www.ligonier.org/learn/articles/athanasian-creed/.

Eternal

Perlman, Howard. "Summary of the Water Cycle." USGS Water Science School. December 15, 2016. https://water.usgs.gov/edu/watercyclesummary.html.

US Department of Commerce, National Oceanic and Atmospheric Administration. "How Much Water Is in the Ocean?" NOAA's National Ocean Service. June 01, 2013. http://oceanservice.noaa.gov/facts/oceanwater.html.

Wu, Vernon. "Volume of Earth's Annual Precipitation." The Physics Factbook. 2008. http://hypertextbook.com/facts/2008/VernonWu.shtml.

Self-Existent and Self-Sufficient

Lawson, Steven. "Lecture 2: The Aseity of God." From *The Attributes of God: A Teaching Series by Dr. Steven Lawson*. Ligonier Ministries. First released in 2013. Video, 23:15. http://www.ligonier.org/learn/series/attributes-god/aseity-of-god/.

Piper, John. "How Is God's Passion for His Own Glory Not Selfishness?" Desiring God. November 24, 2007. http://www.desiringgod.org/articles/how-is-gods-passion-for-his-own-glory-not-selfishness.

Piper, John. "Is God for Us or for Himself?" Desiring God. August 10, 1980. http://www.desiringgod.org/messages/is-god-for-us-or-for-himself.

Spirit and Infinite

Gerstner, John. "Chapters 2–3, Sec. 3." *The Westminster Confession of Faith: A Teaching Series by Dr. John Gerstner*. Ligonier Ministries. First released in 1986. Video, 30:37. http://www.ligonier.org/learn/series/westminster-confession-of-faith/chapters-2-3-sec3.

Hameroff, Stuart. "Is Your Brain Really a Computer, or Is It a Quantum Orchestra?" *The Huffington Post*. July 08, 2015. http://www.huffingtonpost.com/stuart-hameroff/is-your-brain-really-a-co_b_7756700.html.

Sovereign

Moo, Douglas J. *Encountering the Book of Romans: A Theological Survey*. Grand Rapids, MI: Baker Academic, 2014.

Unchanging

Lawson, Steven. "Lecture 9: The Immutability of God." From *The Attributes of God: A Teaching Series by Dr. Steven Lawson*. Ligonier Ministries. First released in 2013. Video, 23:32. http://www.ligonier.org/learn/series/attributes-god/the-immutability-of-god/.

Far Above Creation and Intimately Involved in Creation

"Crafty Sheep Conquer Cattle Grids." BBC News. July 30, 2004. http://news.bbc.co.uk/2/hi/uk_news/3938591.stm.

History.com Staff. "Challenger Explosion." History.com. February 15, 2010. http://www.history.com/topics/challenger-disaster.

Father

MacLaren, Alexander. *MacLaren's Commentary: Expositions of Holy Scripture*. Delmarva Publications, 2013. Kindle.

Packer, J. I. *Knowing God*. Downers Grove, IL: InterVarsity Press, 1973. See esp. chap. 19, "Sons of God."

Sanders, Fred. *The Deep Things of God: How the Trinity Changes Everything*. Wheaton, IL: Crossway Books, 2010. See esp. p. 86 in chap. 2, "Within the Happy Land of the Trinity" and pp. 150–166 in chap. 4, "The Shape of the Gospel.".

Sanders, Fred. *The Triune God*. Grand Rapids, MI: Zondervan, 2016. See esp. p. 113 in chap. 4, "Incarnation and Pentecost."

"The Roman Empire in the First Century." PBS. http://www.pbs.org/empires/romans/empire/women.html.

When God's Nature Meets Human Brokenness

Lawson, Stephen J. *Job*. Vol. 10 of *Holman Old Testament Commentary*, edited by Max Anders. Nashville, TN: B&H Publishing Group, 2004.

Piper, John. *God is the Gospel: Meditations on God's Love as the Gift of Himself.* Wheaton, IL: Crossway Books, 2005. http://www.desiringgod.org/books/god-is-the-gospel.

Love

Grapevine illustration photo reference: Adapted from photograph by user Winniepix on Flickr Creative Commons, see license at https://creativecommons.org/licenses/by/2.0/legalcode.

Spurgeon, Charles Haddon. C. H. Spurgeon: Spurgeon's Sermons Volume 51: 1905 - Christian Classics Ethereal Library. https://ccel.org/ccel/spurgeon/sermons51.xliv.html.

Knowledge

"Neurogenesis in the Adult Brain." *The Journal of Neuroscience.* February 1, 2002. http://www.jneurosci.org/content/22/3/612.

"Neuroscience and How Students Learn." GSI Teaching Resource Center. 2011. http://gsi.berkeley.edu/gsi-guide-contents/learning-theory- research/neuroscience/.

Wolf, Maryanne, and Catherine J. Stoodley. *Proust and the Squid: The Story and Science of the Reading Brain.* New York, NY: Harper, 2007.

Power

Mark, Joshua J. "Pharaoh." Ancient History Encyclopedia. September 2, 2009. https://www.ancient.eu/pharaoh/.

Mercy

Piper, John. "Blessed Are the Merciful." Desiring God. February 23, 1986. https://www.desiringgod.org/messages/blessed-are-the-merciful.

Stevenson, Bryan. *Just Mercy.* New York, NY: Spiegel & Grau, 2015.

Justice

Mackie, Tim, and Jon Collins. "Biblical Justice." The Bible Project. https://thebibleproject.com/explore/justice/.

Faithful

Koessler, John. *The Surprising Grace of Disappointment.* Chicago, IL: Moody Publishers, 2013.

"Pervasive Gloom About the World Economy." Pew Research Center's Global Attitudes Project. July 12, 2012. http://www.pewglobal.org/2012/07/12/chapter-4-the-casualties-faith-in-hard-work-and-capitalism/.

Grace

Bridges, Jerry. *The Discipline of Grace.* Colorado Springs, CO: NavPress, 2006.

Piper, John. *Future Grace.* Colorado Springs, CO: Multnomah, 2012.

Sanders, Fred. *The Deep Things of God: How the Trinity Changes Everything.* Wheaton, IL: Crossway Books, 2010.

Yancy, Phillip. *What's So Amazing About Grace?* Grand Rapids, MI: Zondervan, 1997.

Holy

Piper, John. "What Is God's Glory?" Desiring God. July 22, 2014. https://www.desiringgod.org/interviews/what-is-gods-glory--2.

Sproul, RC. *The Holiness of God.* Carol Stream, IL: Tyndale Momentum, 1998.

Presence

Bavinck, Herman. *Holy Spirit, Church, and New Creation.* Vol. 4 of *Reformed Dogmatics,* edited by John Bolt. Translated by John Vriend. Grand Rapids, MI: Baker Academic, 2008.

"What Is Union with Christ?" Desiring God. October 31, 2018. https://www.desiringgod.org/interviews/what-is-union-with-christ.

"What Does It Mean to Be One with Christ?" Desiring God. November 21, 2016. https://www.desiringgod.org/articles/what-does-it-mean-to-be-one-with-christ.

Wilbourne, Rankin. *Union with Christ: The Way to Know and Enjoy God.* Colorado Springs, CO: David C. Cook, 2018.

Good

Koessler, John. *True Discipleship: The Art of Following Jesus.* Chicago, IL: Moody Publishers, 2003.

Piper, John. *Future Grace.* Colorado Springs, CO: Multnomah, 2012.

Sanders, Fred. *The Deep Things of God: How the Trinity Changes Everything.* Wheaton, IL: Crossway Books, 2010.

The God Who Suffers with Us

Billings, J. Todd. "Can Anger at God Be Righteous?" ChristianityToday.com. December 28, 2018. https://www.christianitytoday.com/ct/2019/january-february/can-anger-at-god-be-righteous-psalms-suffering.html.

Frame, John M. *The Doctrine of God.* Phillipsburg, NJ: P&R Publishing, 2002.

Keller, Timothy. *Walking with God through Pain and Suffering.* New York, NY: Penguin Books, 2013.

Lutzer, Erwin W. *Cries from the Cross: A Journey into the Heart of Jesus.* Chicago, IL: Moody Publishers, 2015.